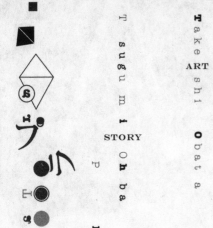

PLATINVM END

13

STORY Tsugumi Ohba

ART Takeshi Obata

Platinum End

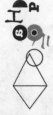

CHARACTERS

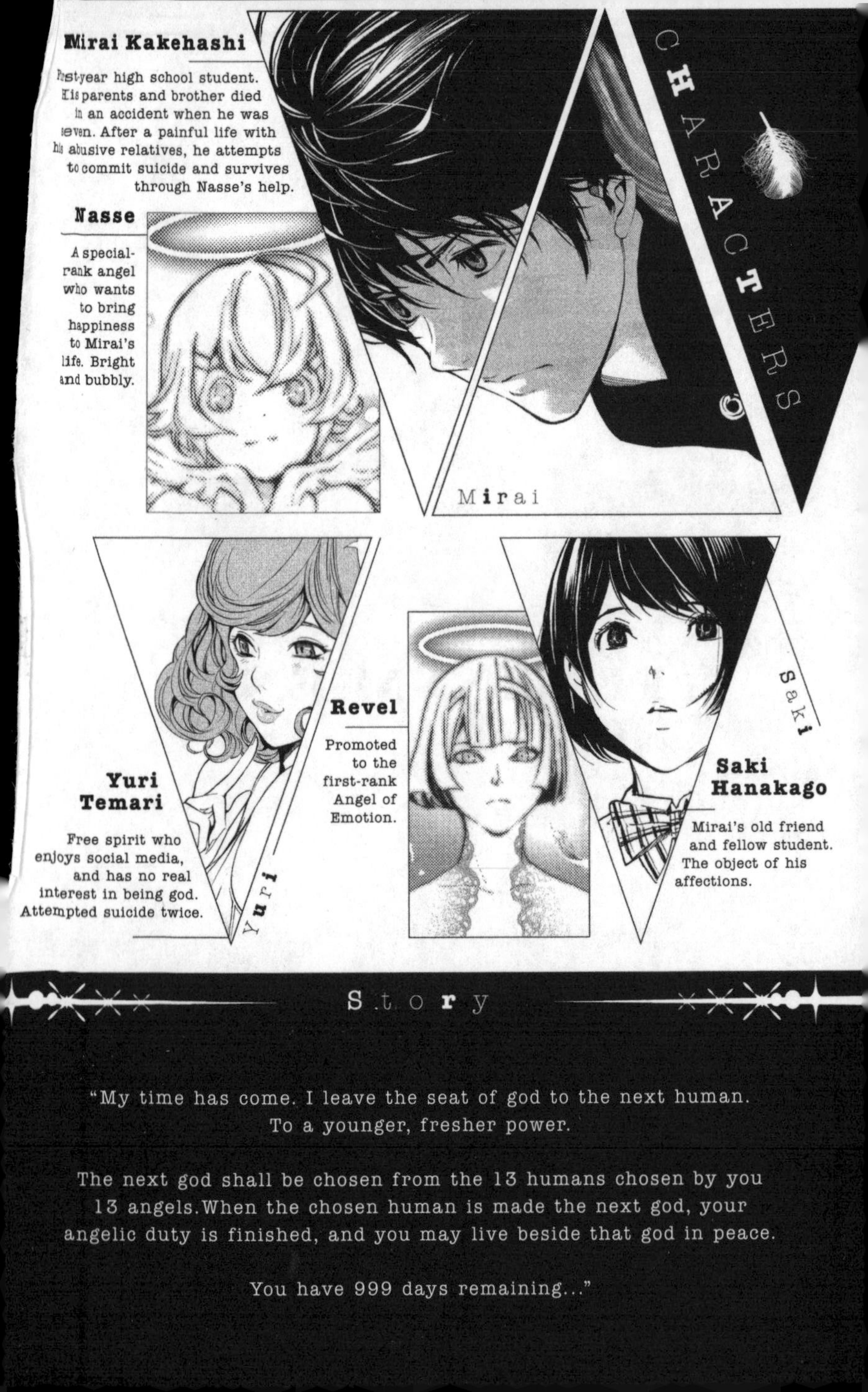

Mirai
Yuri
Saki

Mirai Kakehashi

First-year high school student. His parents and brother died in an accident when he was seven. After a painful life with his abusive relatives, he attempts to commit suicide and survives through Nasse's help.

Nasse

A special-rank angel who wants to bring happiness to Mirai's life. Bright and bubbly.

Saki Hanakago

Mirai's old friend and fellow student. The object of his affections.

Revel

Promoted to the first-rank Angel of Emotion.

Yuri Temari

Free spirit who enjoys social media, and has no real interest in being god. Attempted suicide twice.

Story

"My time has come. I leave the seat of god to the next human. To a younger, fresher power.

The next god shall be chosen from the 13 humans chosen by you 13 angels.When the chosen human is made the next god, your angelic duty is finished, and you may live beside that god in peace.

You have 999 days remaining..."

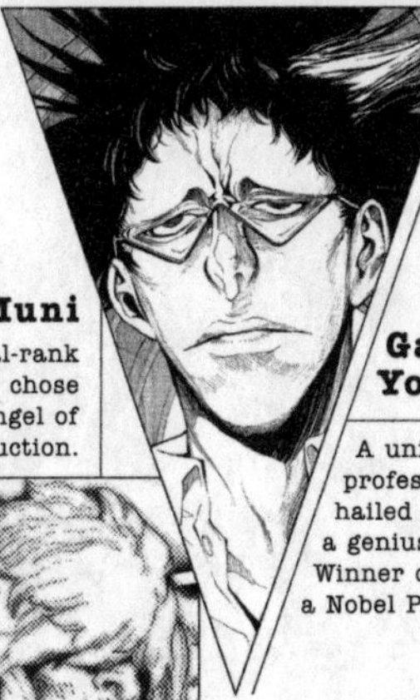

GAKU

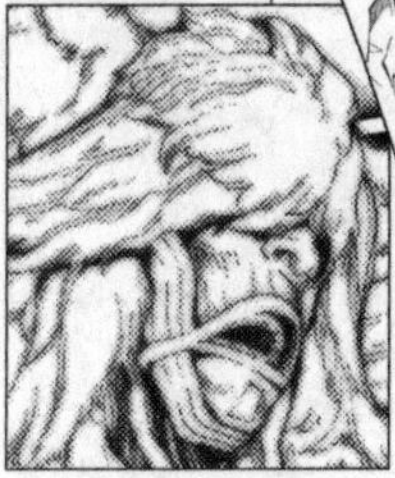

Muni

The special-rank angel who chose Yoneda. Angel of Destruction.

Gaku Yoneda

A university professor hailed as a genius. Winner of a Nobel Prize.

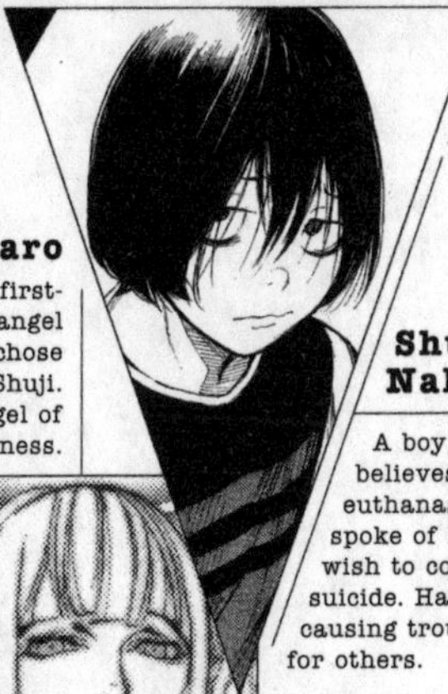

Shuji

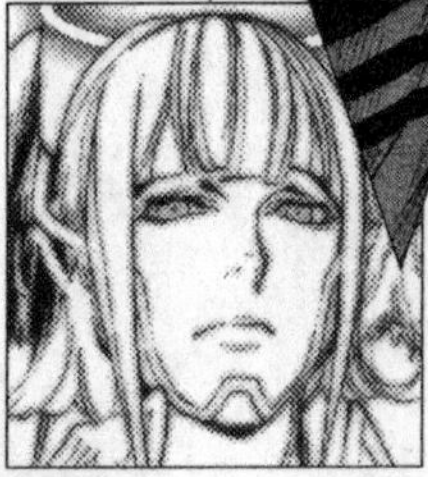

Ogaro

The first-rank angel who chose Shuji. Angel of Darkness.

Shuji Nakaumi

A boy who believes in euthanasia and spoke of his own wish to commit suicide. Hates causing trouble for others.

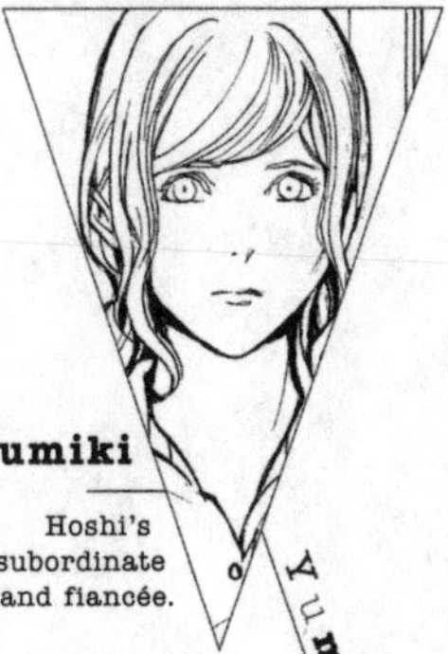

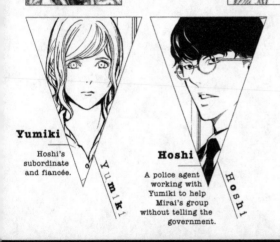

Yumiki

Hoshi's subordinate and fiancée.

Yumiki

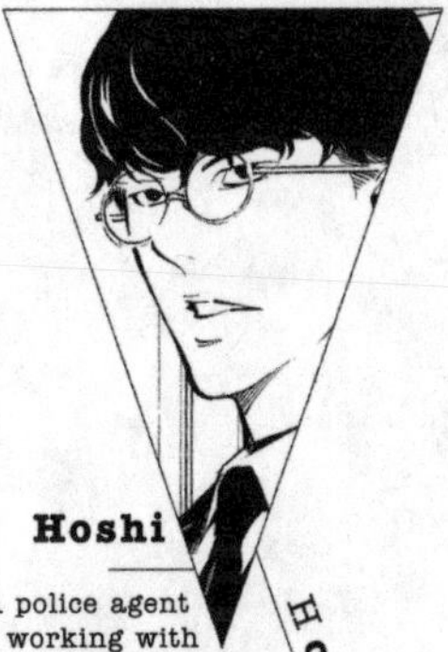

Hoshi

A police agent working with Yumiki to help Mirai's group without telling the government.

Hoshi

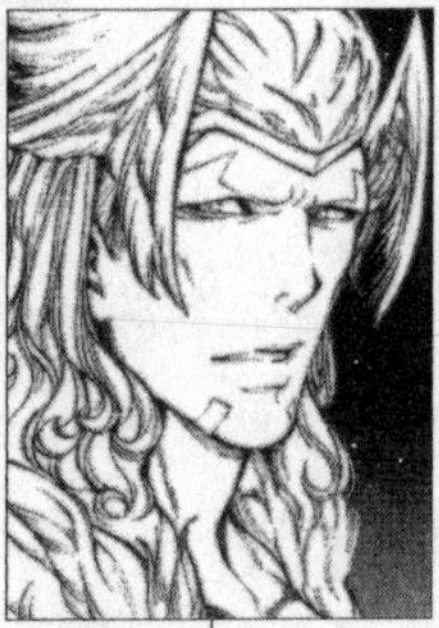

Yazeli

The second-rank angel who chose Yuri. Angel of Truth.

Story

WHAT MUST BE DONE...

At Yoneda's request, another meeting of god candidates is convened. "We'll end it all here," he says...

A SPECIAL ANGEL

Yoneda asks Ogaro about any angels with special powers. Nasse's name is mentioned—she can touch the human world directly.

AS IT SHOULD BE

The public agrees that god is unnecessary. Yoneda has red arrows in Shuji and the prime minister in a plot to wipe out the god candidates.

CONTENTS

13

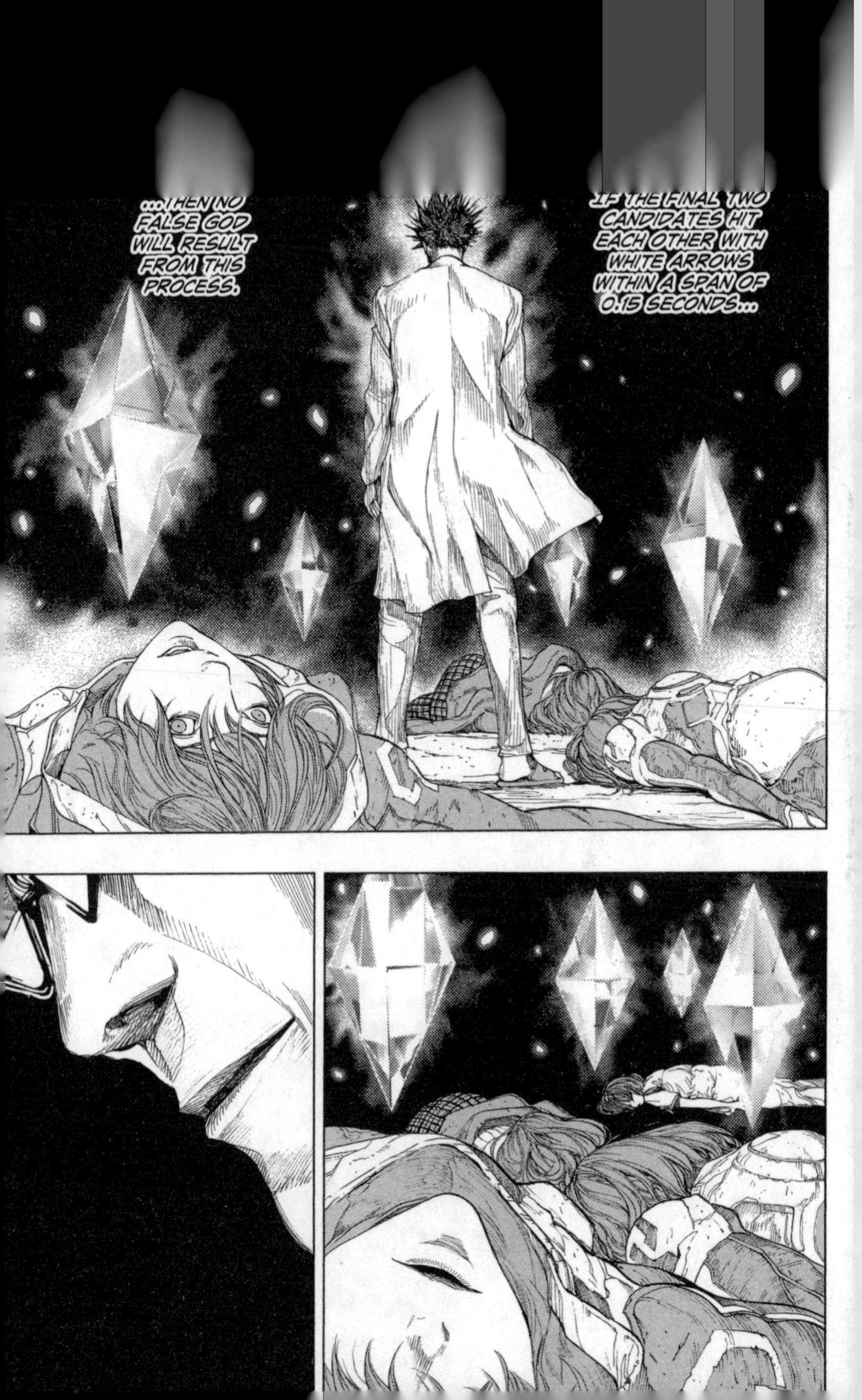
IF THE FINAL TWO CANDIDATES HIT EACH OTHER WITH WHITE ARROWS WITHIN A SPAN OF 0.15 SECONDS...
...THEN NO FALSE GOD WILL RESULT FROM THIS PROCESS.

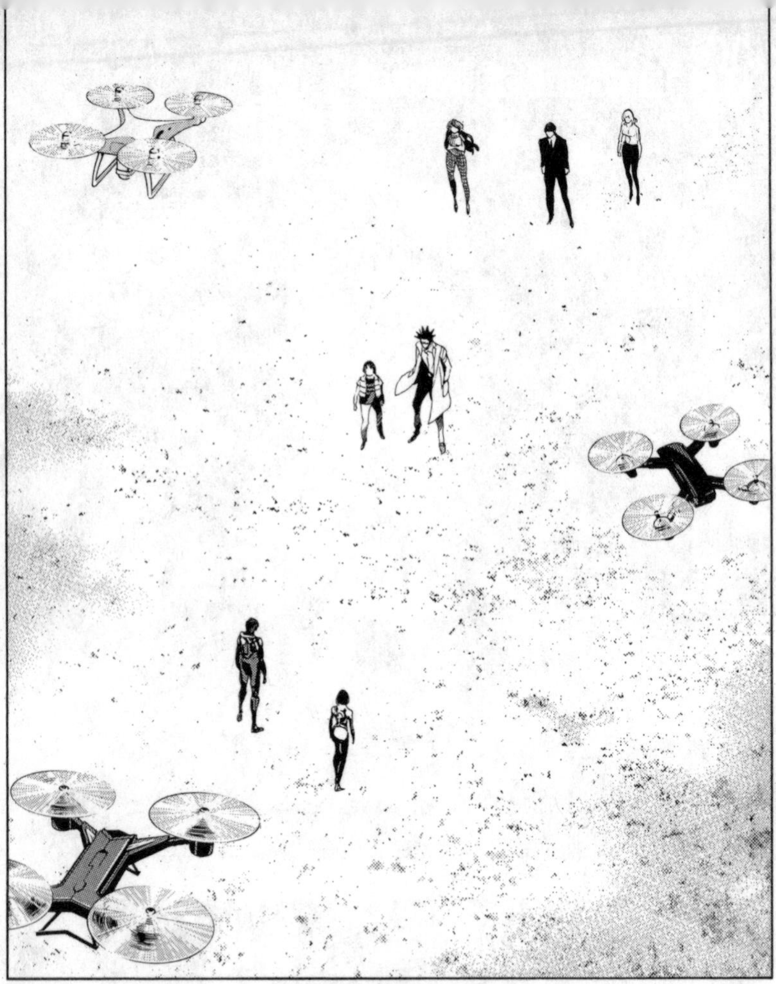
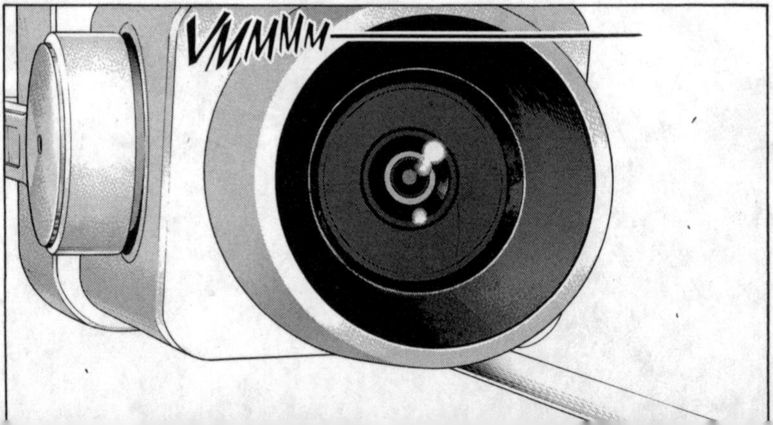
VMMMM

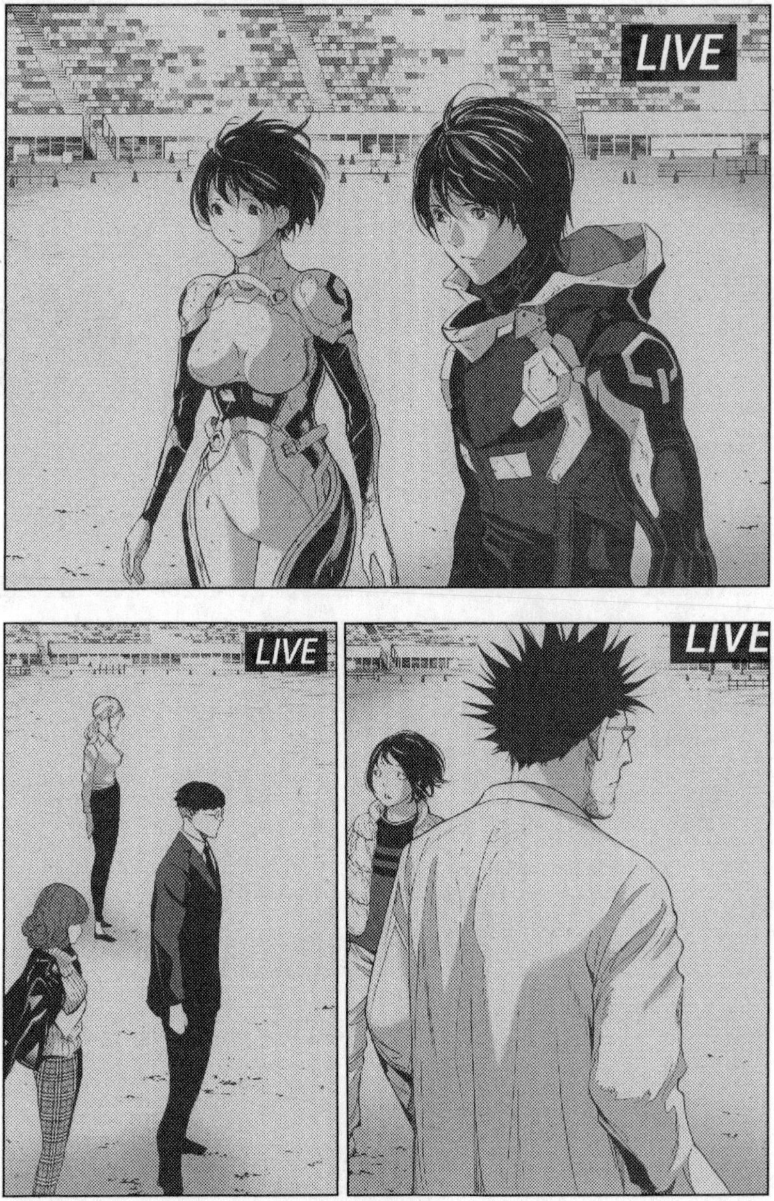
LIVE
LIVE
LIVE

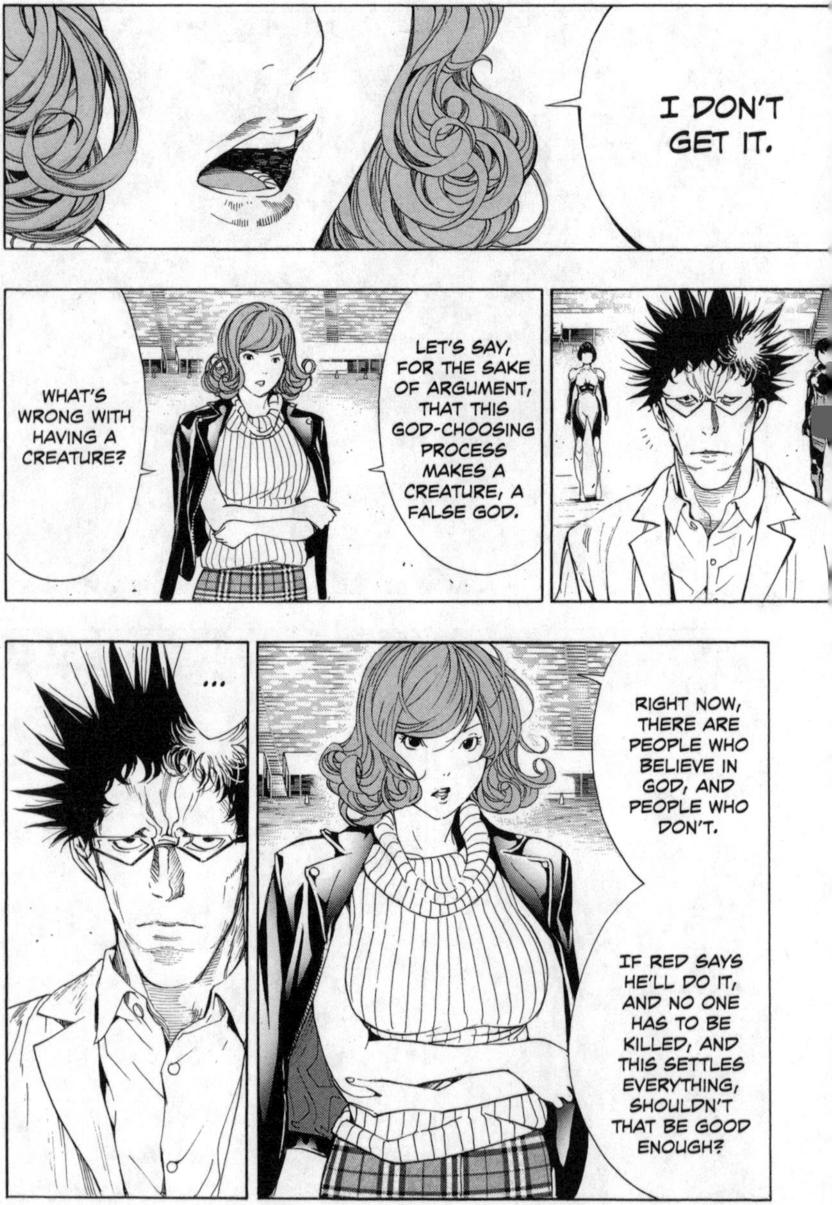
I DON'T GET IT.
LET'S SAY, FOR THE SAKE OF ARGUMENT, THAT THIS GOD-CHOOSING PROCESS MAKES A CREATURE, A FALSE GOD.
WHAT'S WRONG WITH HAVING A CREATURE?
RIGHT NOW, THERE ARE PEOPLE WHO BELIEVE IN GOD, AND PEOPLE WHO DON'T.
IF RED SAYS HE'LL DO IT, AND NO ONE HAS TO BE KILLED, AND THIS SETTLES EVERYTHING, SHOULDN'T THAT BE GOOD ENOUGH?
...

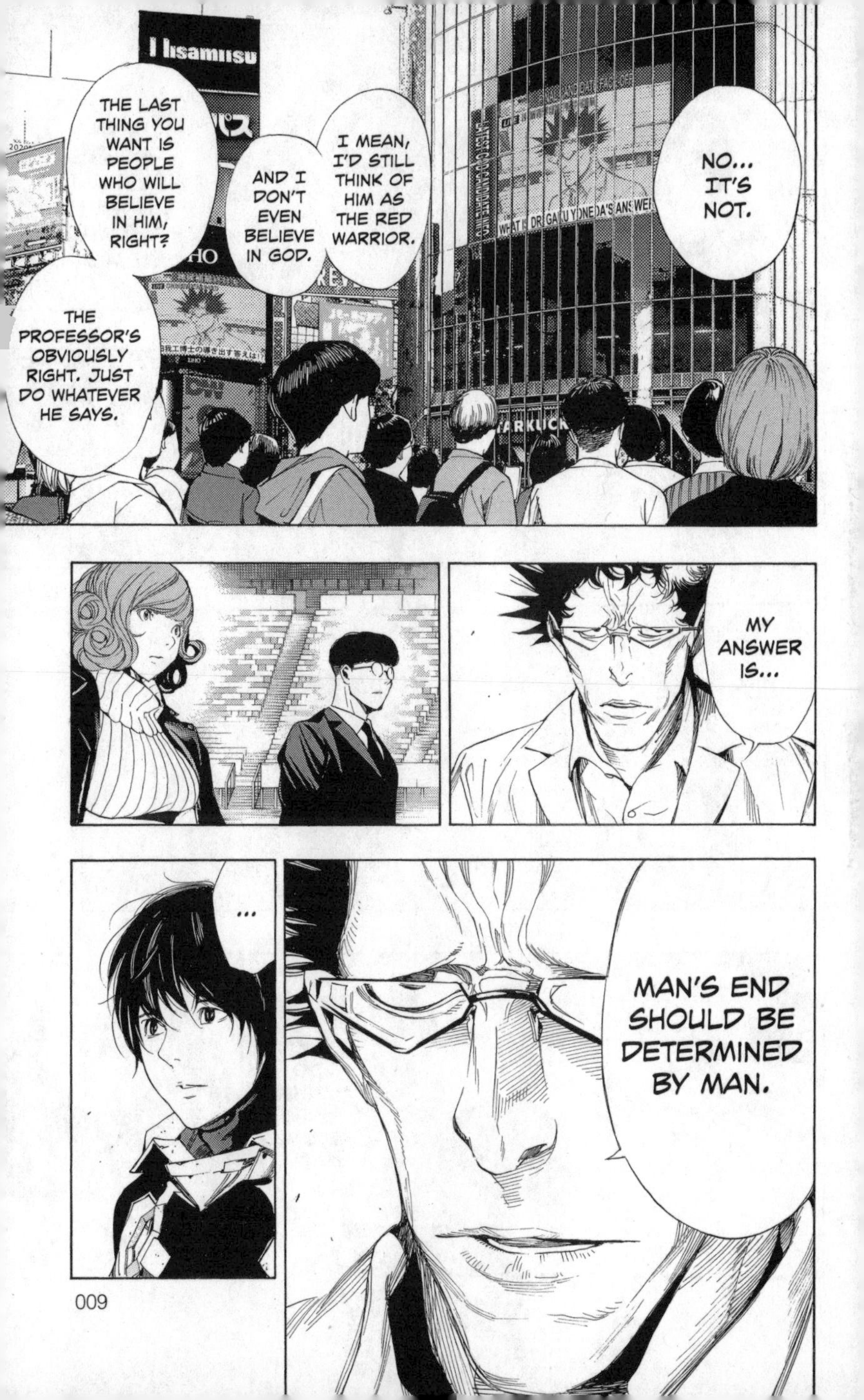
NO... IT'S NOT.
I MEAN, I'D STILL THINK OF HIM AS THE RED WARRIOR.
AND I DON'T EVEN BELIEVE IN GOD.
THE LAST THING YOU WANT IS PEOPLE WHO WILL BELIEVE IN HIM, RIGHT?
THE PROFESSOR'S OBVIOUSLY RIGHT. JUST DO WHATEVER HE SAYS.
MY ANSWER IS...
MAN'S END SHOULD BE DETERMINED BY MAN.
...

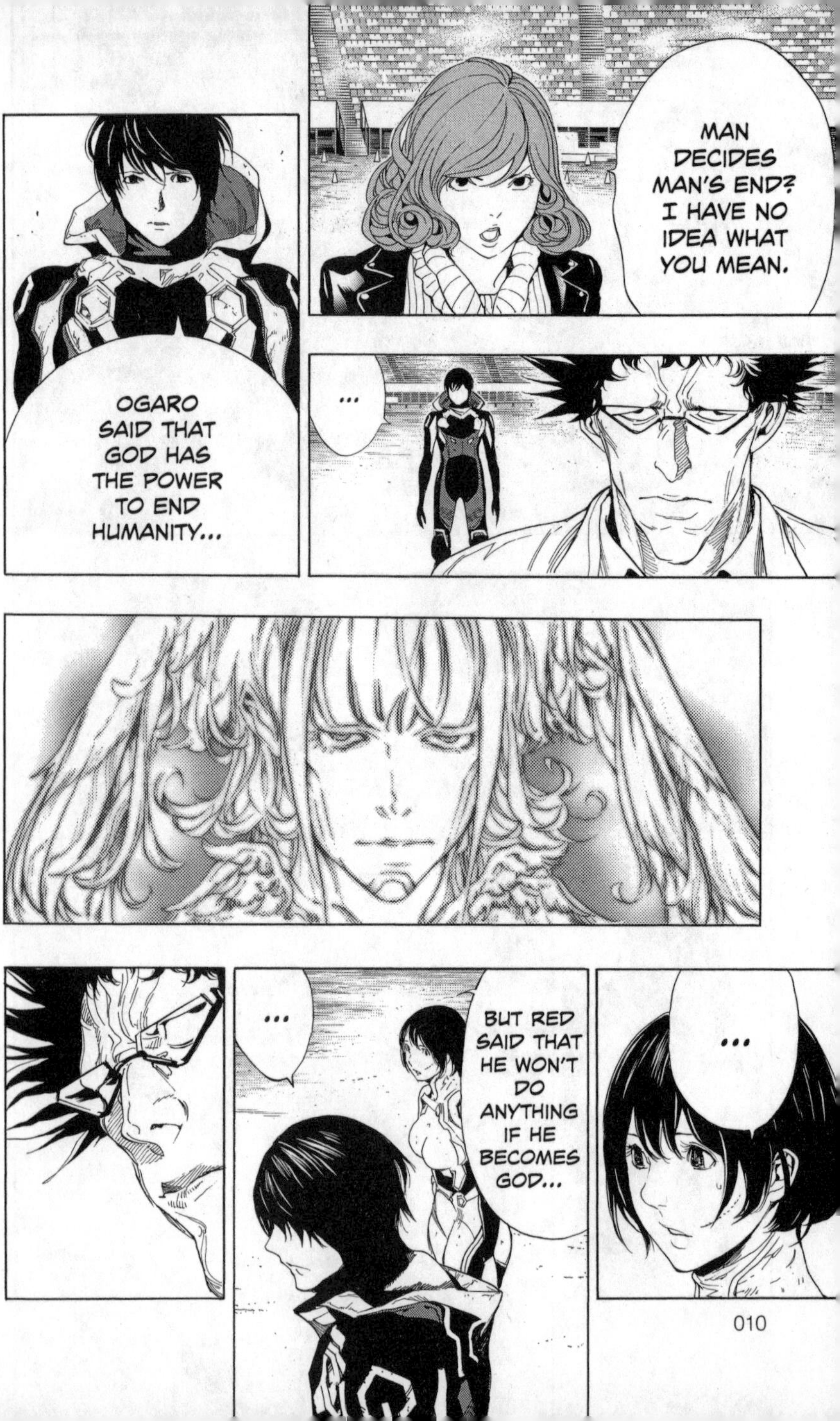
MAN DECIDES MAN'S END? I HAVE NO IDEA WHAT YOU MEAN.
...
OGARO SAID THAT GOD HAS THE POWER TO END HUMANITY...
...
BUT RED SAID THAT HE WON'T DO ANYTHING IF HE BECOMES GOD...
...

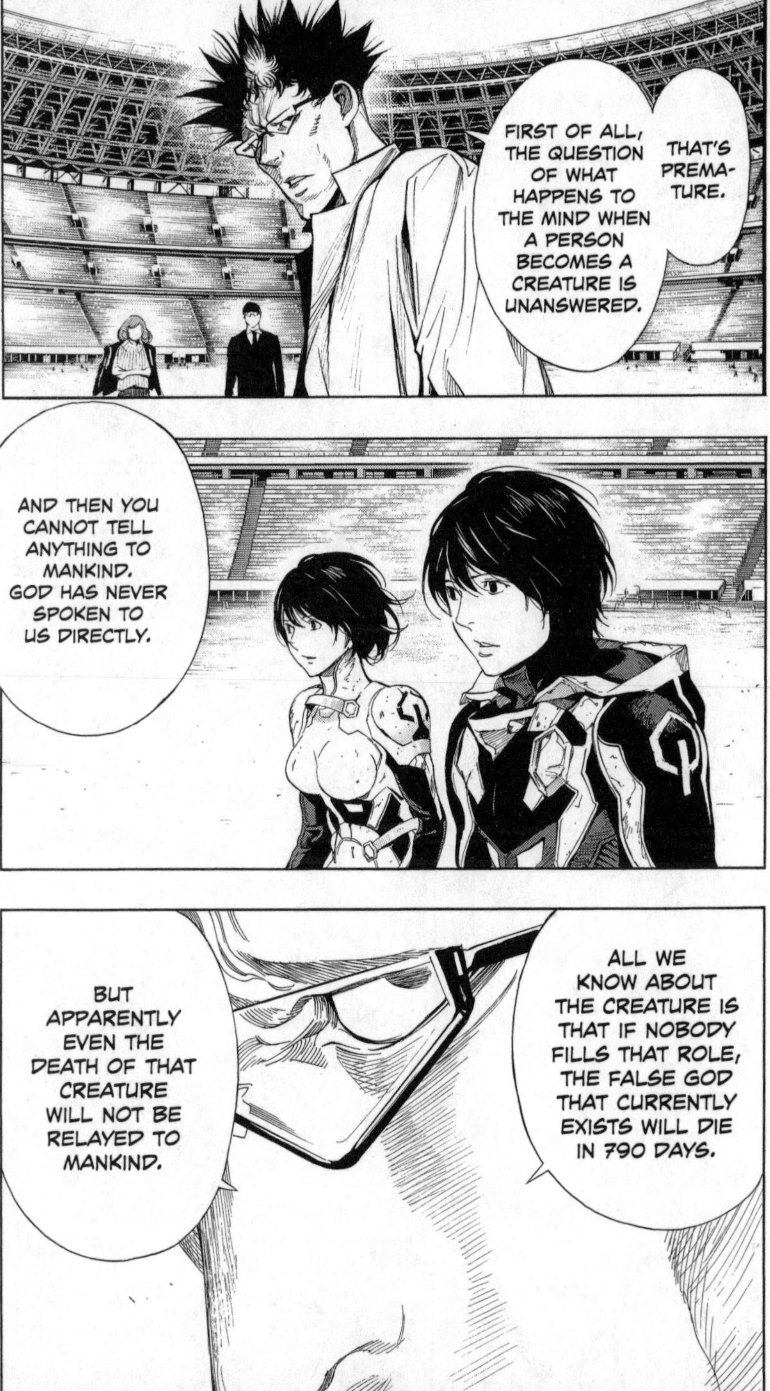
THAT'S PREMATURE.
FIRST OF ALL, THE QUESTION OF WHAT HAPPENS TO THE MIND WHEN A PERSON BECOMES A CREATURE IS UNANSWERED.
AND THEN YOU CANNOT TELL ANYTHING TO MANKIND. GOD HAS NEVER SPOKEN TO US DIRECTLY.
ALL WE KNOW ABOUT THE CREATURE IS THAT IF NOBODY FILLS THAT ROLE, THE FALSE GOD THAT CURRENTLY EXISTS WILL DIE IN 790 DAYS.
BUT APPARENTLY EVEN THE DEATH OF THAT CREATURE WILL NOT BE RELAYED TO MANKIND.

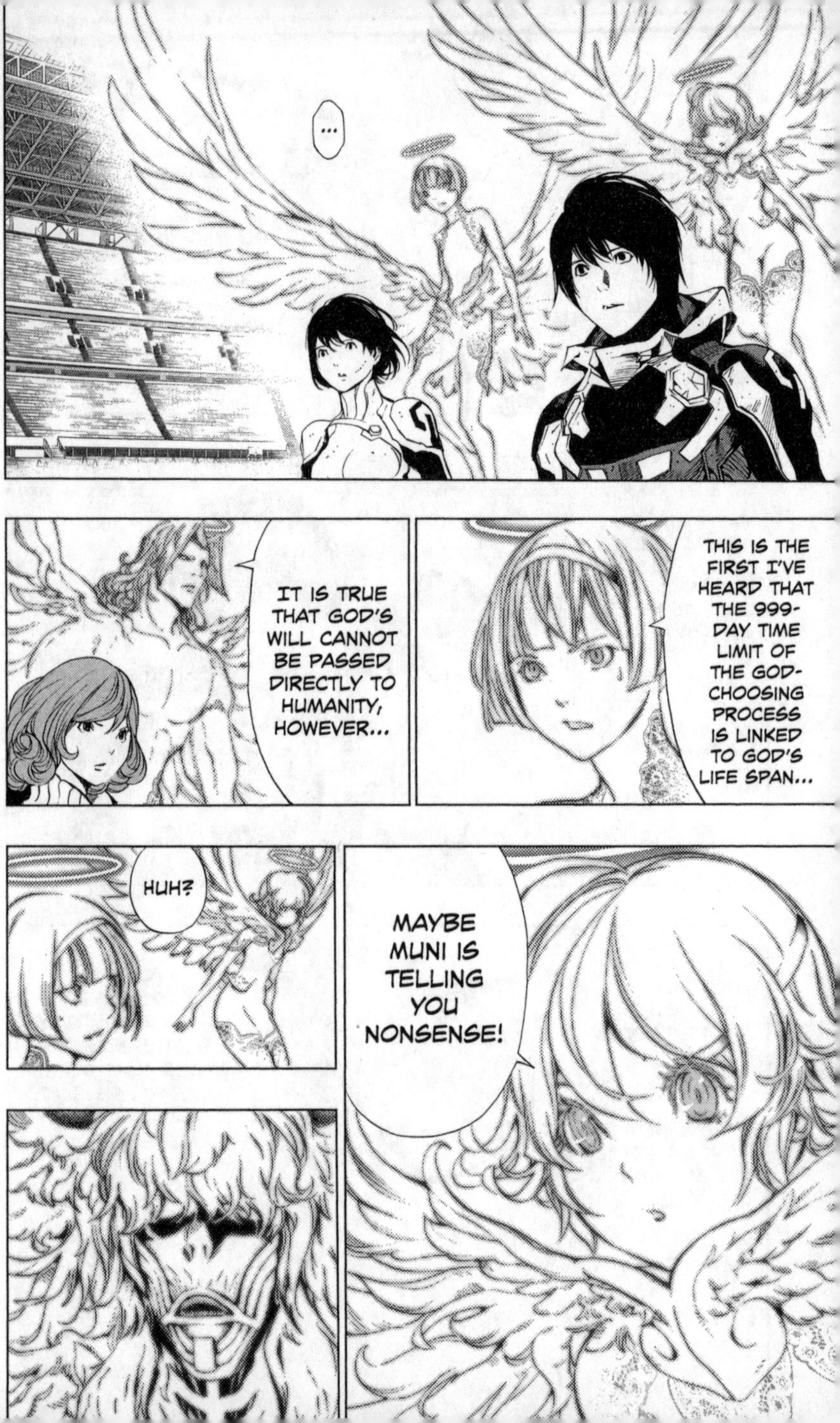
...
THIS IS THE FIRST I'VE HEARD THAT THE 999-DAY TIME LIMIT OF THE GOD-CHOOSING PROCESS IS LINKED TO GOD'S LIFE SPAN...
IT IS TRUE THAT GOD'S WILL CANNOT BE PASSED DIRECTLY TO HUMANITY, HOWEVER...
MAYBE MUNI IS TELLING YOU NONSENSE!
HUH?

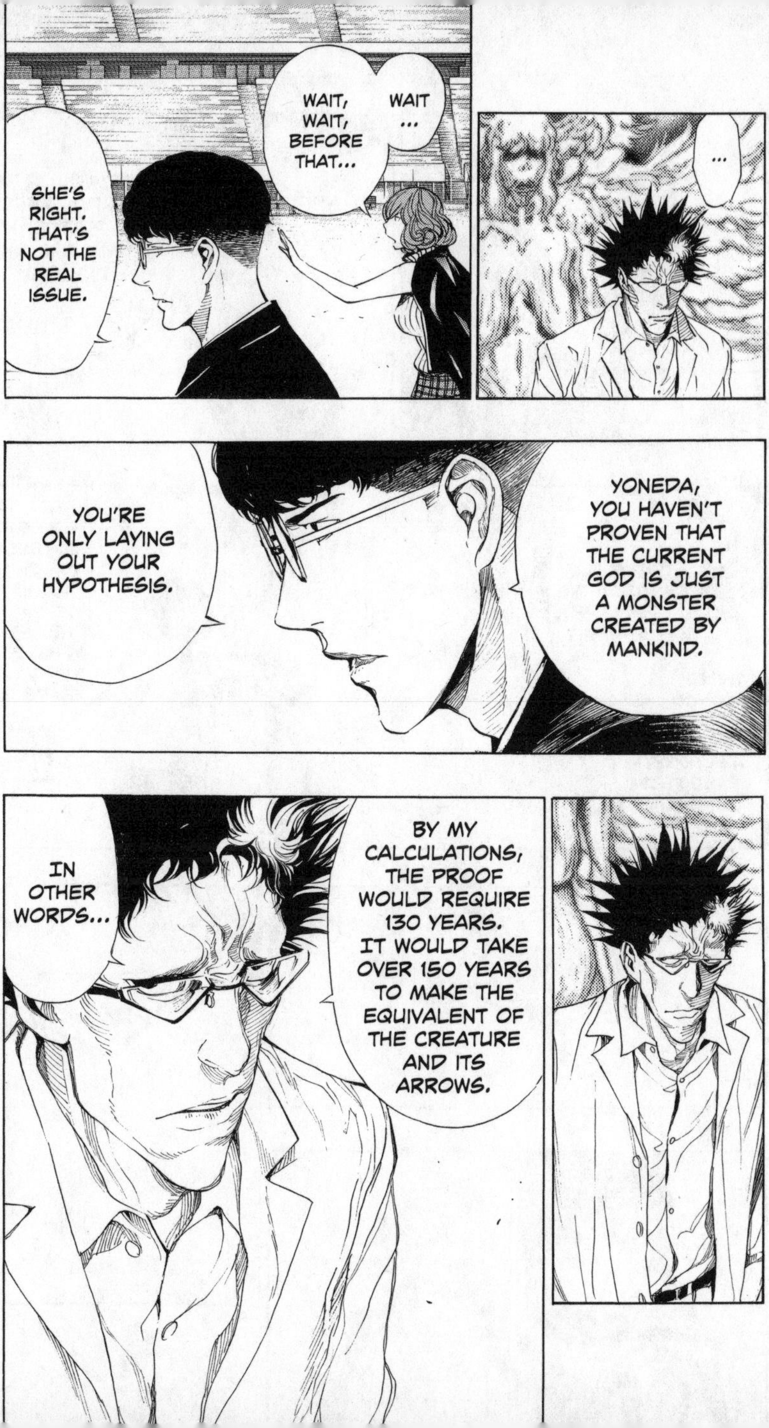
...
WAIT ...
WAIT, WAIT, BEFORE THAT...
SHE'S RIGHT. THAT'S NOT THE REAL ISSUE.
YONEDA, YOU HAVEN'T PROVEN THAT THE CURRENT GOD IS JUST A MONSTER CREATED BY MANKIND.
YOU'RE ONLY LAYING OUT YOUR HYPOTHESIS.
BY MY CALCULATIONS, THE PROOF WOULD REQUIRE 130 YEARS. IT WOULD TAKE OVER 150 YEARS TO MAKE THE EQUIVALENT OF THE CREATURE AND ITS ARROWS.
IN OTHER WORDS...

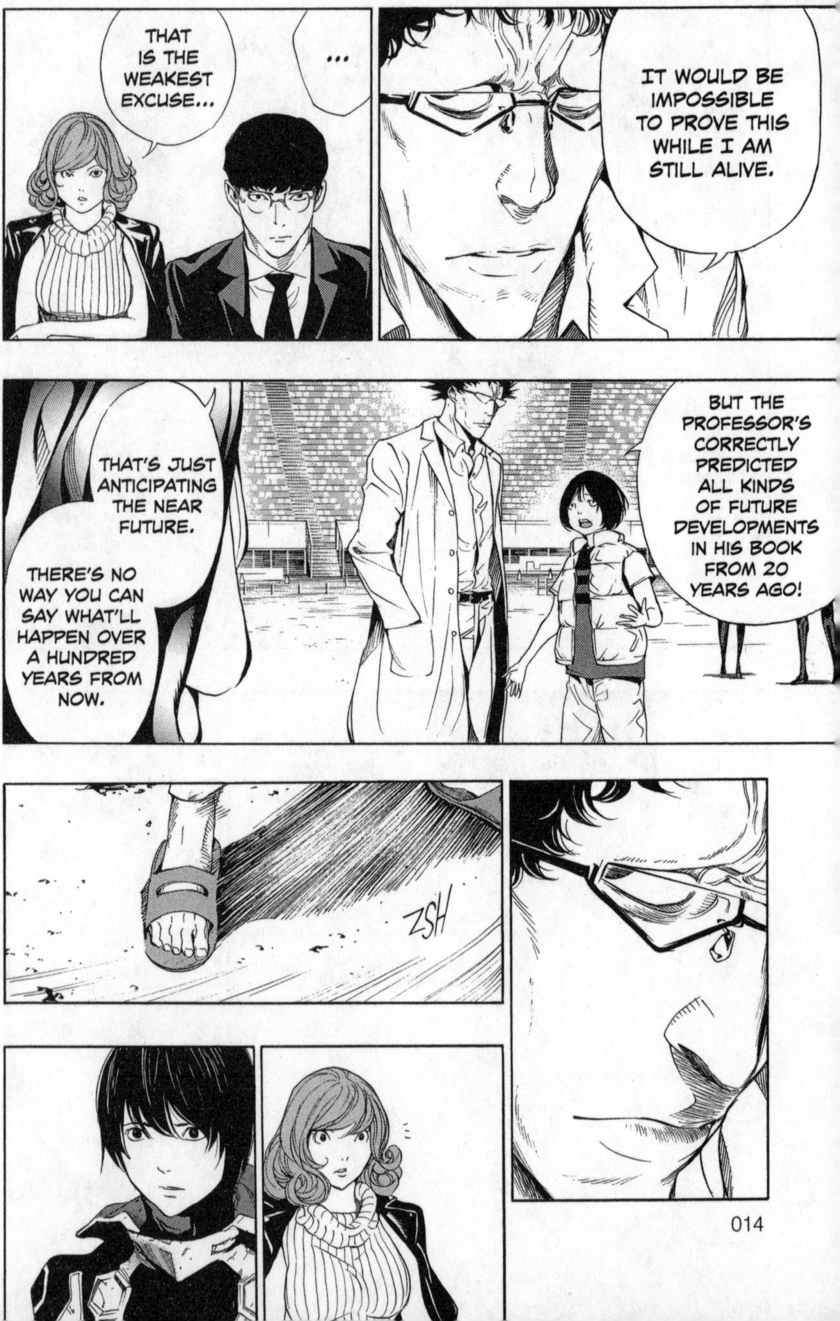
IT WOULD BE IMPOSSIBLE TO PROVE THIS WHILE I AM STILL ALIVE.
...
THAT IS THE WEAKEST EXCUSE...
BUT THE PROFESSOR'S CORRECTLY PREDICTED ALL KINDS OF FUTURE DEVELOPMENTS IN HIS BOOK FROM 20 YEARS AGO!
THAT'S JUST ANTICIPATING THE NEAR FUTURE.
THERE'S NO WAY YOU CAN SAY WHAT'LL HAPPEN OVER A HUNDRED YEARS FROM NOW.
ZSH

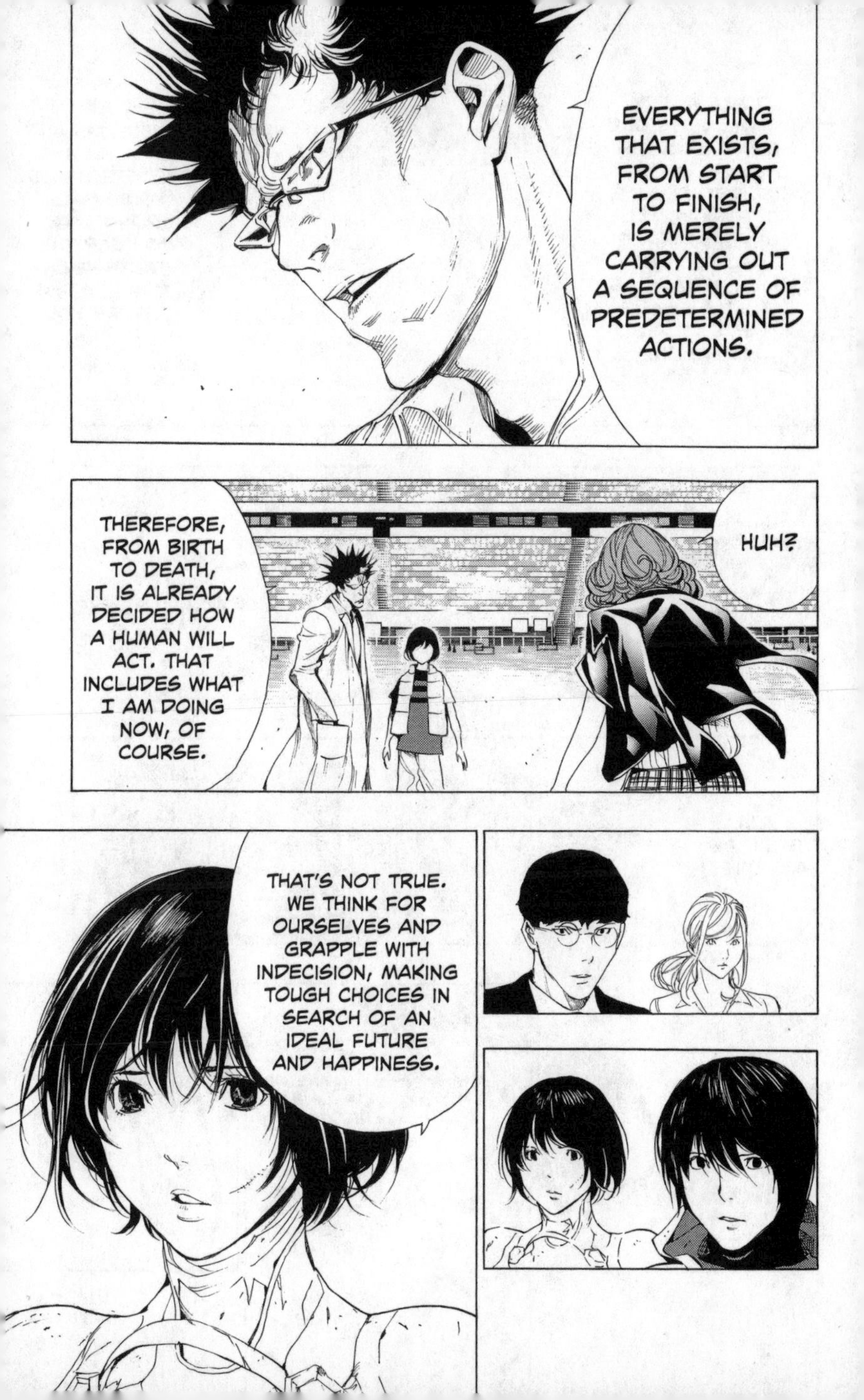
EVERYTHING THAT EXISTS, FROM START TO FINISH, IS MERELY CARRYING OUT A SEQUENCE OF PREDETERMINED ACTIONS.
HUH?
THEREFORE, FROM BIRTH TO DEATH, IT IS ALREADY DECIDED HOW A HUMAN WILL ACT. THAT INCLUDES WHAT I AM DOING NOW, OF COURSE.
THAT'S NOT TRUE. WE THINK FOR OURSELVES AND GRAPPLE WITH INDECISION, MAKING TOUGH CHOICES IN SEARCH OF AN IDEAL FUTURE AND HAPPINESS.

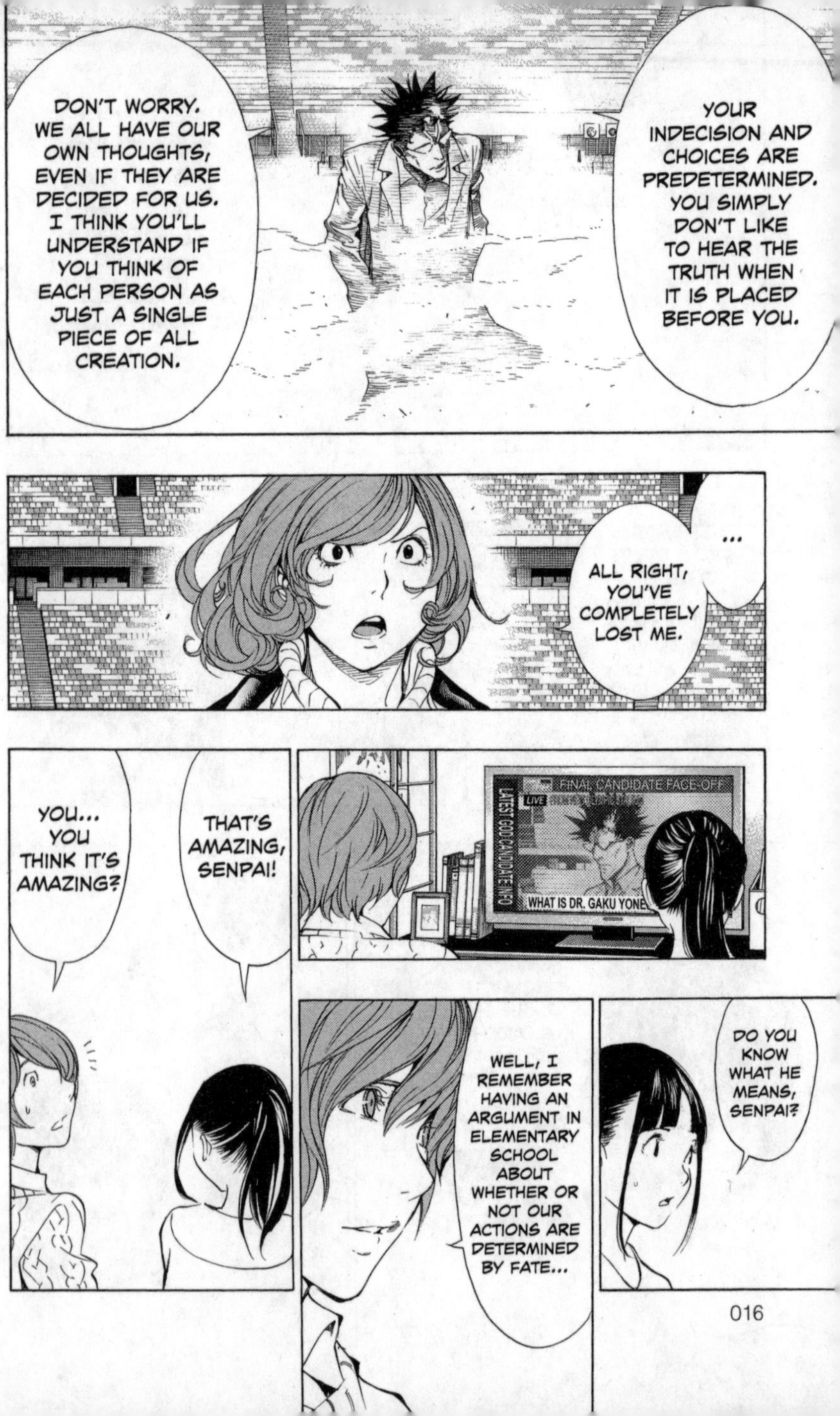
YOUR INDECISION AND CHOICES ARE PREDETERMINED. YOU SIMPLY DON'T LIKE TO HEAR THE TRUTH WHEN IT IS PLACED BEFORE YOU.
DON'T WORRY. WE ALL HAVE OUR OWN THOUGHTS, EVEN IF THEY ARE DECIDED FOR US. I THINK YOU'LL UNDERSTAND IF YOU THINK OF EACH PERSON AS JUST A SINGLE PIECE OF ALL CREATION.
...
ALL RIGHT, YOU'VE COMPLETELY LOST ME.
FINAL CANDIDATE FACE-OFF
LIVE
LATEST GOD CANDIDATE INFO
WHAT IS DR. GAKU YONE
DO YOU KNOW WHAT HE MEANS, SENPAI?
WELL, I REMEMBER HAVING AN ARGUMENT IN ELEMENTARY SCHOOL ABOUT WHETHER OR NOT OUR ACTIONS ARE DETERMINED BY FATE...
THAT'S AMAZING, SENPAI!
YOU... YOU THINK IT'S AMAZING?

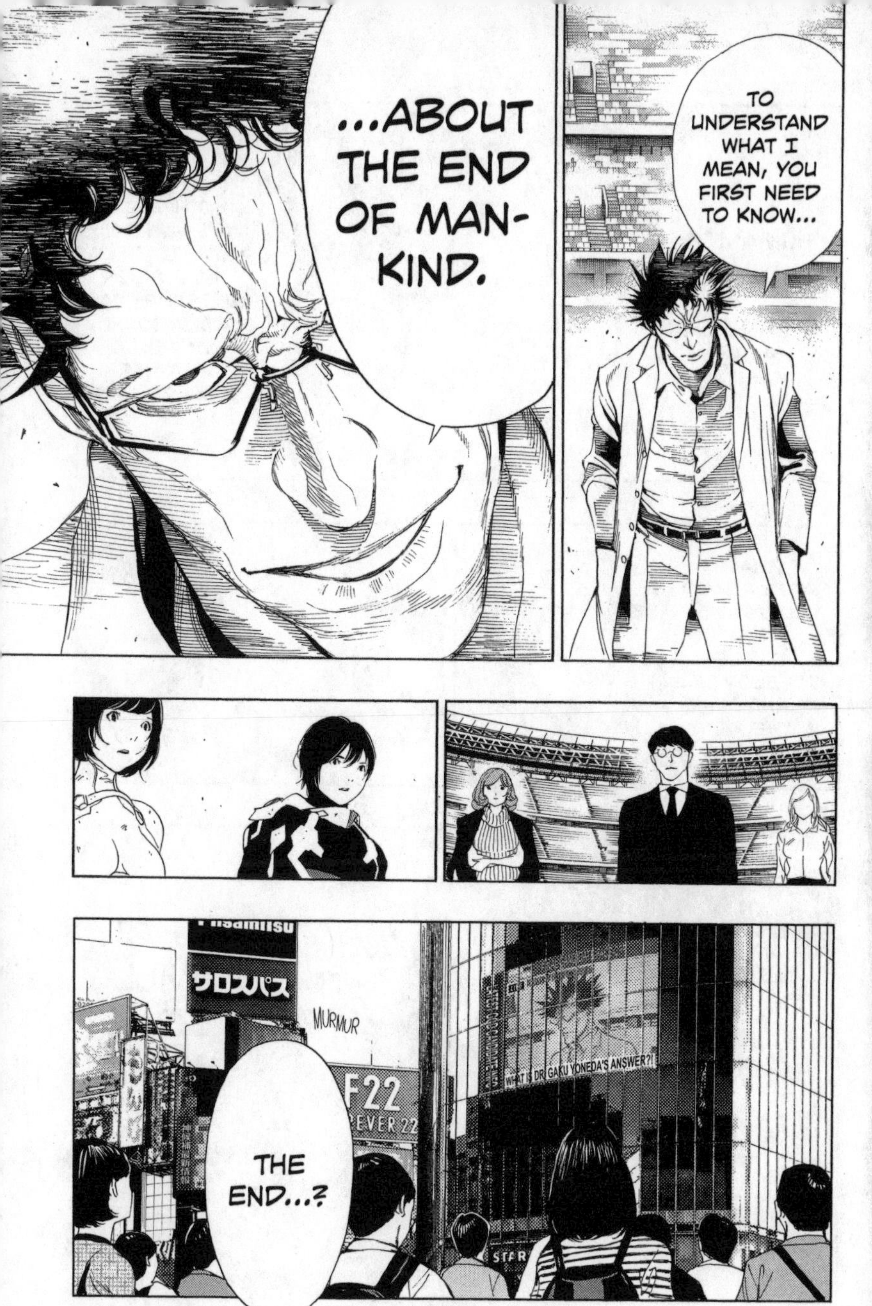
TO UNDERSTAND WHAT I MEAN, YOU FIRST NEED TO KNOW...
...ABOUT THE END OF MAN-KIND.
WHAT IS DR GAKU YONEDA'S ANSWER?!
MURMUR
サロンパス
F22
THE END...?

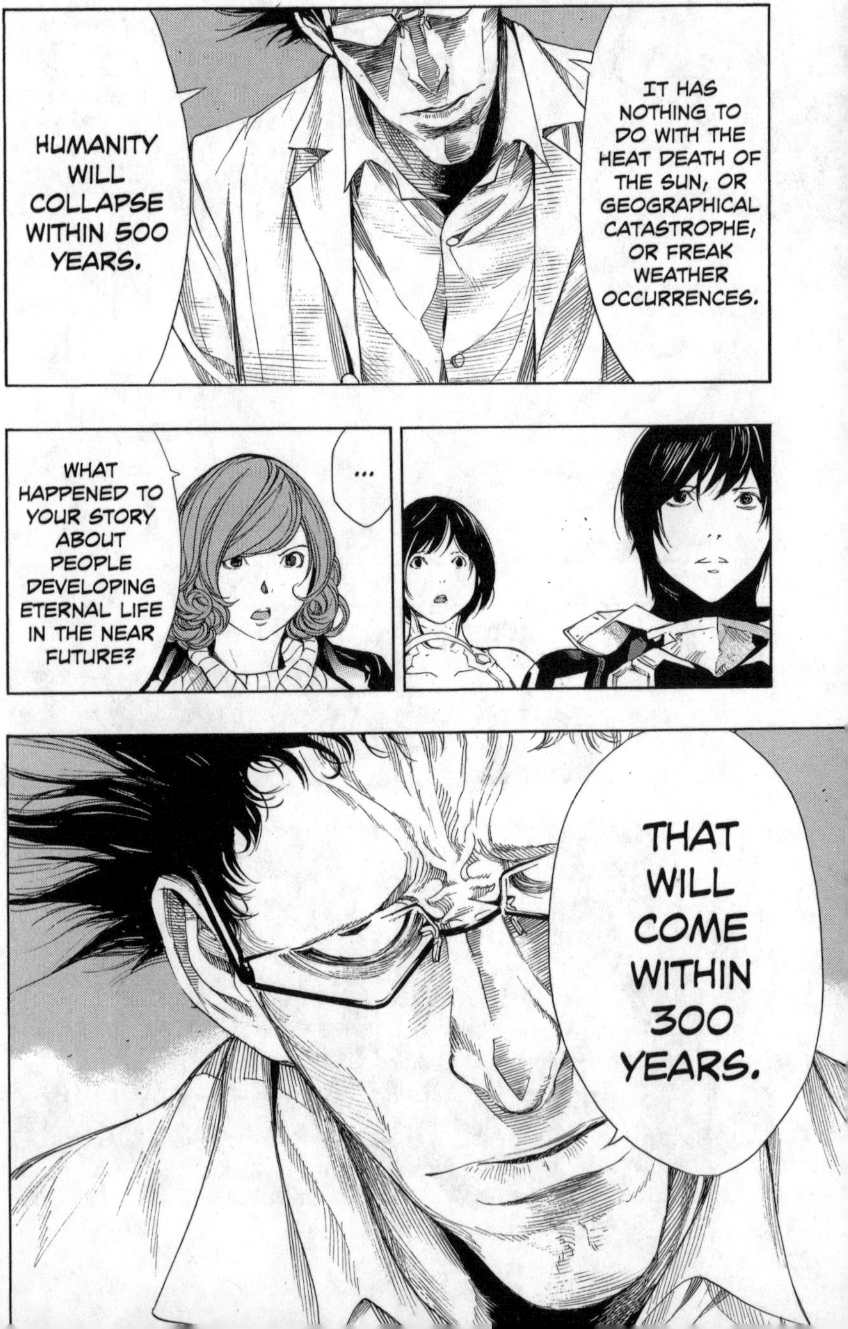
IT HAS NOTHING TO DO WITH THE HEAT DEATH OF THE SUN, OR GEOGRAPHICAL CATASTROPHE, OR FREAK WEATHER OCCURRENCES.
HUMANITY WILL COLLAPSE WITHIN 500 YEARS.
...
WHAT HAPPENED TO YOUR STORY ABOUT PEOPLE DEVELOPING ETERNAL LIFE IN THE NEAR FUTURE?
THAT WILL COME WITHIN 300 YEARS.

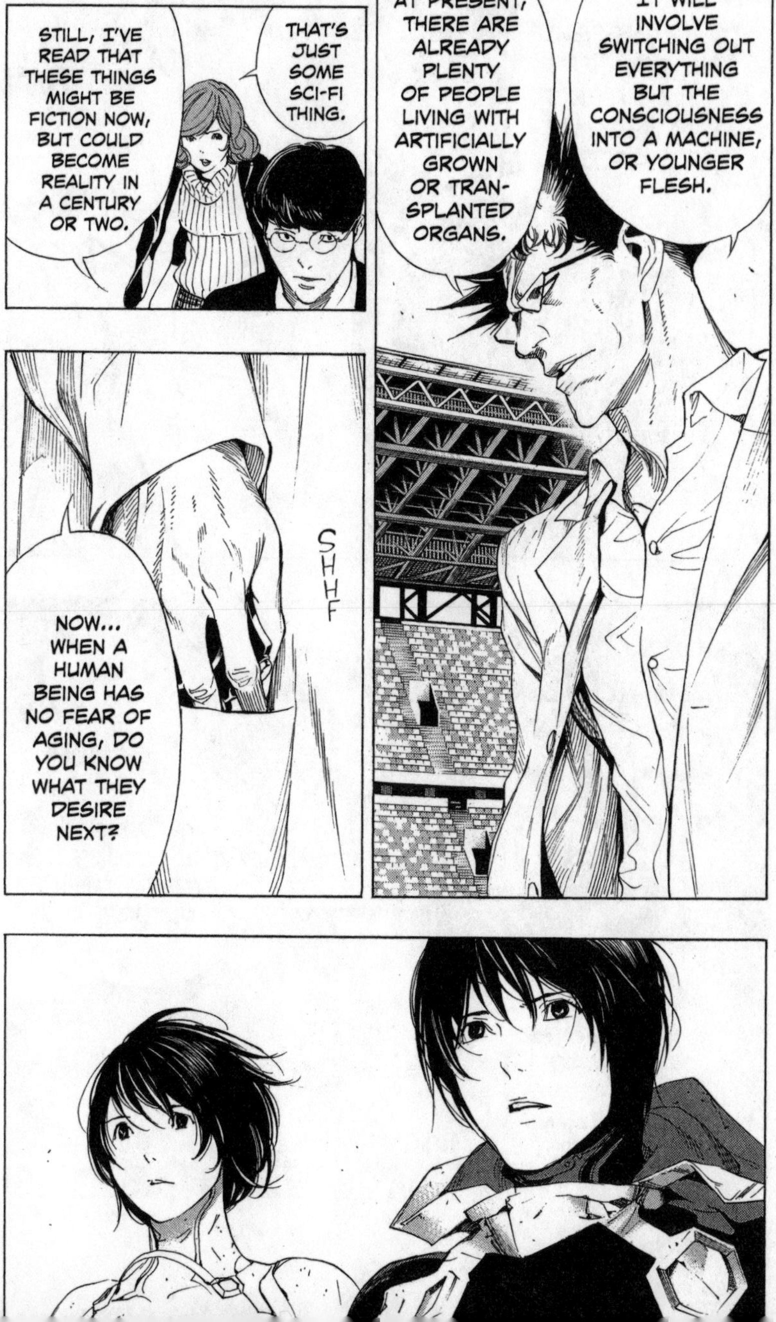
IT WILL INVOLVE SWITCHING OUT EVERYTHING BUT THE CONSCIOUSNESS INTO A MACHINE, OR YOUNGER FLESH.
AT PRESENT, THERE ARE ALREADY PLENTY OF PEOPLE LIVING WITH ARTIFICIALLY GROWN OR TRAN-SPLANTED ORGANS.
THAT'S JUST SOME SCI-FI THING.
STILL, I'VE READ THAT THESE THINGS MIGHT BE FICTION NOW, BUT COULD BECOME REALITY IN A CENTURY OR TWO.
SHHF
NOW... WHEN A HUMAN BEING HAS NO FEAR OF AGING, DO YOU KNOW WHAT THEY DESIRE NEXT?

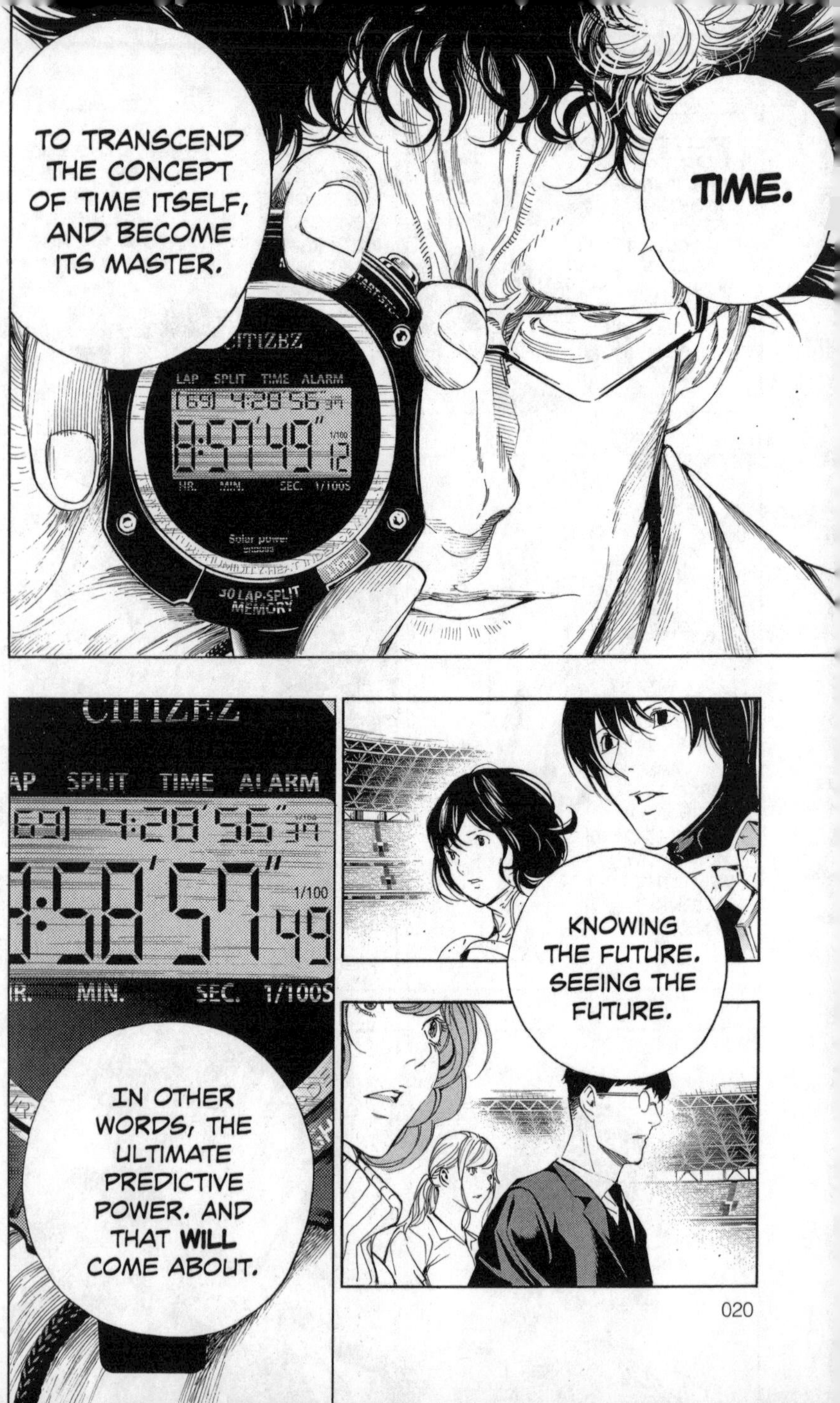
TIME.
TO TRANSCEND THE CONCEPT OF TIME ITSELF, AND BECOME ITS MASTER.
KNOWING THE FUTURE. SEEING THE FUTURE.
IN OTHER WORDS, THE ULTIMATE PREDICTIVE POWER. AND THAT **WILL** COME ABOUT.

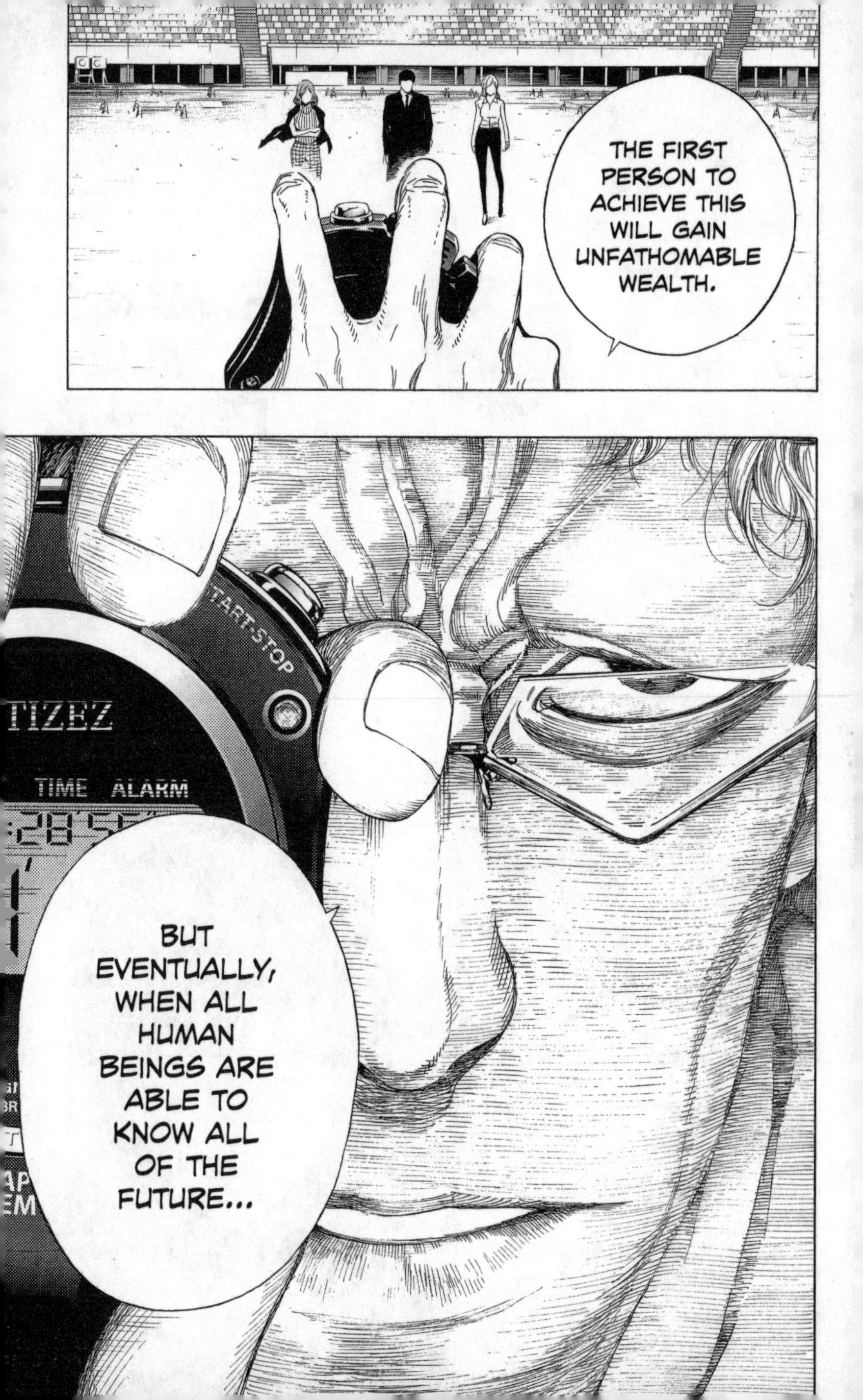
THE FIRST PERSON TO ACHIEVE THIS WILL GAIN UNFATHOMABLE WEALTH.
START-STOP
TIME ALARM
BUT EVENTUALLY, WHEN ALL HUMAN BEINGS ARE ABLE TO KNOW ALL OF THE FUTURE...

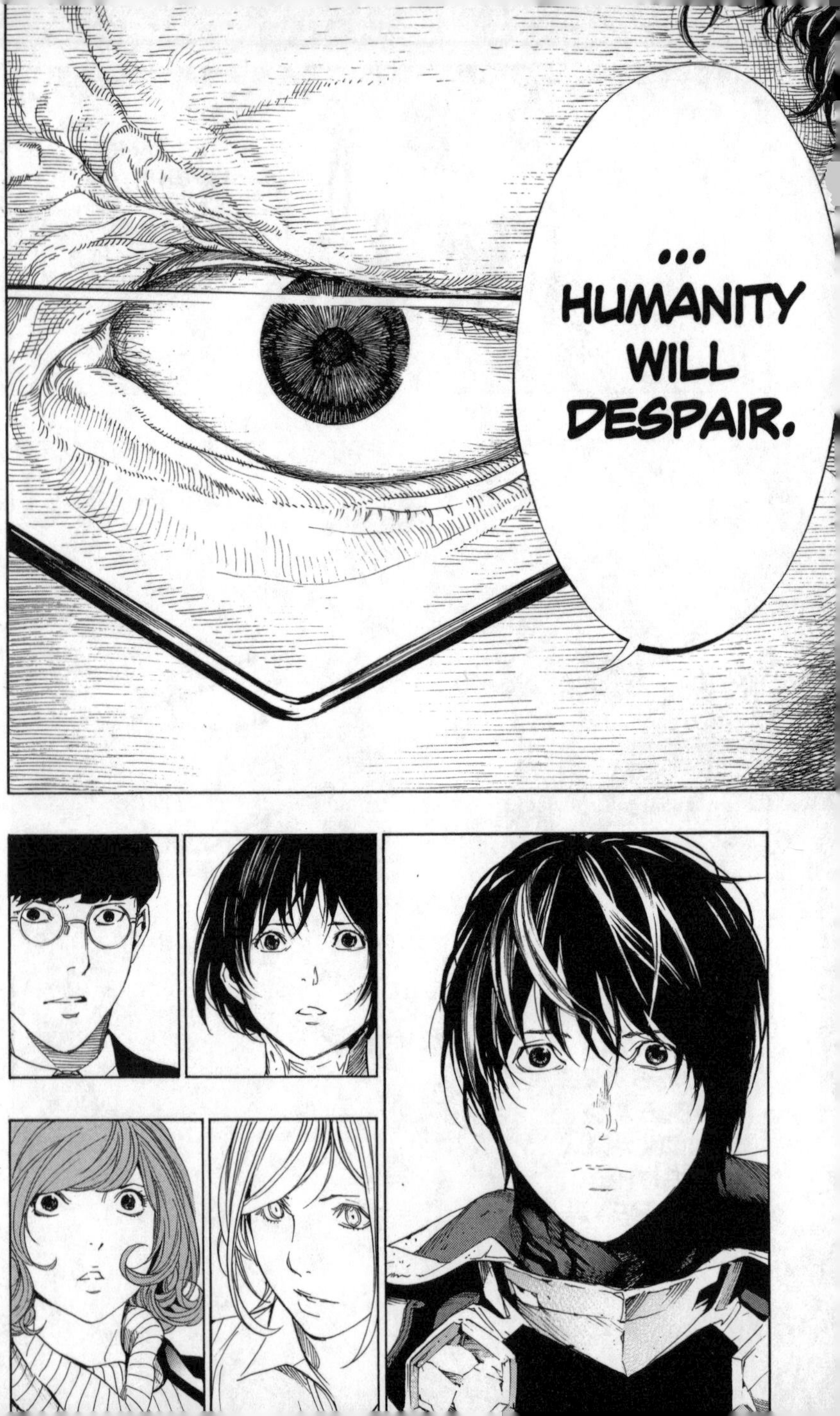
... HUMANITY WILL DESPAIR.

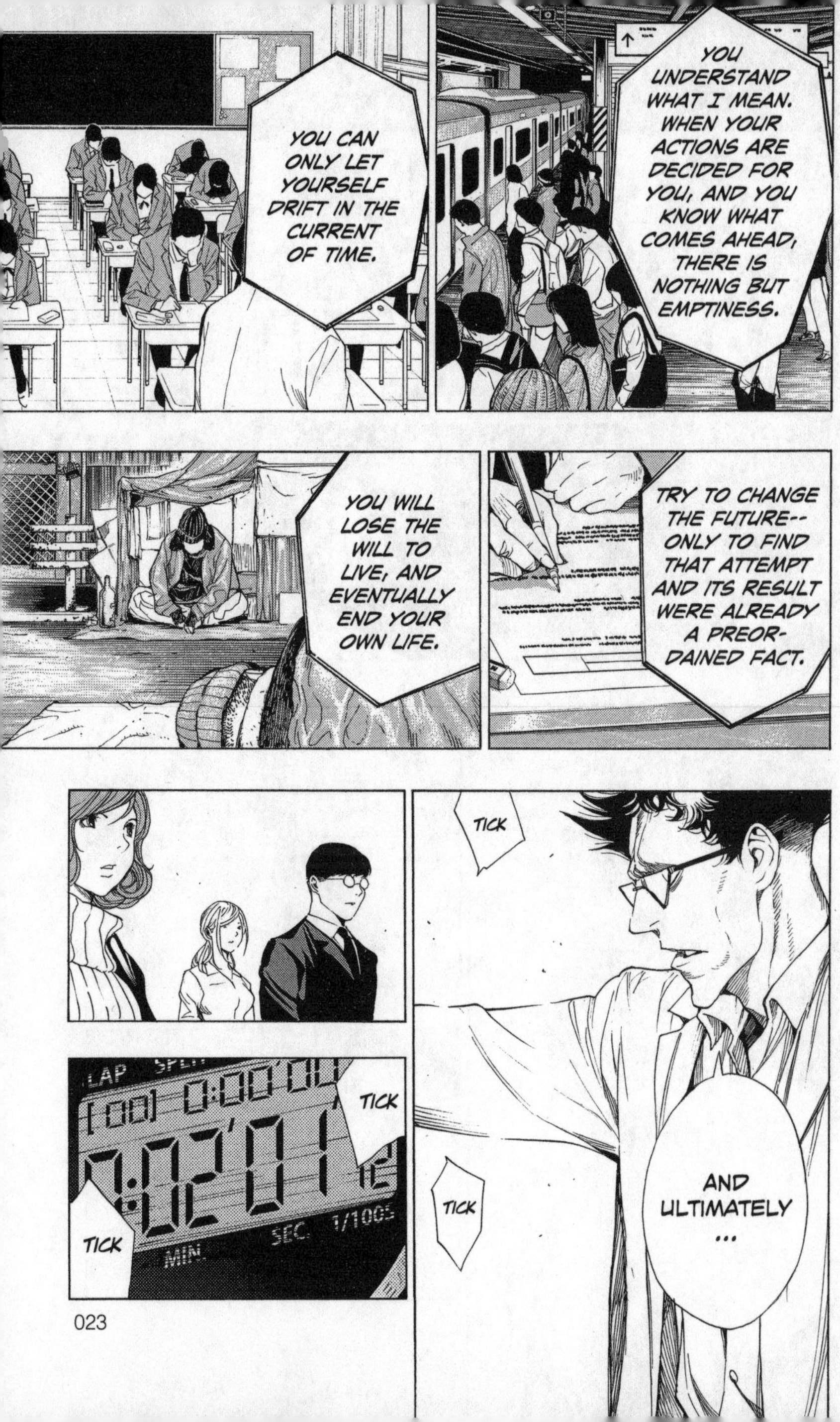
YOU UNDERSTAND WHAT I MEAN. WHEN YOUR ACTIONS ARE DECIDED FOR YOU, AND YOU KNOW WHAT COMES AHEAD, THERE IS NOTHING BUT EMPTINESS.
YOU CAN ONLY LET YOURSELF DRIFT IN THE CURRENT OF TIME.
TRY TO CHANGE THE FUTURE-- ONLY TO FIND THAT ATTEMPT AND ITS RESULT WERE ALREADY A PREOR-DAINED FACT.
YOU WILL LOSE THE WILL TO LIVE, AND EVENTUALLY END YOUR OWN LIFE.
TICK
TICK
AND ULTIMATELY ...
LAP
MIN.
SEC.
TICK
TICK

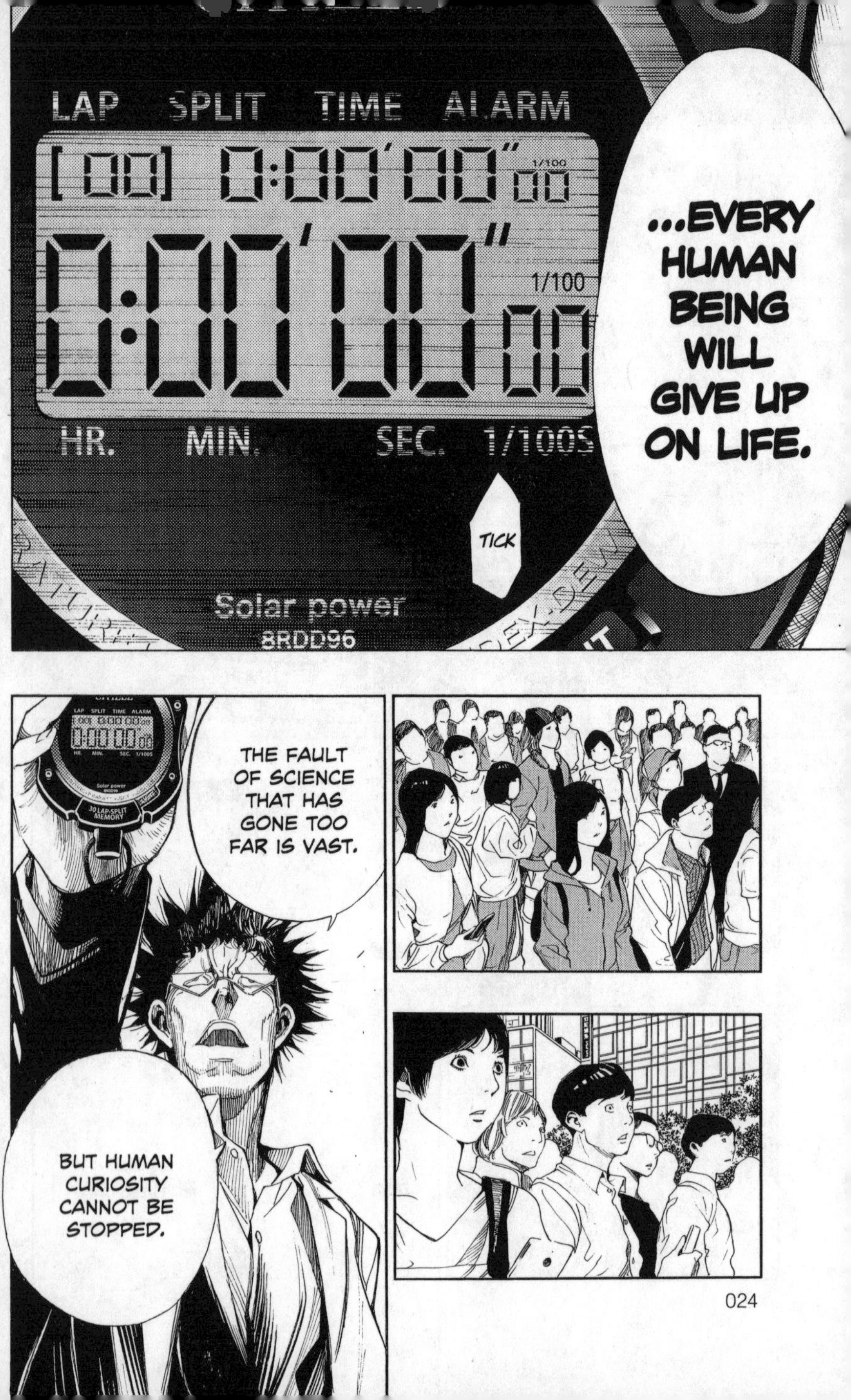
...EVERY HUMAN BEING WILL GIVE UP ON LIFE.
LAP SPLIT TIME ALARM
HR. MIN. SEC. 1/100S
TICK
Solar power
8RDD96
THE FAULT OF SCIENCE THAT HAS GONE TOO FAR IS VAST.
BUT HUMAN CURIOSITY CANNOT BE STOPPED.

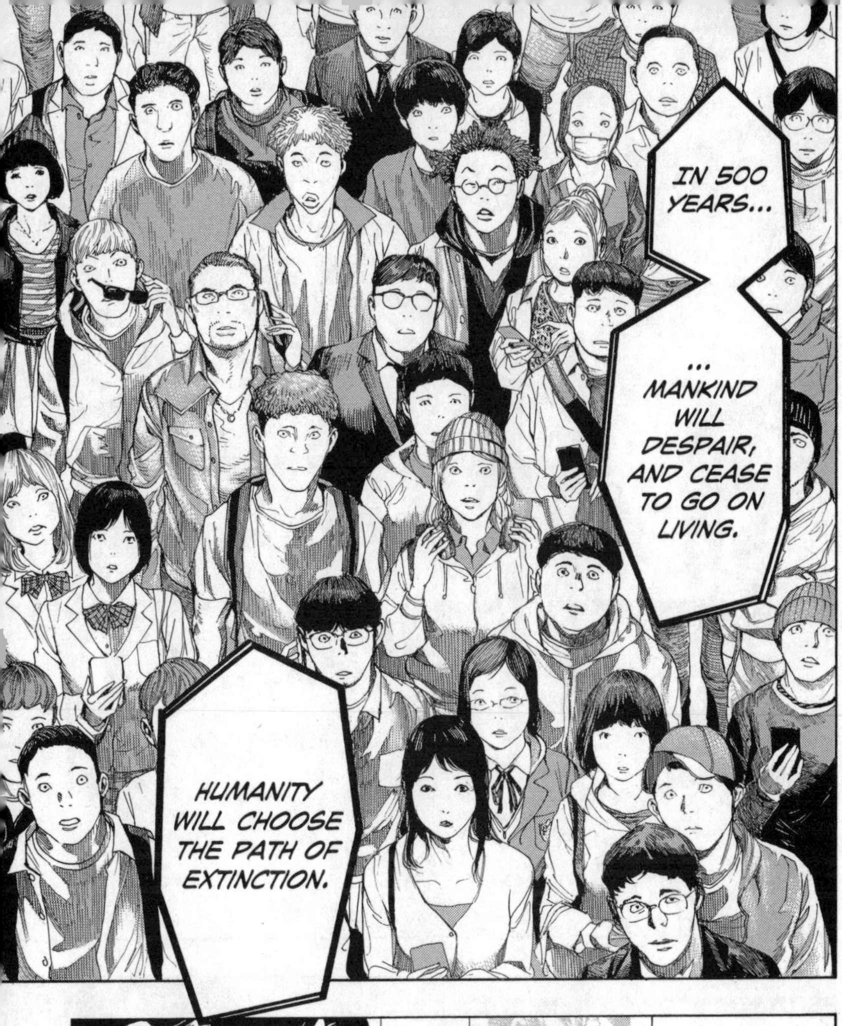
IN 500 YEARS...
... MANKIND WILL DESPAIR, AND CEASE TO GO ON LIVING.
HUMANITY WILL CHOOSE THE PATH OF EXTINCTION.
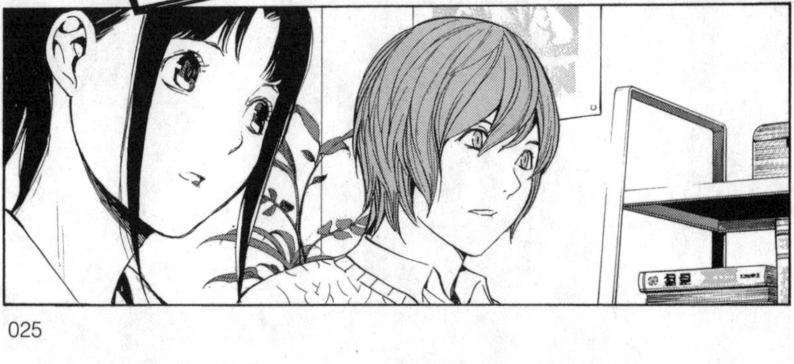

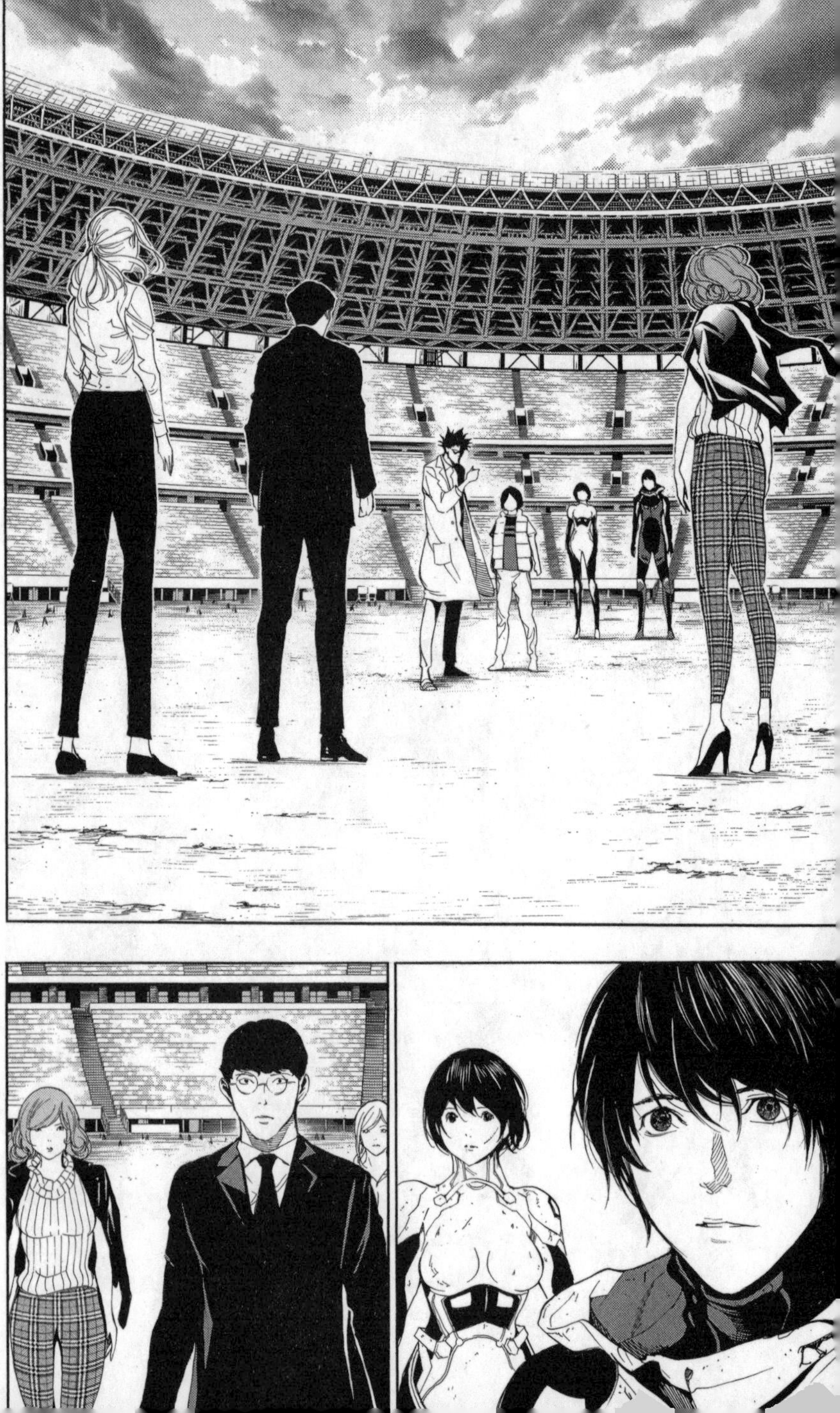

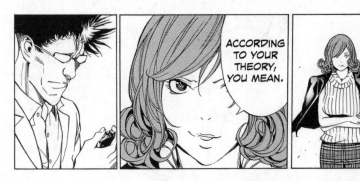

...
ACCORDING TO YOUR THEORY, YOU MEAN.
CONSIDERING THE SPEED AND DIRECTION OF SCIENCE'S ADVANCEMENT, IT IS CERTAIN THAT HUMANITY WILL STAND ABOVE THE CONSTRAINTS OF SPACE-TIME.
IF WE GAIN SCIENCE THAT CAN KNOW AND SEE THE FUTURE, IT WILL BE LESS THAN A CENTURY BEFORE WE CAN CREATE A TIME MACHINE...
...
FOR REAL?
...
I WANT ONE...
A TIME MACHINE ...
...OR SO IT WOULD HAVE SEEMED.

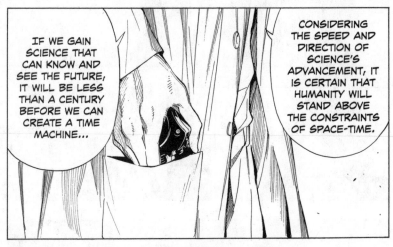

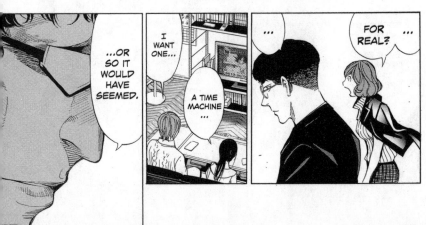

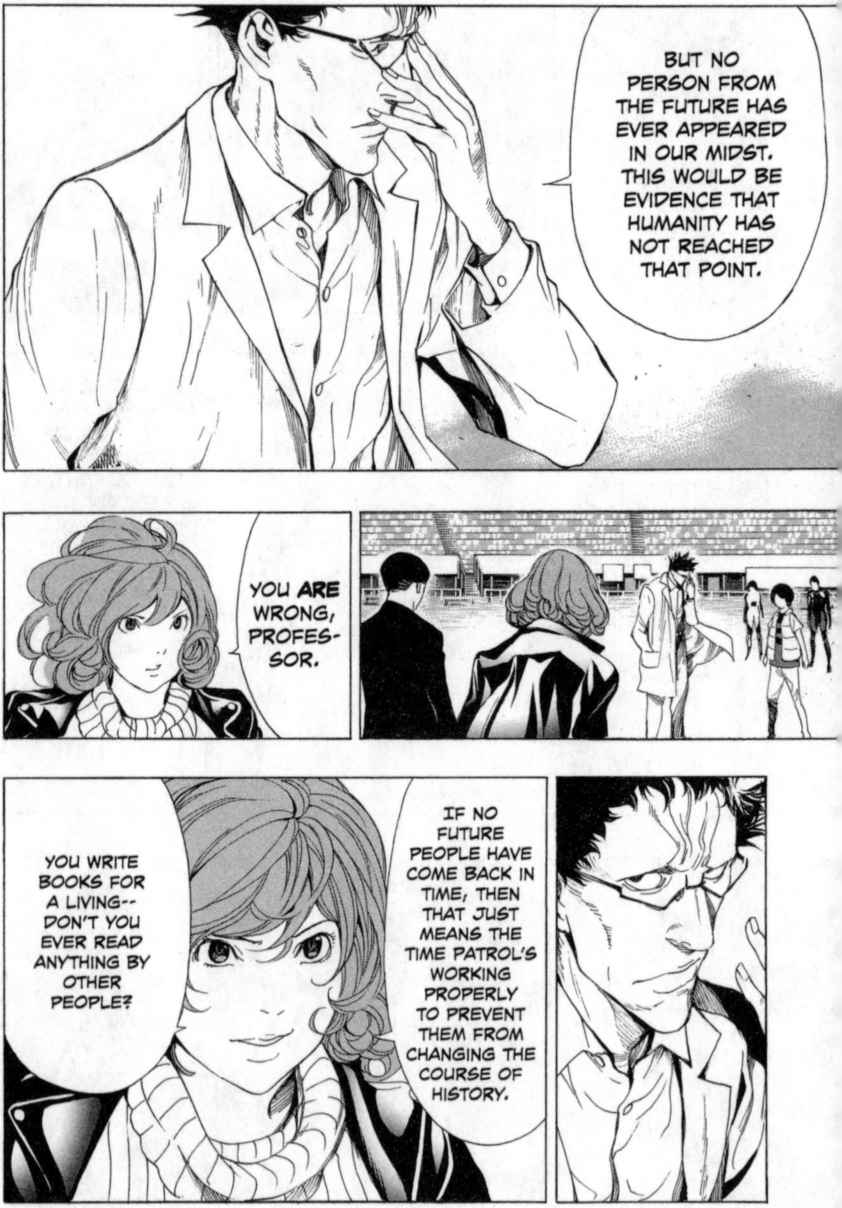
BUT NO PERSON FROM THE FUTURE HAS EVER APPEARED IN OUR MIDST. THIS WOULD BE EVIDENCE THAT HUMANITY HAS NOT REACHED THAT POINT.
YOU **ARE** WRONG, PROFES-SOR.
IF NO FUTURE PEOPLE HAVE COME BACK IN TIME, THEN THAT JUST MEANS THE TIME PATROL'S WORKING PROPERLY TO PREVENT THEM FROM CHANGING THE COURSE OF HISTORY.
YOU WRITE BOOKS FOR A LIVING--DON'T YOU EVER READ ANYTHING BY OTHER PEOPLE?

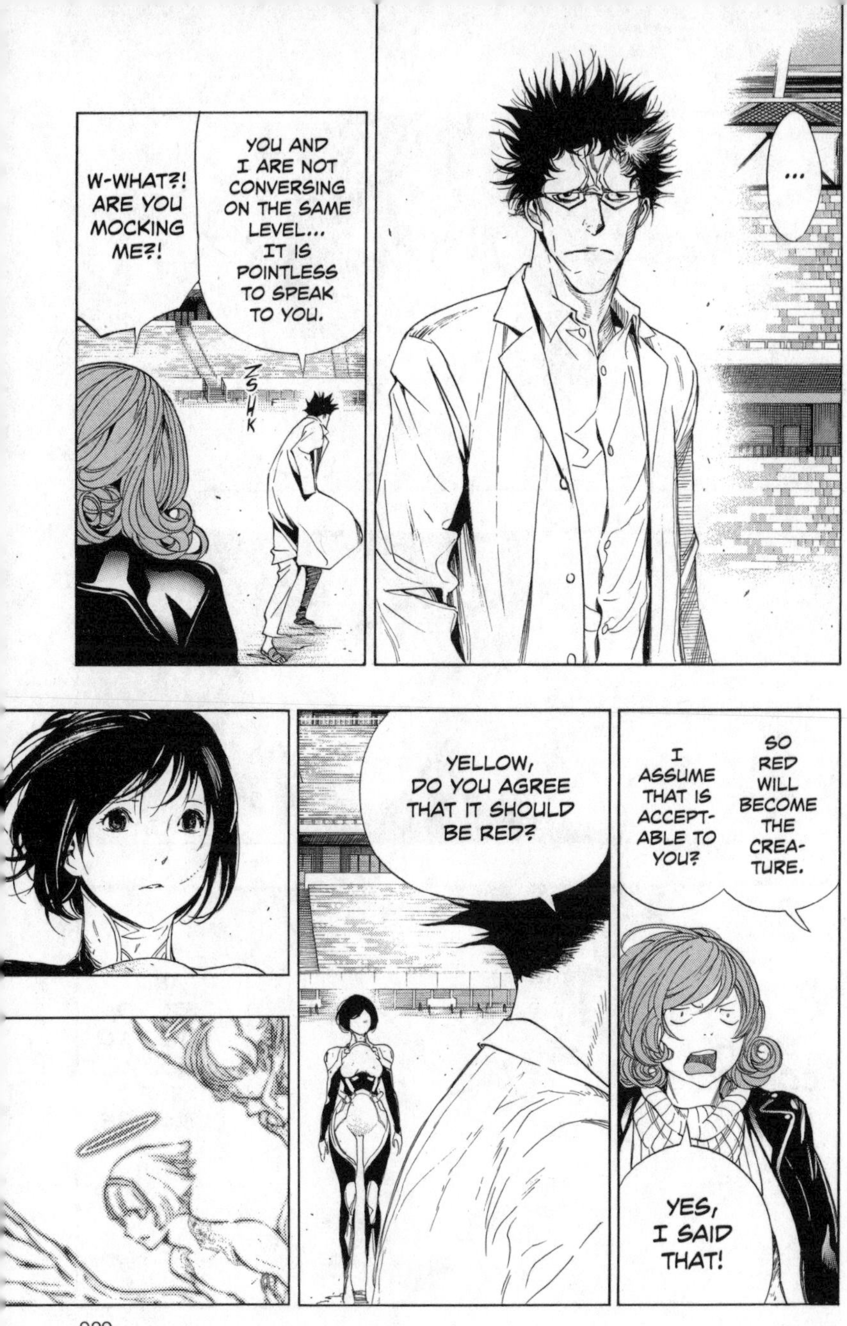
...
YOU AND I ARE NOT CONVERSING ON THE SAME LEVEL... IT IS POINTLESS TO SPEAK TO YOU.
ZSHK
W-WHAT?! ARE YOU MOCKING ME?!
SO RED WILL BECOME THE CREA-TURE.
I ASSUME THAT IS ACCEPT-ABLE TO YOU?
YES, I SAID THAT!
YELLOW, DO YOU AGREE THAT IT SHOULD BE RED?

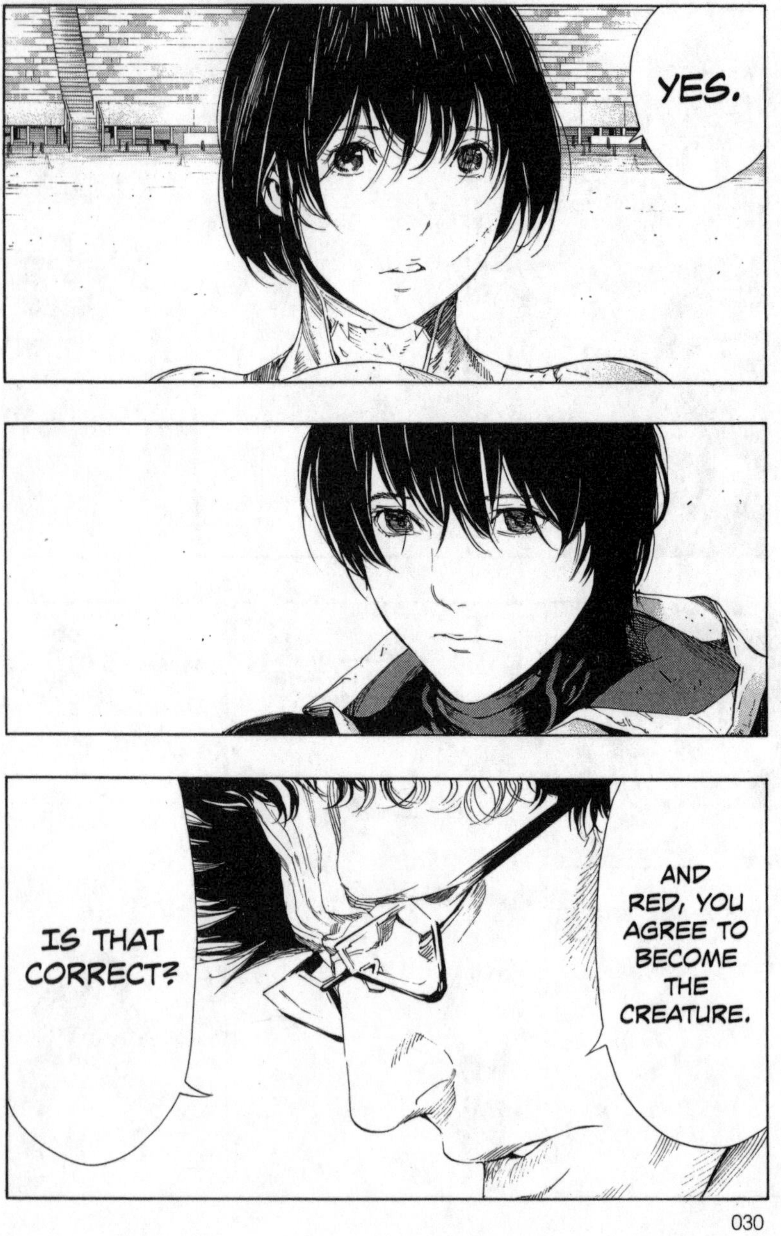
YES.
AND RED, YOU AGREE TO BECOME THE CREATURE.
IS THAT CORRECT?

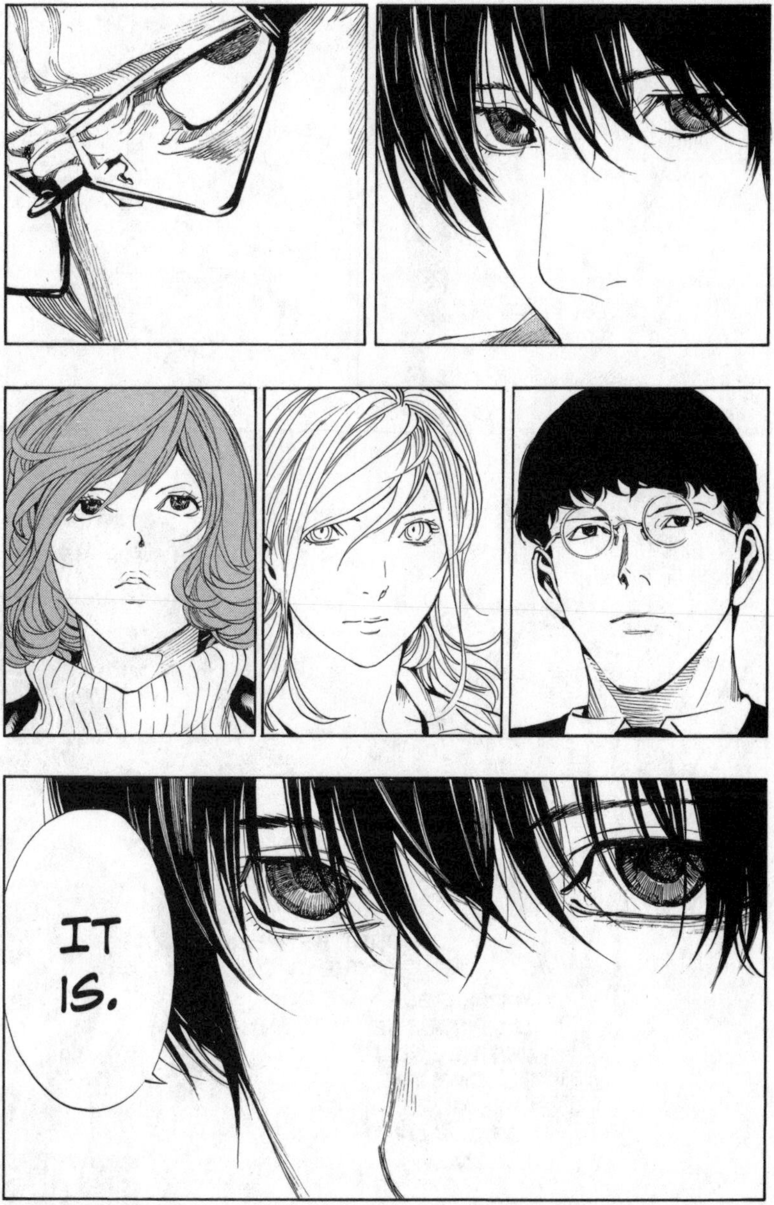
IT IS.

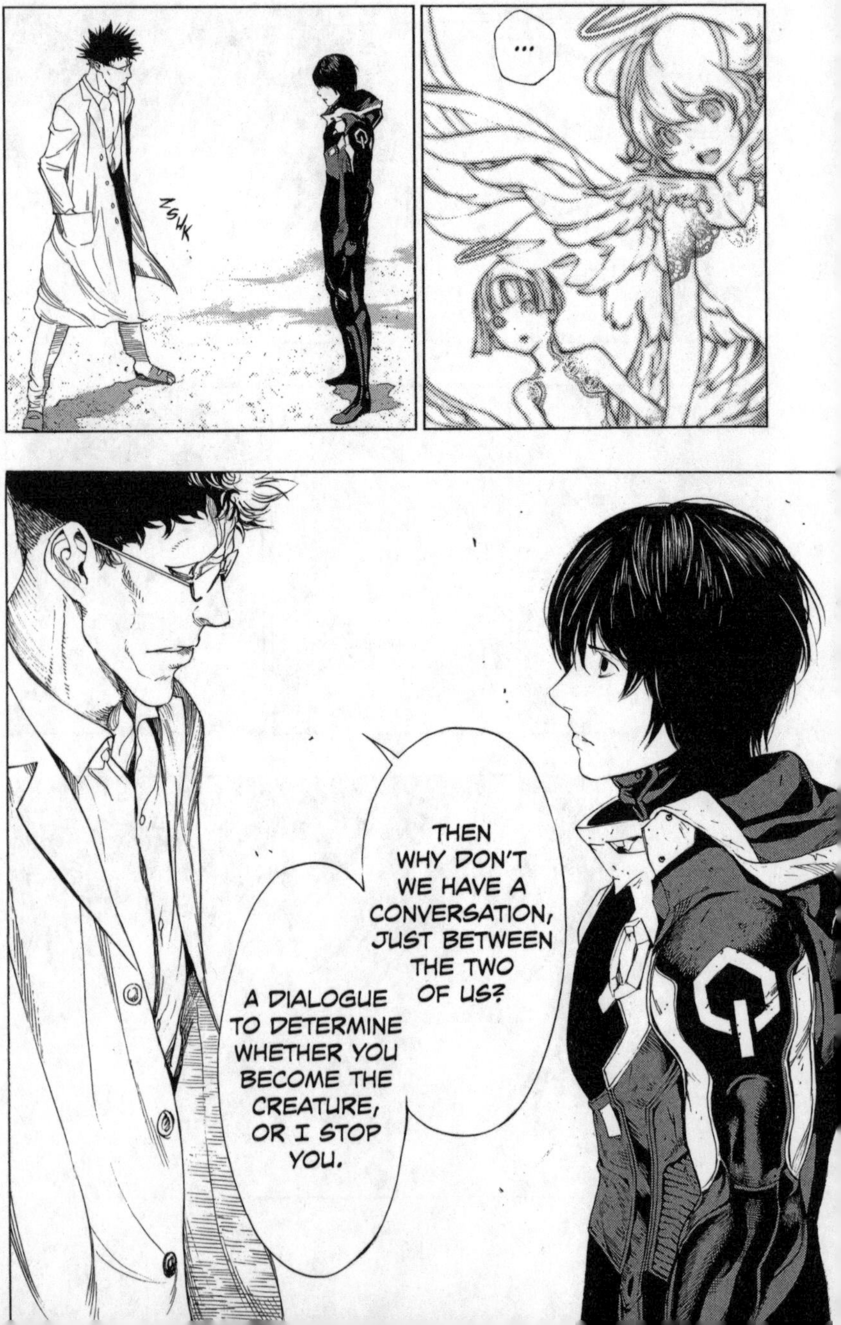
...
ZSHK
THEN WHY DON'T WE HAVE A CONVERSATION, JUST BETWEEN THE TWO OF US?
A DIALOGUE TO DETERMINE WHETHER YOU BECOME THE CREATURE, OR I STOP YOU.

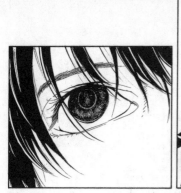

...

I DON'T MIND.

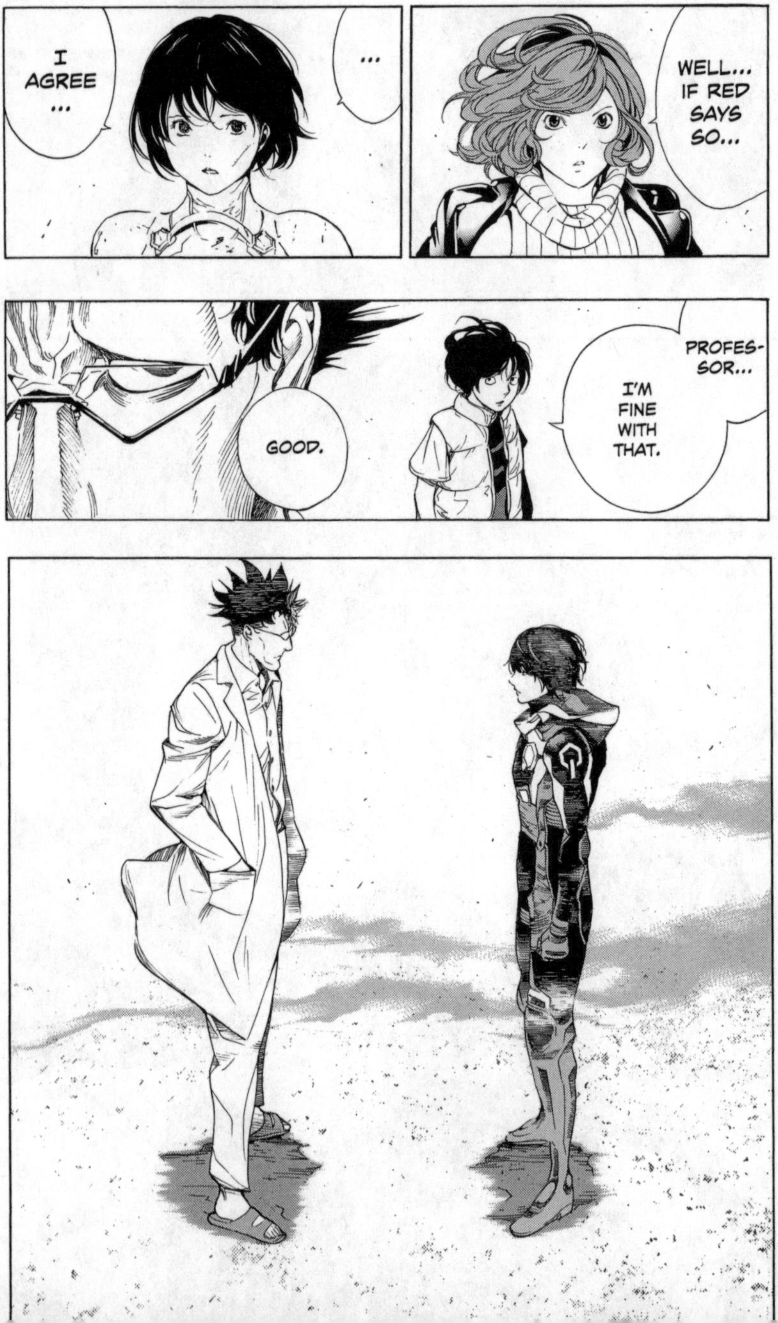
WELL... IF RED SAYS SO...
...
I AGREE ...
PROFES-SOR...
I'M FINE WITH THAT.
GOOD.

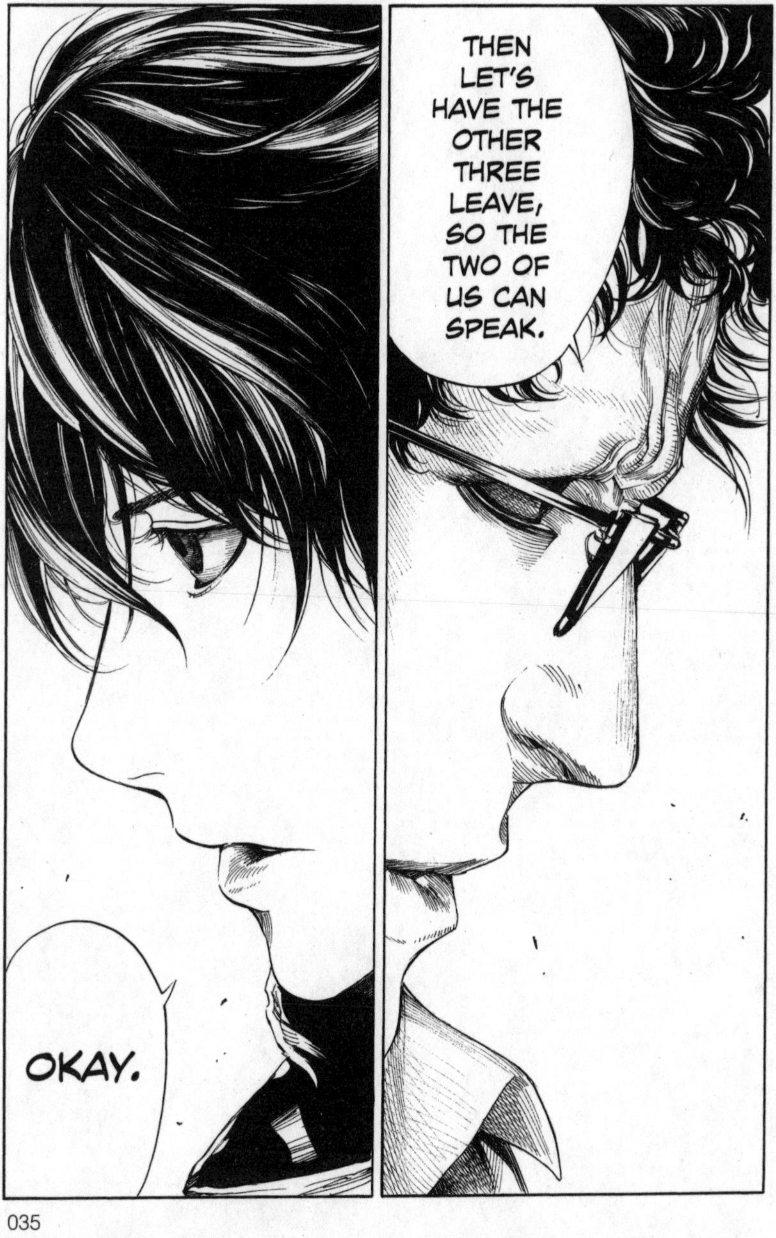
THEN LET'S HAVE THE OTHER THREE LEAVE, SO THE TWO OF US CAN SPEAK.
OKAY.

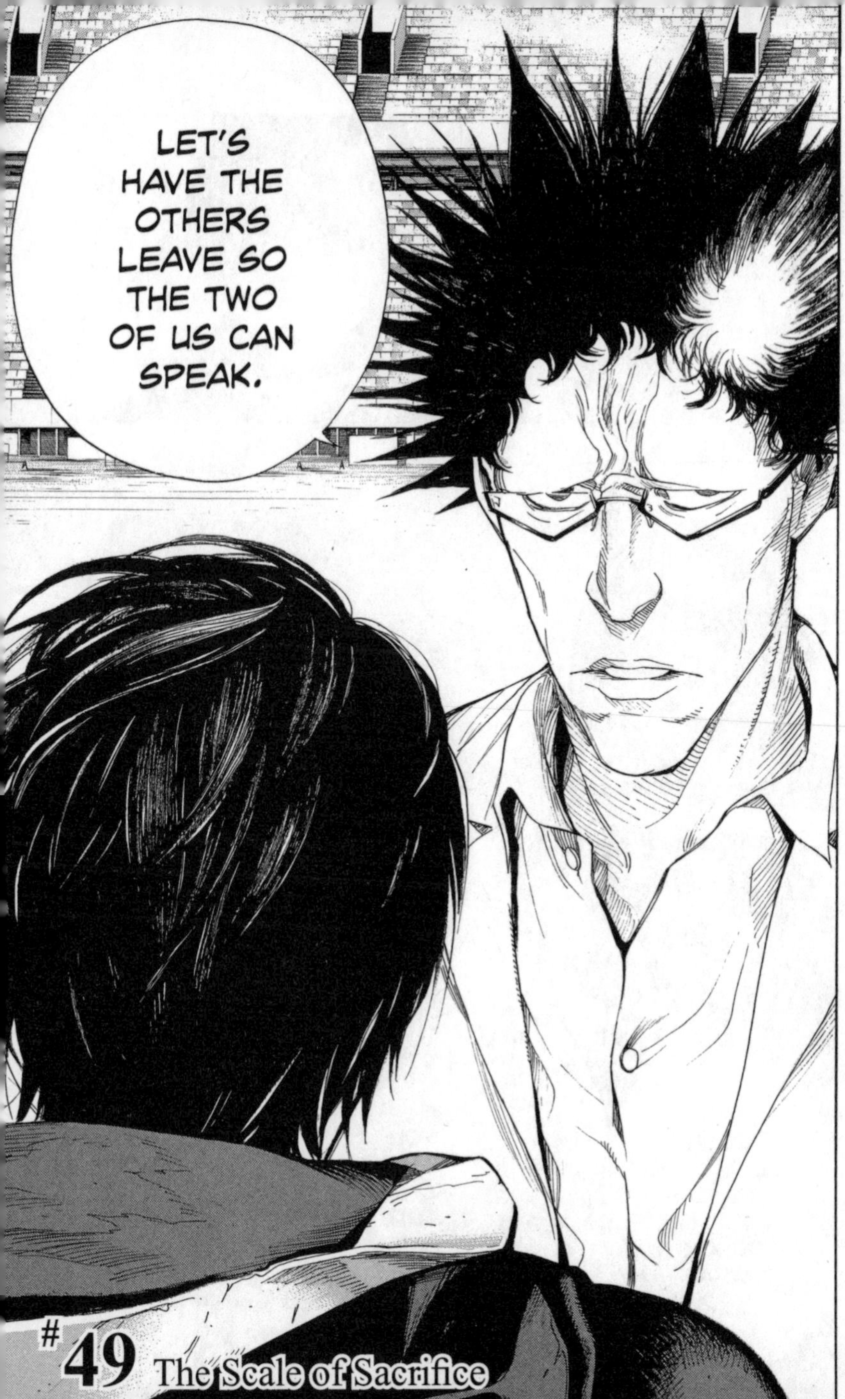
LET'S HAVE THE OTHERS LEAVE SO THE TWO OF US CAN SPEAK.
#49 The Scale of Sacrifice

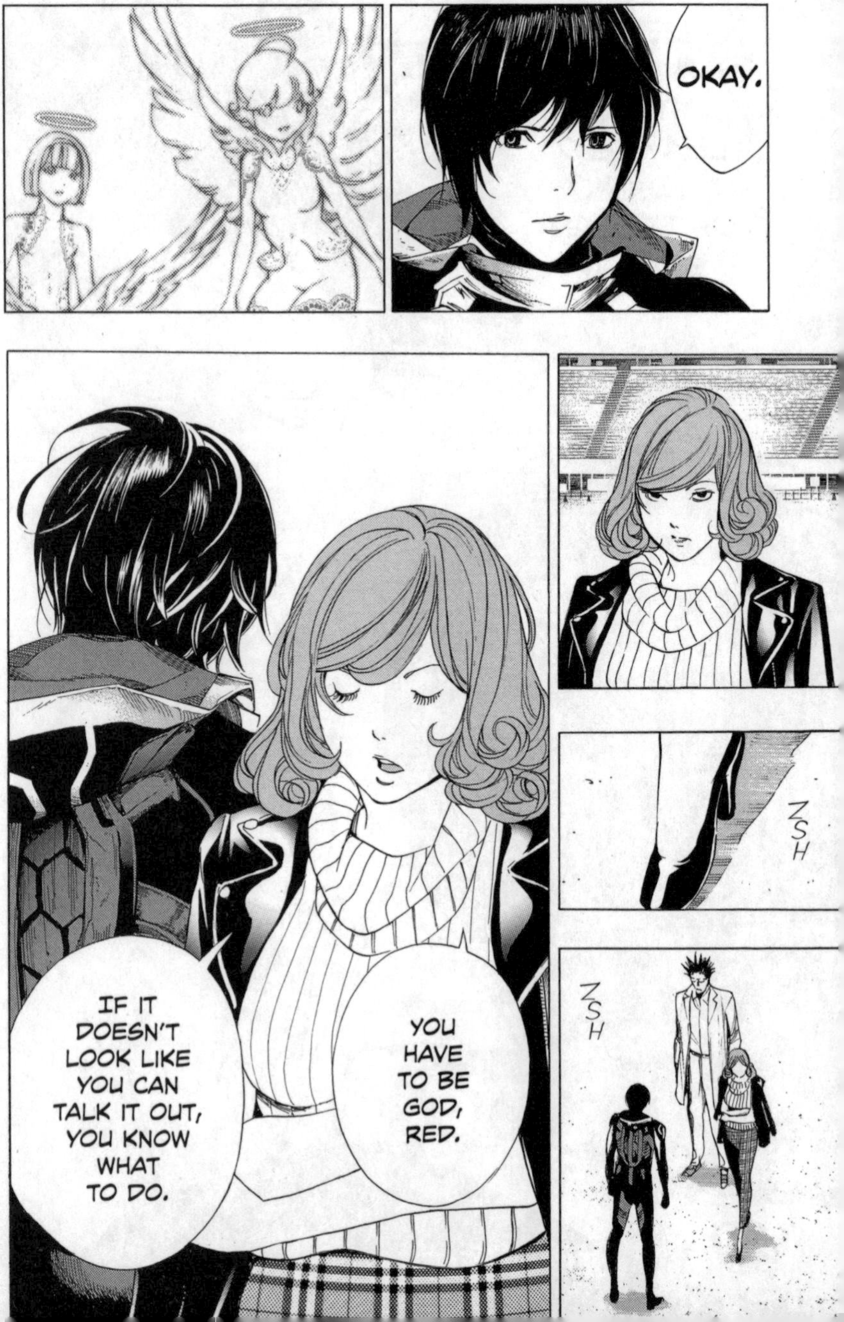
OKAY.
ZSH
ZSH
YOU HAVE TO BE GOD, RED.
IF IT DOESN'T LOOK LIKE YOU CAN TALK IT OUT, YOU KNOW WHAT TO DO.

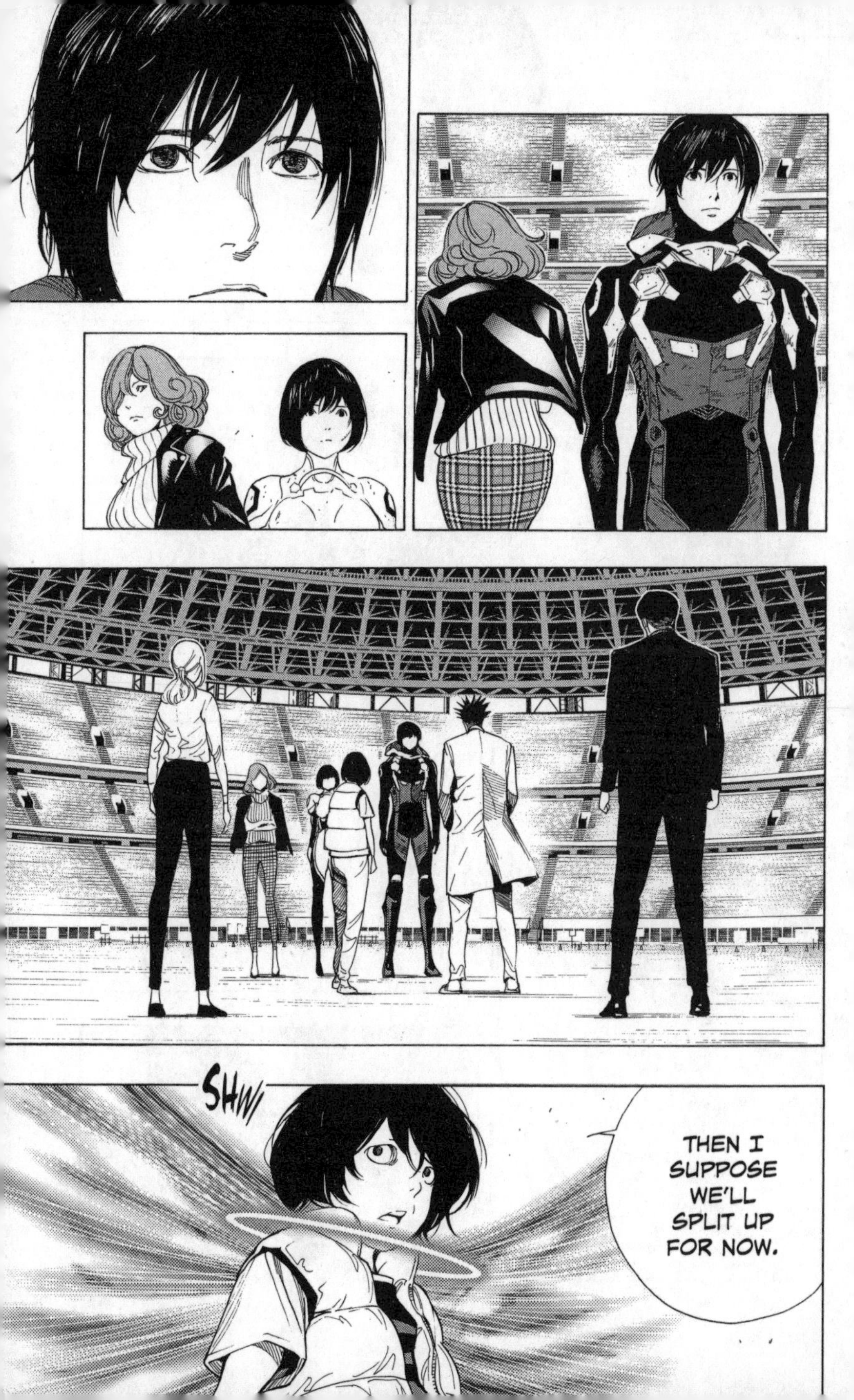
THEN I SUPPOSE WE'LL SPLIT UP FOR NOW.
SHW

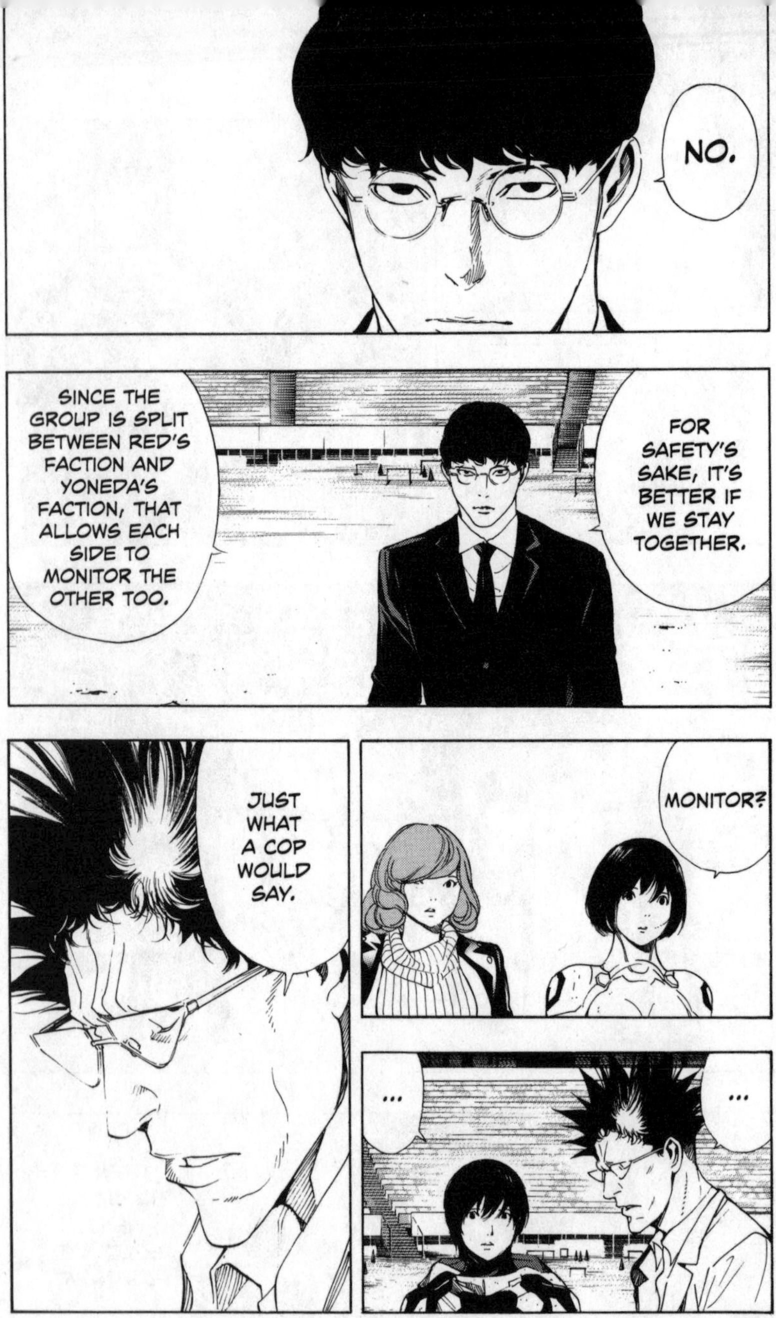
NO.
FOR SAFETY'S SAKE, IT'S BETTER IF WE STAY TOGETHER.
SINCE THE GROUP IS SPLIT BETWEEN RED'S FACTION AND YONEDA'S FACTION, THAT ALLOWS EACH SIDE TO MONITOR THE OTHER TOO.
MONITOR?
...
...
JUST WHAT A COP WOULD SAY.

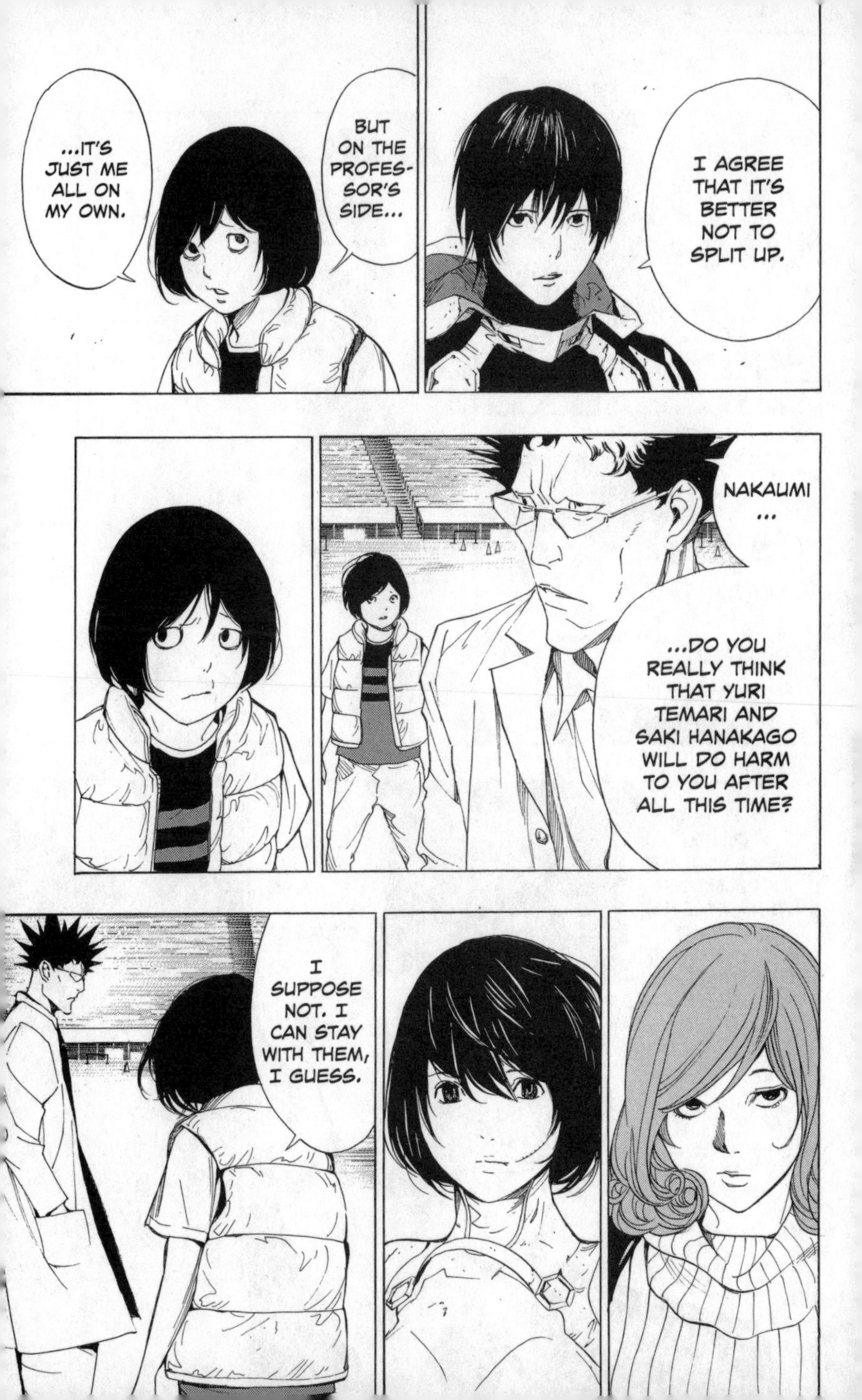
I AGREE THAT IT'S BETTER NOT TO SPLIT UP.
BUT ON THE PROFES-SOR'S SIDE...
...IT'S JUST ME ALL ON MY OWN.
NAKAUMI ...
...DO YOU REALLY THINK THAT YURI TEMARI AND SAKI HANAKAGO WILL DO HARM TO YOU AFTER ALL THIS TIME?
I SUPPOSE NOT. I CAN STAY WITH THEM, I GUESS.

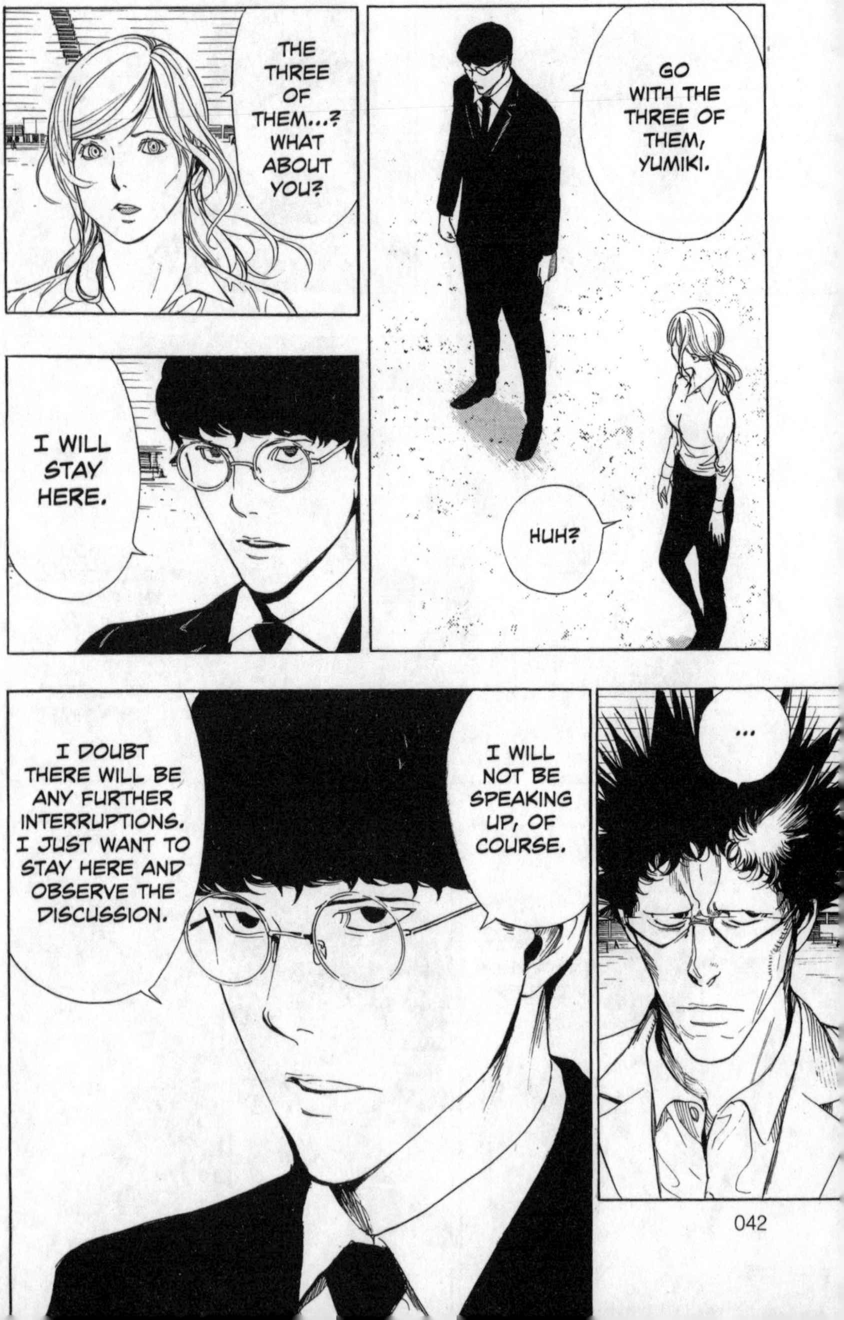
GO WITH THE THREE OF THEM, YUMIKI.
HUH?
THE THREE OF THEM...? WHAT ABOUT YOU?
I WILL STAY HERE.
...
I WILL NOT BE SPEAKING UP, OF COURSE.
I DOUBT THERE WILL BE ANY FURTHER INTERRUPTIONS. I JUST WANT TO STAY HERE AND OBSERVE THE DISCUSSION.

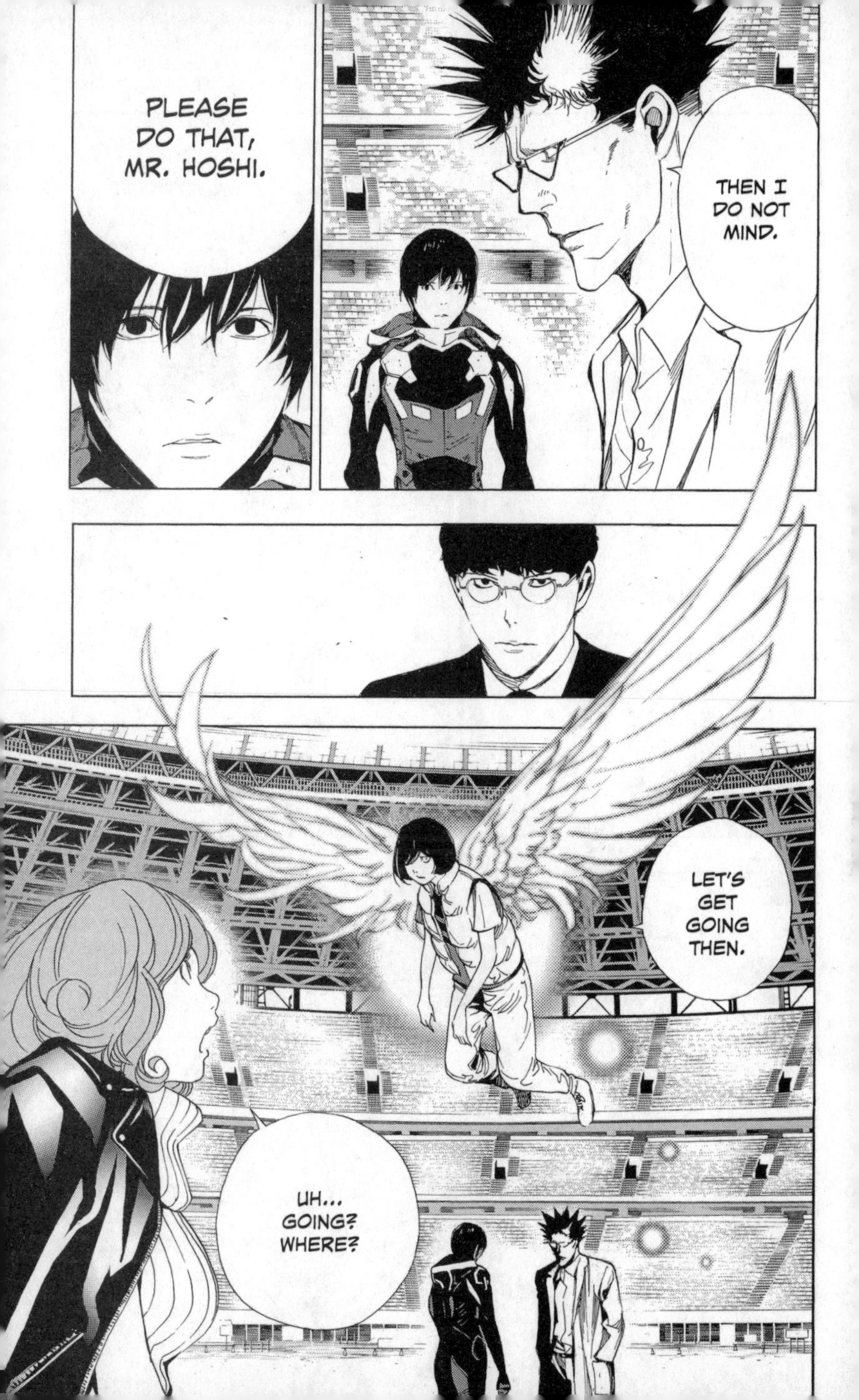
THEN I DO NOT MIND.
PLEASE DO THAT, MR. HOSHI.
LET'S GET GOING THEN.
UH... GOING? WHERE?

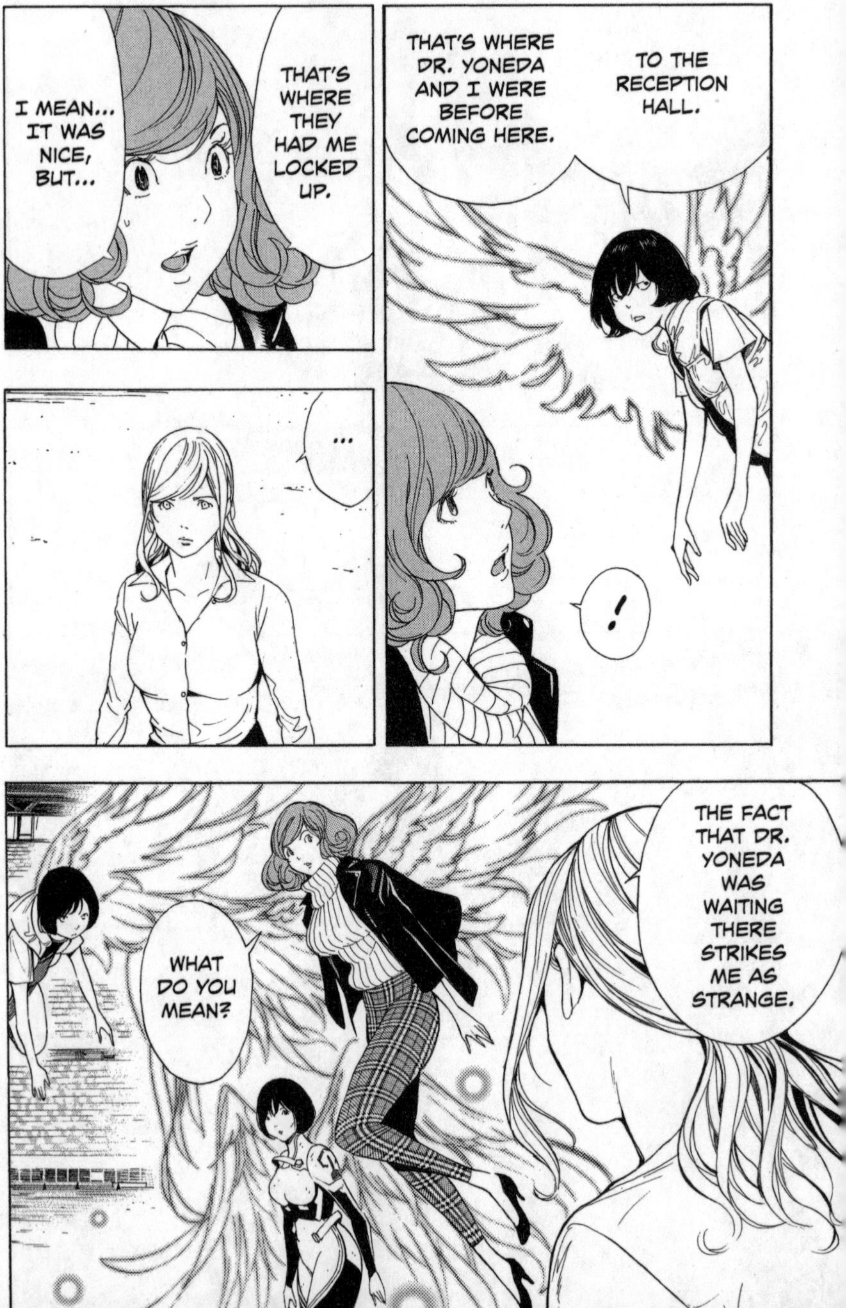
TO THE RECEPTION HALL.
THAT'S WHERE DR. YONEDA AND I WERE BEFORE COMING HERE.
!
THAT'S WHERE THEY HAD ME LOCKED UP.
I MEAN... IT WAS NICE, BUT...
...
THE FACT THAT DR. YONEDA WAS WAITING THERE STRIKES ME AS STRANGE.
WHAT DO YOU MEAN?

NO, IT'S FINE. THERE'S SECURITY THERE, BUT WE HAVE A RED ARROW IN THE PRIME MINISTER SO THAT THE NEGOTIATIONS CAN GO SMOOTHLY. HE'S NOT ALLOWED TO DEFY THE GOD CANDIDATES.
THERE'S AN UNLOCKED WINDOW SO THAT THEY CAN'T DETECT US COMING AND GOING.
WELL, YOU DON'T HAVE TO COME IF YOU DON'T WANT TO.
YOU'RE NOT A CANDIDATE ANYWAY.
FWOOSH
...

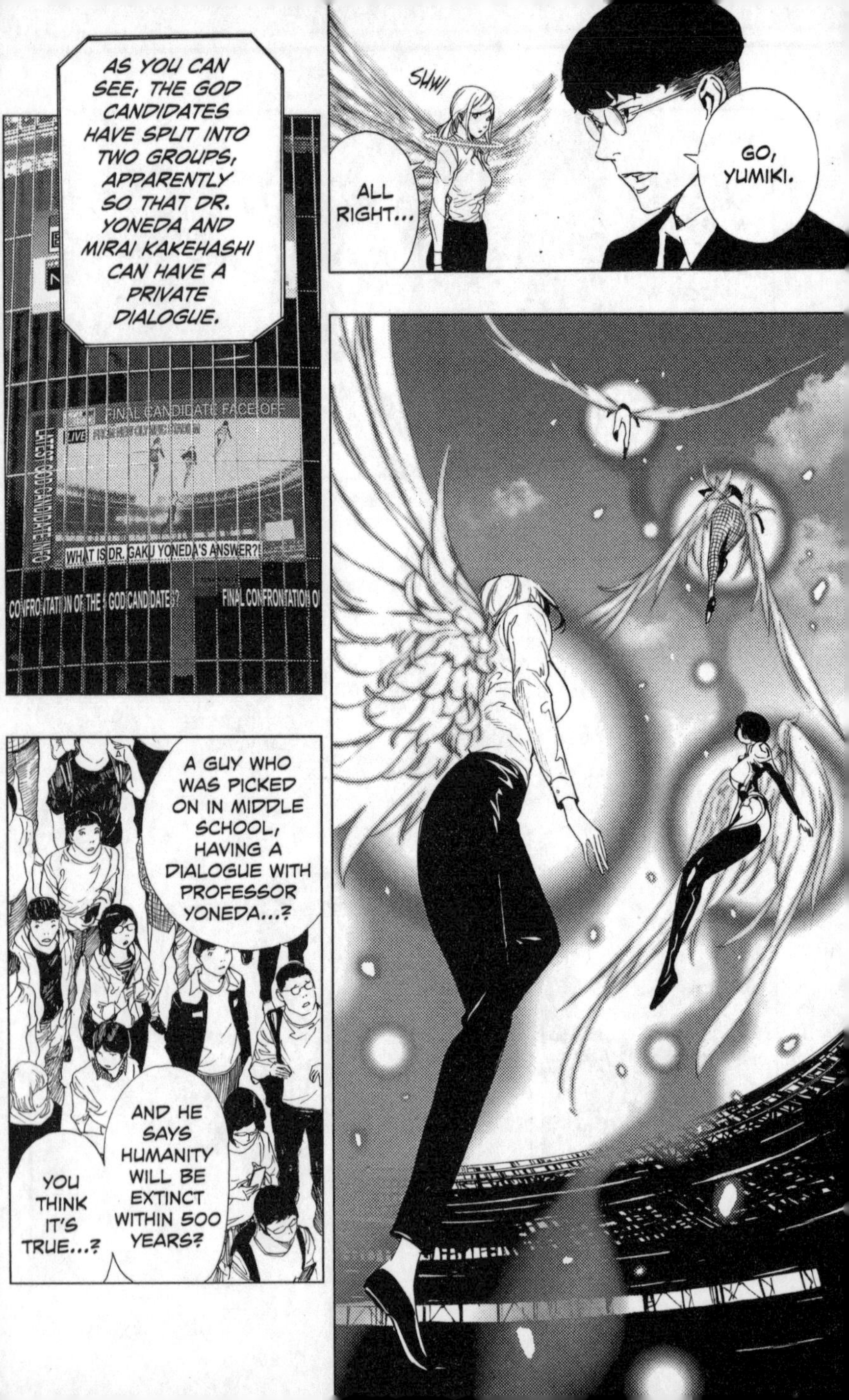
GO, YUMIKI.
SHWI
ALL RIGHT...
AS YOU CAN SEE, THE GOD CANDIDATES HAVE SPLIT INTO TWO GROUPS, APPARENTLY SO THAT DR. YONEDA AND MIRAI KAKEHASHI CAN HAVE A PRIVATE DIALOGUE.
FINAL CANDIDATE FACE-OFF
LIVE
LATEST GOD CANDIDATE INFO
WHAT IS DR. GAKU YONEDA'S ANSWER?!
CONFRONTATION OF THE GOD CANDIDATES?
FINAL CONFRONTATION O
A GUY WHO WAS PICKED ON IN MIDDLE SCHOOL, HAVING A DIALOGUE WITH PROFESSOR YONEDA...?
AND HE SAYS HUMANITY WILL BE EXTINCT WITHIN 500 YEARS?
YOU THINK IT'S TRUE...?

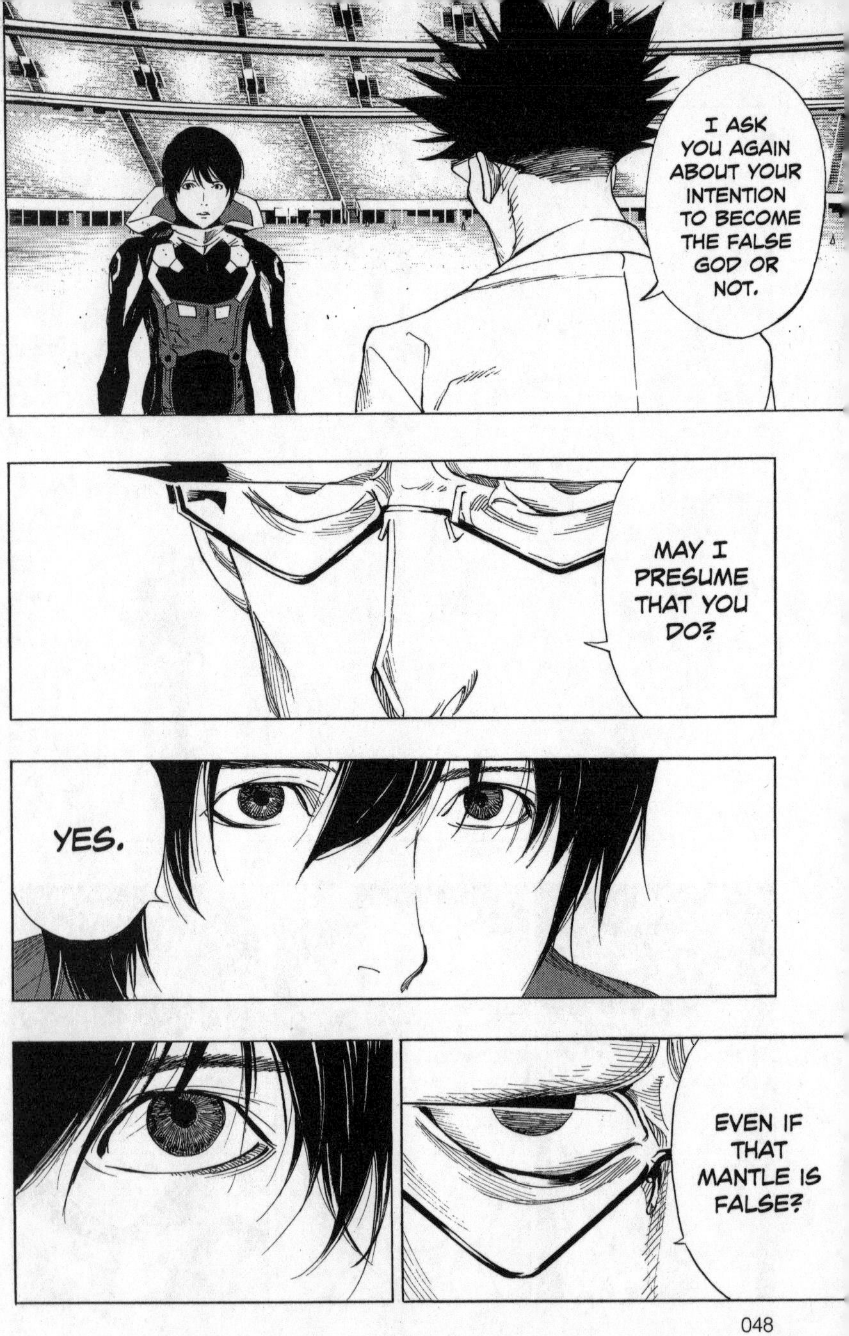
I ASK YOU AGAIN ABOUT YOUR INTENTION TO BECOME THE FALSE GOD OR NOT.
MAY I PRESUME THAT YOU DO?
YES.
EVEN IF THAT MANTLE IS FALSE?

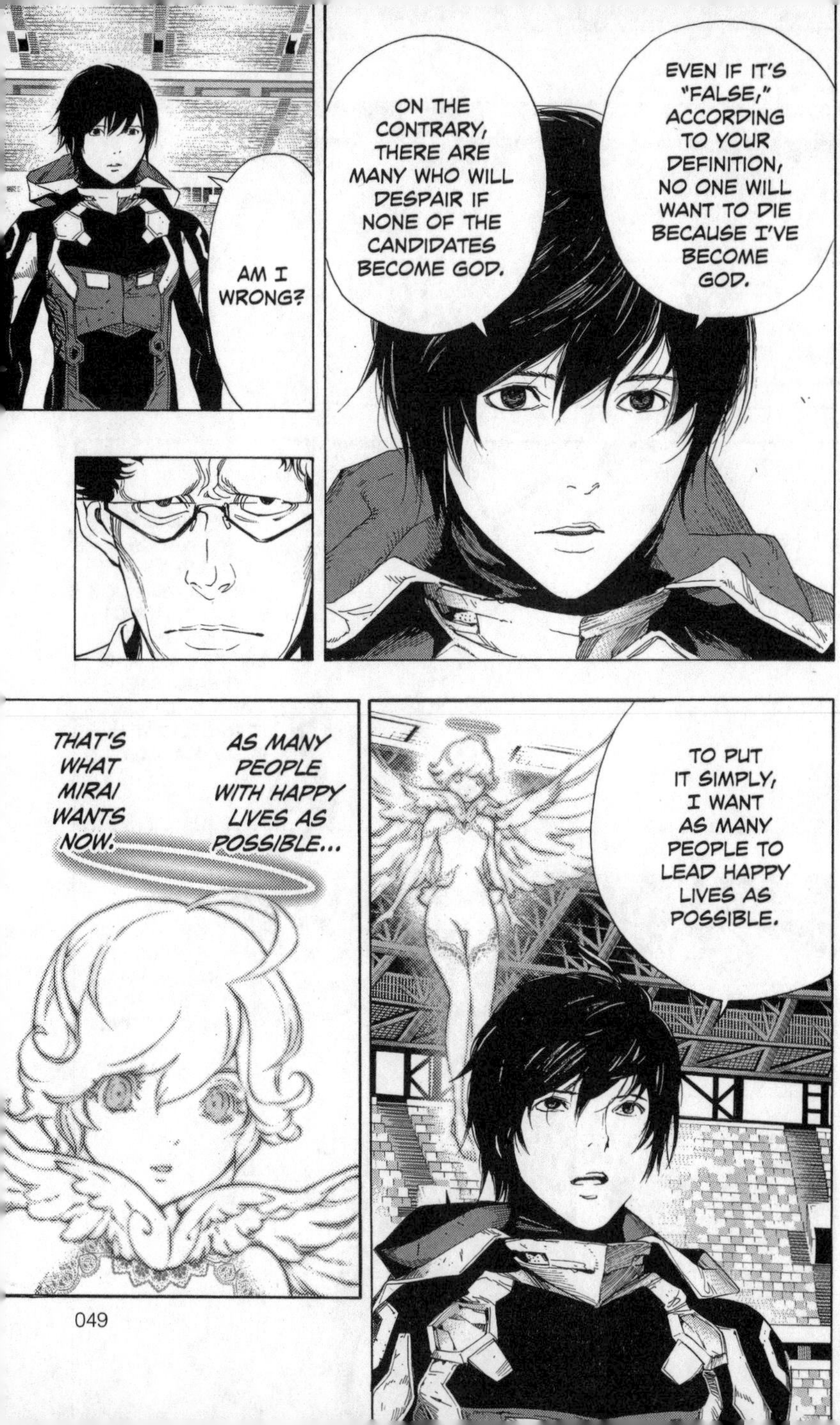
EVEN IF IT'S "FALSE," ACCORDING TO YOUR DEFINITION, NO ONE WILL WANT TO DIE BECAUSE I'VE BECOME GOD.
ON THE CONTRARY, THERE ARE MANY WHO WILL DESPAIR IF NONE OF THE CANDIDATES BECOME GOD.
AM I WRONG?
TO PUT IT SIMPLY, I WANT AS MANY PEOPLE TO LEAD HAPPY LIVES AS POSSIBLE.
AS MANY PEOPLE WITH HAPPY LIVES AS POSSIBLE...
THAT'S WHAT MIRAI WANTS NOW.

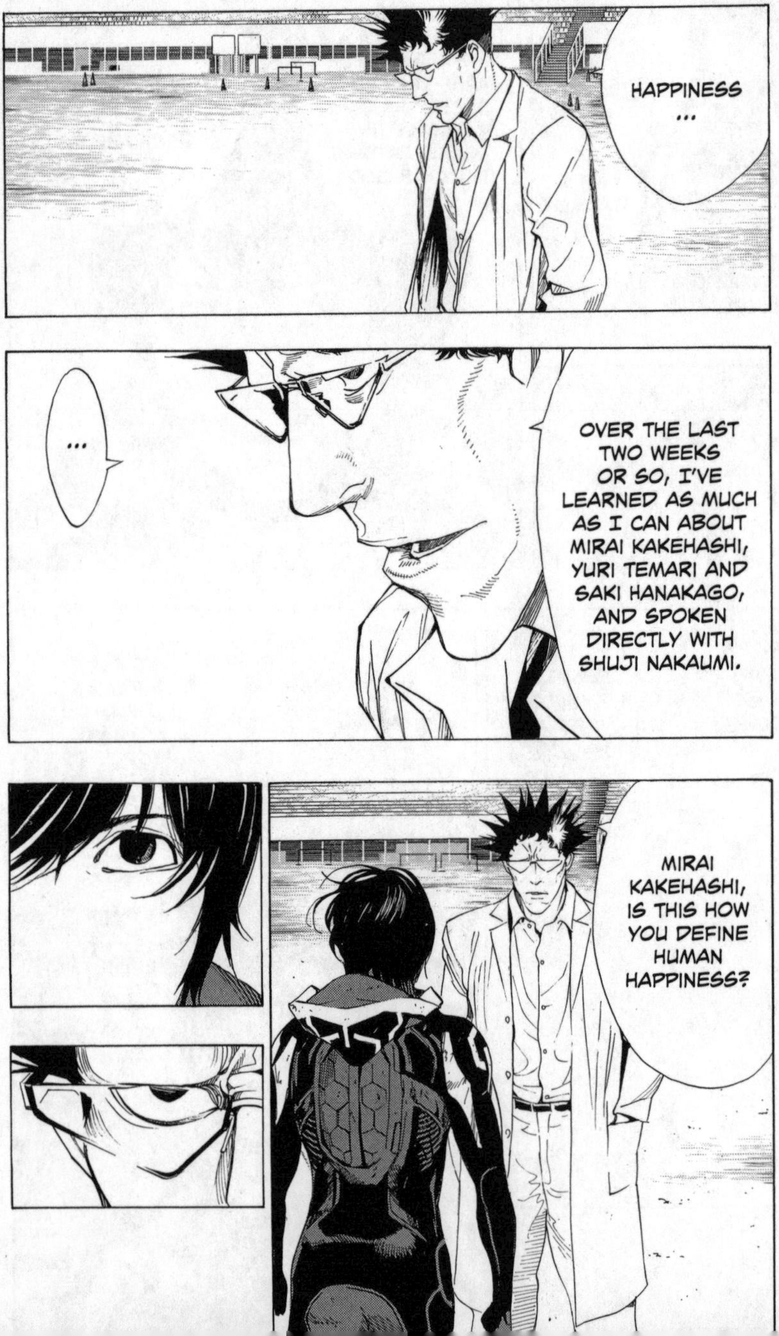
HAPPINESS ...
OVER THE LAST TWO WEEKS OR SO, I'VE LEARNED AS MUCH AS I CAN ABOUT MIRAI KAKEHASHI, YURI TEMARI AND SAKI HANAKAGO, AND SPOKEN DIRECTLY WITH SHUJI NAKAUMI.
...
MIRAI KAKEHASHI, IS THIS HOW YOU DEFINE HUMAN HAPPINESS?

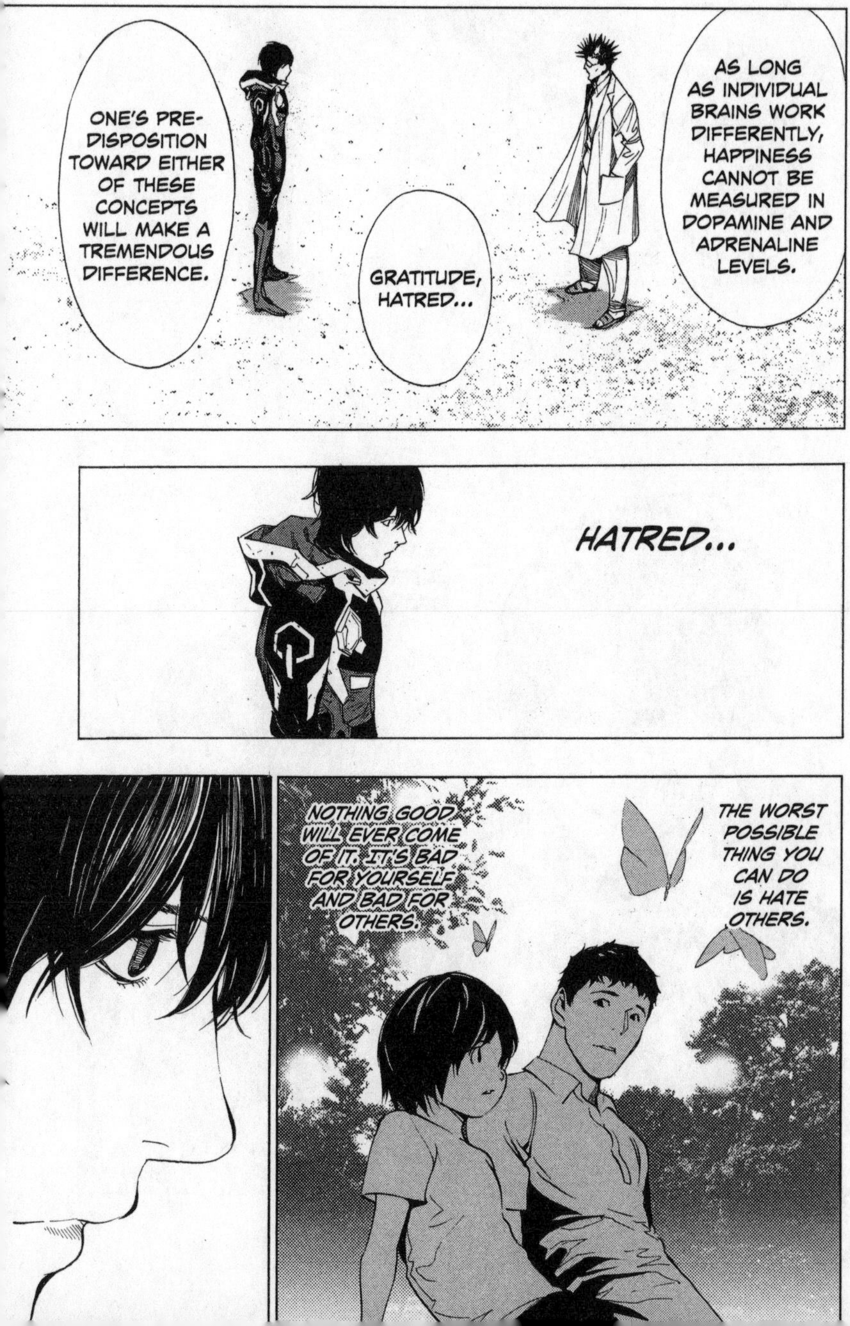
AS LONG AS INDIVIDUAL BRAINS WORK DIFFERENTLY, HAPPINESS CANNOT BE MEASURED IN DOPAMINE AND ADRENALINE LEVELS.
GRATITUDE, HATRED...
ONE'S PRE-DISPOSITION TOWARD EITHER OF THESE CONCEPTS WILL MAKE A TREMENDOUS DIFFERENCE.
HATRED...
THE WORST POSSIBLE THING YOU CAN DO IS HATE OTHERS.
NOTHING GOOD WILL EVER COME OF IT. IT'S BAD FOR YOURSELF AND BAD FOR OTHERS.

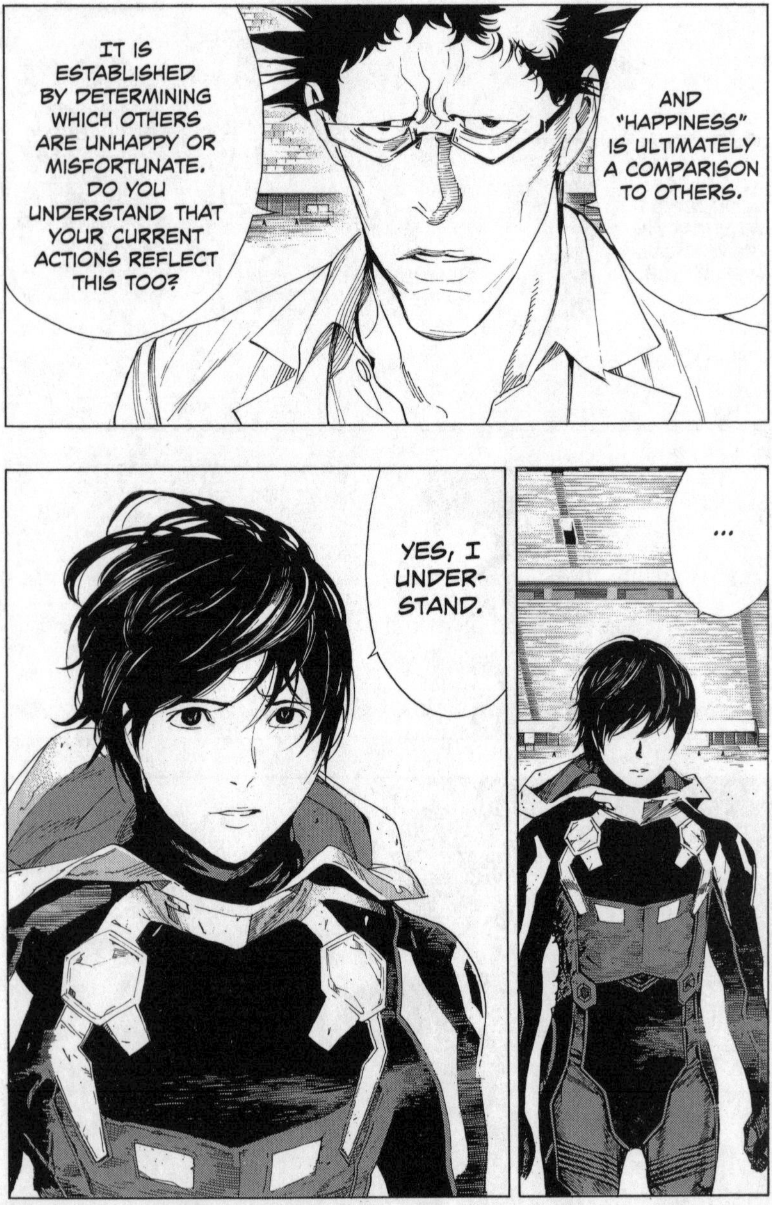
AND "HAPPINESS" IS ULTIMATELY A COMPARISON TO OTHERS.
IT IS ESTABLISHED BY DETERMINING WHICH OTHERS ARE UNHAPPY OR MISFORTUNATE. DO YOU UNDERSTAND THAT YOUR CURRENT ACTIONS REFLECT THIS TOO?
...
YES, I UNDER-STAND.

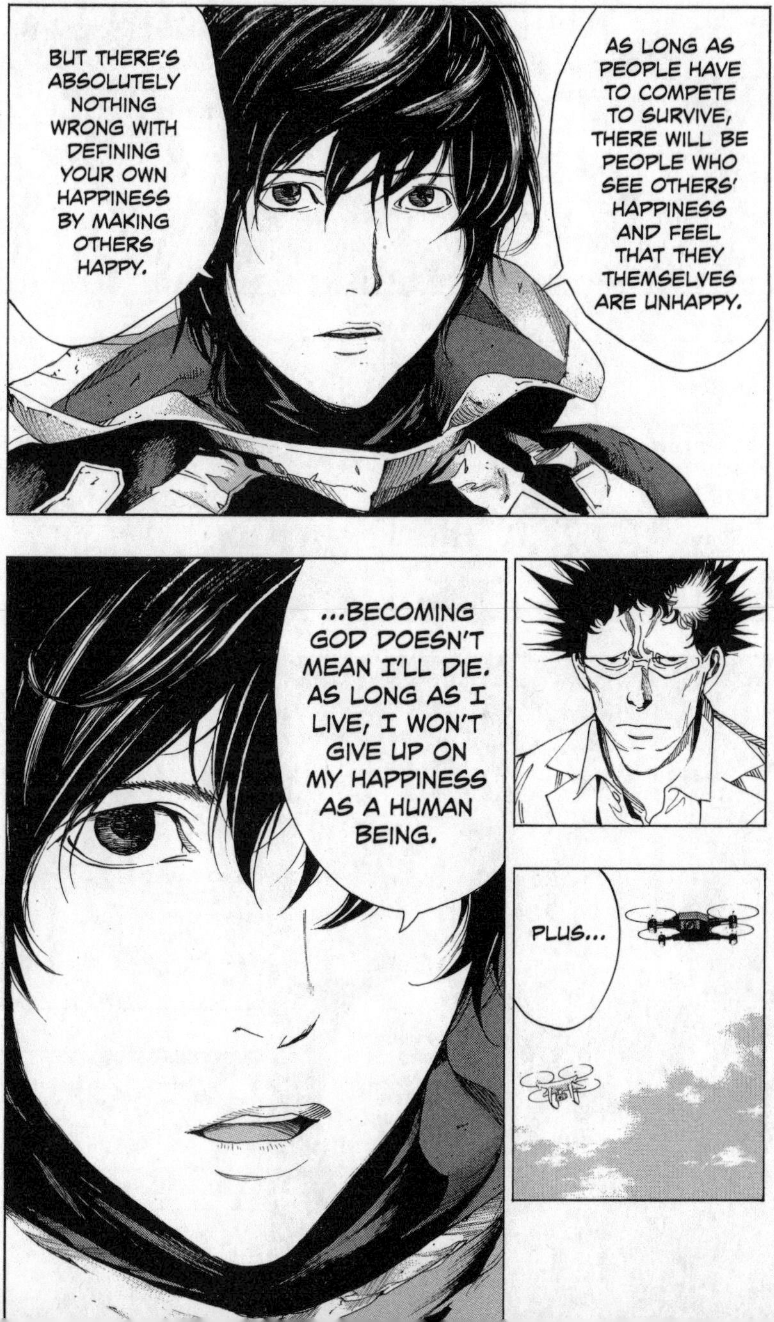
AS LONG AS PEOPLE HAVE TO COMPETE TO SURVIVE, THERE WILL BE PEOPLE WHO SEE OTHERS' HAPPINESS AND FEEL THAT THEY THEMSELVES ARE UNHAPPY.
BUT THERE'S ABSOLUTELY NOTHING WRONG WITH DEFINING YOUR OWN HAPPINESS BY MAKING OTHERS HAPPY.
PLUS...
...BECOMING GOD DOESN'T MEAN I'LL DIE. AS LONG AS I LIVE, I WON'T GIVE UP ON MY HAPPINESS AS A HUMAN BEING.

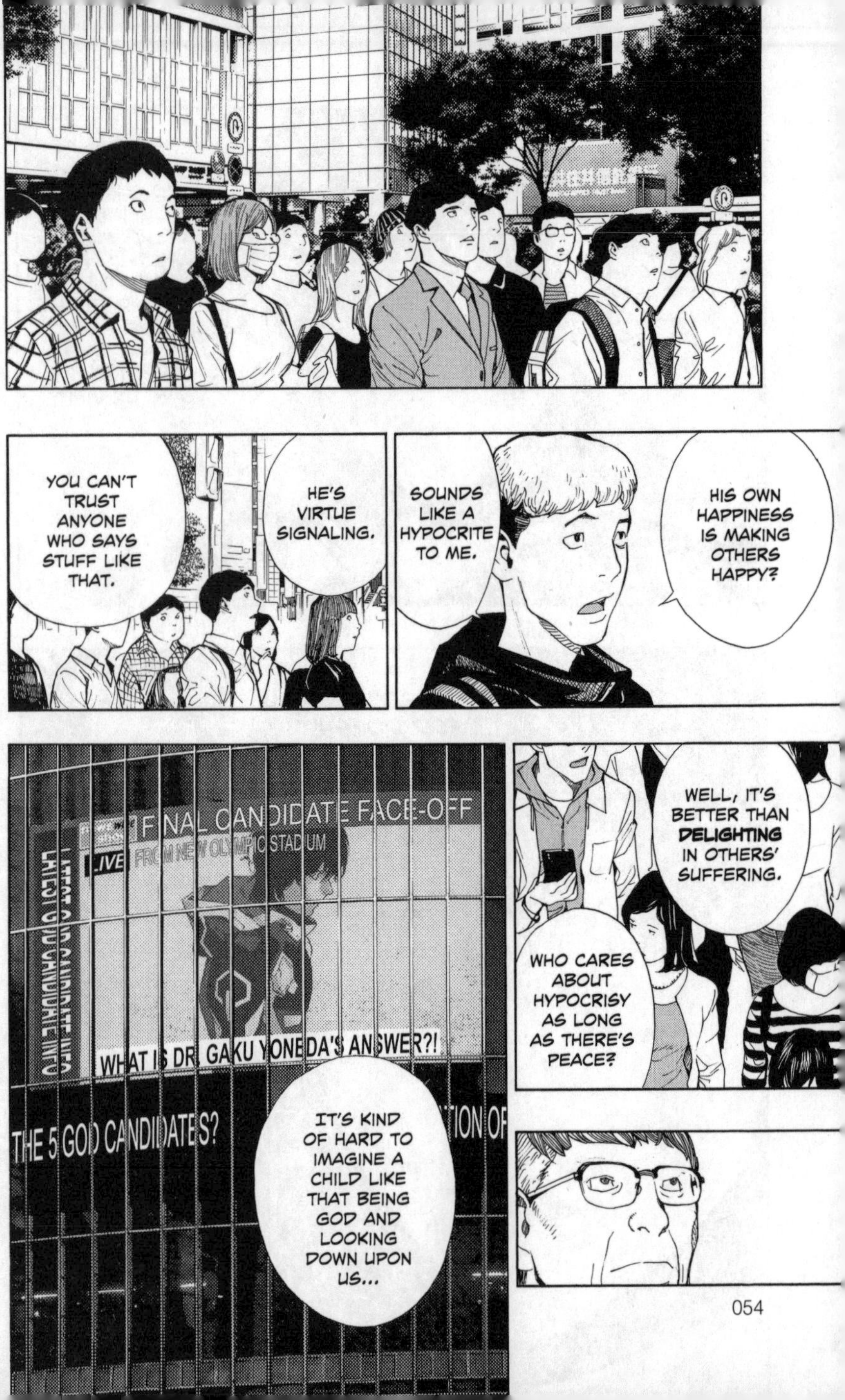
HIS OWN HAPPINESS IS MAKING OTHERS HAPPY?
SOUNDS LIKE A HYPOCRITE TO ME.
HE'S VIRTUE SIGNALING.
YOU CAN'T TRUST ANYONE WHO SAYS STUFF LIKE THAT.
WELL, IT'S BETTER THAN **DELIGHTING** IN OTHERS' SUFFERING.
WHO CARES ABOUT HYPOCRISY AS LONG AS THERE'S PEACE?
FINAL CANDIDATE FACE-OFF
LIVE FROM NEW OLYMPIC STADIUM
LATEST GOD CANDIDATE INFO
WHAT IS DR. GAKU YONEDA'S ANSWER?!
THE 5 GOD CANDIDATES?
IT'S KIND OF HARD TO IMAGINE A CHILD LIKE THAT BEING GOD AND LOOKING DOWN UPON US...

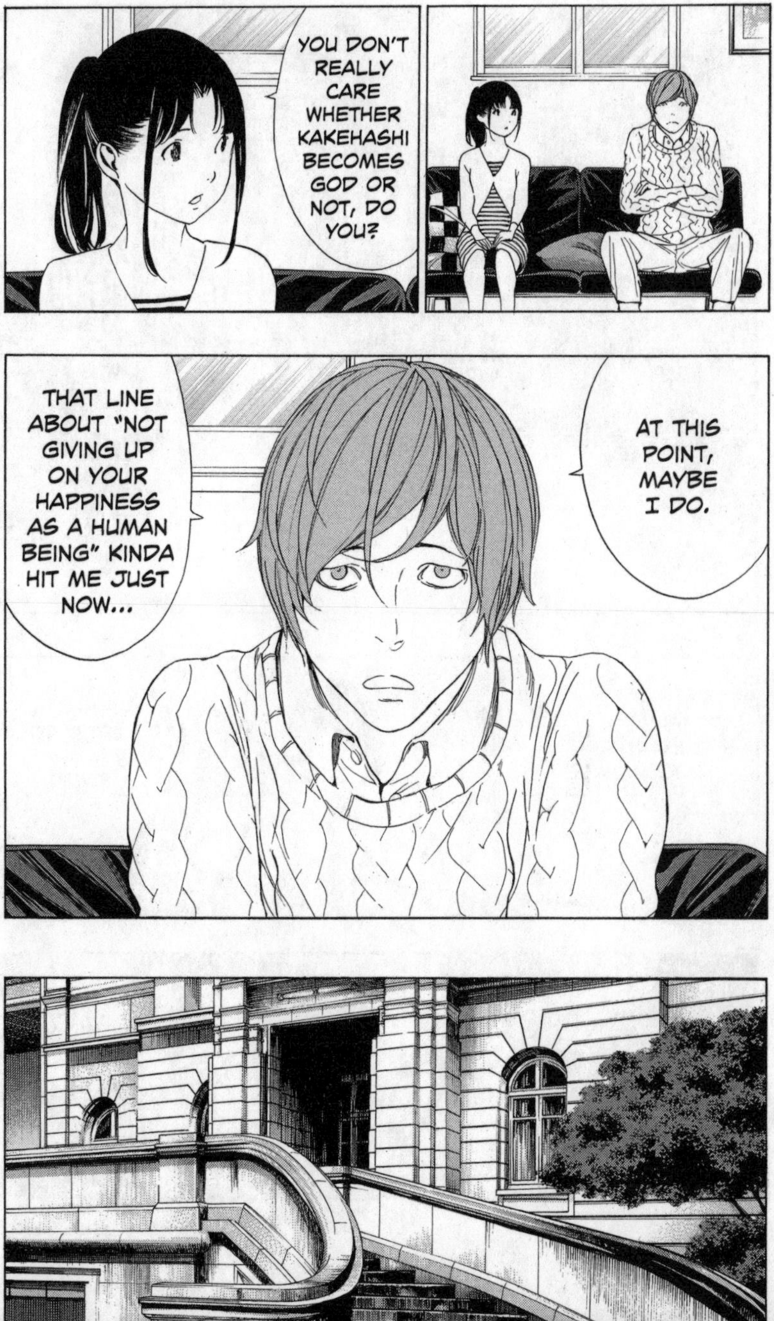
YOU DON'T REALLY CARE WHETHER KAKEHASHI BECOMES GOD OR NOT, DO YOU?
AT THIS POINT, MAYBE I DO.
THAT LINE ABOUT "NOT GIVING UP ON YOUR HAPPINESS AS A HUMAN BEING" KINDA HIT ME JUST NOW...

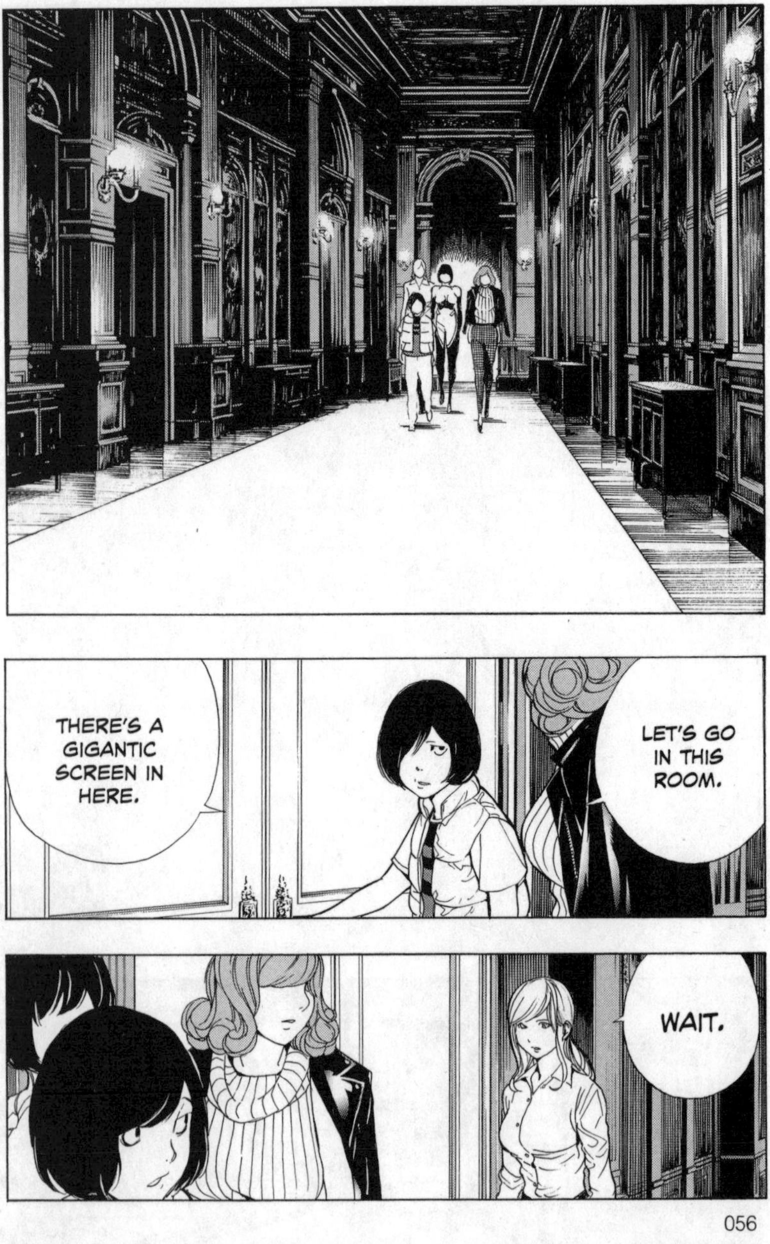
LET'S GO IN THIS ROOM.
THERE'S A GIGANTIC SCREEN IN HERE.
WAIT.

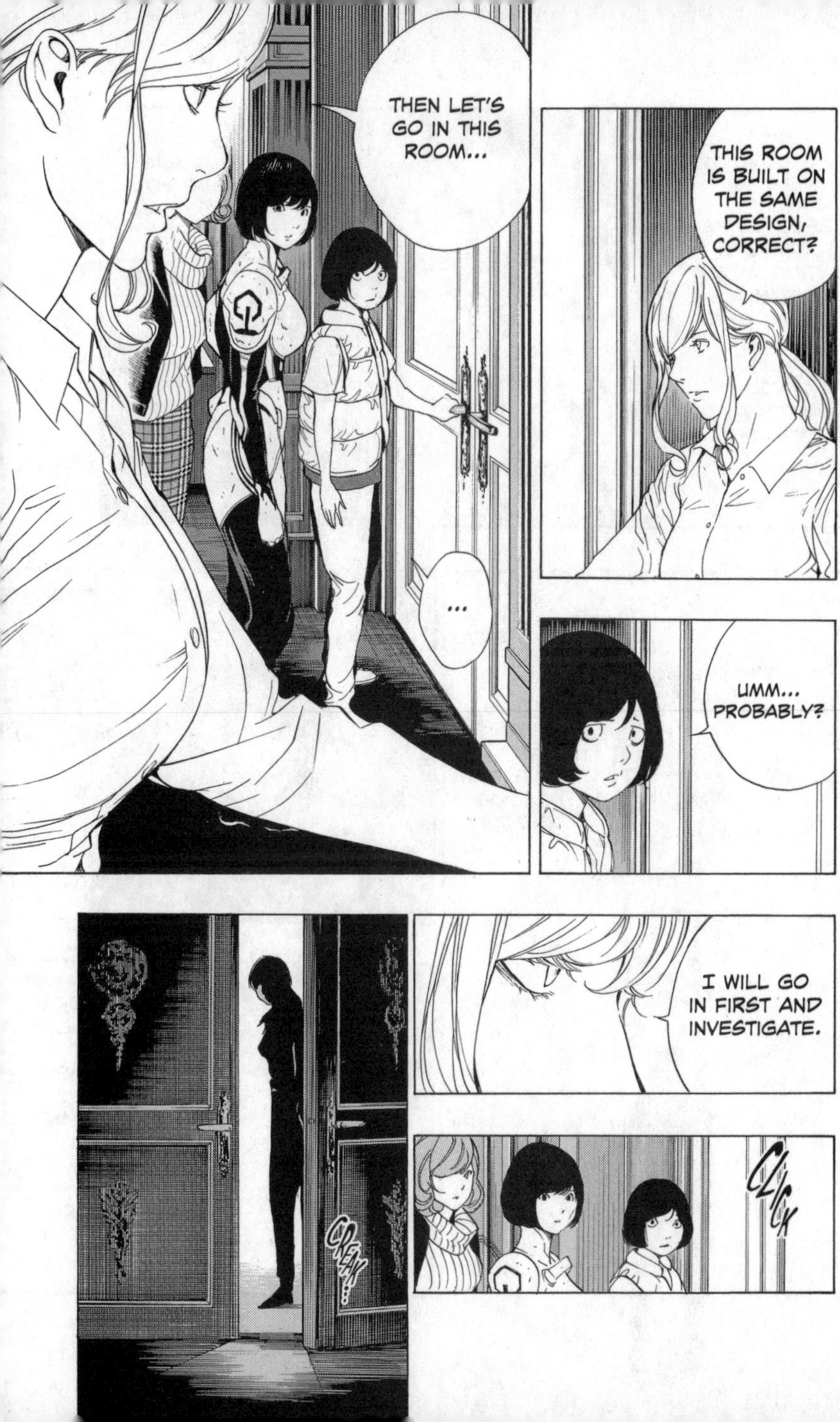
THIS ROOM IS BUILT ON THE SAME DESIGN, CORRECT?
UMM... PROBABLY?
THEN LET'S GO IN THIS ROOM...
...
I WILL GO IN FIRST AND INVESTIGATE.
CLICK
CREAK...

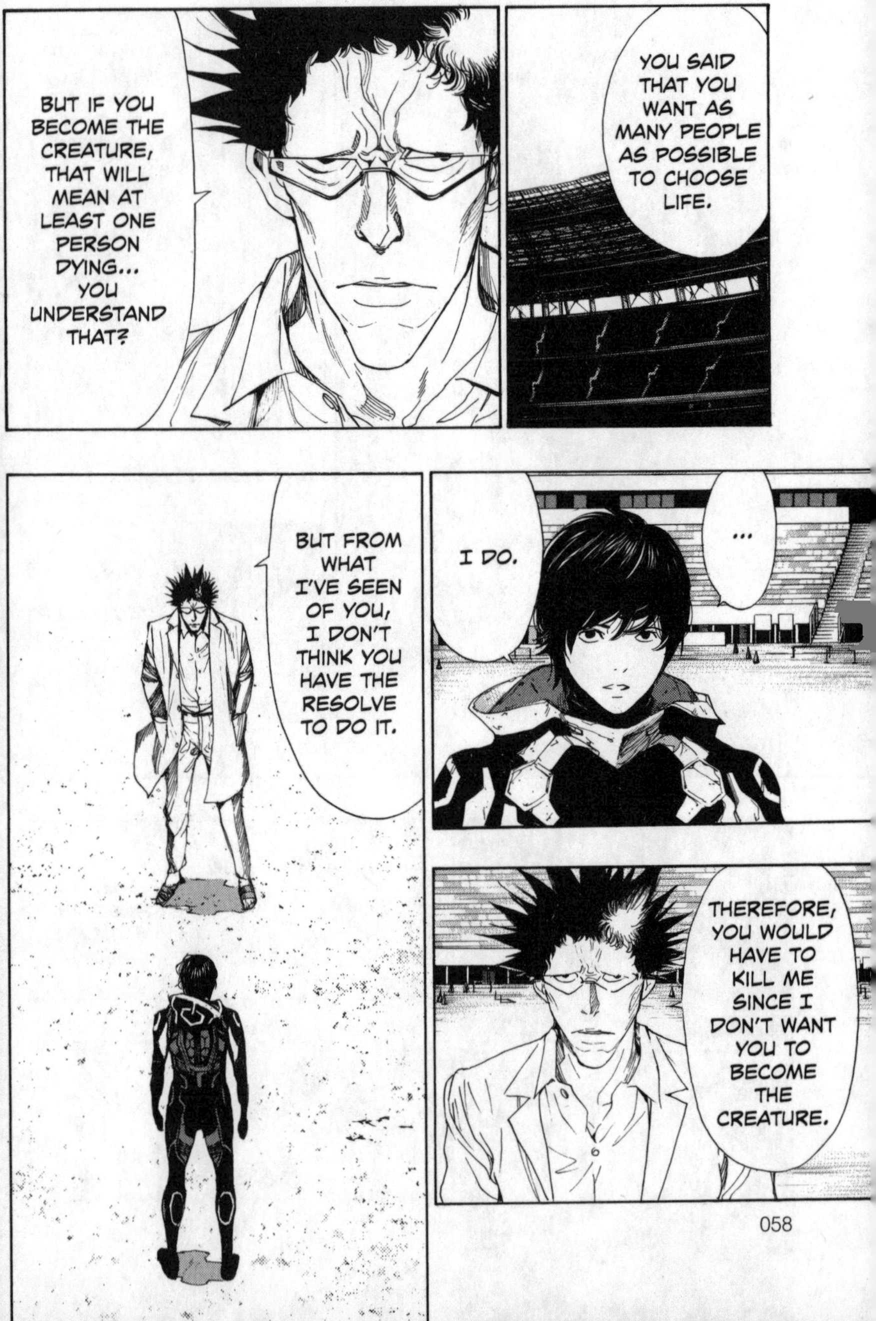
YOU SAID THAT YOU WANT AS MANY PEOPLE AS POSSIBLE TO CHOOSE LIFE.
BUT IF YOU BECOME THE CREATURE, THAT WILL MEAN AT LEAST ONE PERSON DYING... YOU UNDERSTAND THAT?
...
I DO.
THEREFORE, YOU WOULD HAVE TO KILL ME SINCE I DON'T WANT YOU TO BECOME THE CREATURE.
BUT FROM WHAT I'VE SEEN OF YOU, I DON'T THINK YOU HAVE THE RESOLVE TO DO IT.

I DO.

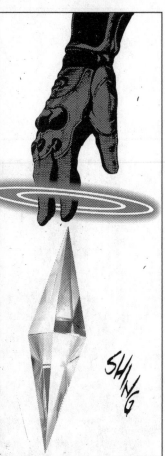

SHING

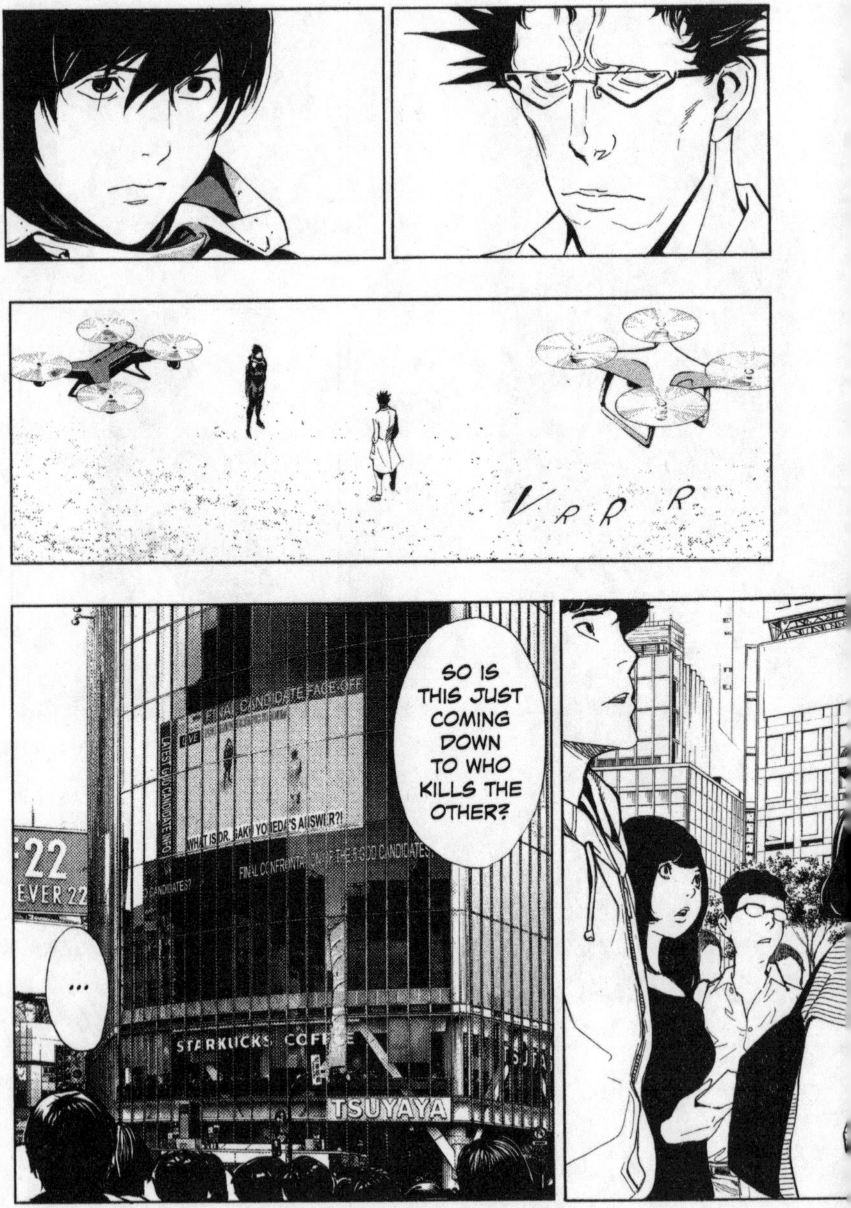
VRRR
SO IS THIS JUST COMING DOWN TO WHO KILLS THE OTHER?
FINAL CANDIDATE FACE-OFF
TSUYAYA
...

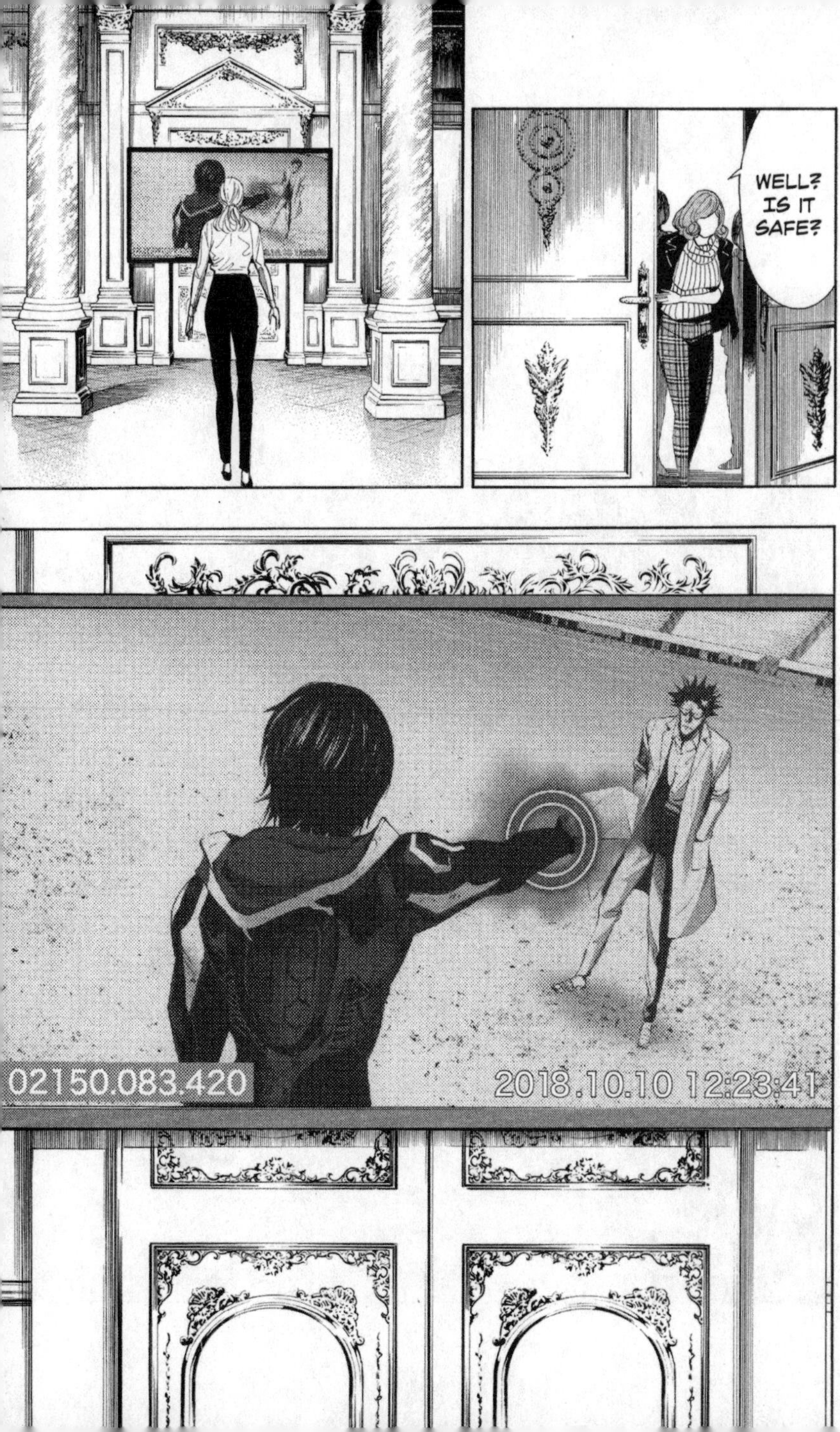
WELL? IS IT SAFE?
2018.10.10 12:23:41
02150.083.420

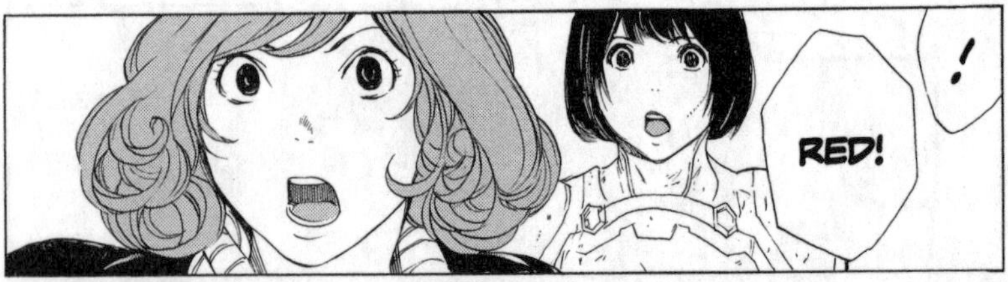
!
RED!

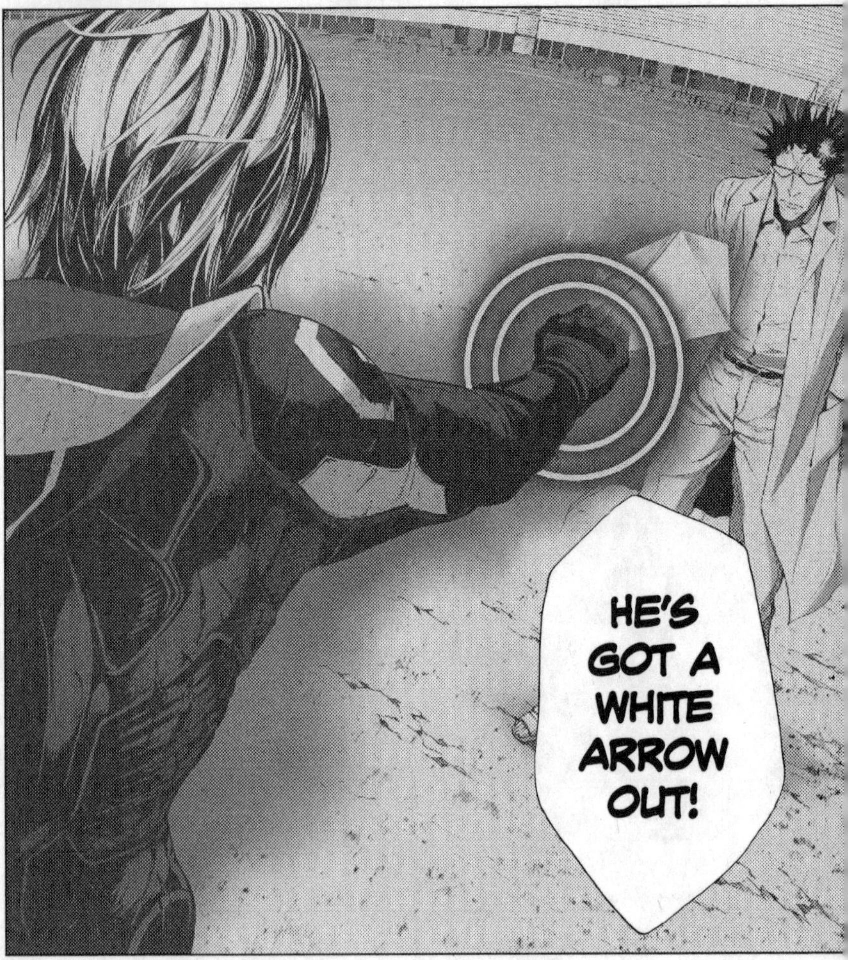
HE'S GOT A WHITE ARROW OUT!

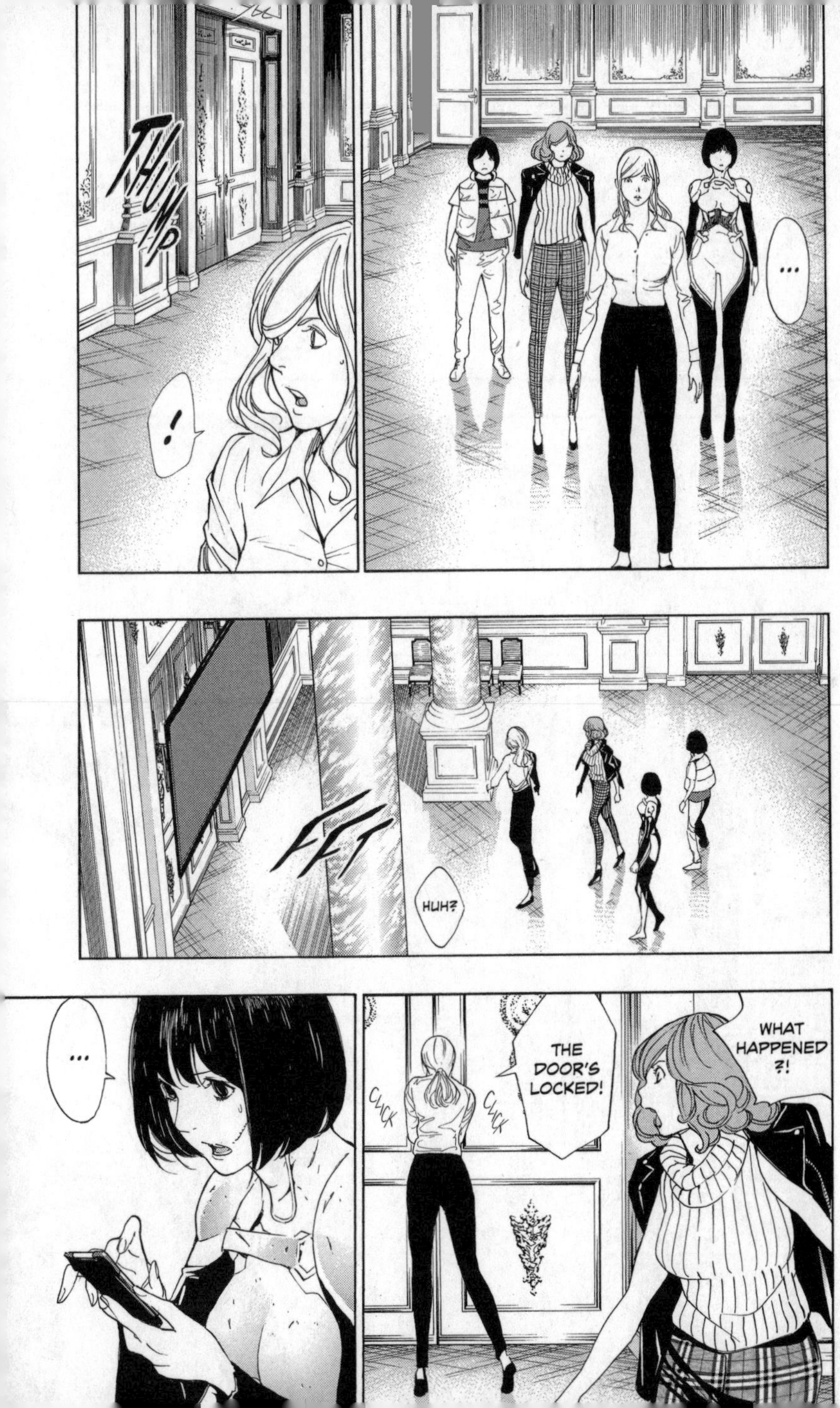
...
THUMP
!
FFT
HUH?
WHAT HAPPENED ?!
THE DOOR'S LOCKED!
CLICK
CLICK
...

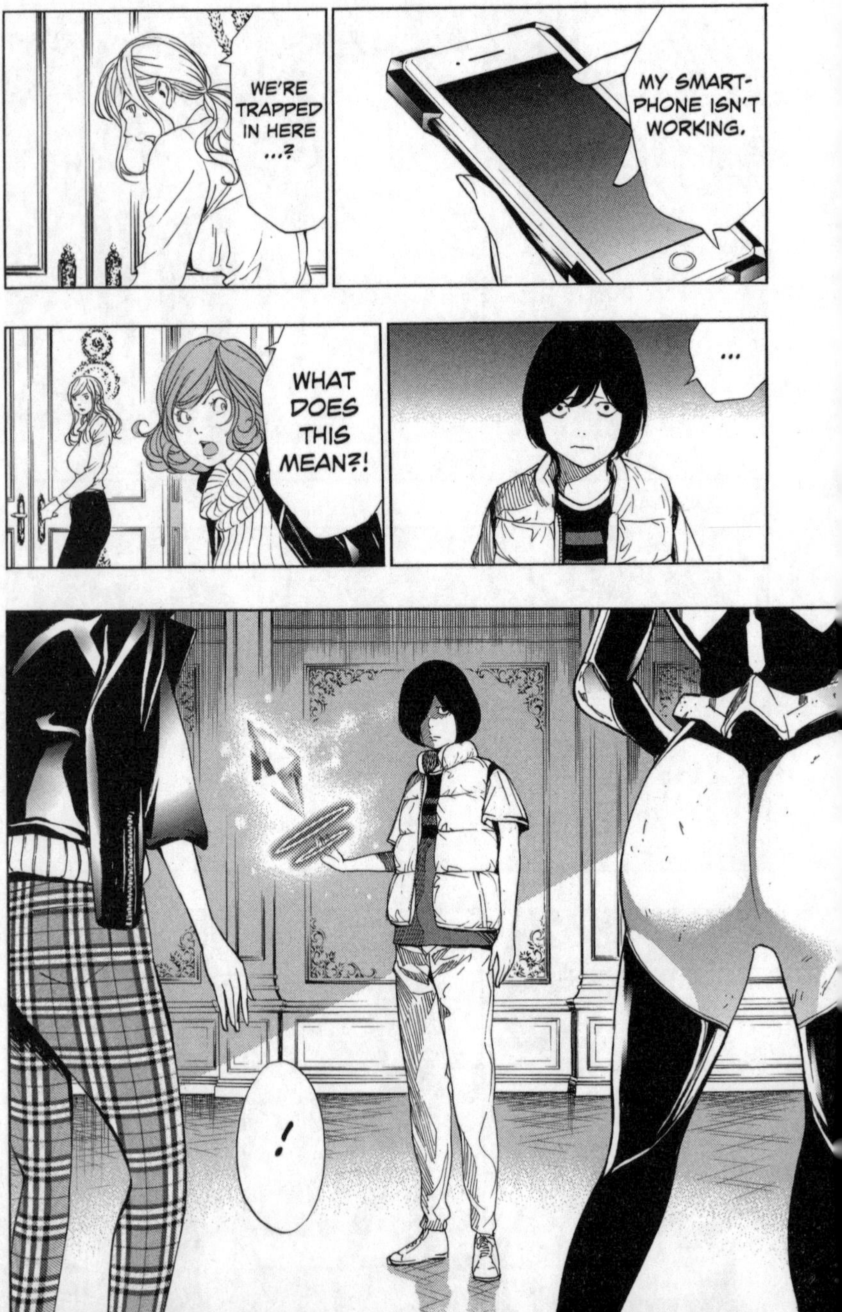
MY SMART-PHONE ISN'T WORKING.
WE'RE TRAPPED IN HERE ...?
...
WHAT DOES THIS MEAN?!
!

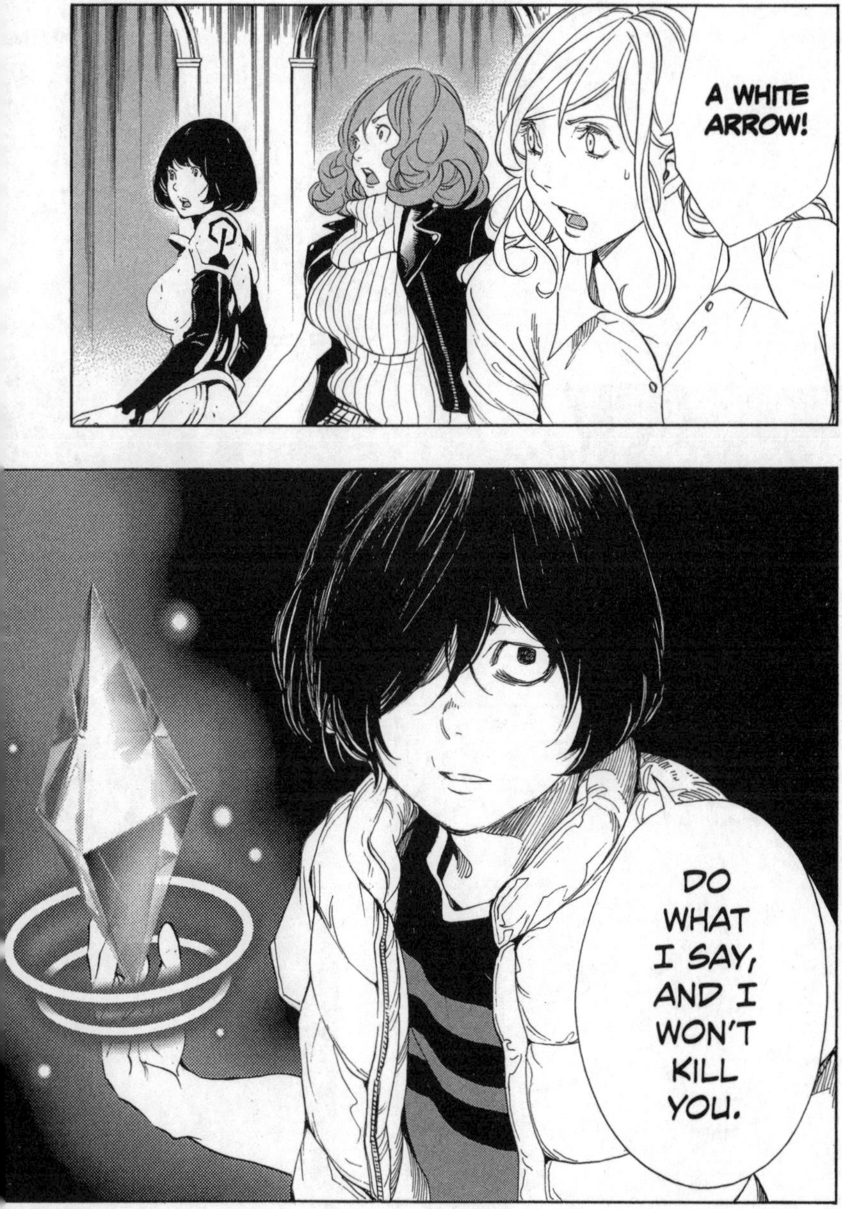
A WHITE ARROW!
DO WHAT I SAY, AND I WON'T KILL YOU.

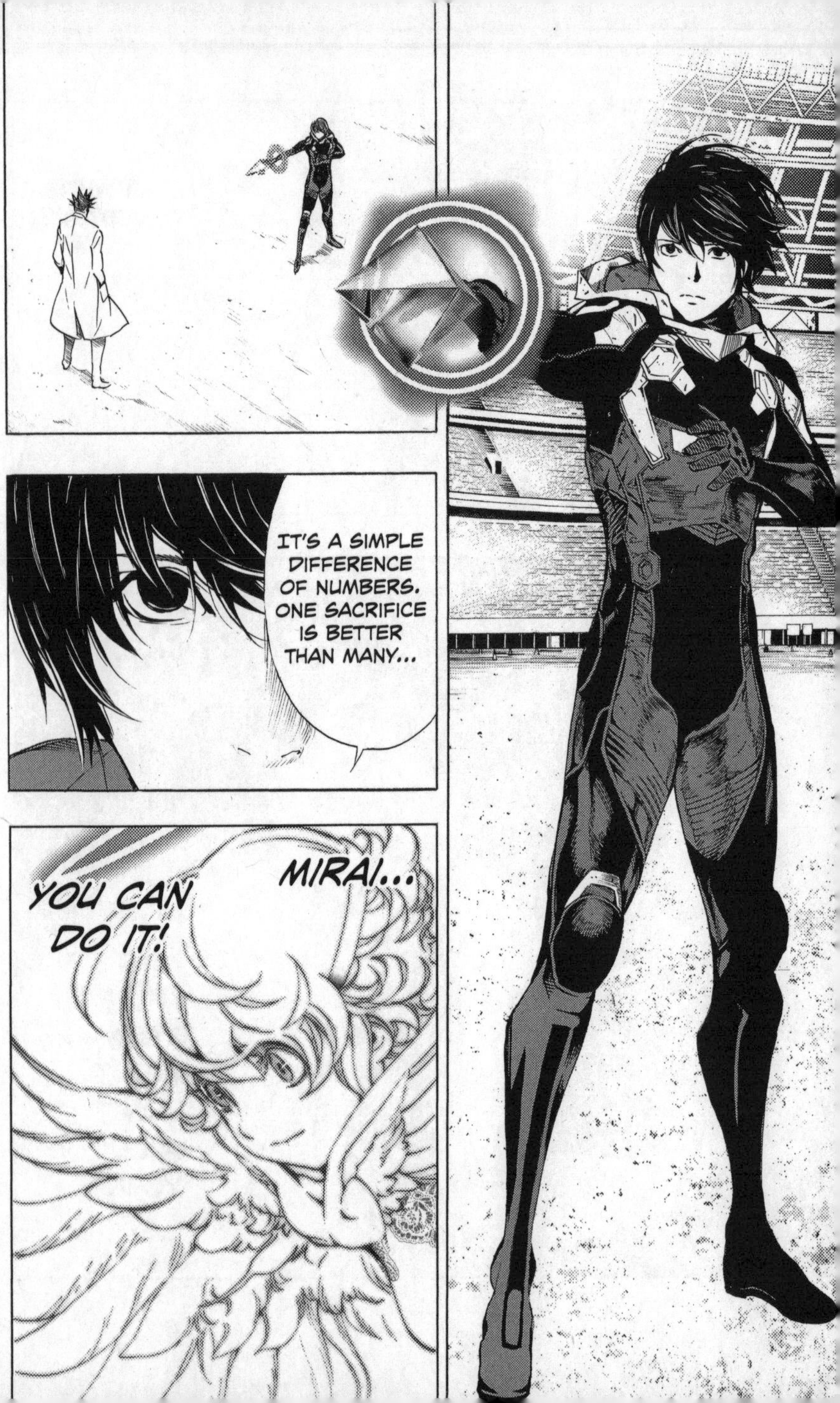
IT'S A SIMPLE DIFFERENCE OF NUMBERS. ONE SACRIFICE IS BETTER THAN MANY...
MIRAI...
YOU CAN DO IT!

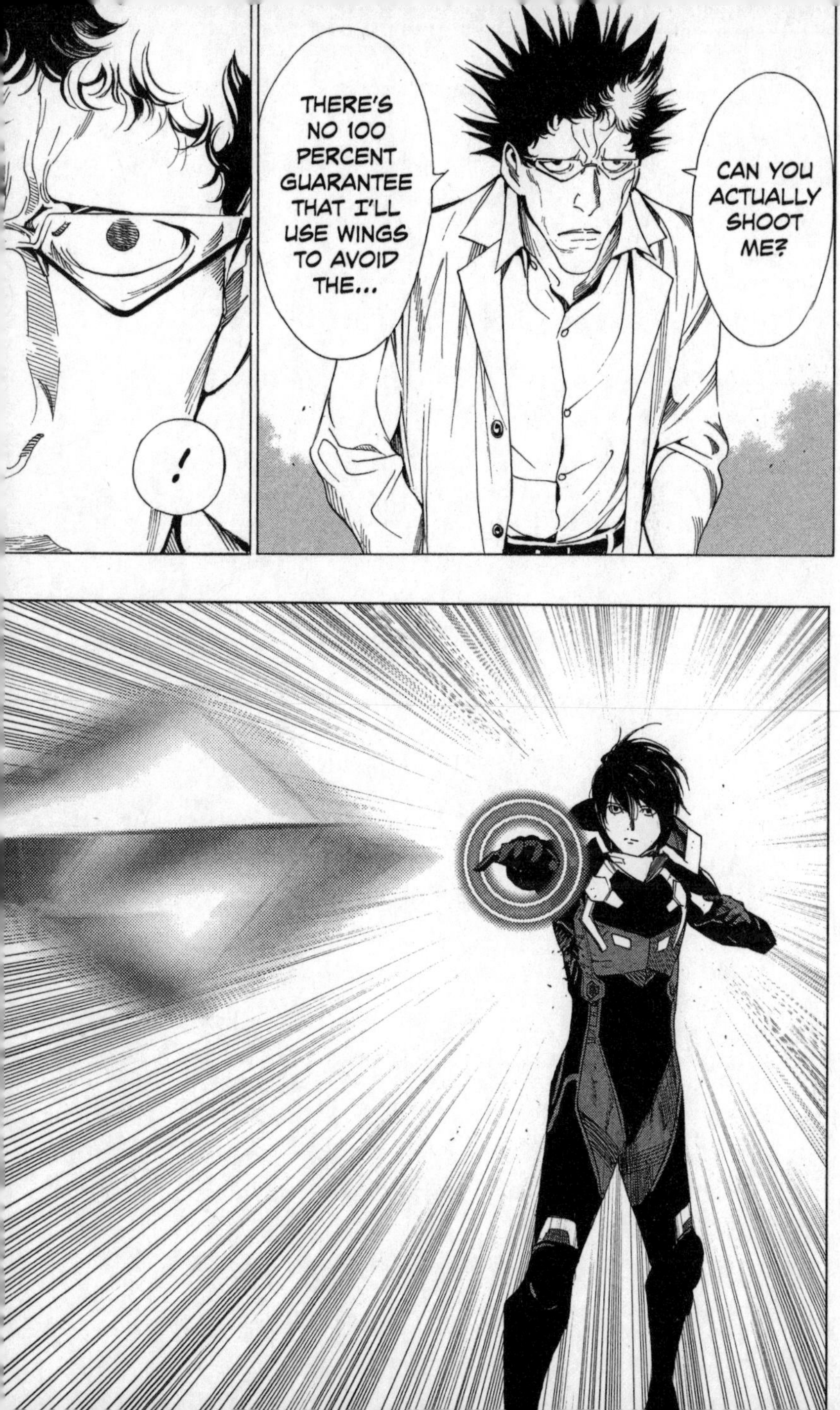
CAN YOU ACTUALLY SHOOT ME?
THERE'S NO 100 PERCENT GUARANTEE THAT I'LL USE WINGS TO AVOID THE...
!

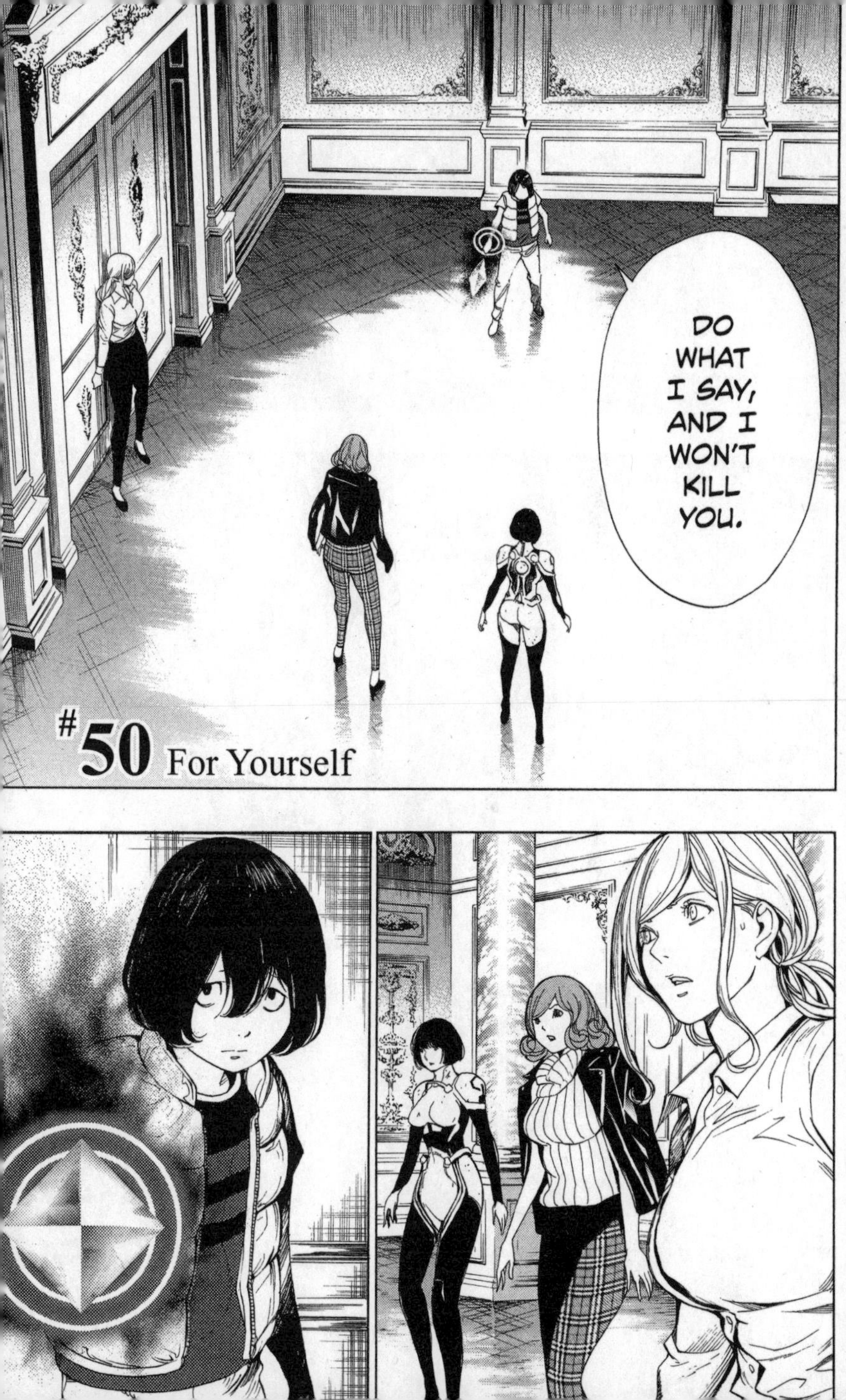
DO WHAT I SAY, AND I WON'T KILL YOU.
#50 For Yourself

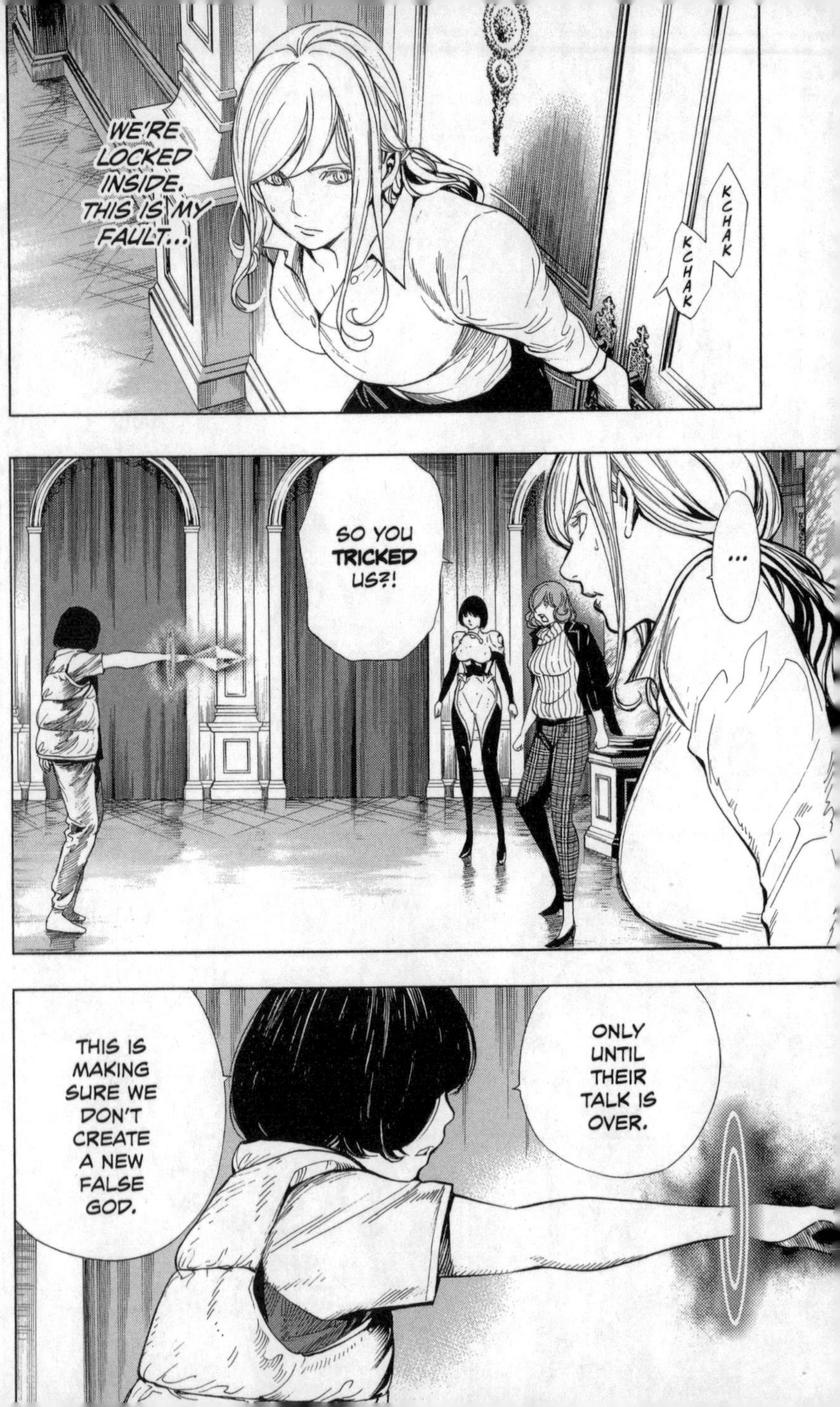
KCHAK
KCHAK
WE'RE LOCKED INSIDE. THIS IS MY FAULT...
...
SO YOU TRICKED US?!
ONLY UNTIL THEIR TALK IS OVER.
THIS IS MAKING SURE WE DON'T CREATE A NEW FALSE GOD.

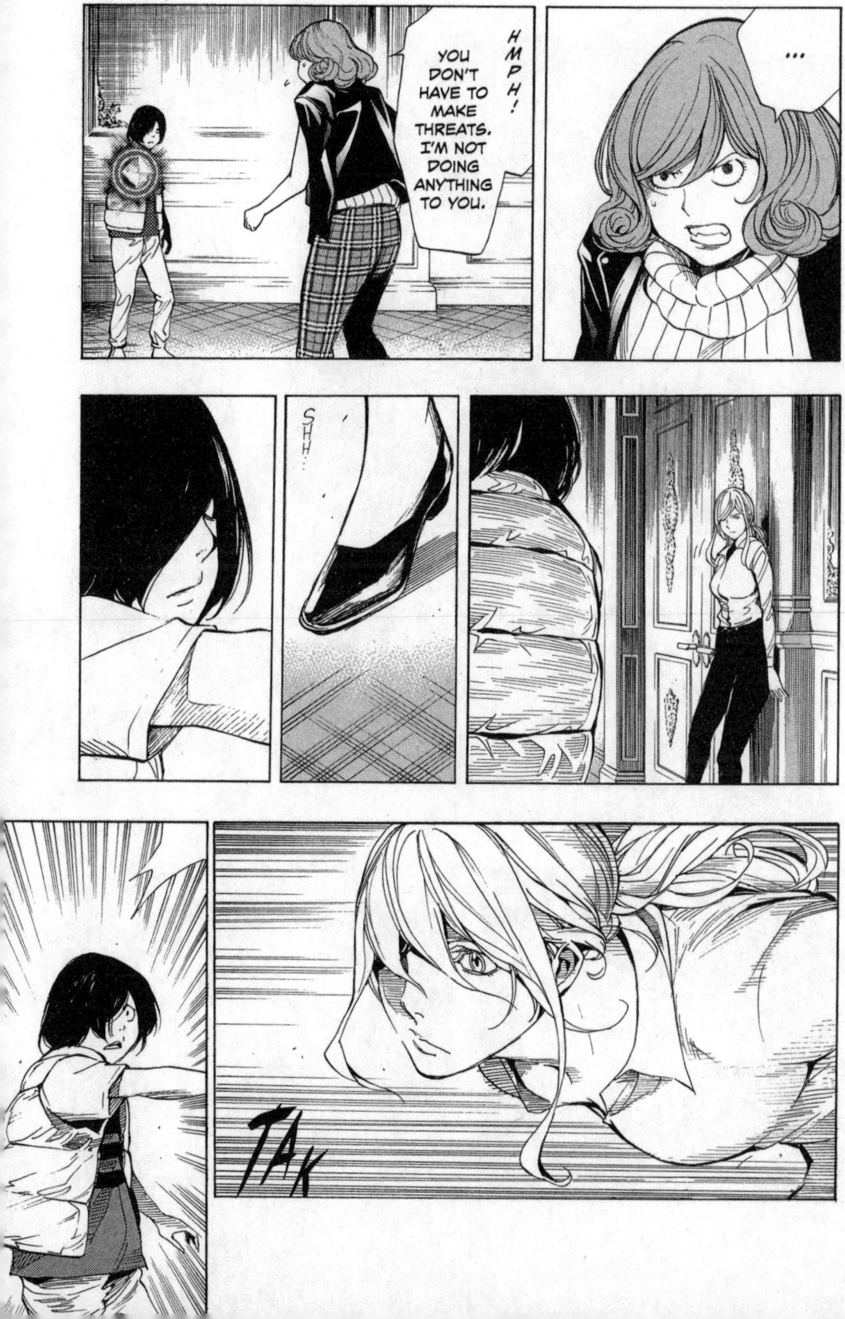
...
HMPH!
YOU DON'T HAVE TO MAKE THREATS. I'M NOT DOING ANYTHING TO YOU.
SHH...
TAK

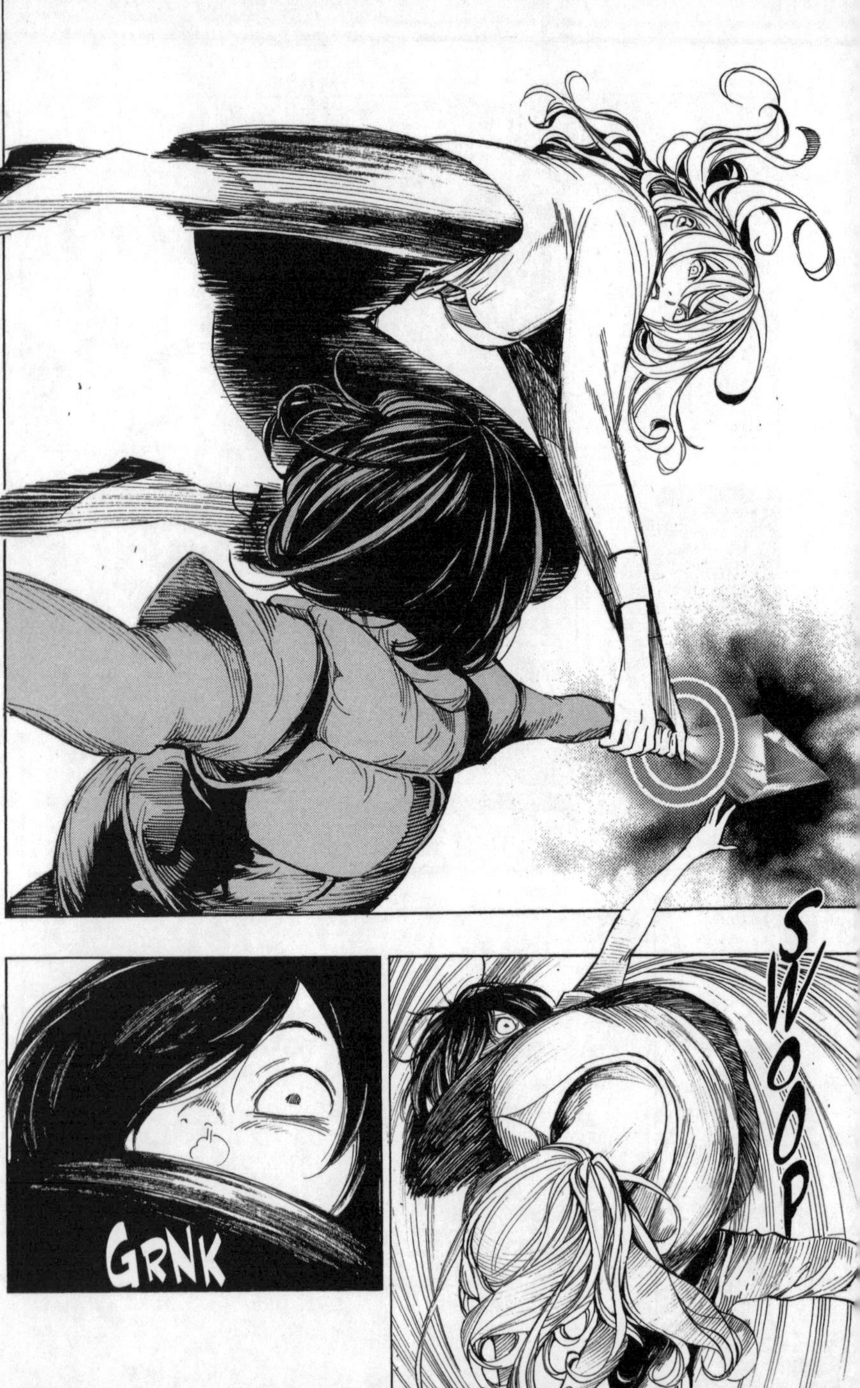
SWOOP
GRNK

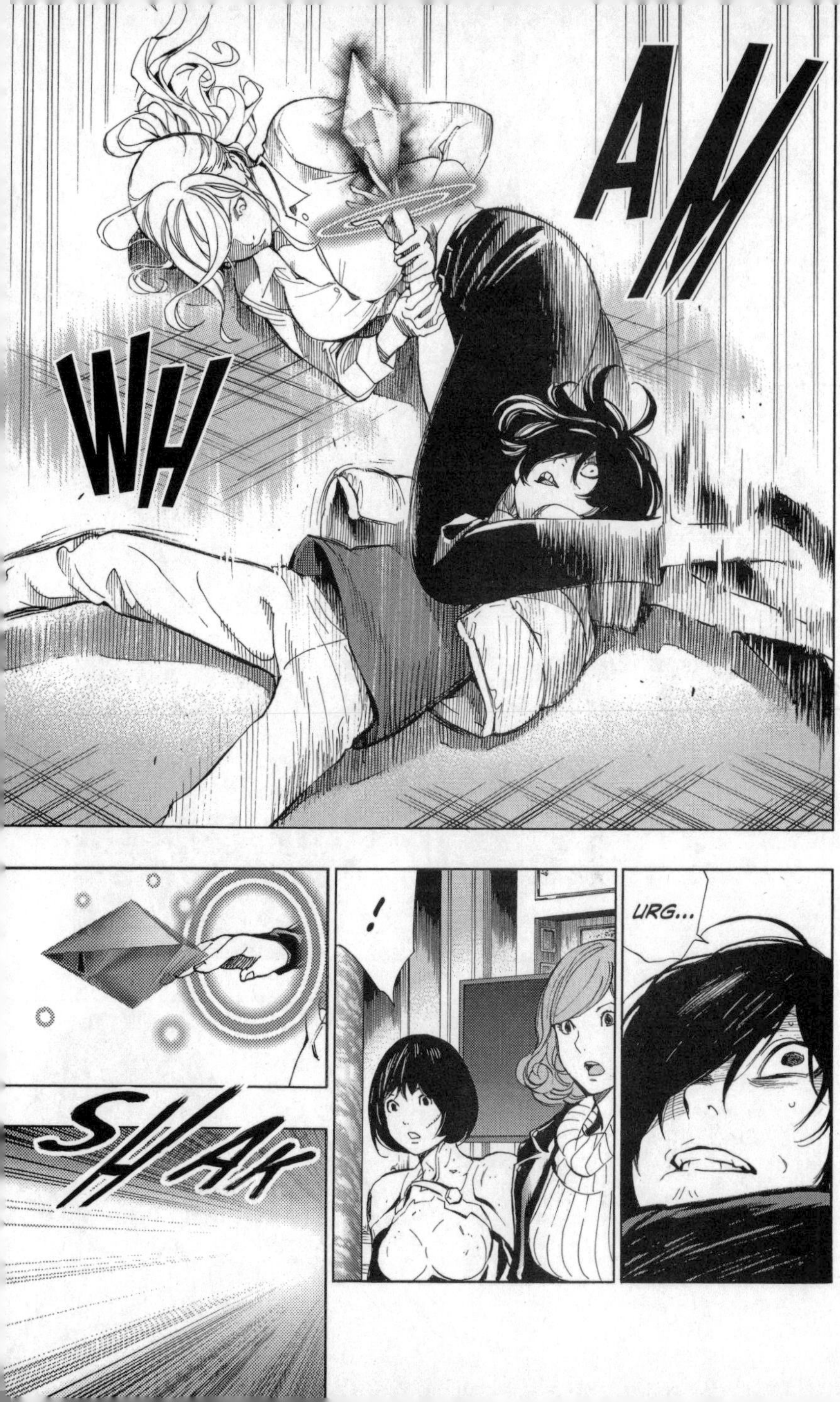
WH
AM
URG...
!
SHAK

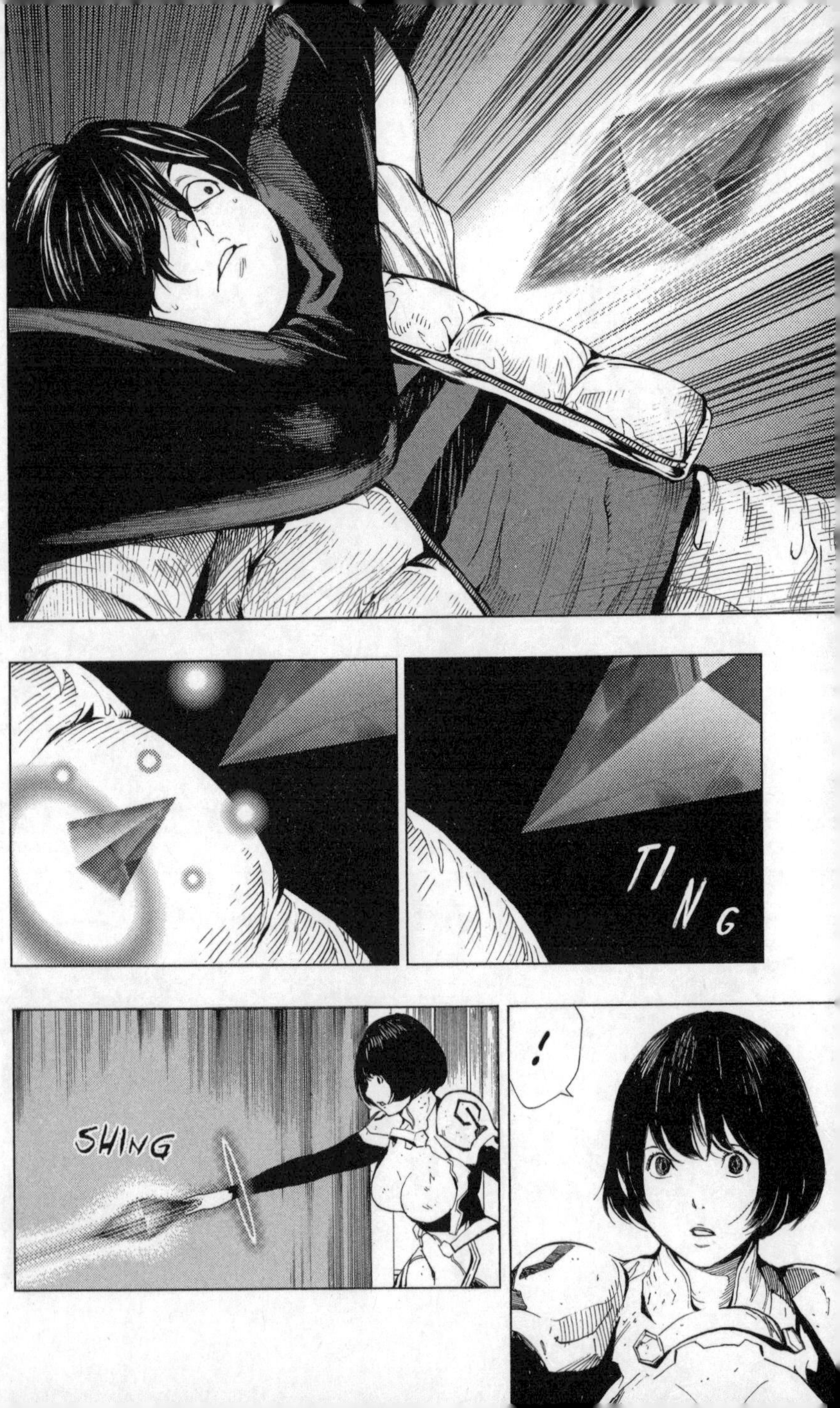
TING
!
SHING

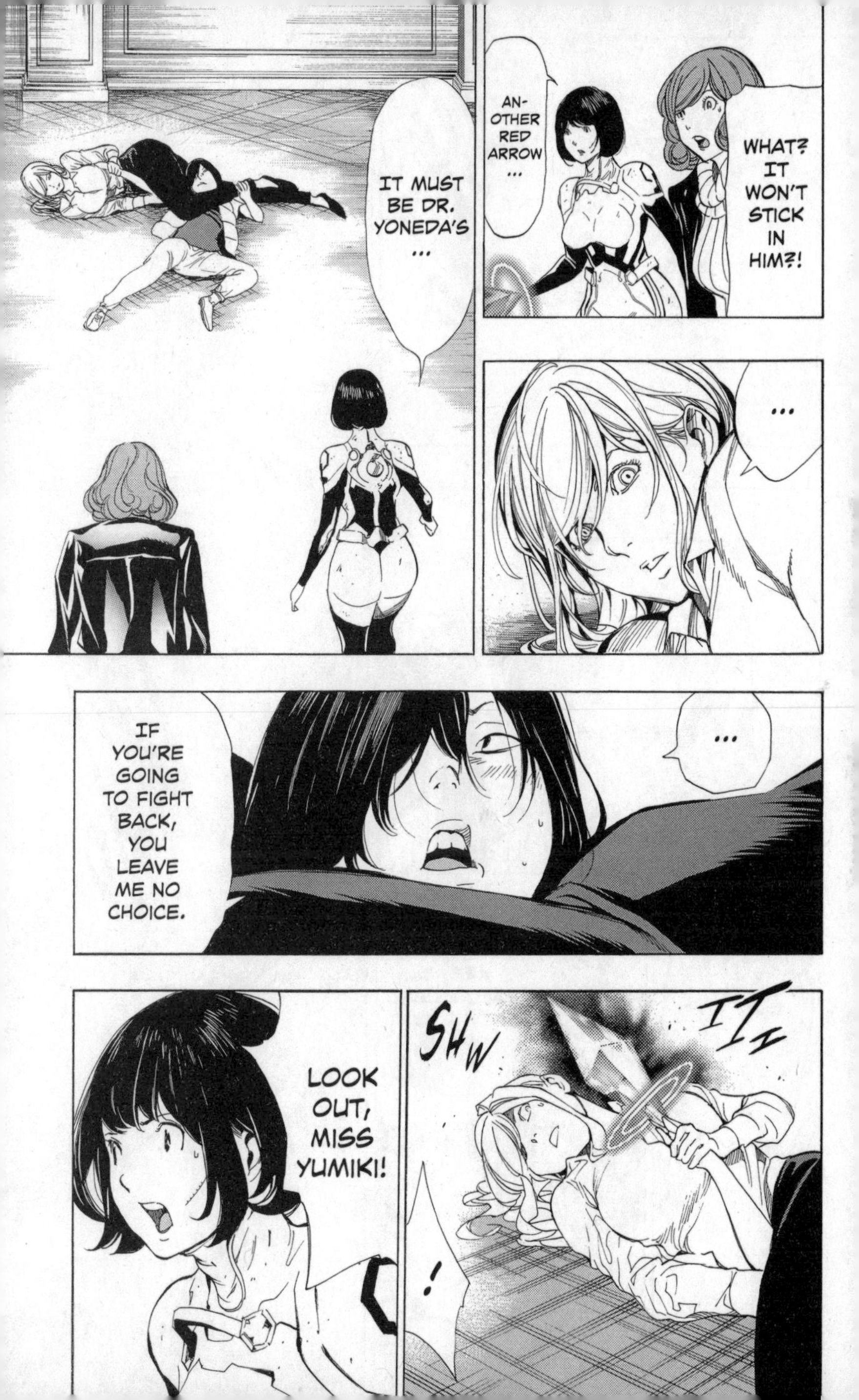
WHAT?! IT WON'T STICK IN HIM?!
AN-OTHER RED ARROW ...
...
IT MUST BE DR. YONEDA'S ...
...
IF YOU'RE GOING TO FIGHT BACK, YOU LEAVE ME NO CHOICE.
SHW
!
LOOK OUT, MISS YUMIKI!

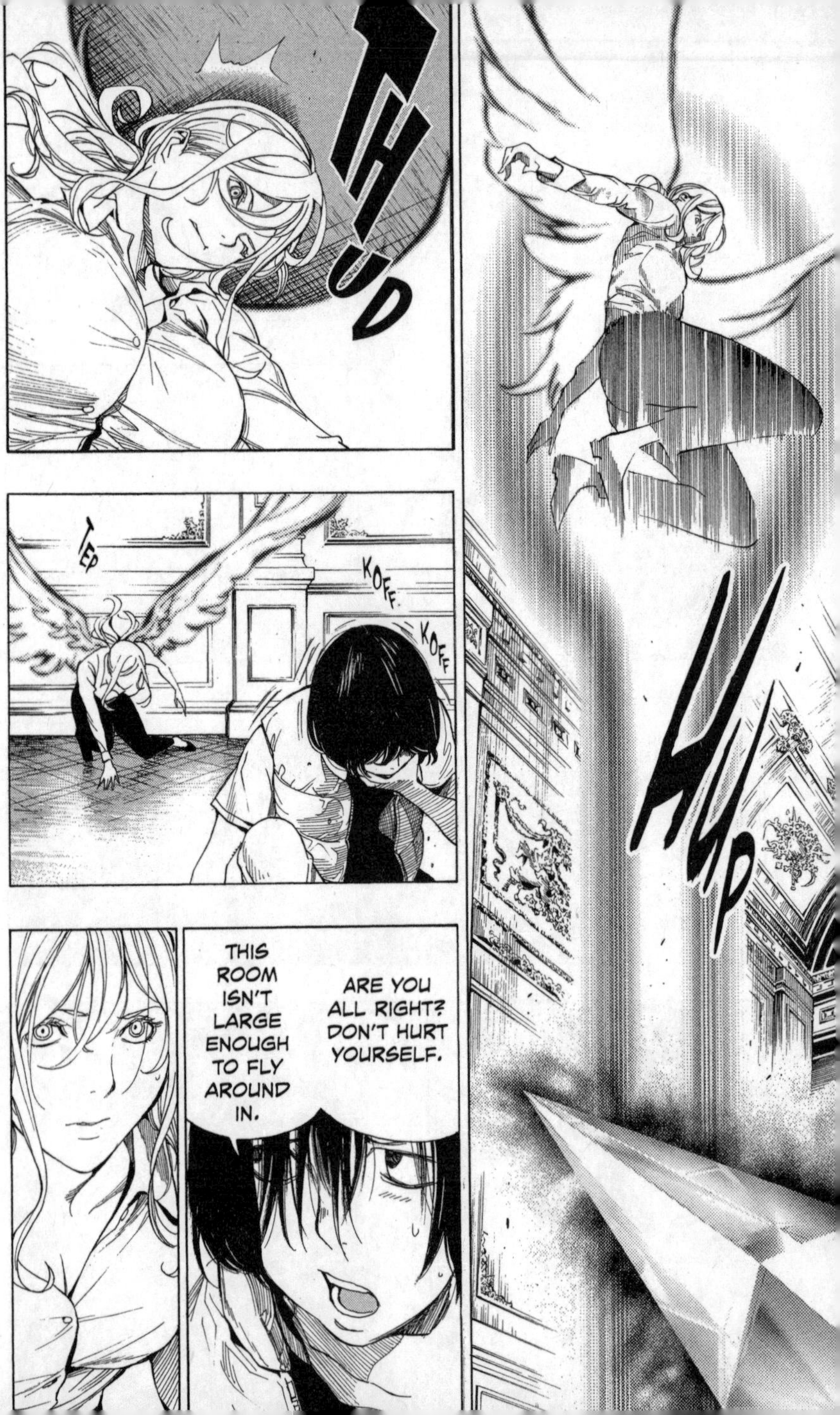
HUP
THUD
TEP
KOFF
KOFF
ARE YOU ALL RIGHT? DON'T HURT YOURSELF.
THIS ROOM ISN'T LARGE ENOUGH TO FLY AROUND IN.

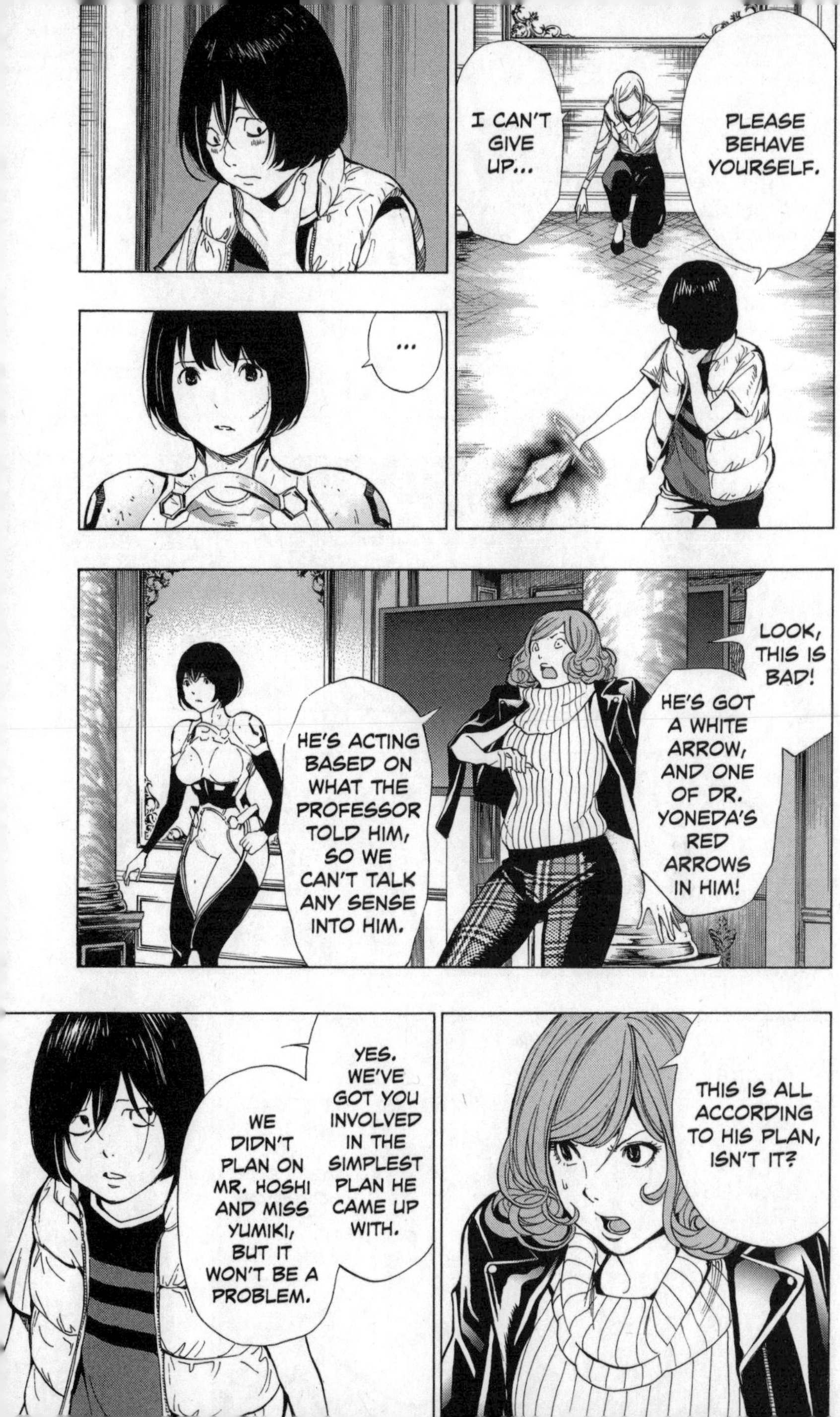
PLEASE BEHAVE YOURSELF.
I CAN'T GIVE UP...
...
LOOK, THIS IS BAD!
HE'S GOT A WHITE ARROW, AND ONE OF DR. YONEDA'S RED ARROWS IN HIM!
HE'S ACTING BASED ON WHAT THE PROFESSOR TOLD HIM, SO WE CAN'T TALK ANY SENSE INTO HIM.
THIS IS ALL ACCORDING TO HIS PLAN, ISN'T IT?
YES. WE'VE GOT YOU INVOLVED IN THE SIMPLEST PLAN HE CAME UP WITH.
WE DIDN'T PLAN ON MR. HOSHI AND MISS YUMIKI, BUT IT WON'T BE A PROBLEM.

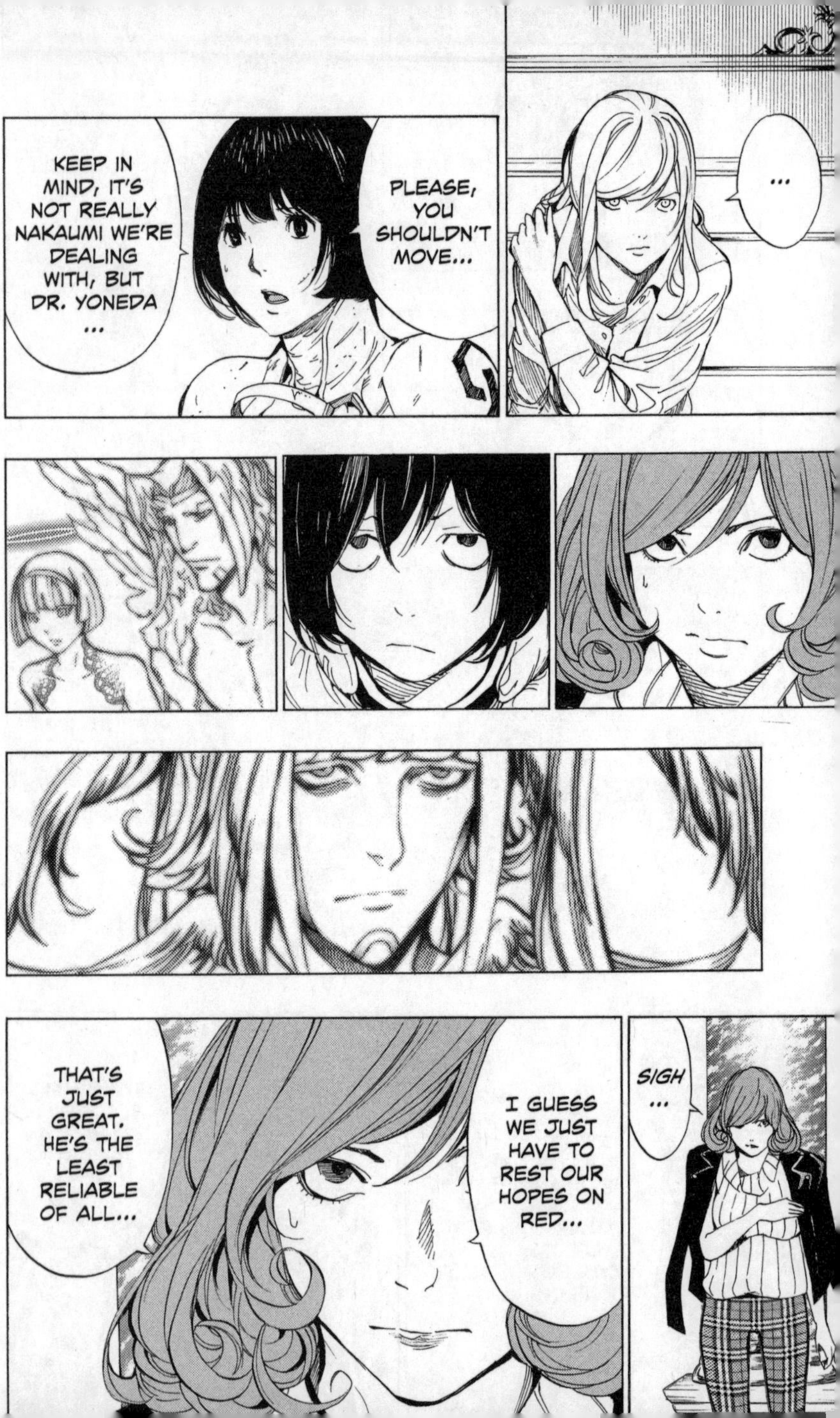
...
PLEASE, YOU SHOULDN'T MOVE...
KEEP IN MIND, IT'S NOT REALLY NAKAUMI WE'RE DEALING WITH, BUT DR. YONEDA ...
SIGH ...
THAT'S JUST GREAT. HE'S THE LEAST RELIABLE OF ALL...
I GUESS WE JUST HAVE TO REST OUR HOPES ON RED...

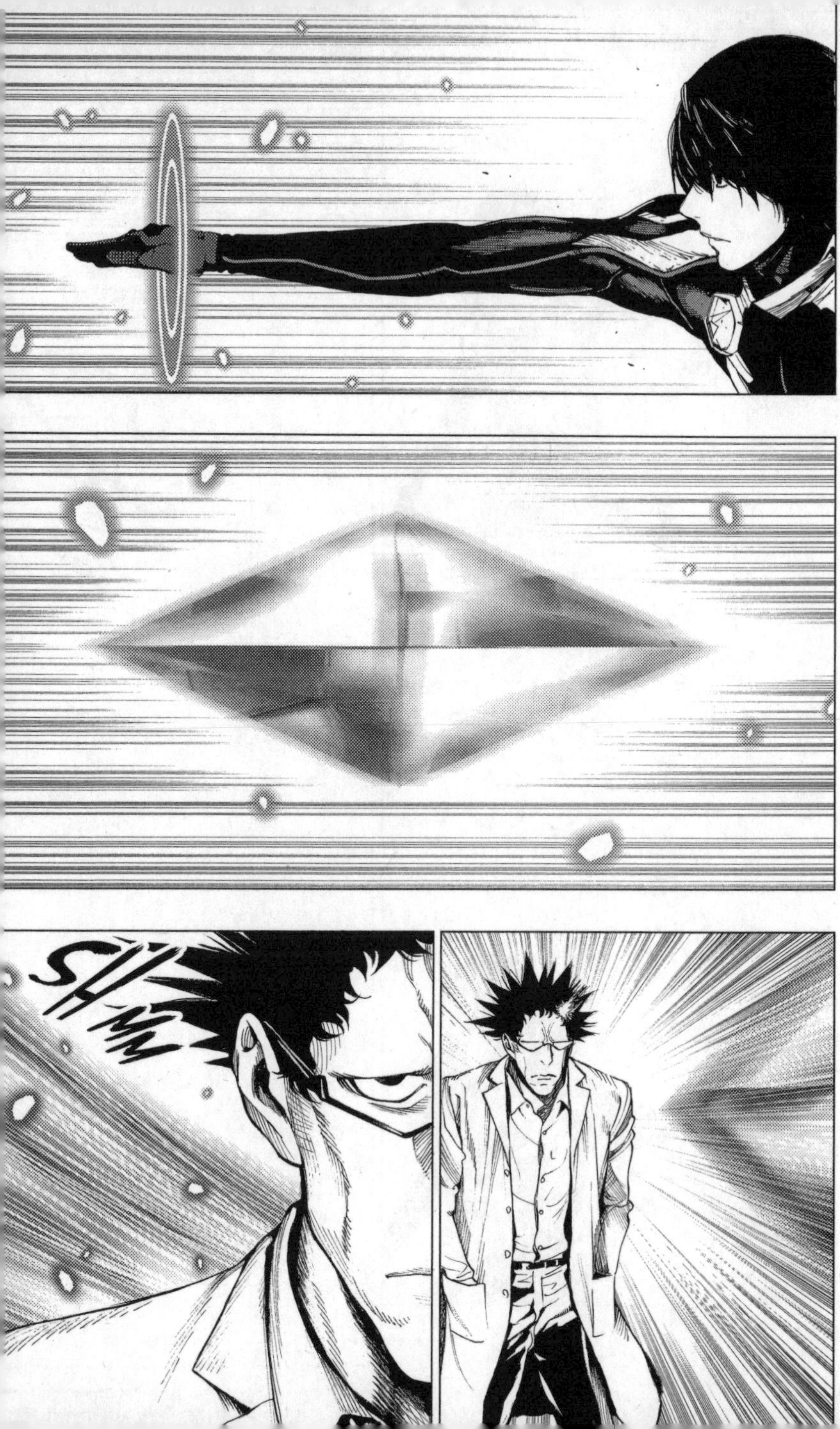
SHMM

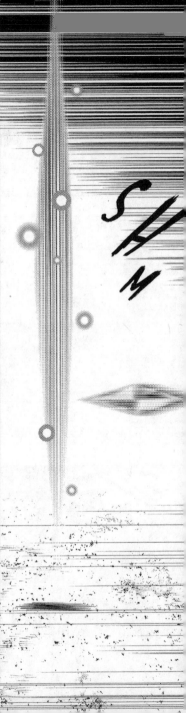

I SHOULD HAVE FIGURED IT WOULD GO THIS WAY.

SHM

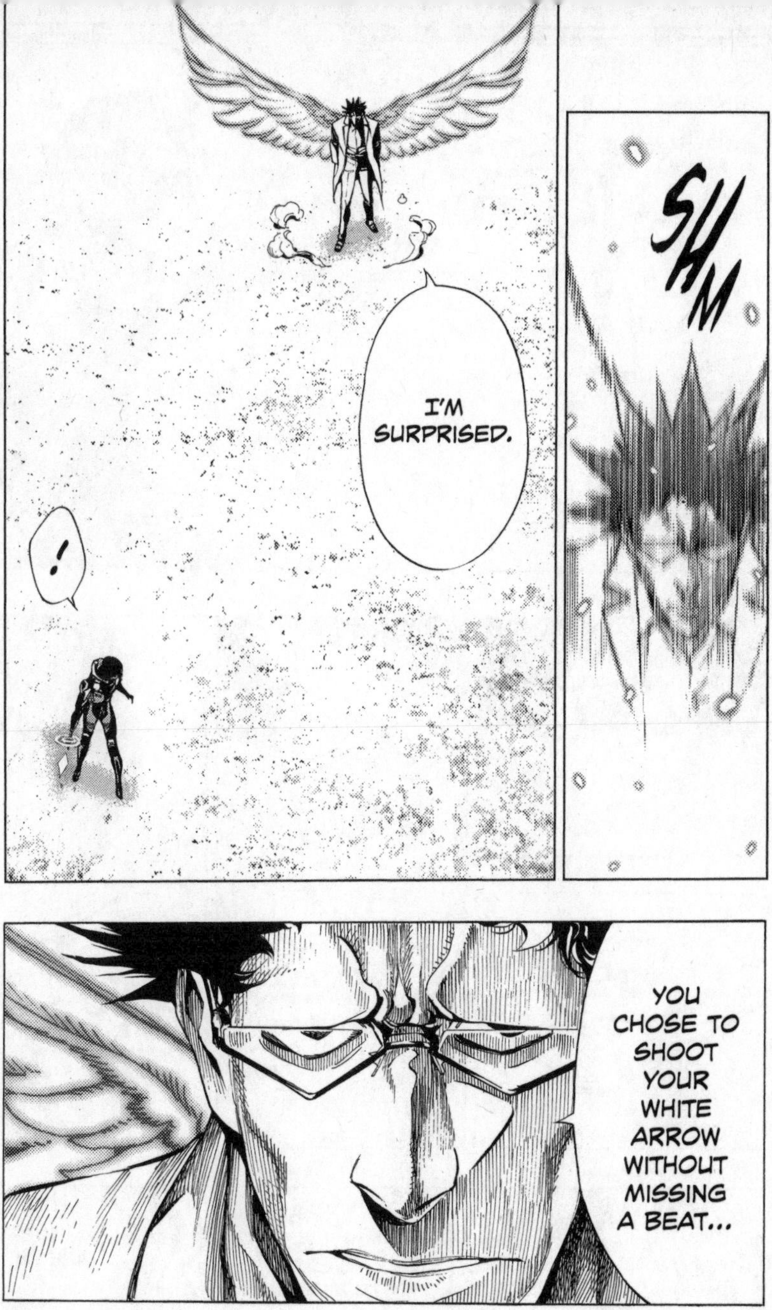
SHM
I'M SURPRISED.
!
YOU CHOSE TO SHOOT YOUR WHITE ARROW WITHOUT MISSING A BEAT...

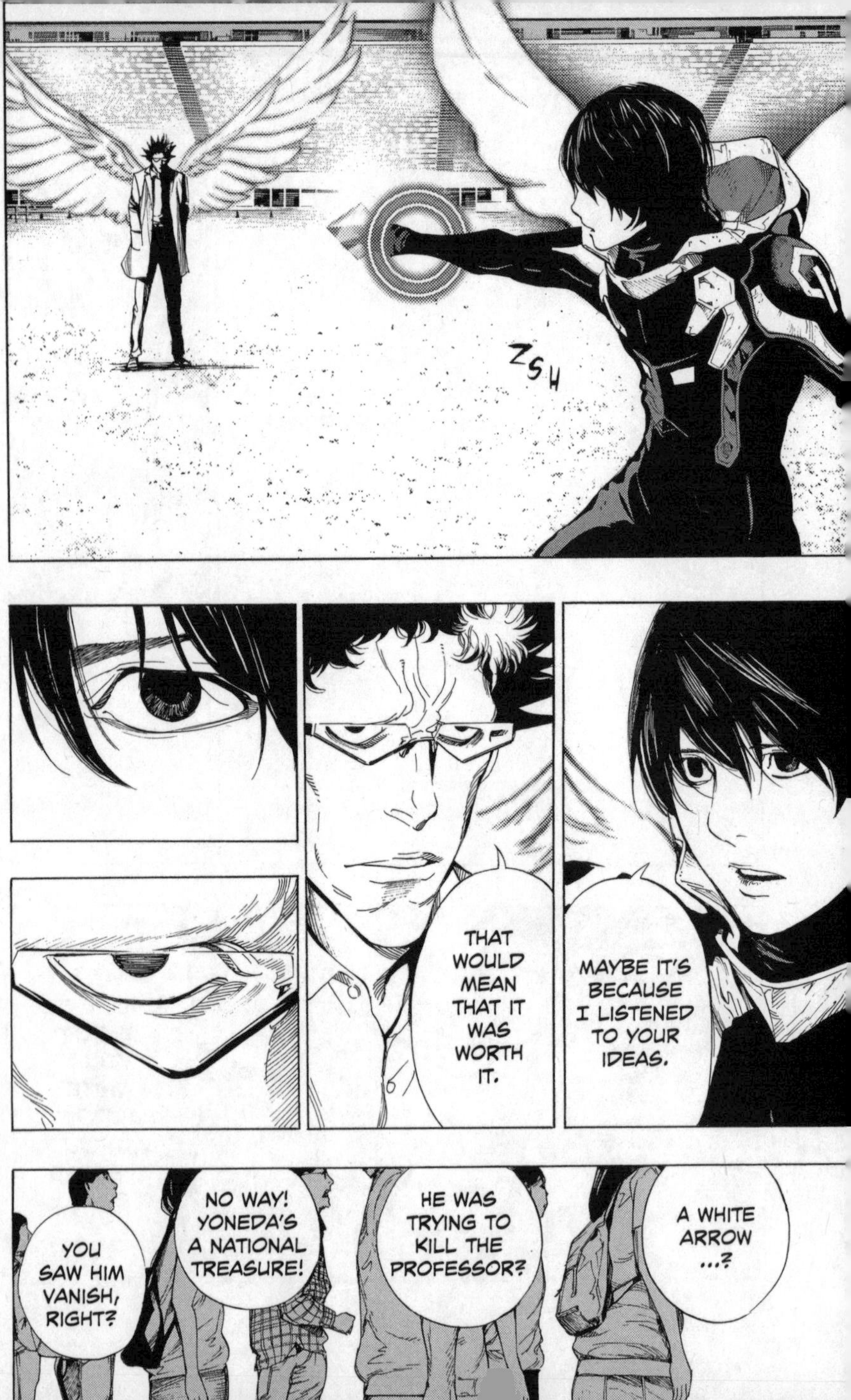
ZSH
MAYBE IT'S BECAUSE I LISTENED TO YOUR IDEAS.
THAT WOULD MEAN THAT IT WAS WORTH IT.
A WHITE ARROW ...?
HE WAS TRYING TO KILL THE PROFESSOR?
NO WAY! YONEDA'S A NATIONAL TREASURE!
YOU SAW HIM VANISH, RIGHT?

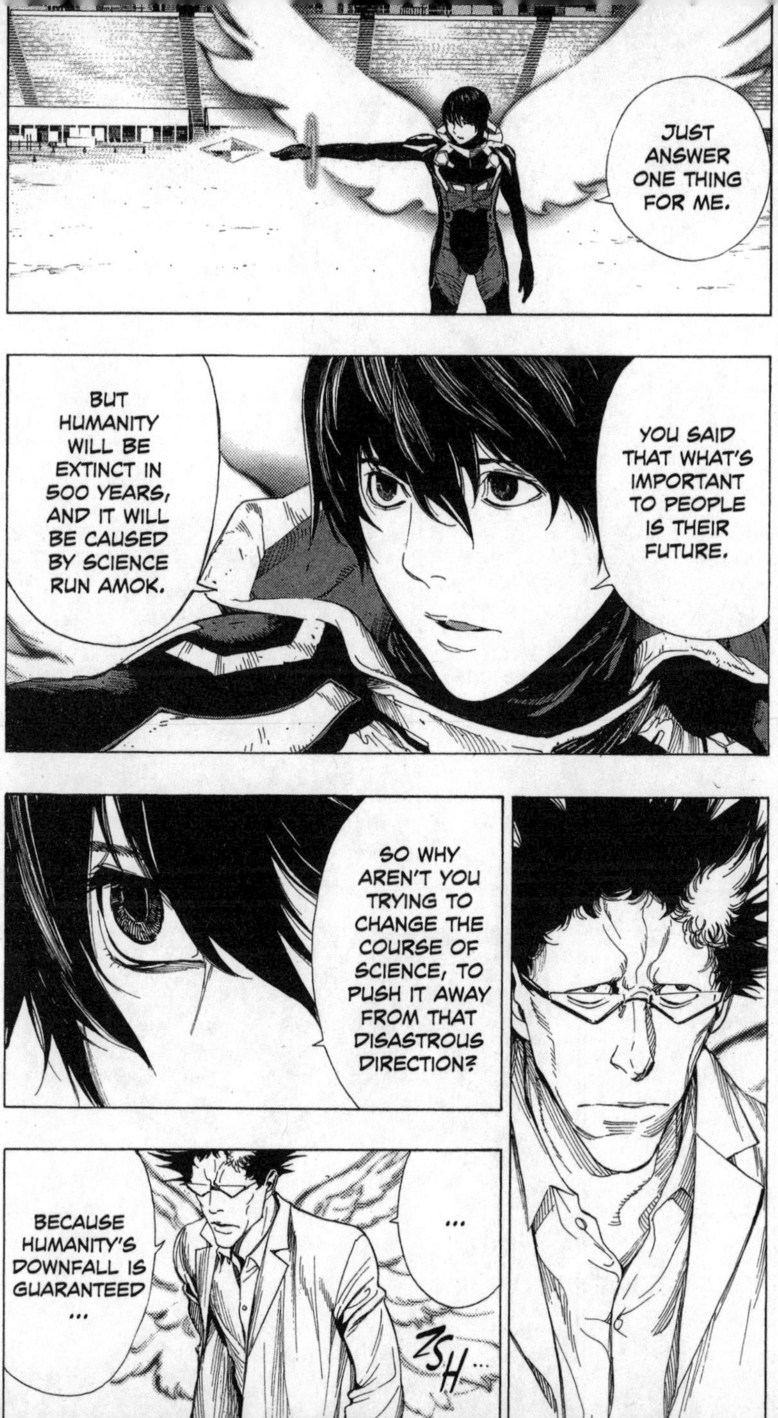
JUST ANSWER ONE THING FOR ME.
YOU SAID THAT WHAT'S IMPORTANT TO PEOPLE IS THEIR FUTURE.
BUT HUMANITY WILL BE EXTINCT IN 500 YEARS, AND IT WILL BE CAUSED BY SCIENCE RUN AMOK.
SO WHY AREN'T YOU TRYING TO CHANGE THE COURSE OF SCIENCE, TO PUSH IT AWAY FROM THAT DISASTROUS DIRECTION?
...
BECAUSE HUMANITY'S DOWNFALL IS GUARANTEED ...
ZSH...

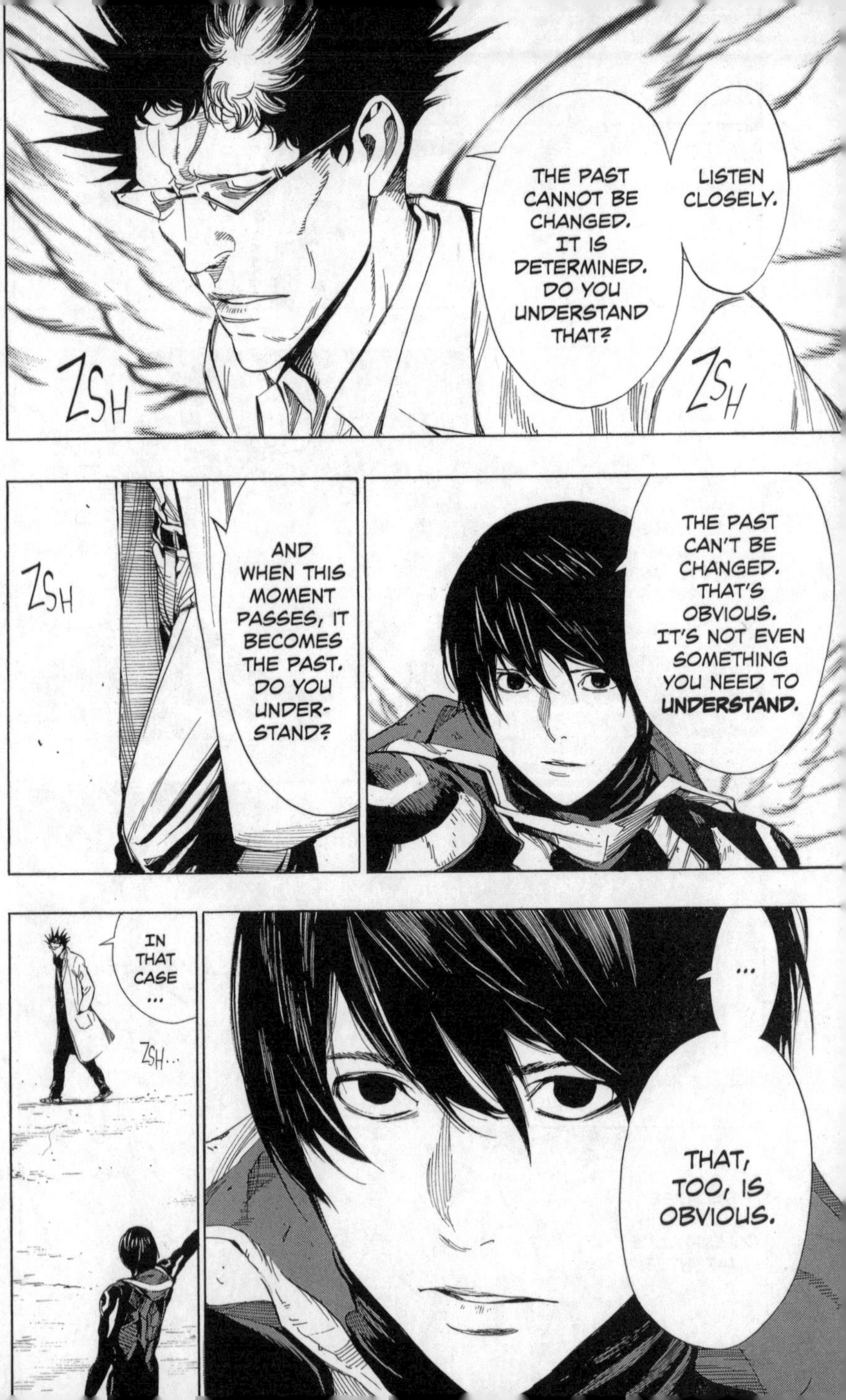
LISTEN CLOSELY.
THE PAST CANNOT BE CHANGED. IT IS DETERMINED. DO YOU UNDERSTAND THAT?
ZSH
ZSH
THE PAST CAN'T BE CHANGED. THAT'S OBVIOUS. IT'S NOT EVEN SOMETHING YOU NEED TO **UNDERSTAND.**
AND WHEN THIS MOMENT PASSES, IT BECOMES THE PAST. DO YOU UNDER-STAND?
ZSH
...
THAT, TOO, IS OBVIOUS.
IN THAT CASE ...
ZSH...

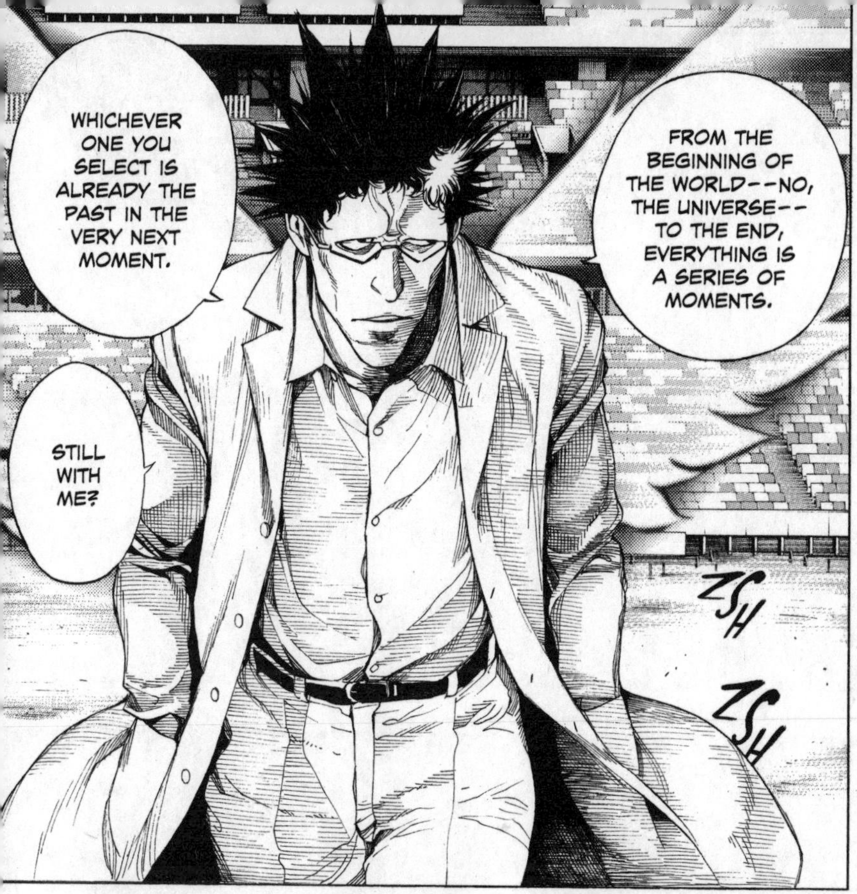
FROM THE BEGINNING OF THE WORLD--NO, THE UNIVERSE--TO THE END, EVERYTHING IS A SERIES OF MOMENTS.
WHICHEVER ONE YOU SELECT IS ALREADY THE PAST IN THE VERY NEXT MOMENT.
ZSH
ZSH
STILL WITH ME?

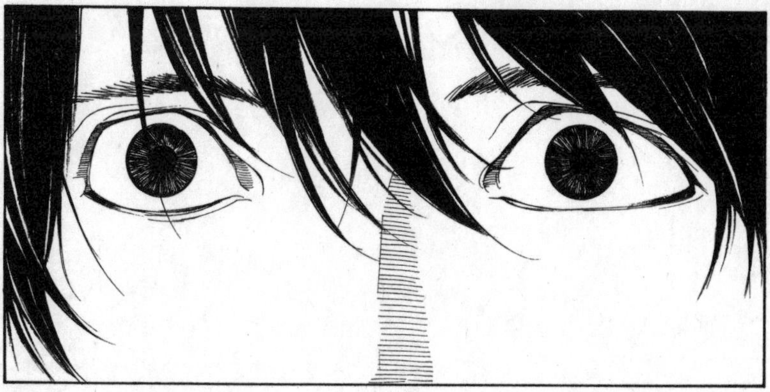

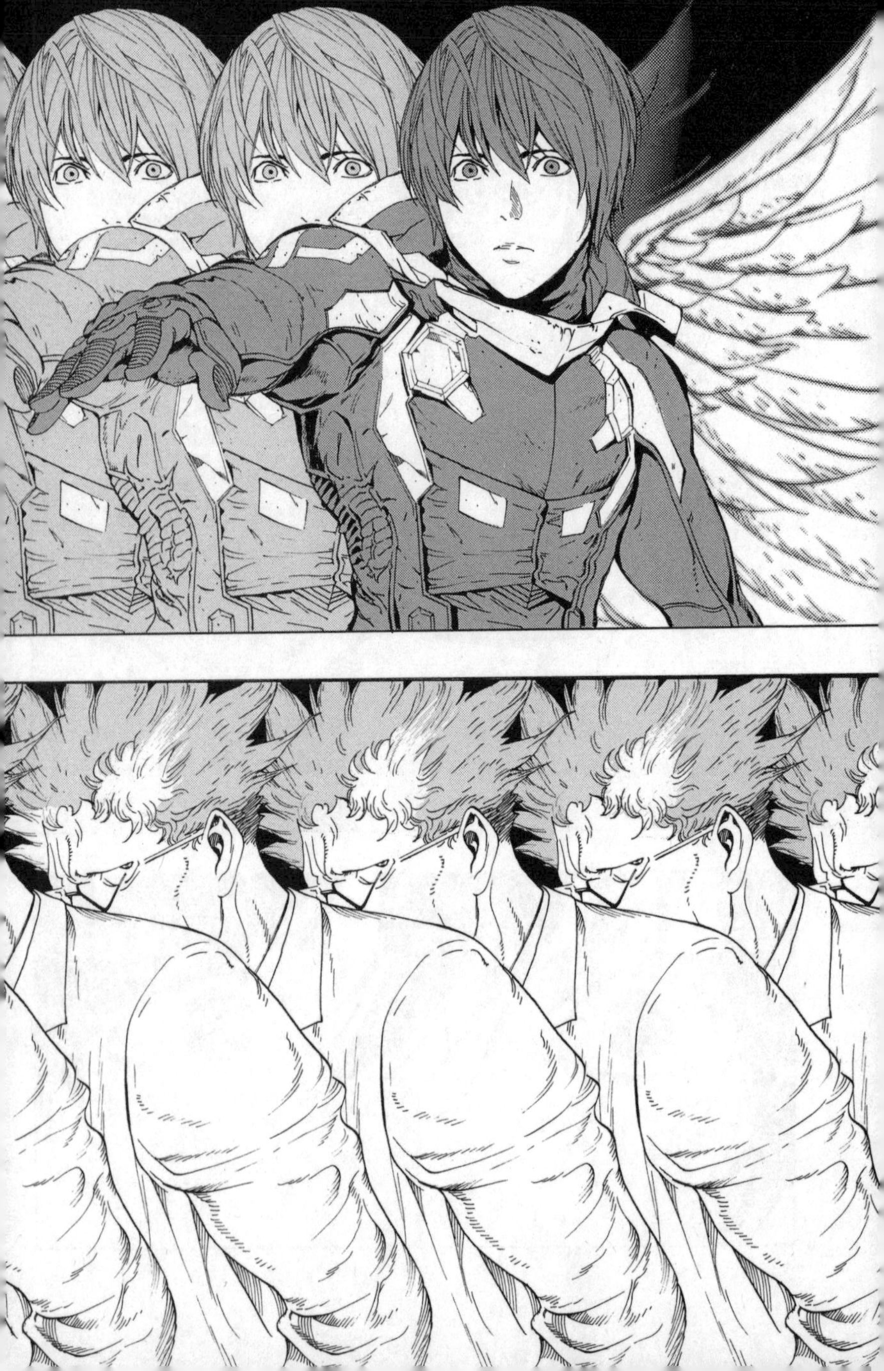

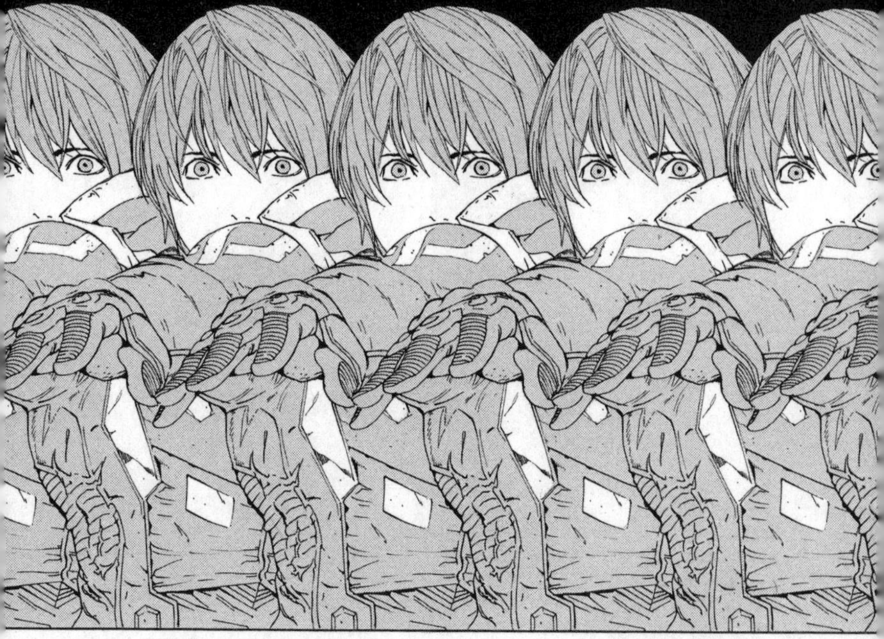
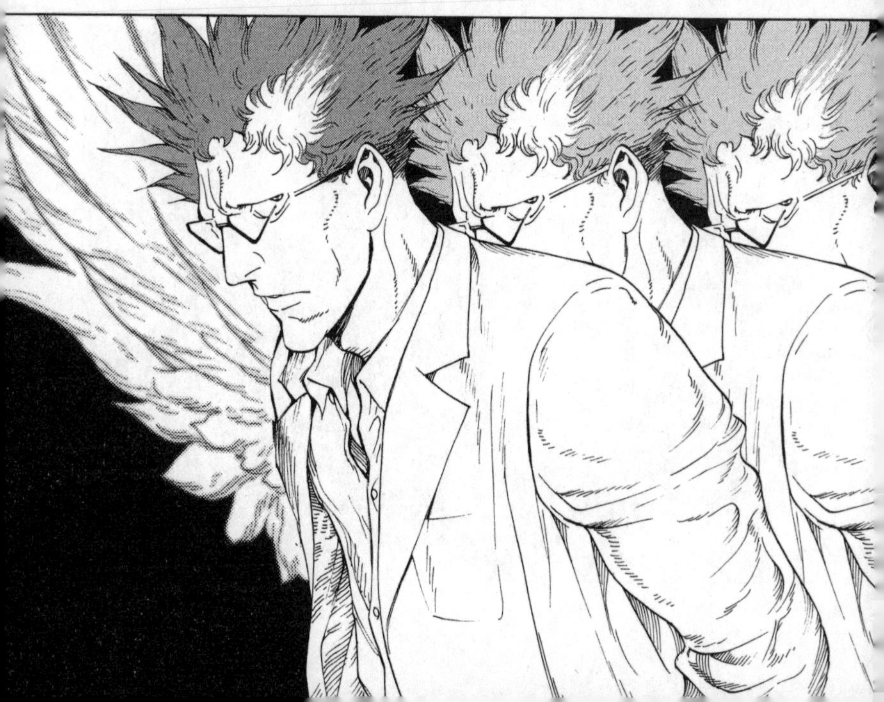

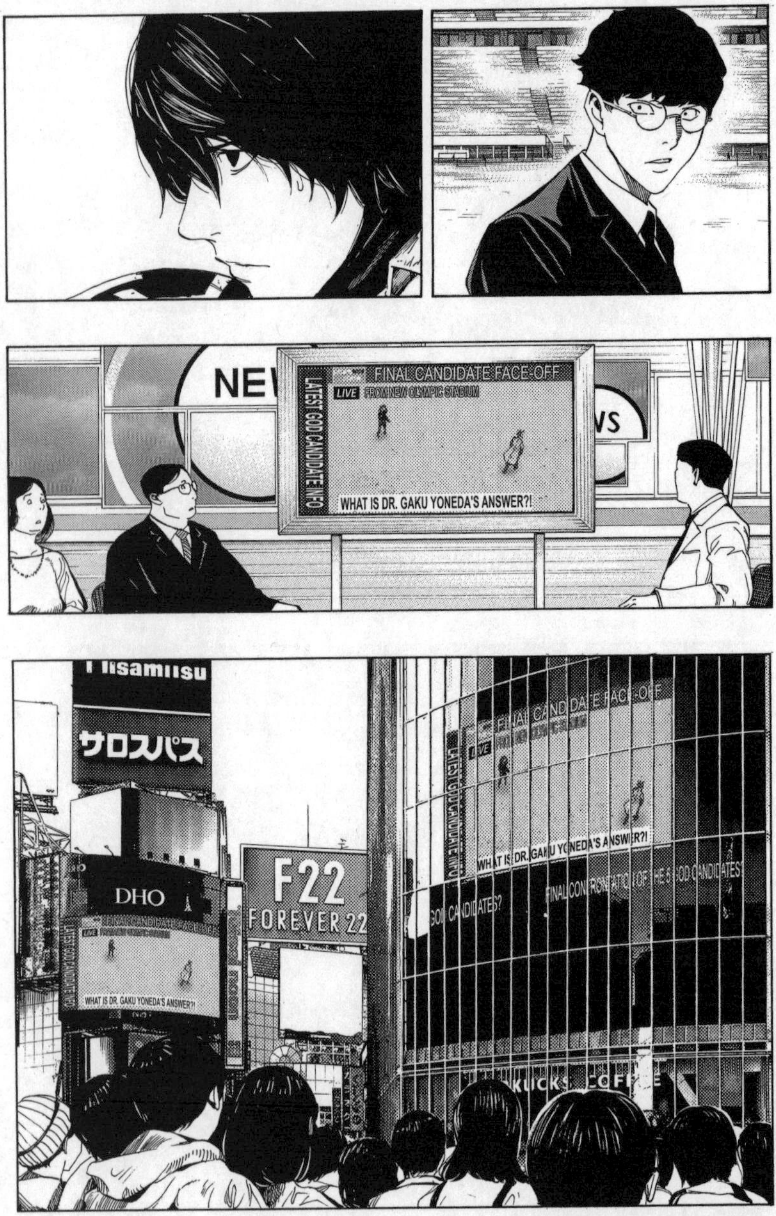
FINAL CANDIDATE FACE-OFF
LIVE
FROM NEW OLYMPIC STADIUM
LATEST GOD CANDIDATE INFO
WHAT IS DR. GAKU YONEDA'S ANSWER?!
サロスパス
F22
FOREVER 22
DHO
WHAT IS DR. GAKU YONEDA'S ANSWER?!
WHAT IS DR. GAKU YONEDA'S ANSWER?!

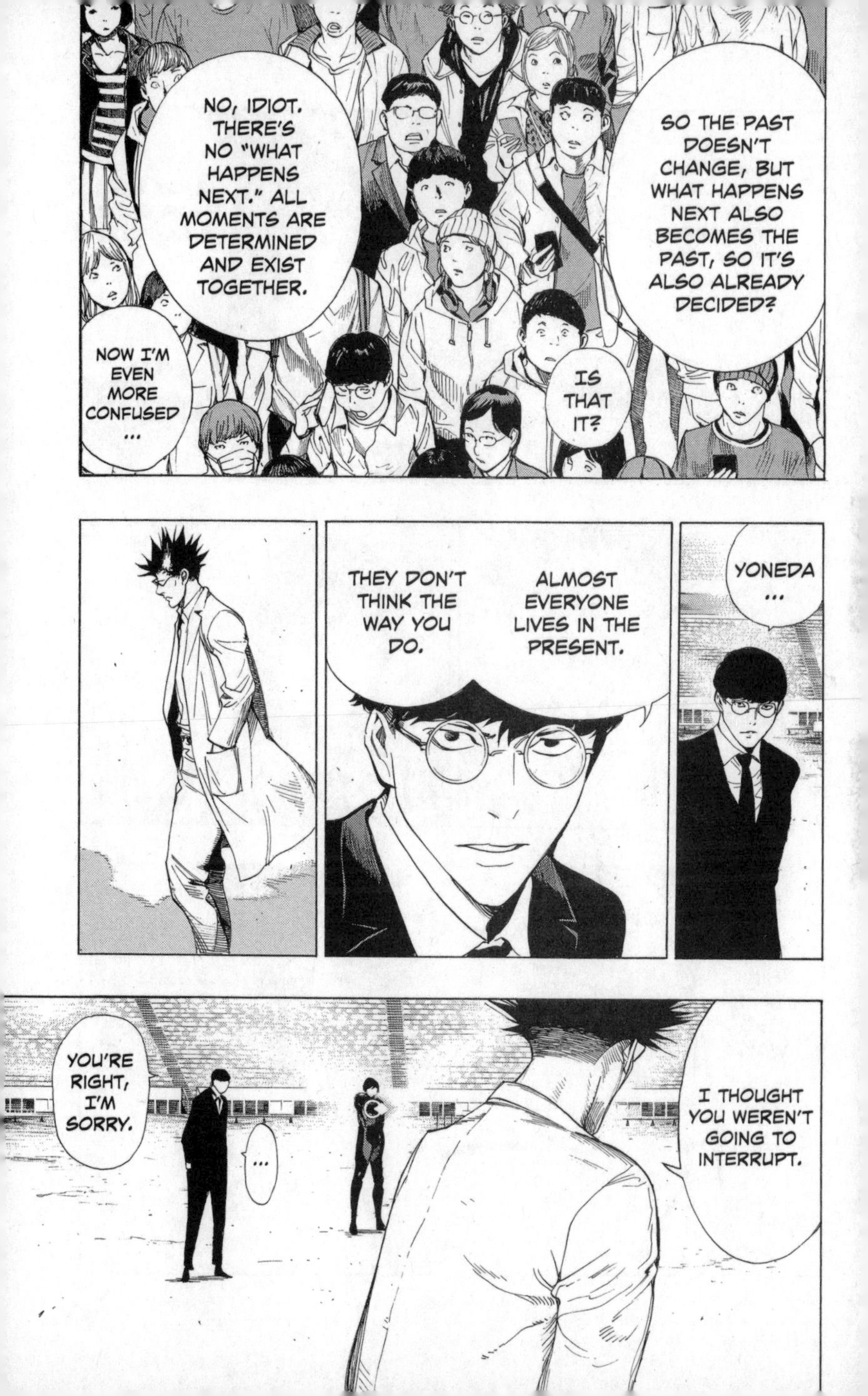
SO THE PAST DOESN'T CHANGE, BUT WHAT HAPPENS NEXT ALSO BECOMES THE PAST, SO IT'S ALSO ALREADY DECIDED?
IS THAT IT?
NO, IDIOT. THERE'S NO "WHAT HAPPENS NEXT." ALL MOMENTS ARE DETERMINED AND EXIST TOGETHER.
NOW I'M EVEN MORE CONFUSED ...
YONEDA ...
THEY DON'T THINK THE WAY YOU DO.
ALMOST EVERYONE LIVES IN THE PRESENT.
I THOUGHT YOU WEREN'T GOING TO INTERRUPT.
...
YOU'RE RIGHT, I'M SORRY.

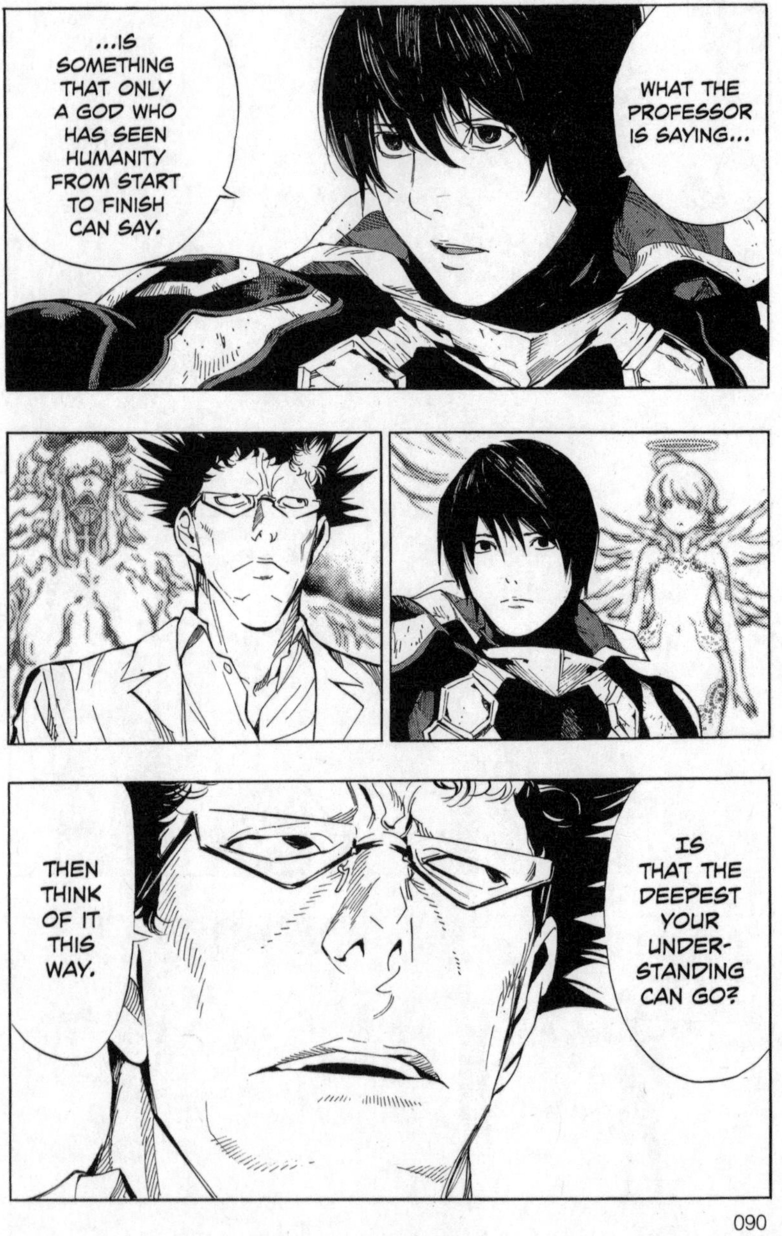
WHAT THE PROFESSOR IS SAYING...
...IS SOMETHING THAT ONLY A GOD WHO HAS SEEN HUMANITY FROM START TO FINISH CAN SAY.
IS THAT THE DEEPEST YOUR UNDER-STANDING CAN GO?
THEN THINK OF IT THIS WAY.

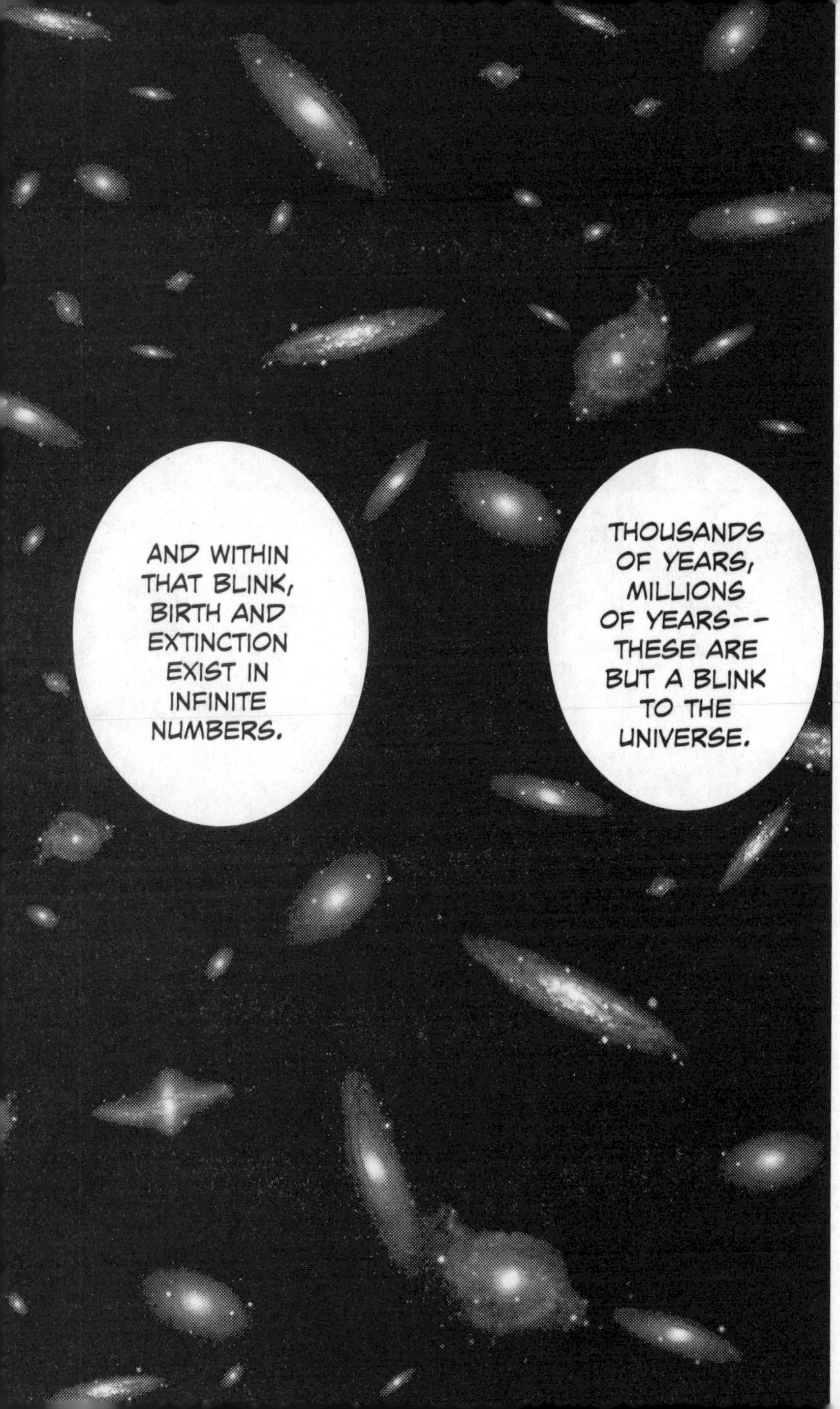
THOUSANDS OF YEARS, MILLIONS OF YEARS-- THESE ARE BUT A BLINK TO THE UNIVERSE.
AND WITHIN THAT BLINK, BIRTH AND EXTINCTION EXIST IN INFINITE NUMBERS.

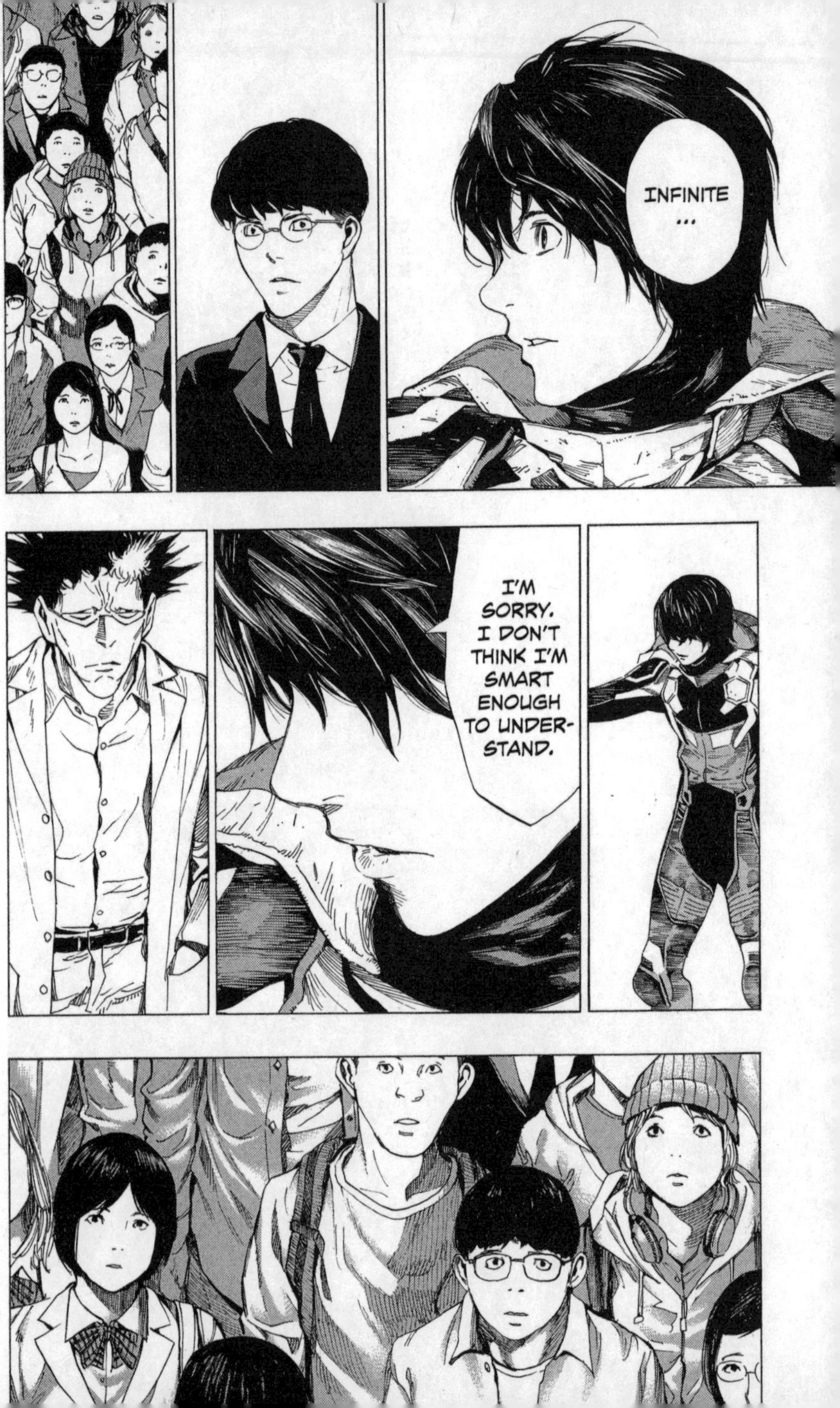
INFINITE ...
I'M SORRY. I DON'T THINK I'M SMART ENOUGH TO UNDER-STAND.

THAT'S FINE. YOUR LACK OF UNDER-STANDING IS NOT A PROBLEM.

ZSH...

BETWEEN 100 AND 200 YEARS FROM NOW, I WILL BE PROVEN CORRECT, AND THEN PEOPLE WILL UNDERSTAND. IT IS ALREADY DETERMINED.

I AM MERELY PURSUING THE ACTIONS NECESSARY FOR THAT MOMENT.

ZSHK...

FOR THE WORLD, FOR OTHERS, FOR THE FUTURE-- WHATEVER CAUSE YOU WANT TO GIVE IT, IT'S ULTIMATELY FOR YOURSELF.

THAT JUST MEANS THAT'S YOUR IDEAL FUTURE.

...

THAT'S FINE.

ALL HUMAN BEINGS, INCLUDING YOURSELF, LIVE ONLY FOR THEIR OWN SAKE.

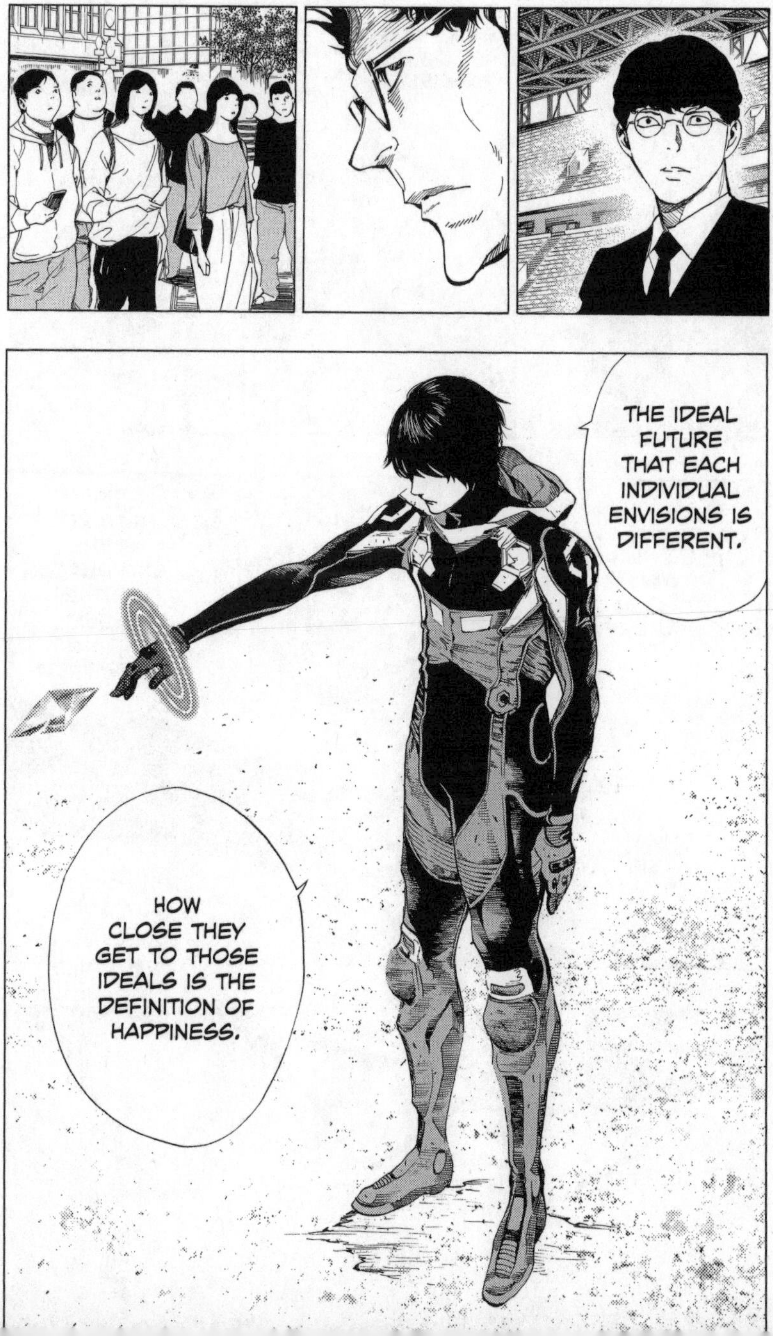
THE IDEAL FUTURE THAT EACH INDIVIDUAL ENVISIONS IS DIFFERENT.
HOW CLOSE THEY GET TO THOSE IDEALS IS THE DEFINITION OF HAPPINESS.

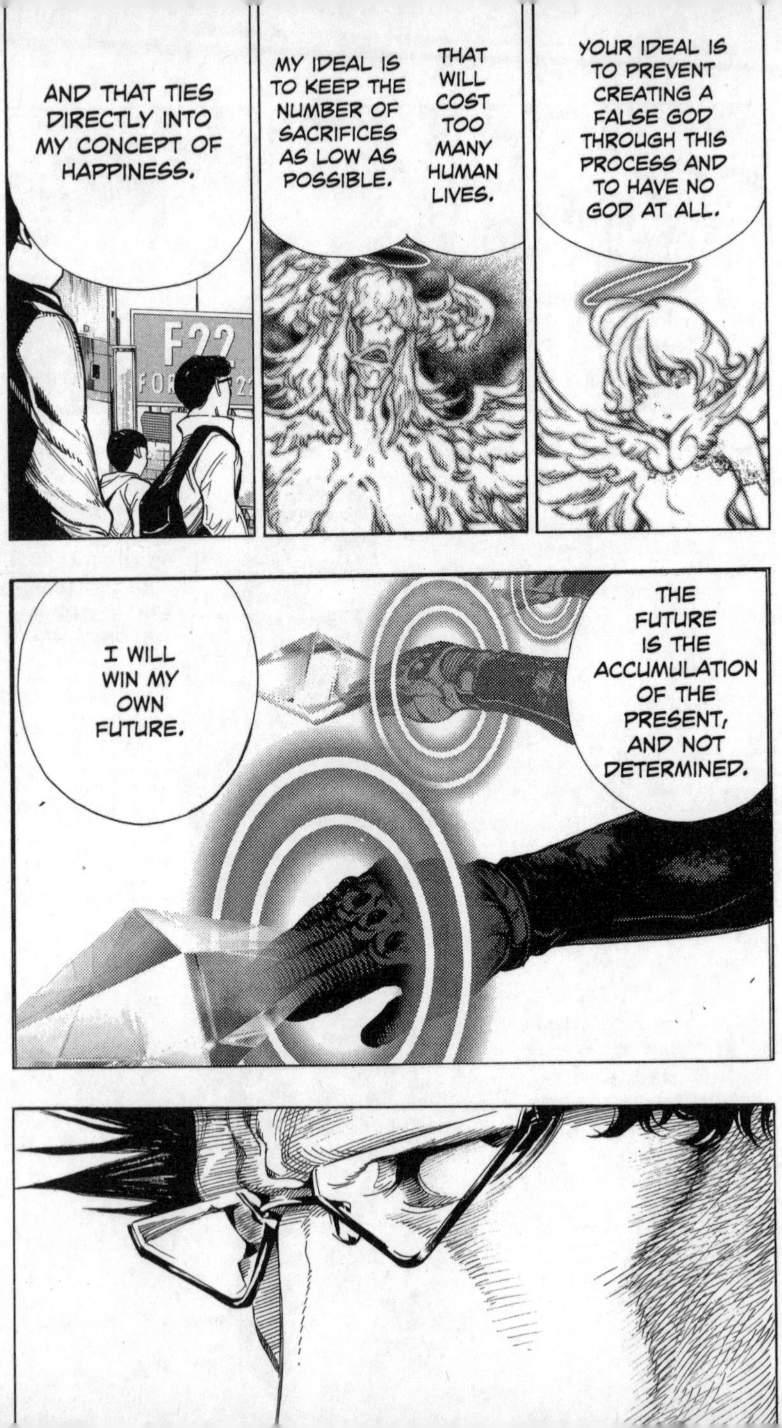
YOUR IDEAL IS TO PREVENT CREATING A FALSE GOD THROUGH THIS PROCESS AND TO HAVE NO GOD AT ALL.
THAT WILL COST TOO MANY HUMAN LIVES.
MY IDEAL IS TO KEEP THE NUMBER OF SACRIFICES AS LOW AS POSSIBLE.
AND THAT TIES DIRECTLY INTO MY CONCEPT OF HAPPINESS.
F22
THE FUTURE IS THE ACCUMULATION OF THE PRESENT, AND NOT DETERMINED.
I WILL WIN MY OWN FUTURE.

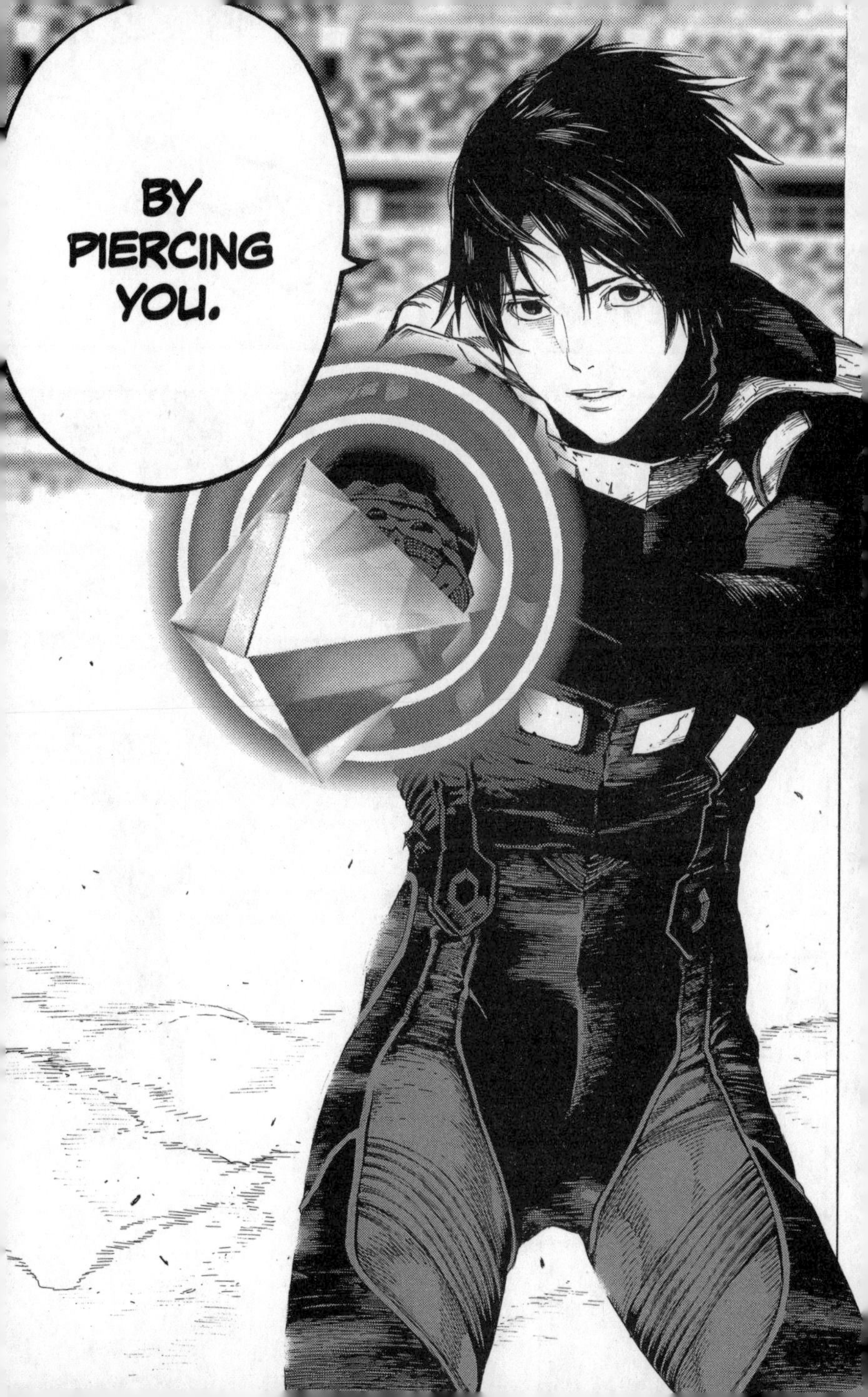
BY PIERCING YOU.

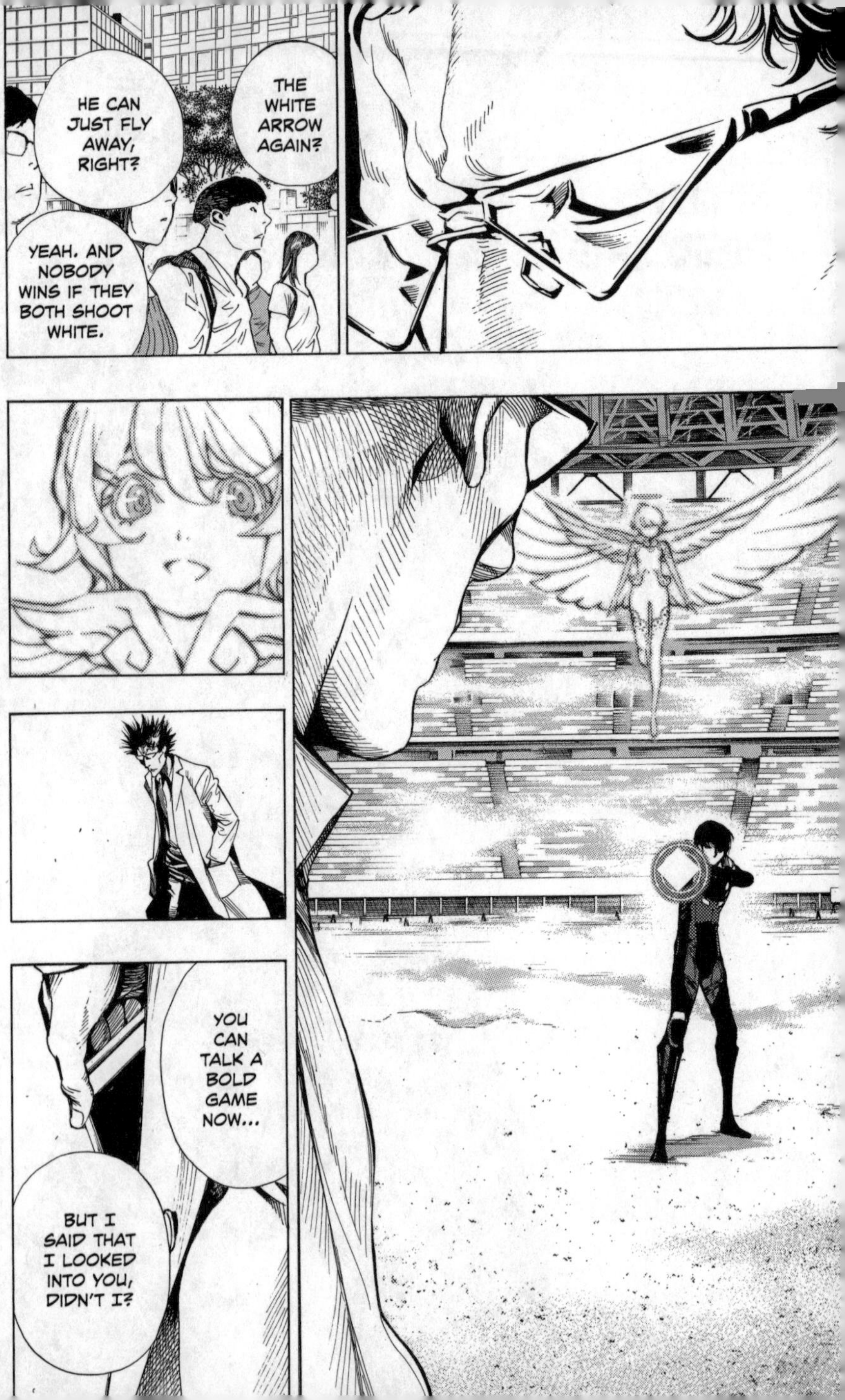
THE WHITE ARROW AGAIN?
HE CAN JUST FLY AWAY, RIGHT?
YEAH. AND NOBODY WINS IF THEY BOTH SHOOT WHITE.
...
YOU CAN TALK A BOLD GAME NOW...
BUT I SAID THAT I LOOKED INTO YOU, DIDN'T I?

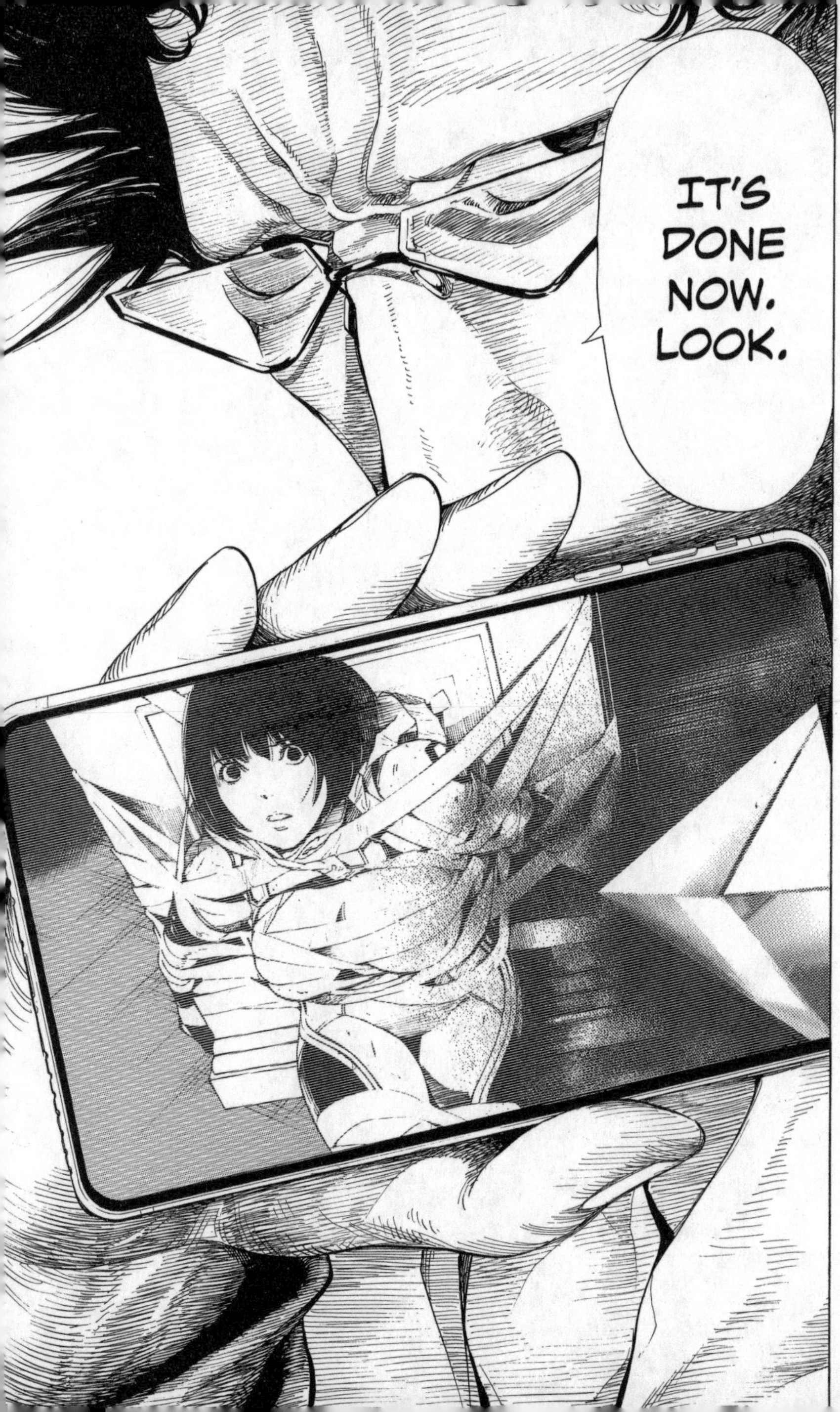
IT'S DONE NOW. LOOK.

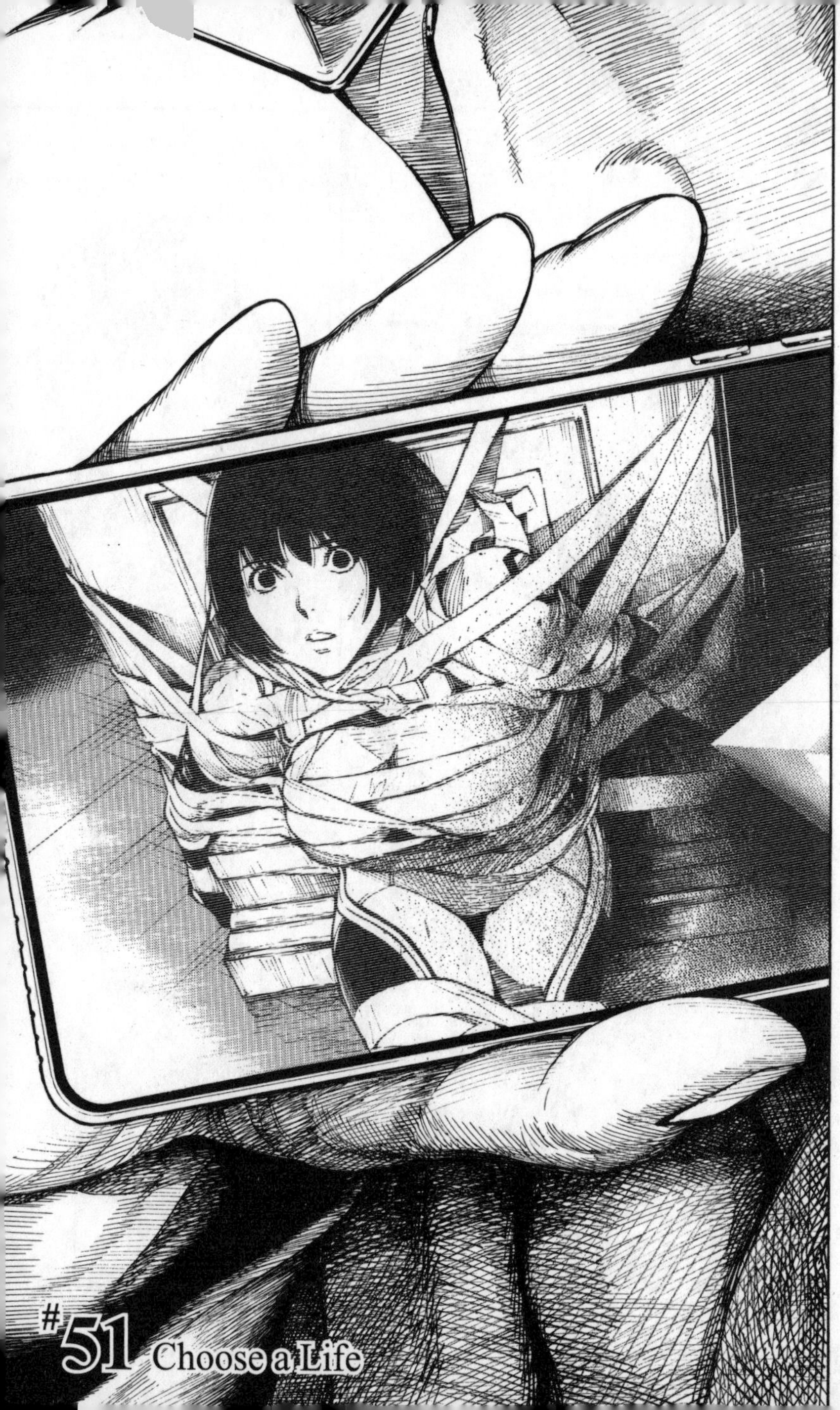

#51 Choose a Life

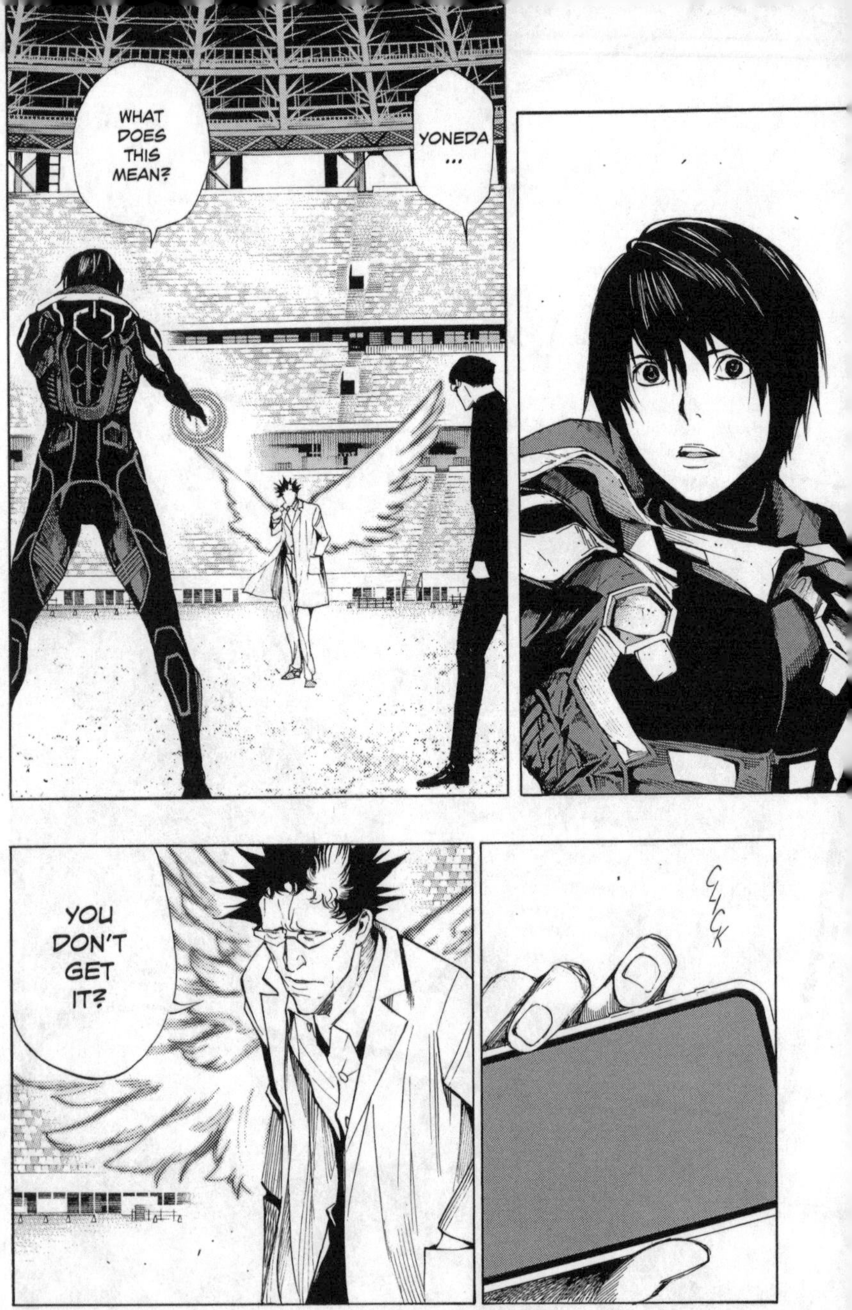
YONEDA ...
WHAT DOES THIS MEAN?
CLICK
YOU DON'T GET IT?

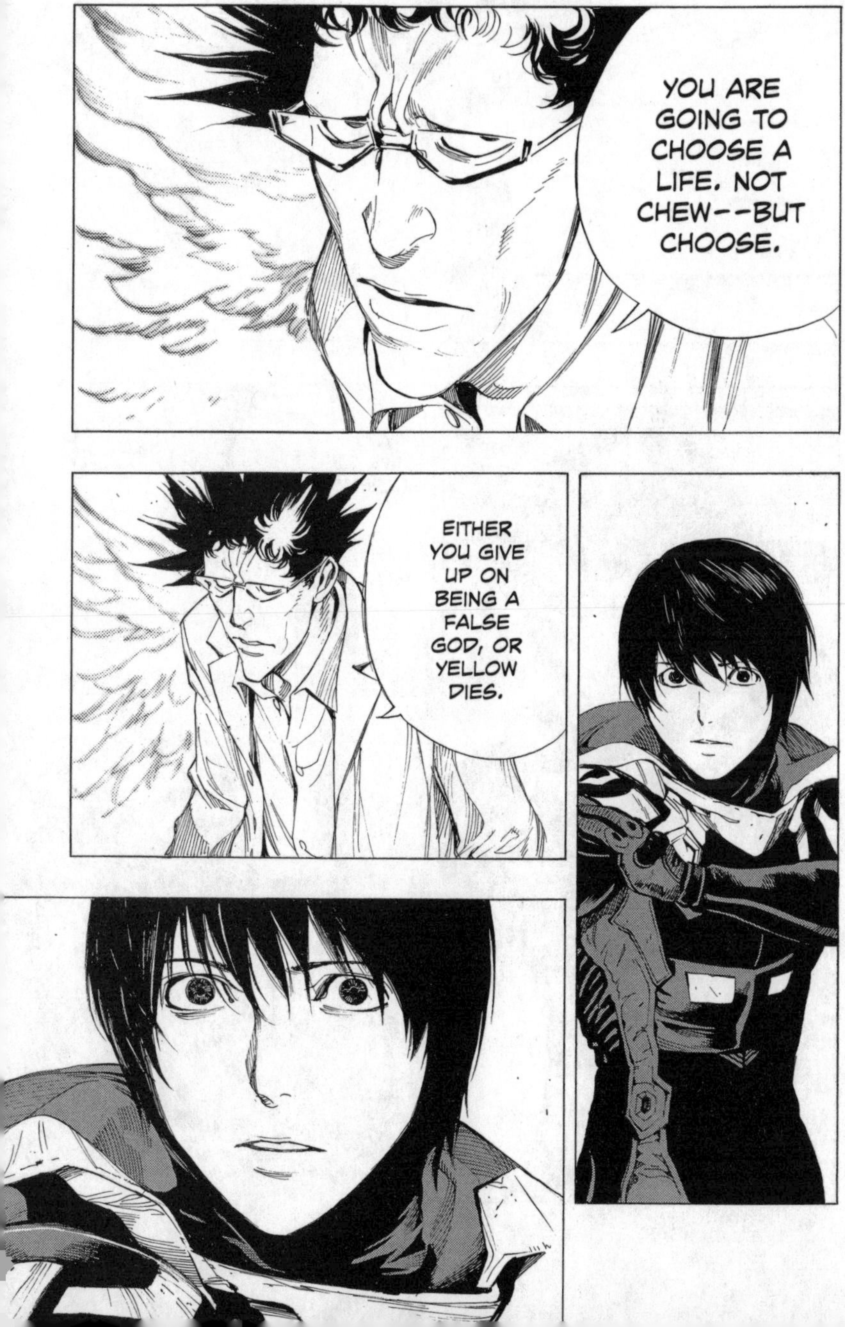
YOU ARE GOING TO CHOOSE A LIFE. NOT CHEW--BUT CHOOSE.
EITHER YOU GIVE UP ON BEING A FALSE GOD, OR YELLOW DIES.

AT THE PRESENT MOMENT, THIS IS THE MOST EFFECTIVE MEANS OF PREVENTING A FALSE GOD.

YOU HAVE 28 SECONDS.

NOW DECIDE.

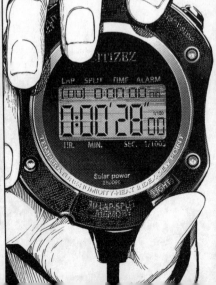

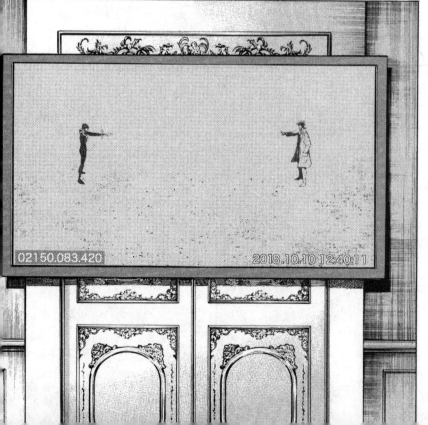

02150.083.420 2018.10.10 12:40:11

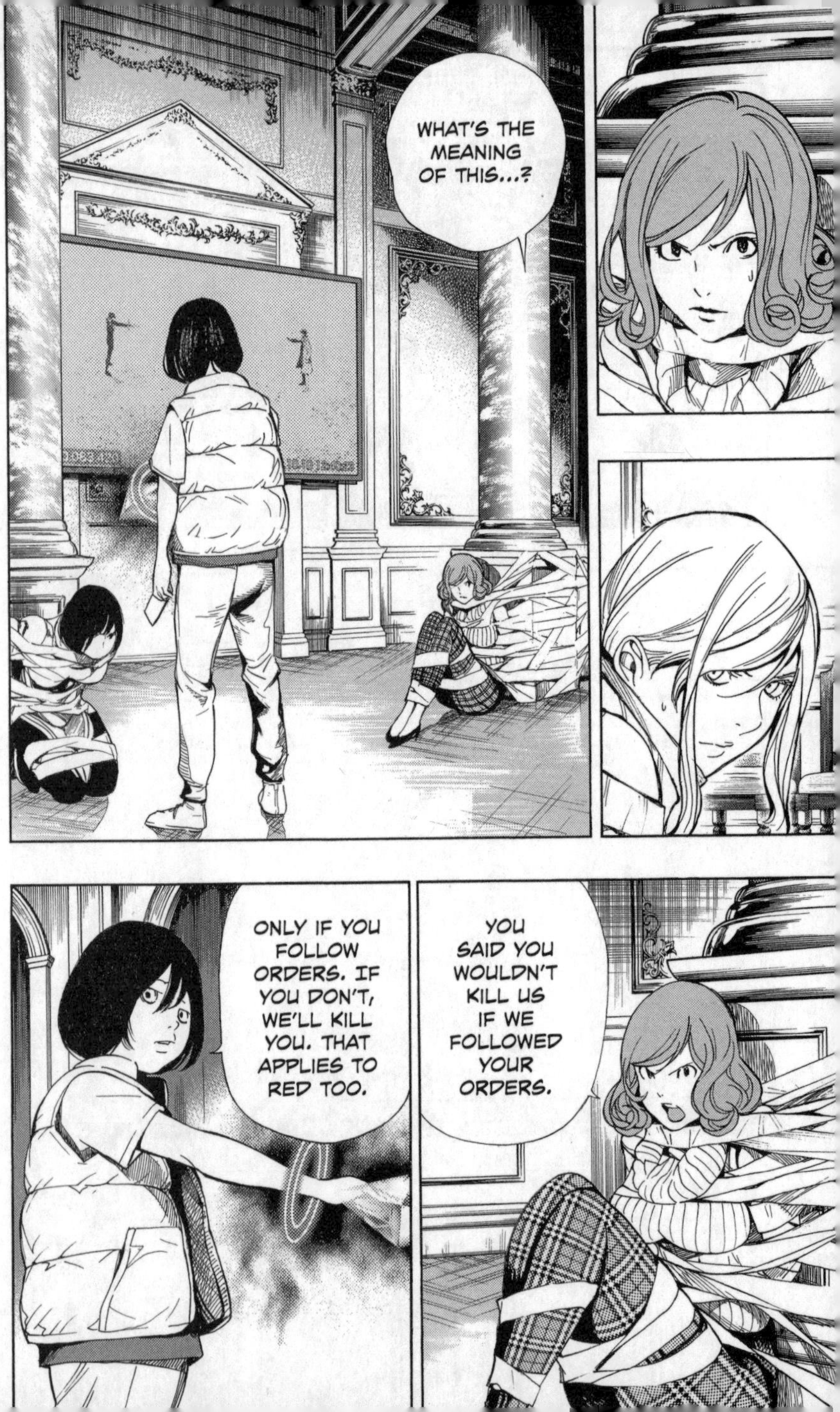
WHAT'S THE MEANING OF THIS...?
YOU SAID YOU WOULDN'T KILL US IF WE FOLLOWED YOUR ORDERS.
ONLY IF YOU FOLLOW ORDERS. IF YOU DON'T, WE'LL KILL YOU. THAT APPLIES TO RED TOO.

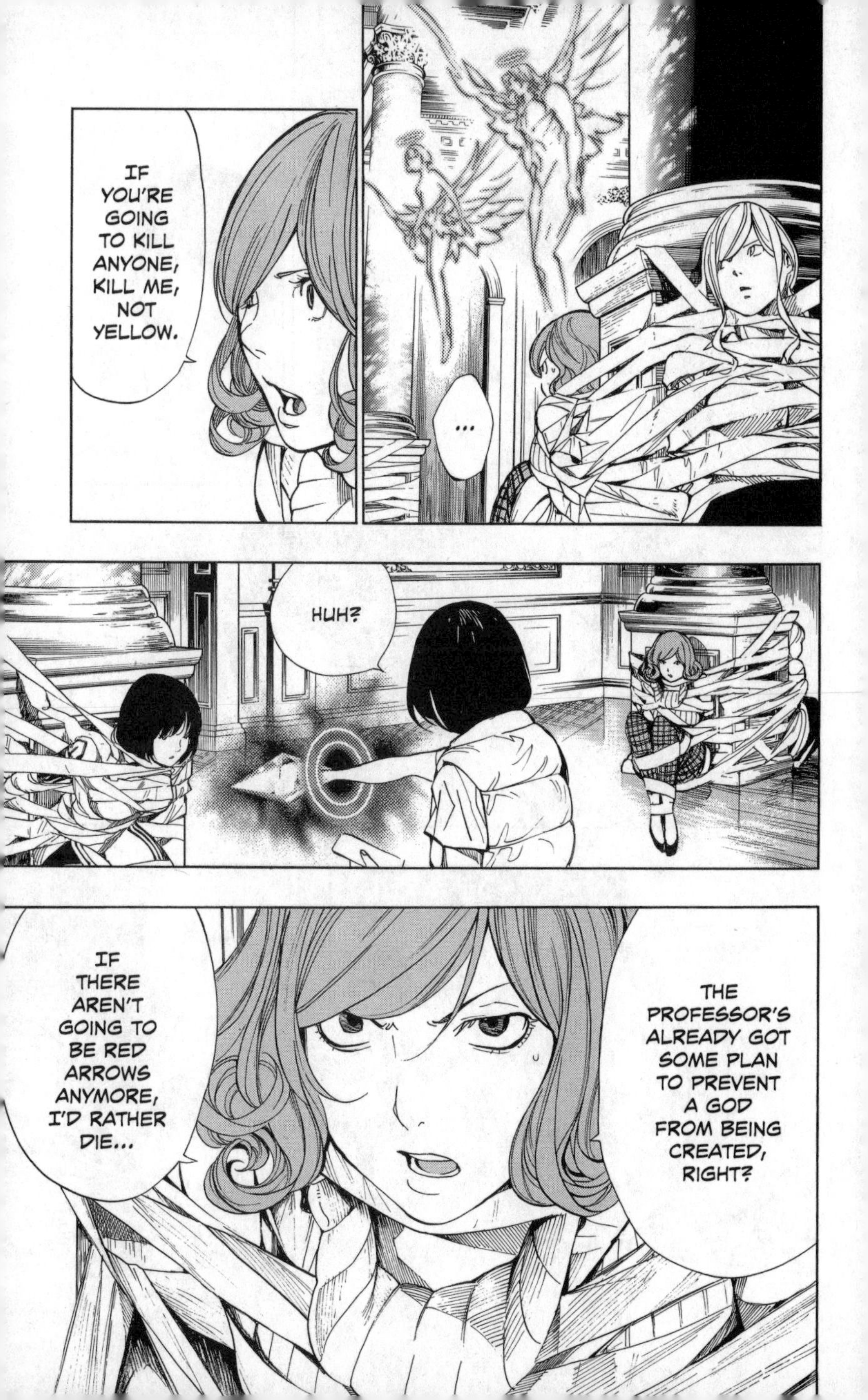
...
IF YOU'RE GOING TO KILL ANYONE, KILL ME, NOT YELLOW.
HUH?
THE PROFESSOR'S ALREADY GOT SOME PLAN TO PREVENT A GOD FROM BEING CREATED, RIGHT?
IF THERE AREN'T GOING TO BE RED ARROWS ANYMORE, I'D RATHER DIE...

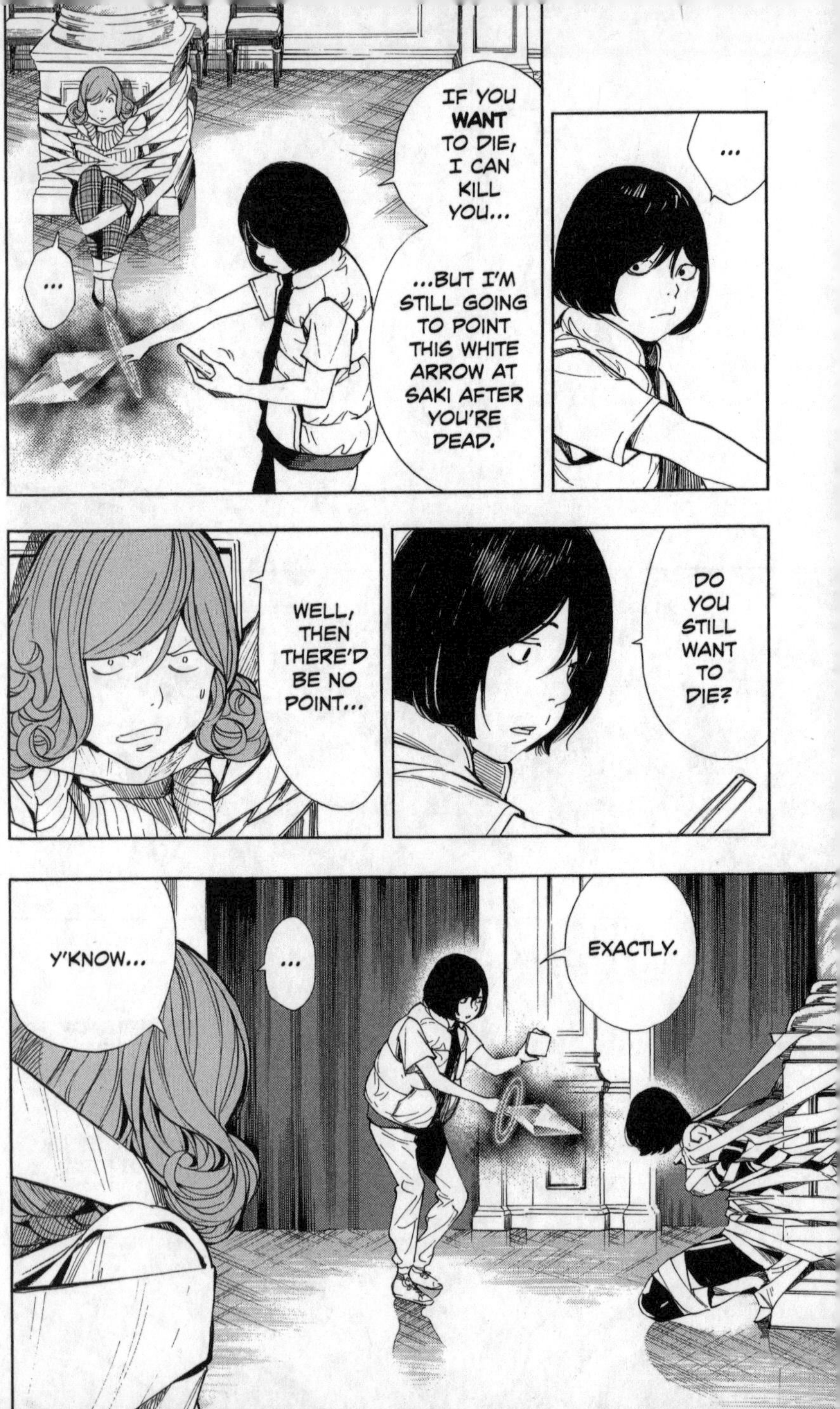
...
IF YOU WANT TO DIE, I CAN KILL YOU...
...BUT I'M STILL GOING TO POINT THIS WHITE ARROW AT SAKI AFTER YOU'RE DEAD.
...
DO YOU STILL WANT TO DIE?
WELL, THEN THERE'D BE NO POINT...
EXACTLY.
...
Y'KNOW...

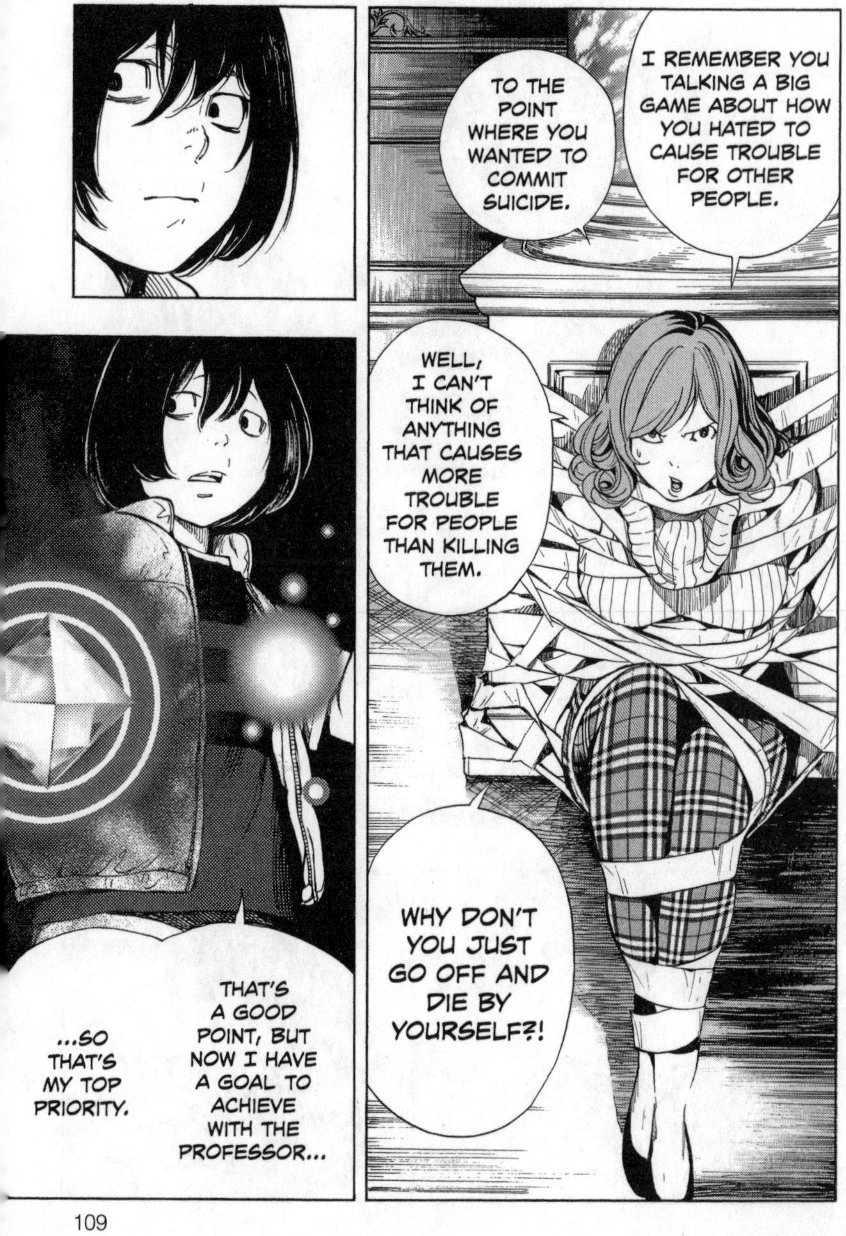
I REMEMBER YOU TALKING A BIG GAME ABOUT HOW YOU HATED TO CAUSE TROUBLE FOR OTHER PEOPLE.
TO THE POINT WHERE YOU WANTED TO COMMIT SUICIDE.
WELL, I CAN'T THINK OF ANYTHING THAT CAUSES MORE TROUBLE FOR PEOPLE THAN KILLING THEM.
WHY DON'T YOU JUST GO OFF AND DIE BY YOURSELF?!
THAT'S A GOOD POINT, BUT NOW I HAVE A GOAL TO ACHIEVE WITH THE PROFESSOR...
...SO THAT'S MY TOP PRIORITY.

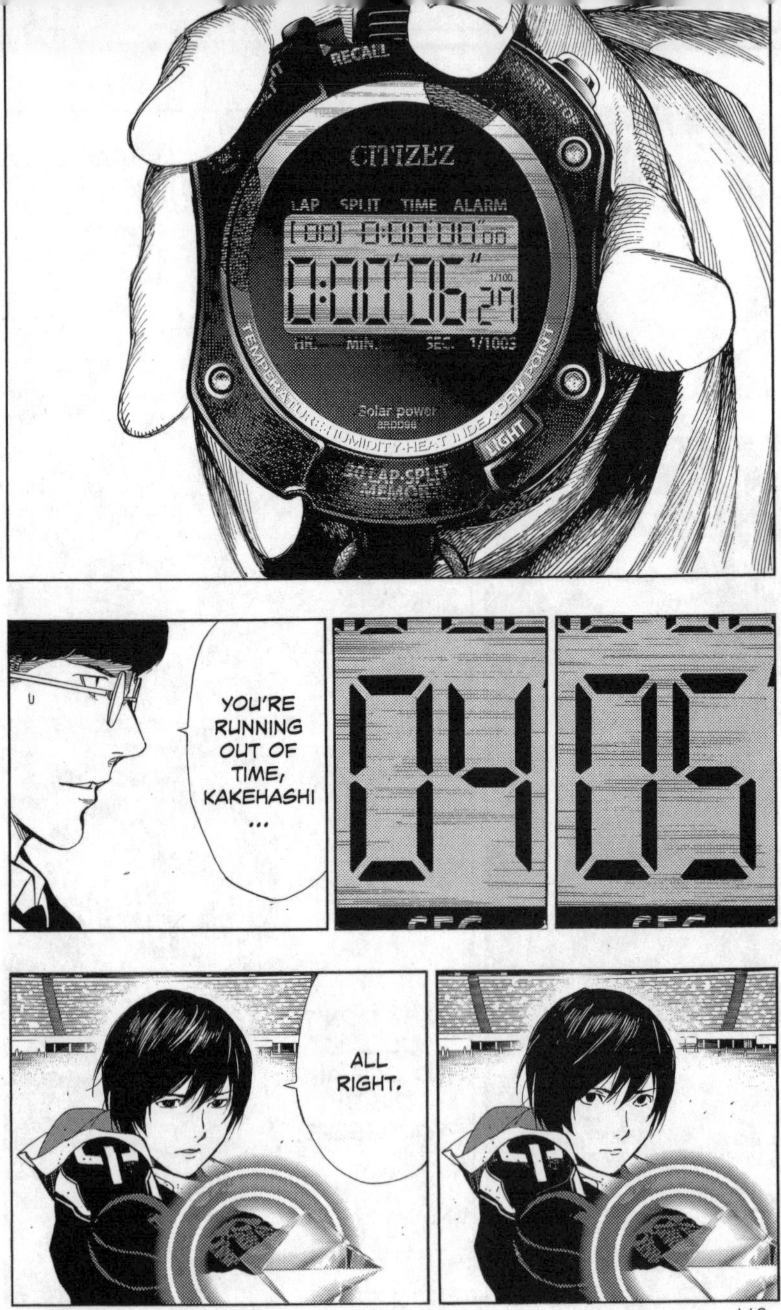
RECALL
CITIZEZ
LAP SPLIT TIME ALARM
0:00'06"27
Solar power
LIGHT
05
04
YOU'RE RUNNING OUT OF TIME, KAKEHASHI ...
ALL RIGHT.

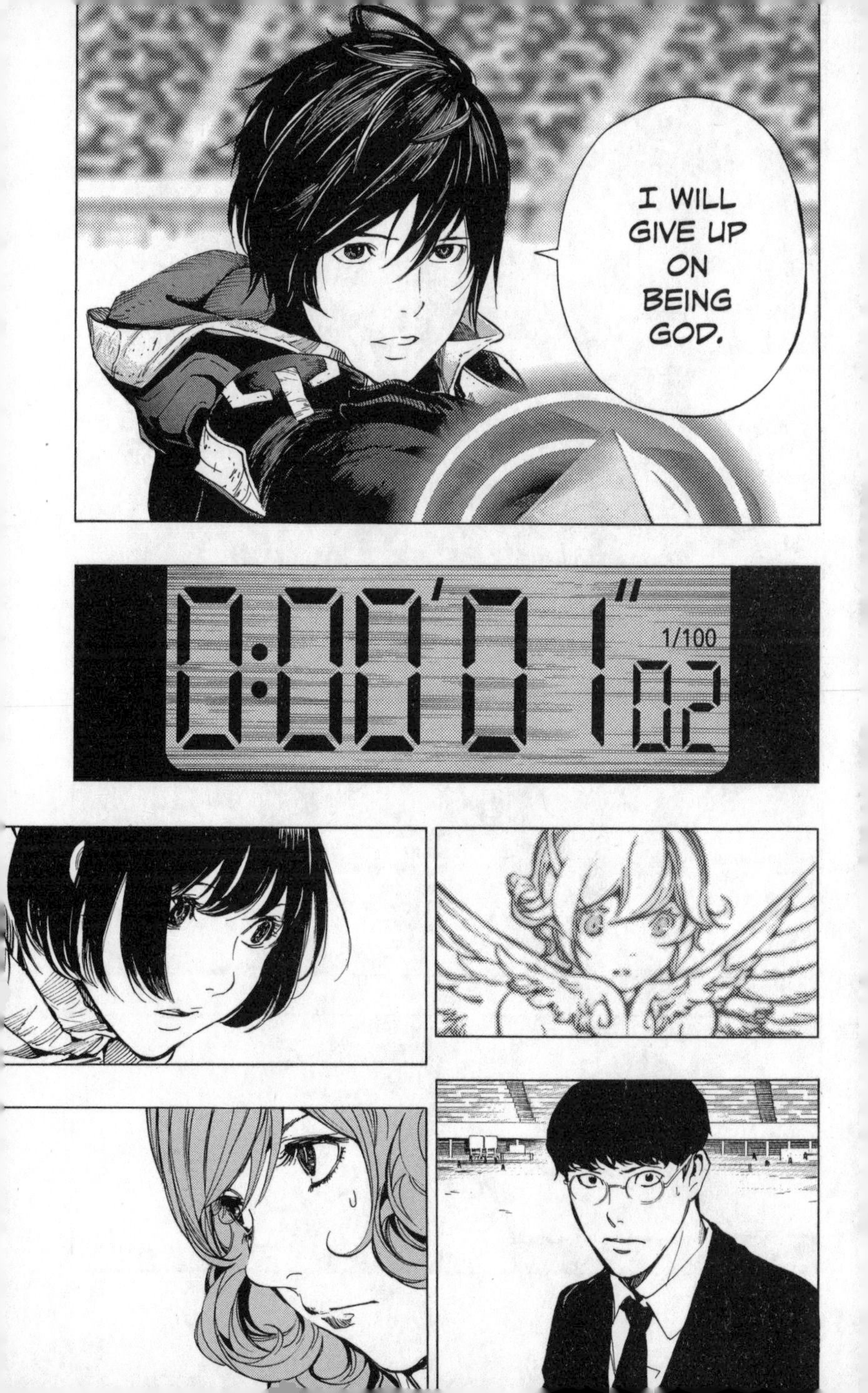
I WILL GIVE UP ON BEING GOD.
0:00'01"02
1/100

FINAL CANDIDATE FACE-OFF

LIVE FROM NEW OLYMPIC STADIUM

LATEST GOD CANDIDATE IN

WHAT IS DR. GAKU YONEDA'S ANSWER?!

FINAL CON

THAT MEANS THERE WILL NOT BE A NEW GOD.

THE CANDIDATE MIRAI KAKEHASHI HAS GIVEN UP ON BEING GOD.

SO THE PROFESSOR'S RIGHT.

OR FALSE GOD, ANYWAY.

HE'D PROBABLY BEND THE RULES TO FAVOR YELLOW IF HE WERE GOD.

ARE RED AND YELLOW AN ITEM, THEN?

THANK GOODNESS.

...

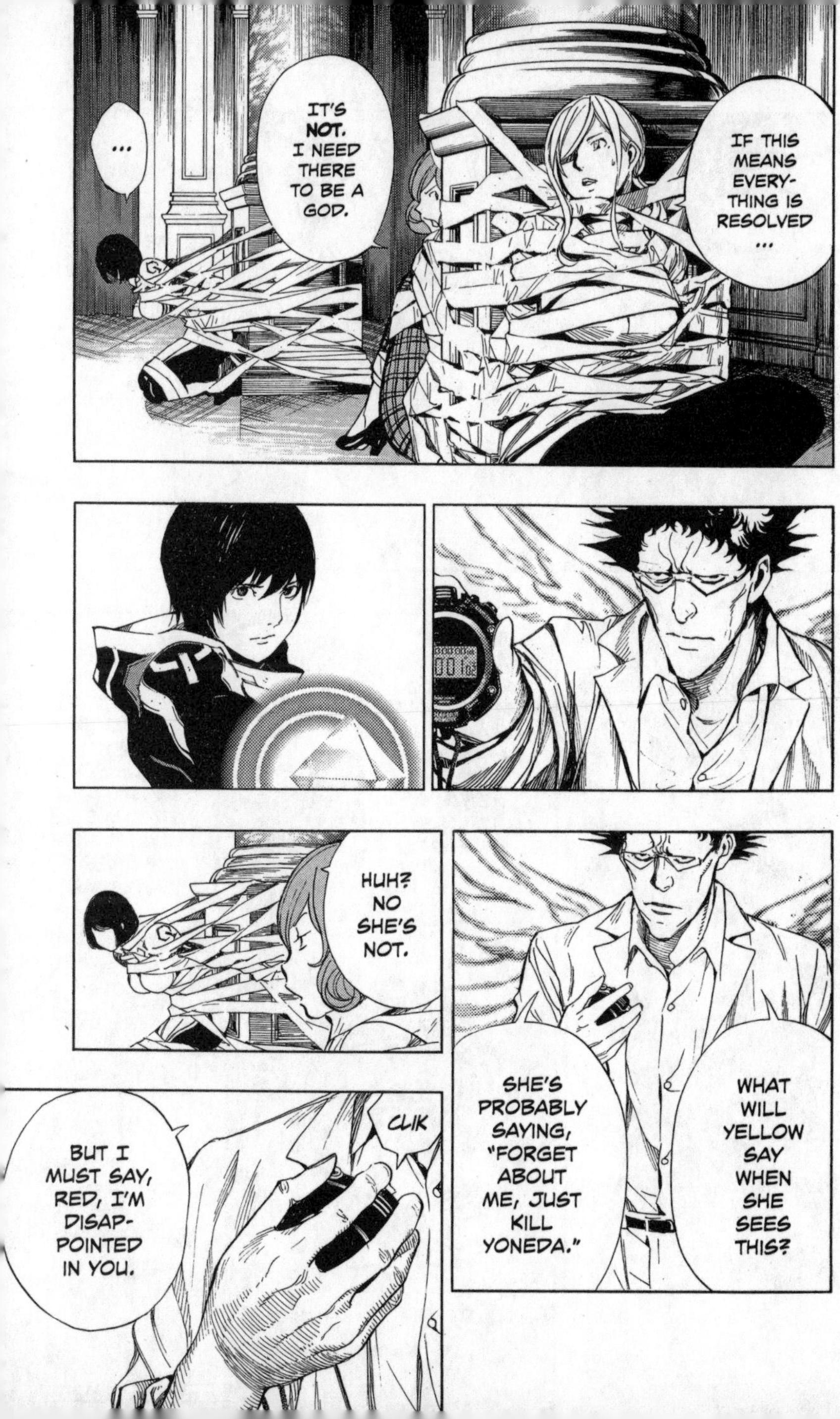
IF THIS MEANS EVERYTHING IS RESOLVED ...
IT'S **NOT.** I NEED THERE TO BE A GOD.
...
WHAT WILL YELLOW SAY WHEN SHE SEES THIS?
SHE'S PROBABLY SAYING, "FORGET ABOUT ME, JUST KILL YONEDA."
HUH? NO SHE'S NOT.
CLIK
BUT I MUST SAY, RED, I'M DISAPPOINTED IN YOU.

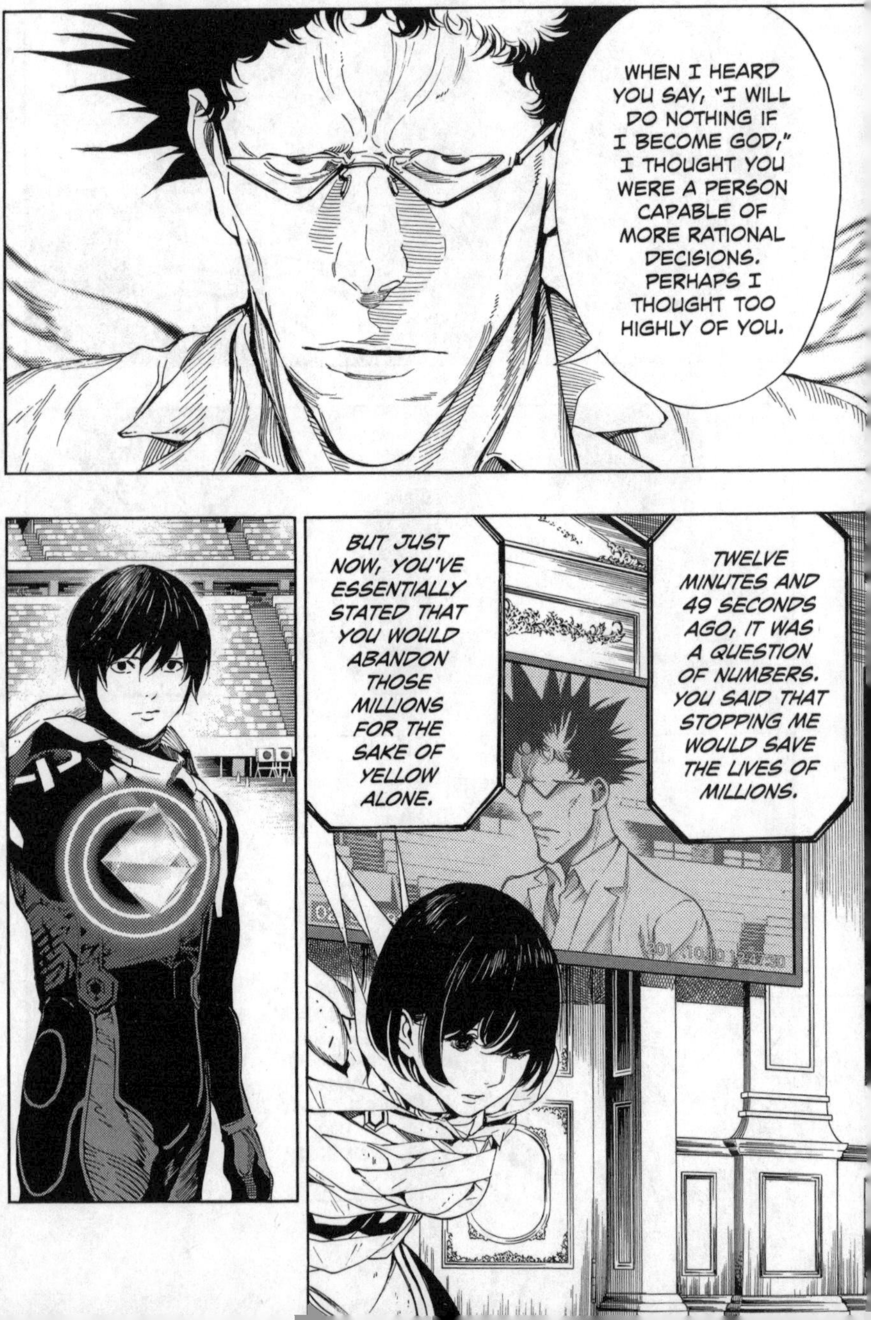
WHEN I HEARD YOU SAY, "I WILL DO NOTHING IF I BECOME GOD," I THOUGHT YOU WERE A PERSON CAPABLE OF MORE RATIONAL DECISIONS. PERHAPS I THOUGHT TOO HIGHLY OF YOU.
TWELVE MINUTES AND 49 SECONDS AGO, IT WAS A QUESTION OF NUMBERS. YOU SAID THAT STOPPING ME WOULD SAVE THE LIVES OF MILLIONS.
BUT JUST NOW, YOU'VE ESSENTIALLY STATED THAT YOU WOULD ABANDON THOSE MILLIONS FOR THE SAKE OF YELLOW ALONE.

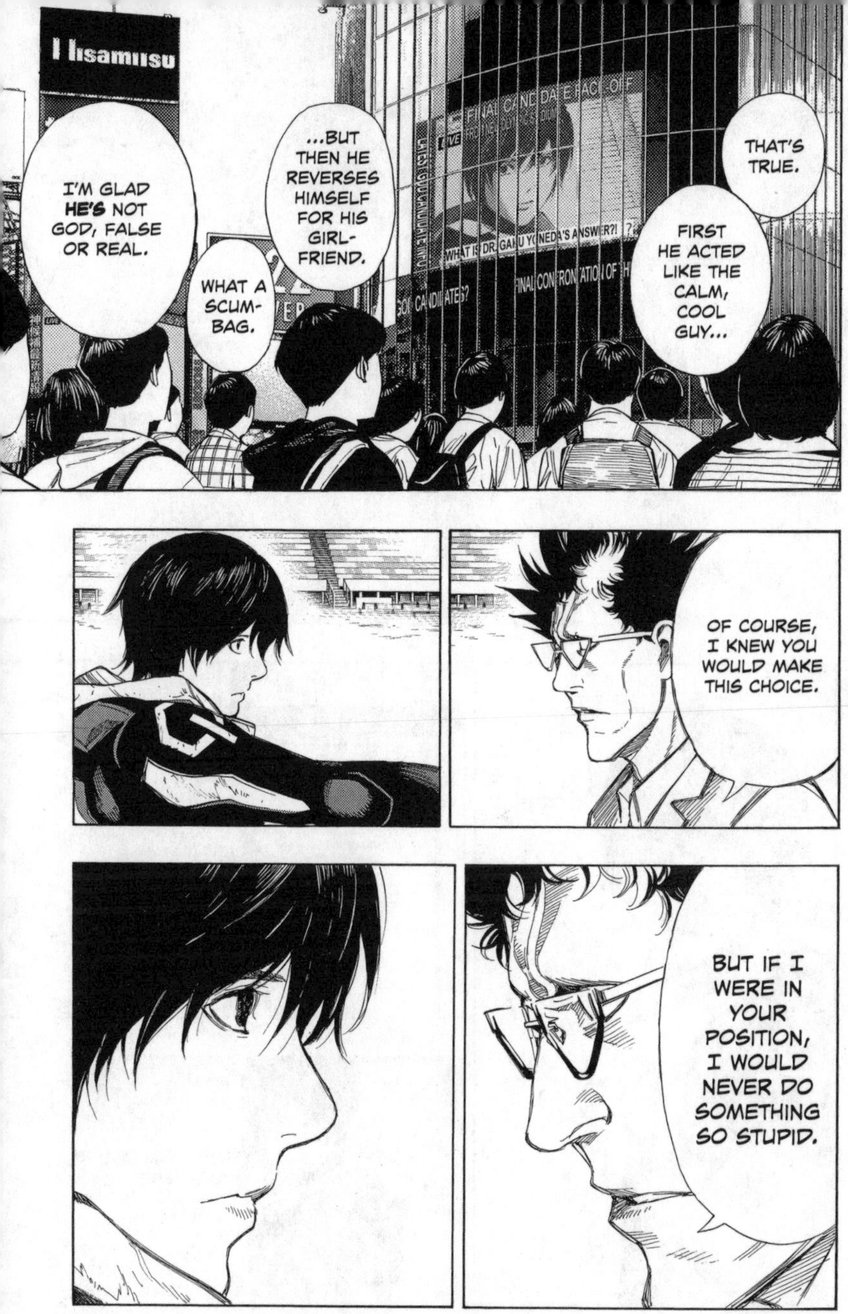
WHAT IS DR. GAHU YONEDA'S ANSWER?!
THAT'S TRUE.
FIRST HE ACTED LIKE THE CALM, COOL GUY...
...BUT THEN HE REVERSES HIMSELF FOR HIS GIRLFRIEND.
WHAT A SCUMBAG.
I'M GLAD **HE'S** NOT GOD, FALSE OR REAL.
OF COURSE, I KNEW YOU WOULD MAKE THIS CHOICE.
BUT IF I WERE IN YOUR POSITION, I WOULD NEVER DO SOMETHING SO STUPID.

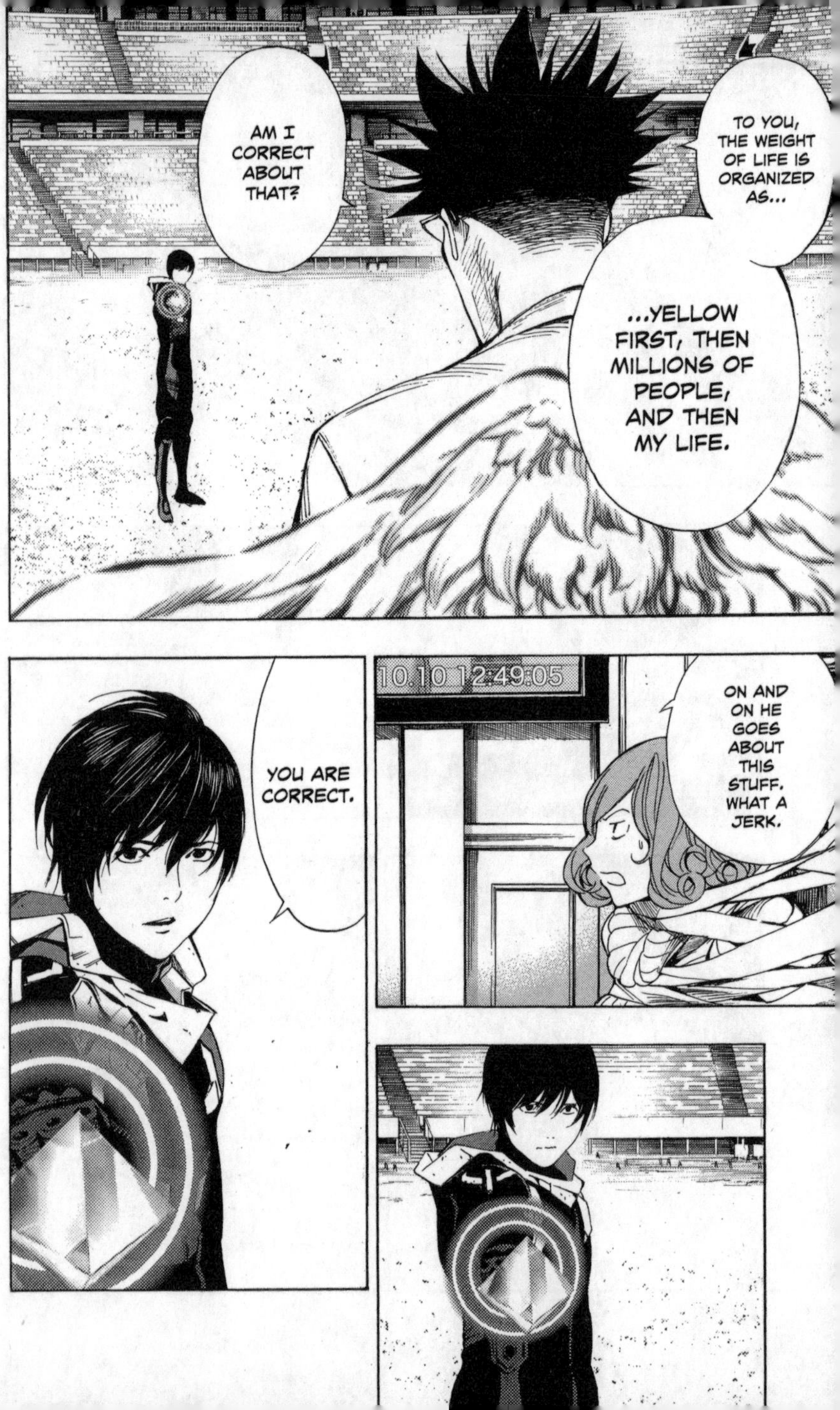
TO YOU, THE WEIGHT OF LIFE IS ORGANIZED AS...
...YELLOW FIRST, THEN MILLIONS OF PEOPLE, AND THEN MY LIFE.
AM I CORRECT ABOUT THAT?
ON AND ON HE GOES ABOUT THIS STUFF. WHAT A JERK.
10.10 12:49:05
YOU ARE CORRECT.

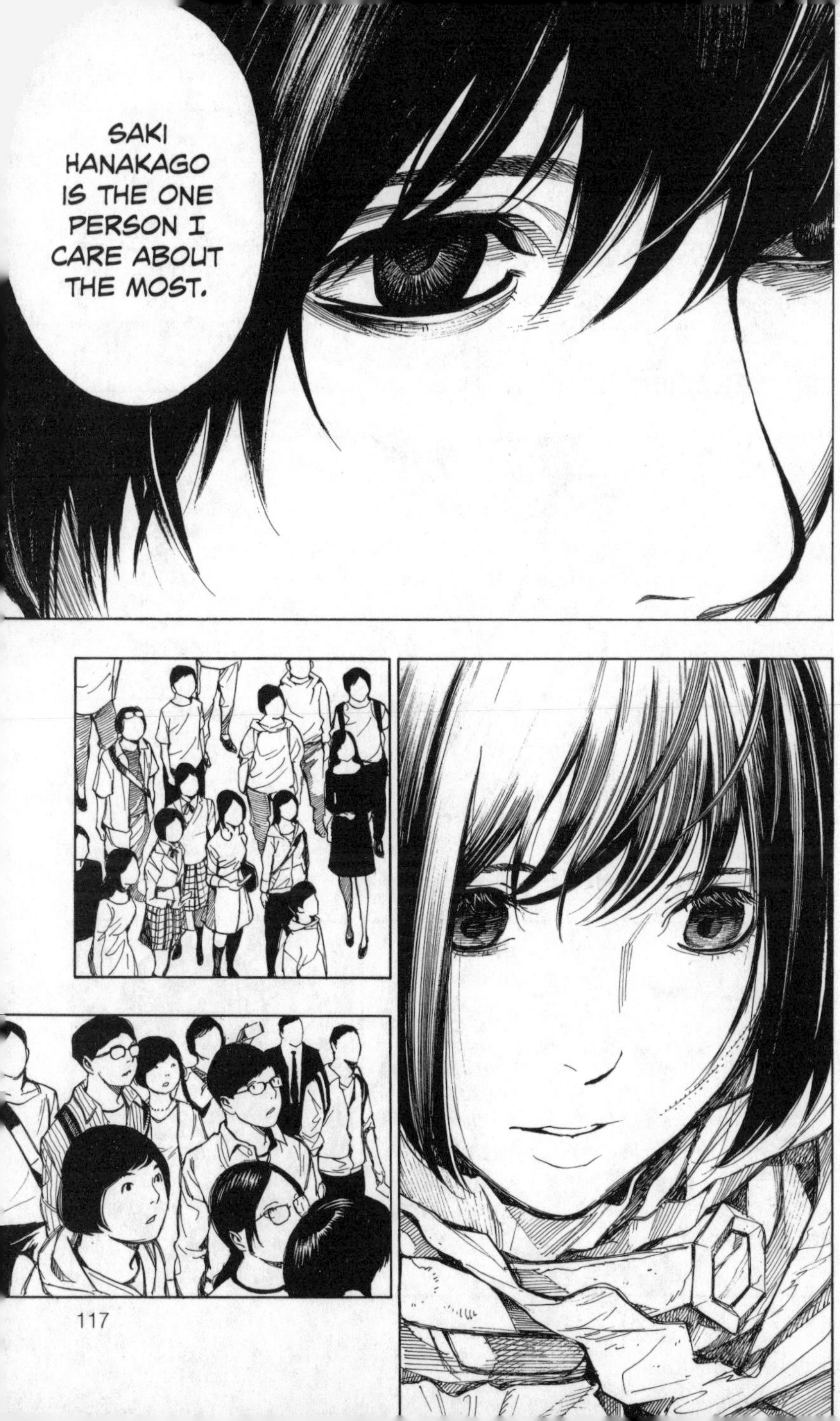
SAKI HANAKAGO IS THE ONE PERSON I CARE ABOUT THE MOST.

THE MOST, EH...?

...

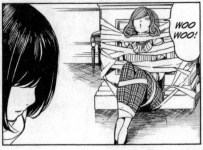

WOO WOO!

I HATE THIS IDEA OF "THE MOST IMPORTANT PERSON." IT HAS NO BASIS IN SCIENCE... OR EVEN BIOLOGY...

"MOST IMPORTANT PERSON." "MY FATED PARTNER." THESE ARE ILLUSIONS THAT THE WEAK-MINDED FALL INTO.

118

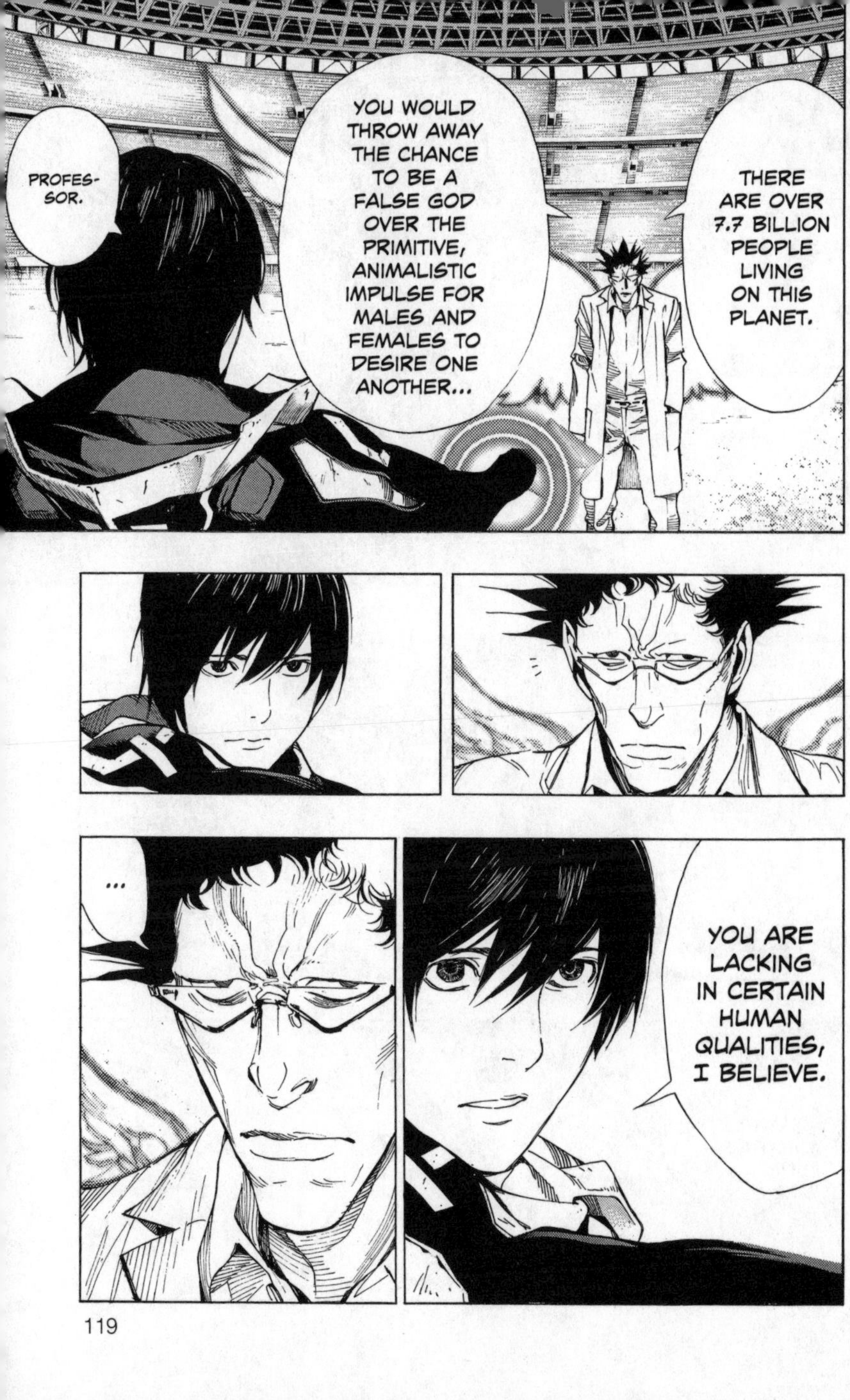
THERE ARE OVER 7.7 BILLION PEOPLE LIVING ON THIS PLANET.
YOU WOULD THROW AWAY THE CHANCE TO BE A FALSE GOD OVER THE PRIMITIVE, ANIMALISTIC IMPULSE FOR MALES AND FEMALES TO DESIRE ONE ANOTHER...
PROFES-SOR.
YOU ARE LACKING IN CERTAIN HUMAN QUALITIES, I BELIEVE.
...

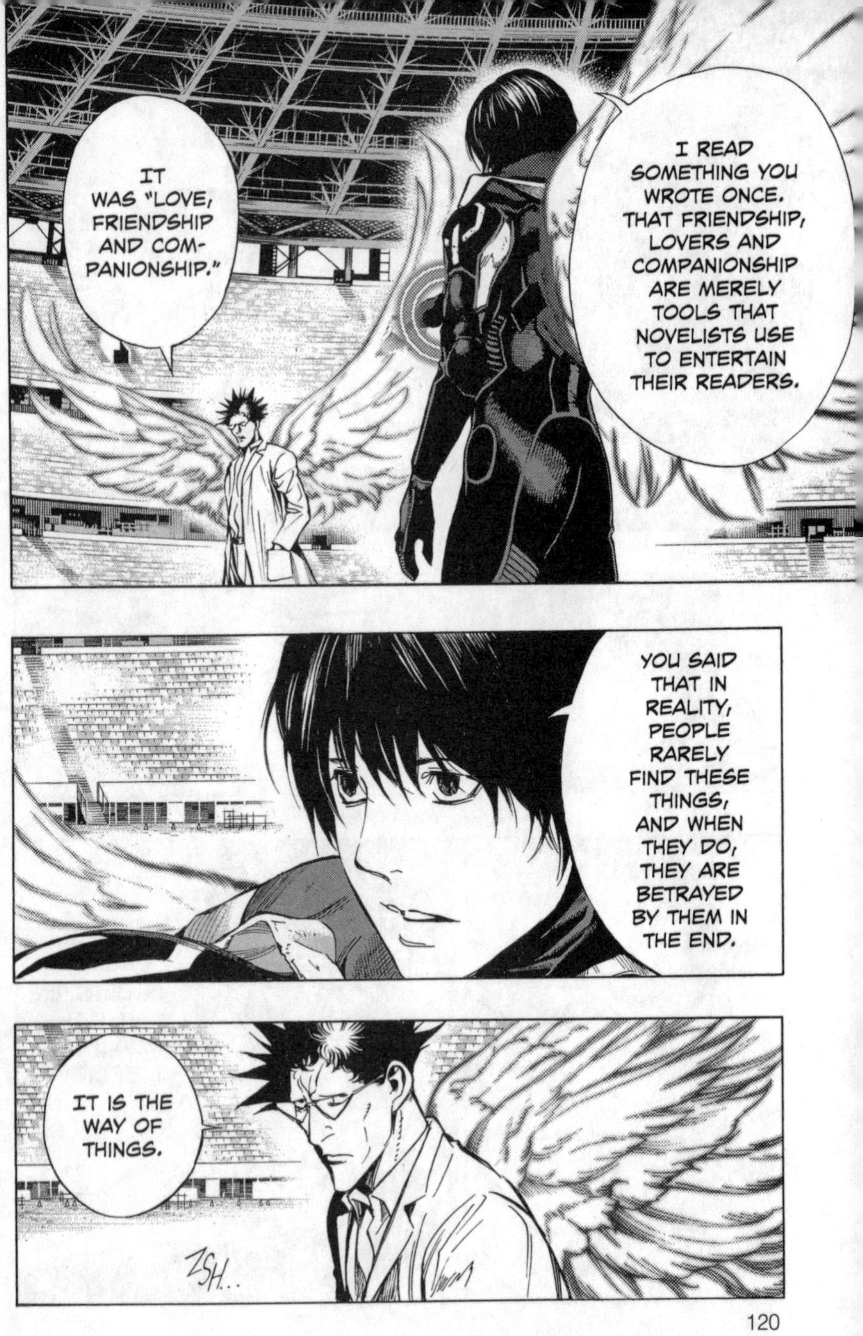
I READ SOMETHING YOU WROTE ONCE. THAT FRIENDSHIP, LOVERS AND COMPANIONSHIP ARE MERELY TOOLS THAT NOVELISTS USE TO ENTERTAIN THEIR READERS.
IT WAS "LOVE, FRIENDSHIP AND COM-PANIONSHIP."
YOU SAID THAT IN REALITY, PEOPLE RARELY FIND THESE THINGS, AND WHEN THEY DO, THEY ARE BETRAYED BY THEM IN THE END.
IT IS THE WAY OF THINGS.
ZSH...

THERE ARE TIMES WHEN I'VE FELT THAT WAY TOO...

HA HA HA!

HOLD YOUR NOSE AROUND HIM!

PIG-STY!

PIG-STY!

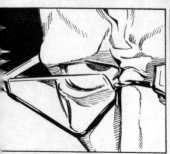

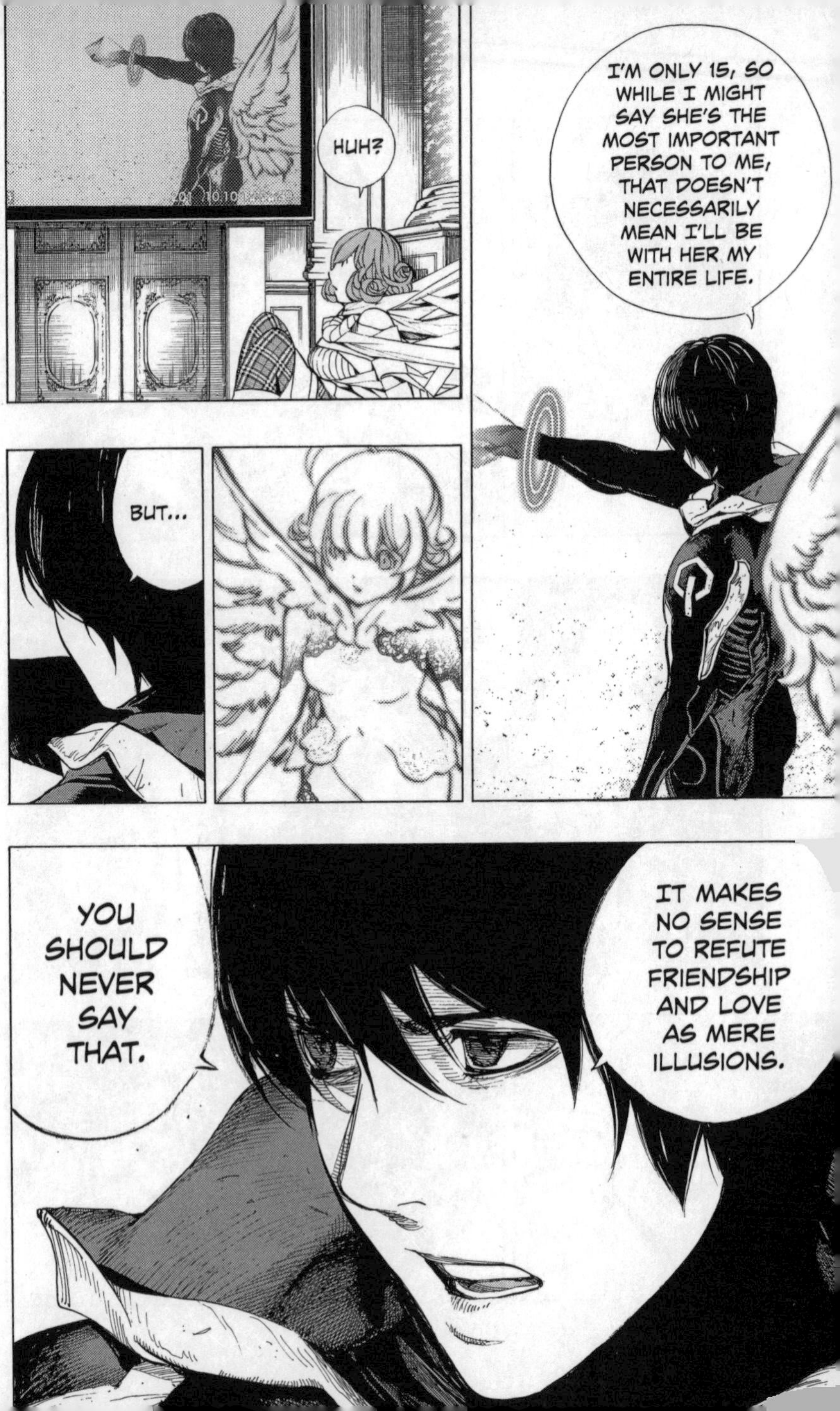
I'M ONLY 15, SO WHILE I MIGHT SAY SHE'S THE MOST IMPORTANT PERSON TO ME, THAT DOESN'T NECESSARILY MEAN I'LL BE WITH HER MY ENTIRE LIFE.
HUH?
BUT...
IT MAKES NO SENSE TO REFUTE FRIENDSHIP AND LOVE AS MERE ILLUSIONS.
YOU SHOULD NEVER SAY THAT.

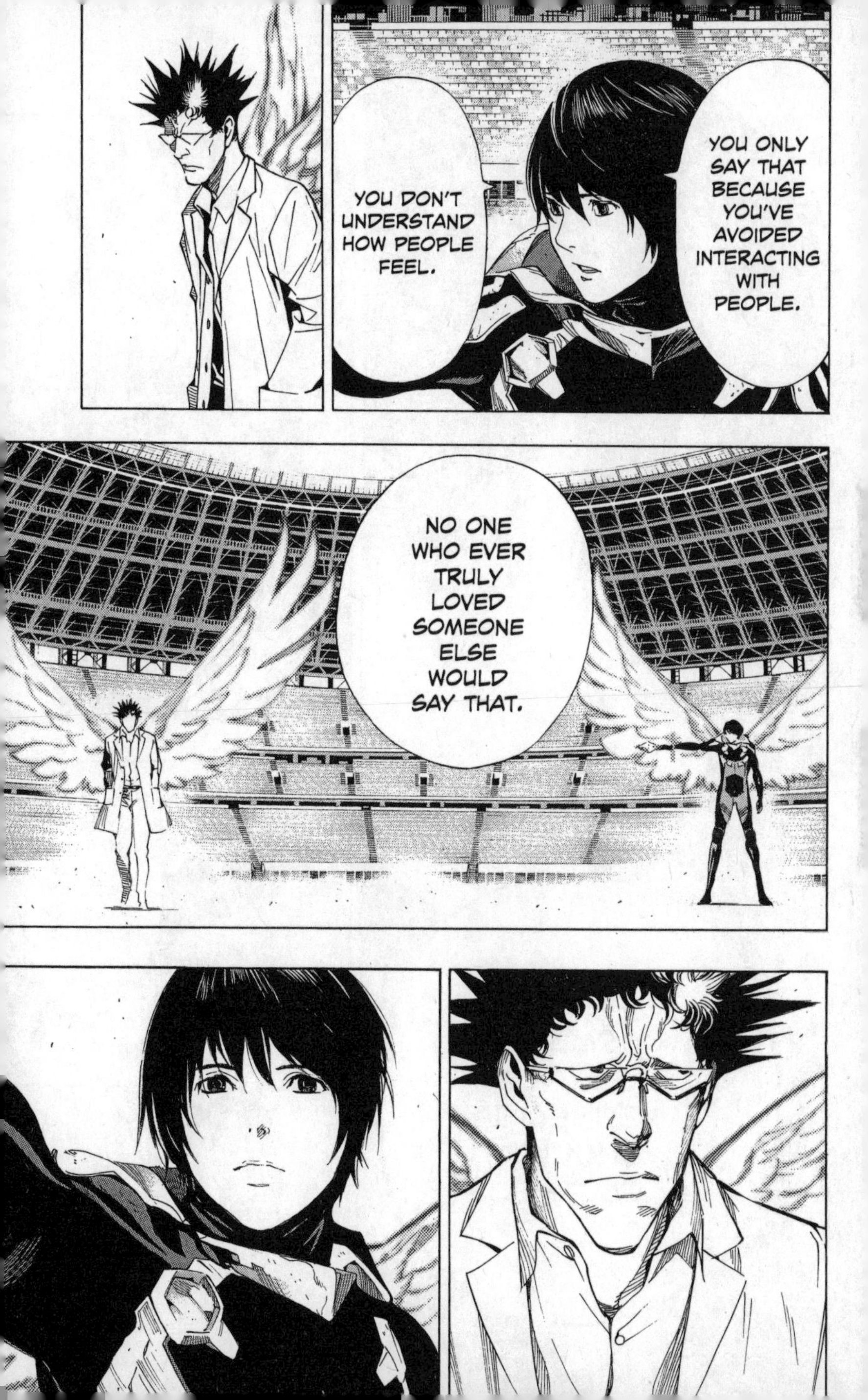
YOU ONLY SAY THAT BECAUSE YOU'VE AVOIDED INTERACTING WITH PEOPLE.
YOU DON'T UNDERSTAND HOW PEOPLE FEEL.
NO ONE WHO EVER TRULY LOVED SOMEONE ELSE WOULD SAY THAT.

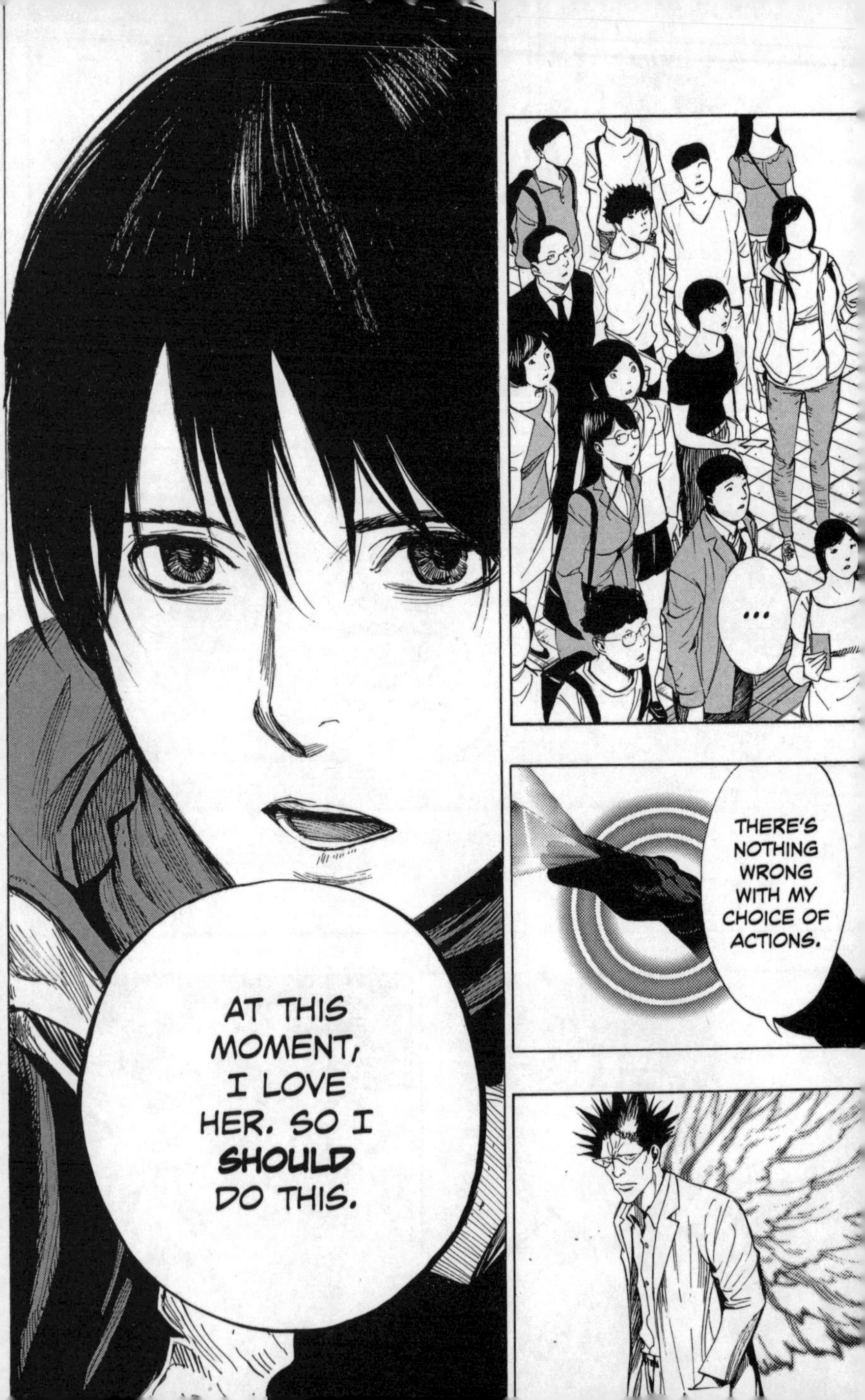
...
THERE'S NOTHING WRONG WITH MY CHOICE OF ACTIONS.
AT THIS MOMENT, I LOVE HER. SO I **SHOULD** DO THIS.

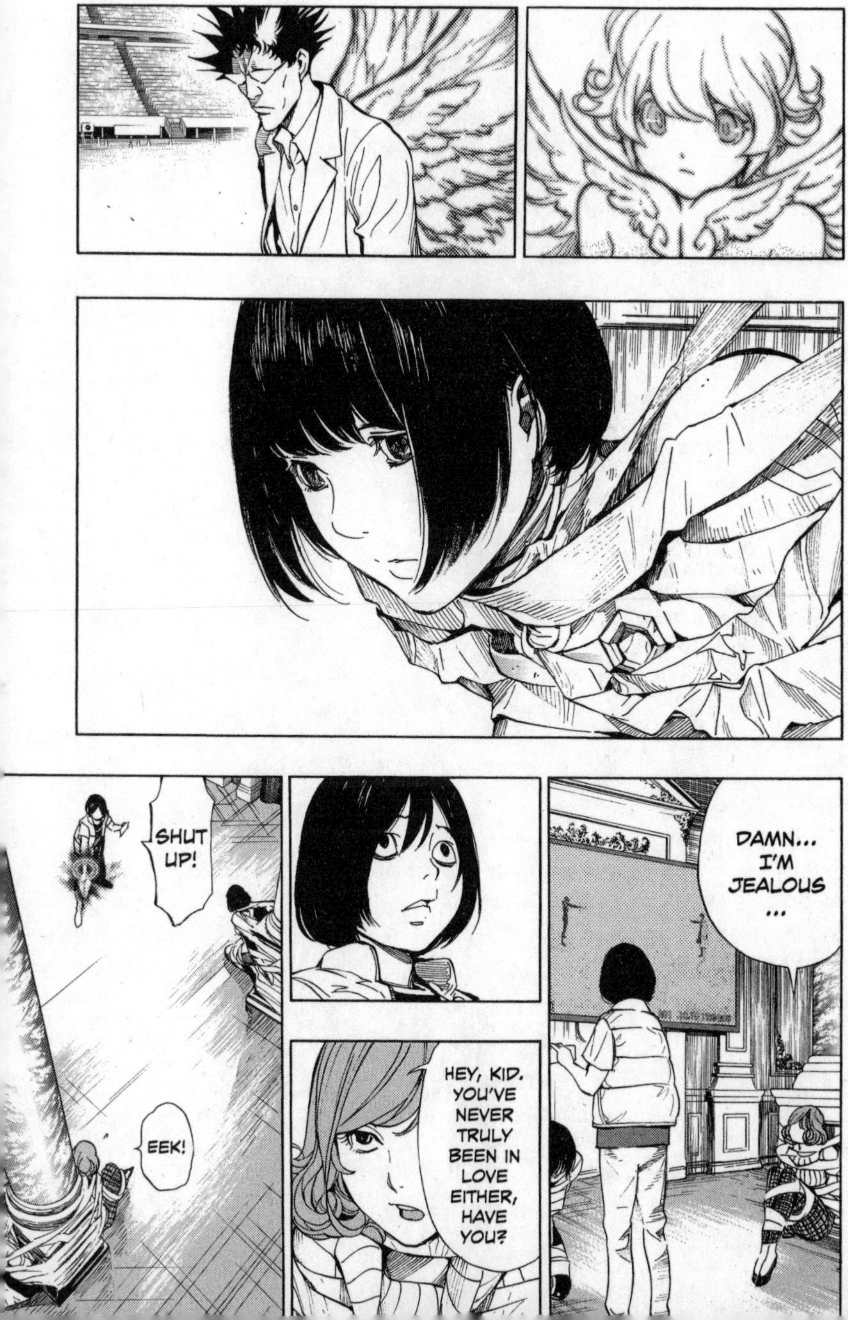
DAMN... I'M JEALOUS ...
HEY, KID. YOU'VE NEVER TRULY BEEN IN LOVE EITHER, HAVE YOU?
SHUT UP!
EEK!

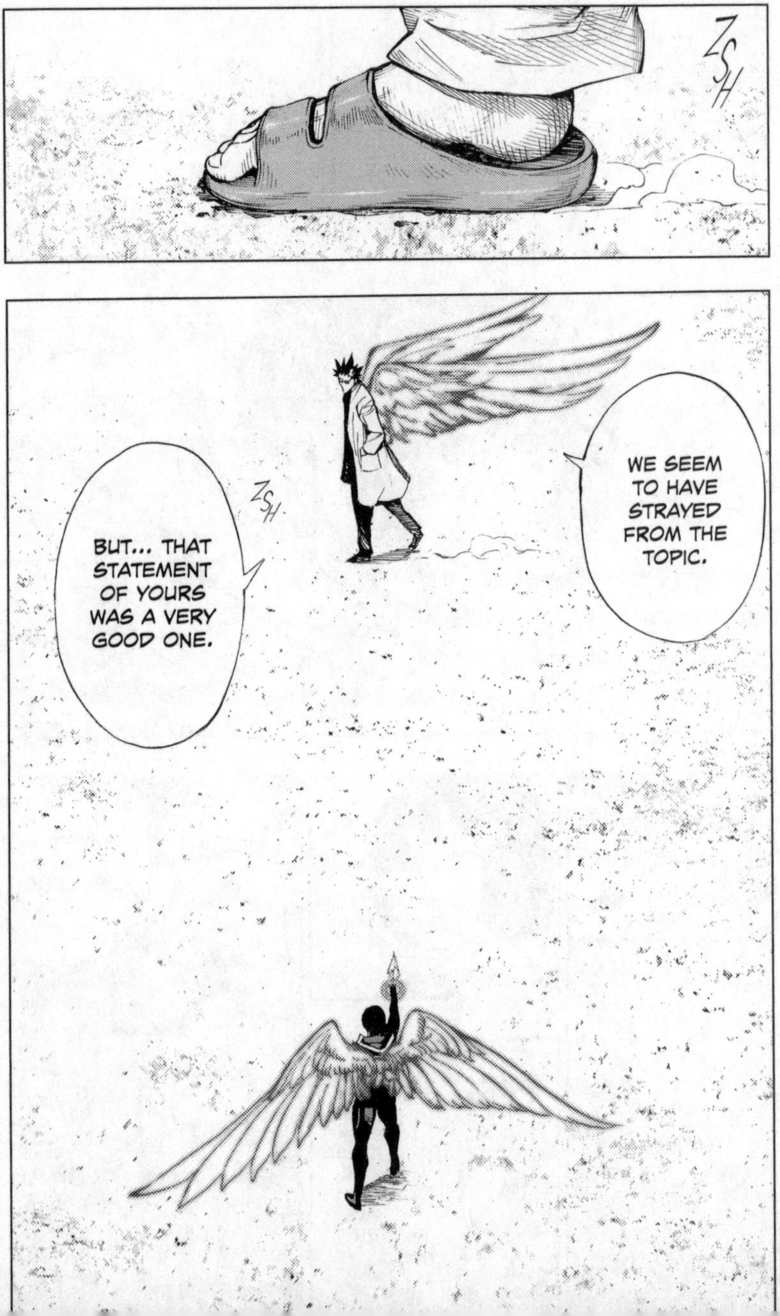
ZSH
WE SEEM TO HAVE STRAYED FROM THE TOPIC.
ZSH
BUT... THAT STATEMENT OF YOURS WAS A VERY GOOD ONE.

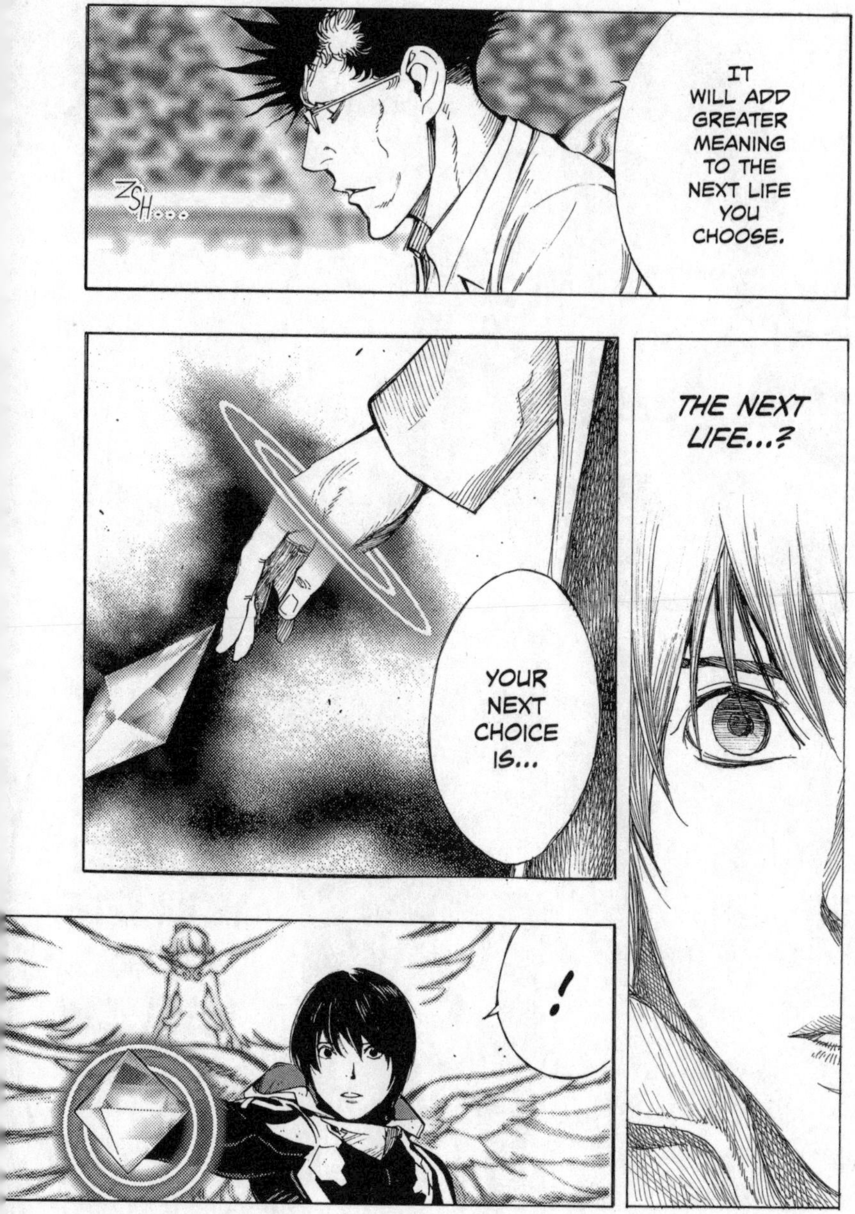
IT WILL ADD GREATER MEANING TO THE NEXT LIFE YOU CHOOSE.
ZSH...
THE NEXT LIFE...?
YOUR NEXT CHOICE IS...
!

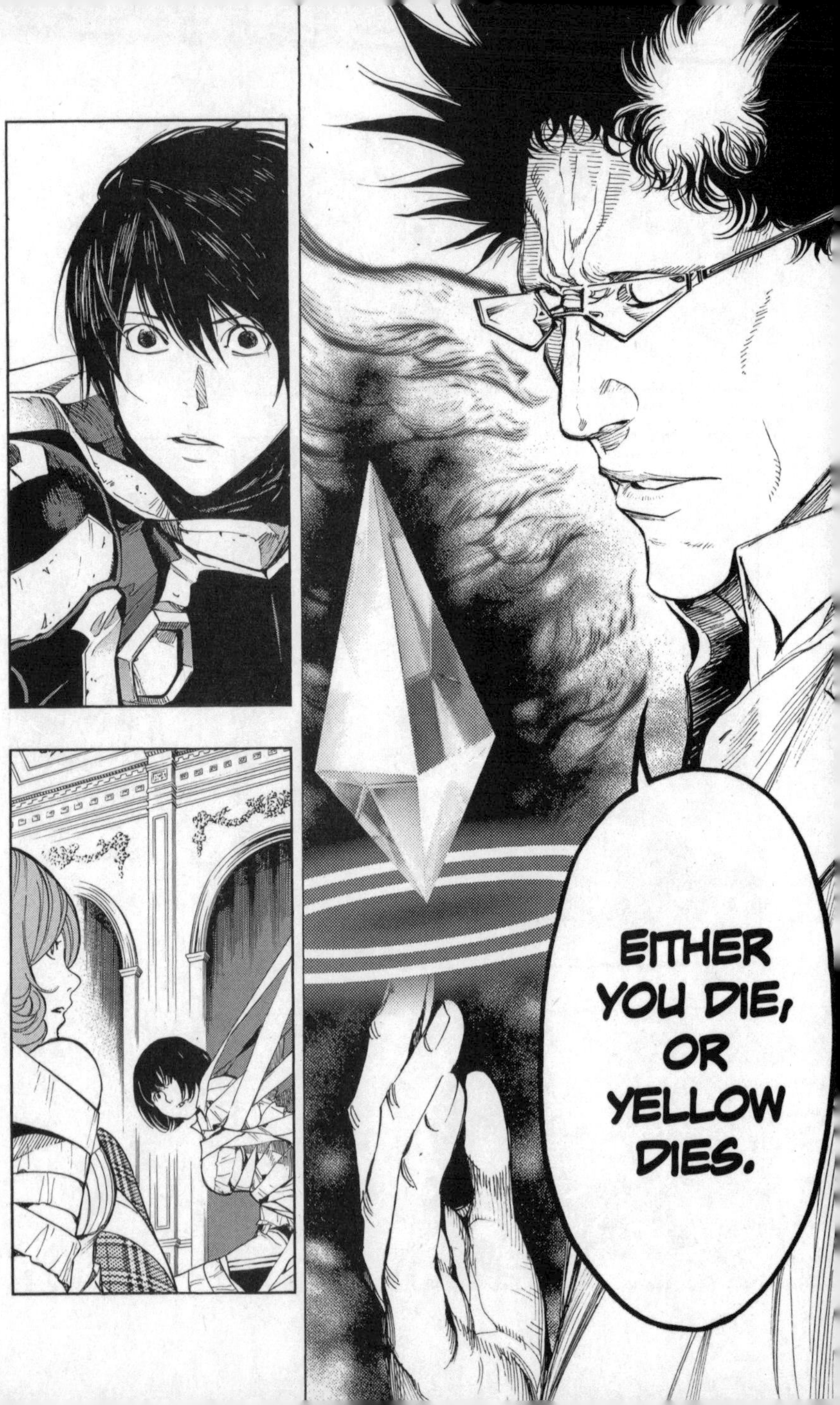
EITHER YOU DIE, OR YELLOW DIES.

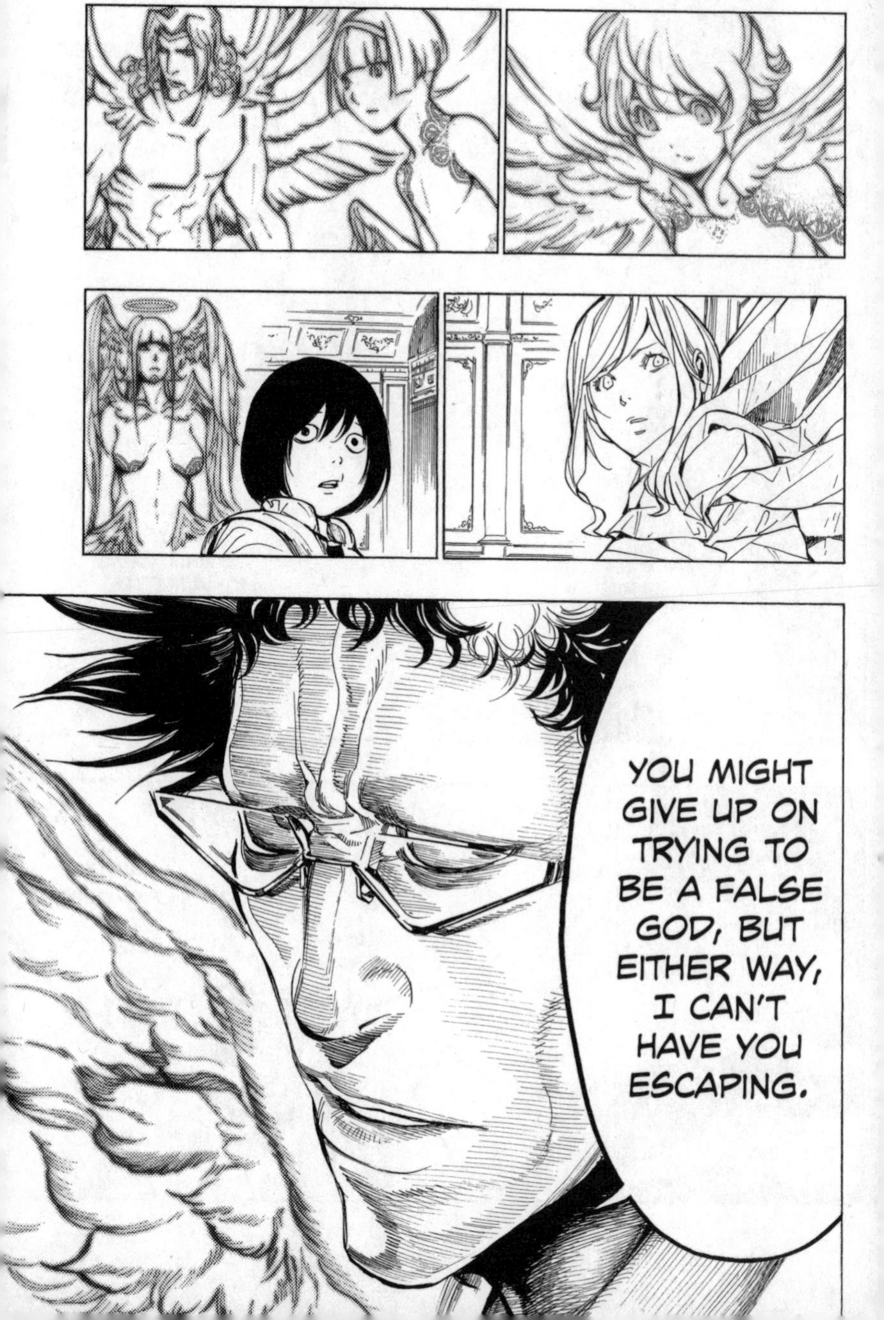
YOU MIGHT GIVE UP ON TRYING TO BE A FALSE GOD, BUT EITHER WAY, I CAN'T HAVE YOU ESCAPING.

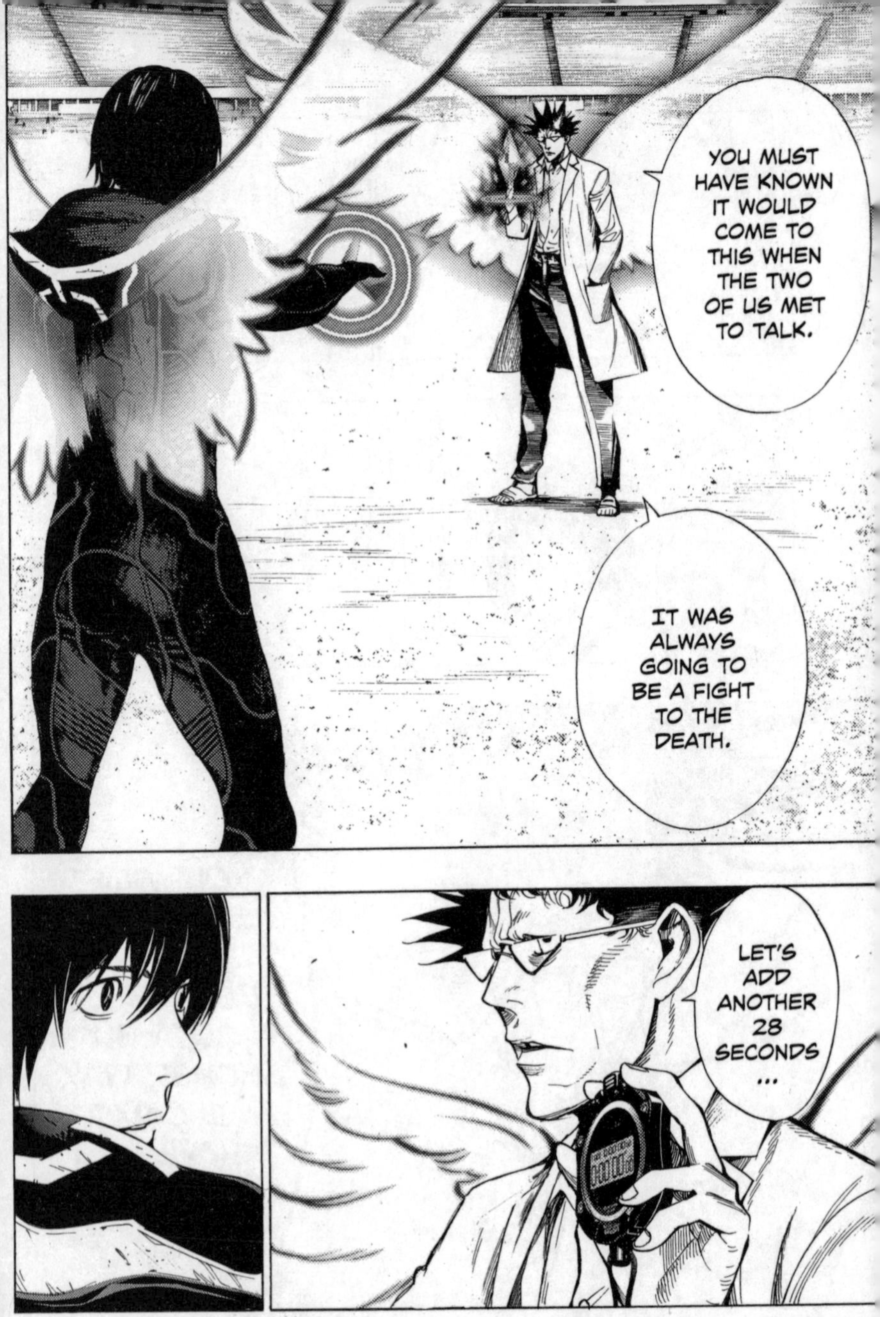
YOU MUST HAVE KNOWN IT WOULD COME TO THIS WHEN THE TWO OF US MET TO TALK.
IT WAS ALWAYS GOING TO BE A FIGHT TO THE DEATH.
LET'S ADD ANOTHER 28 SECONDS ...

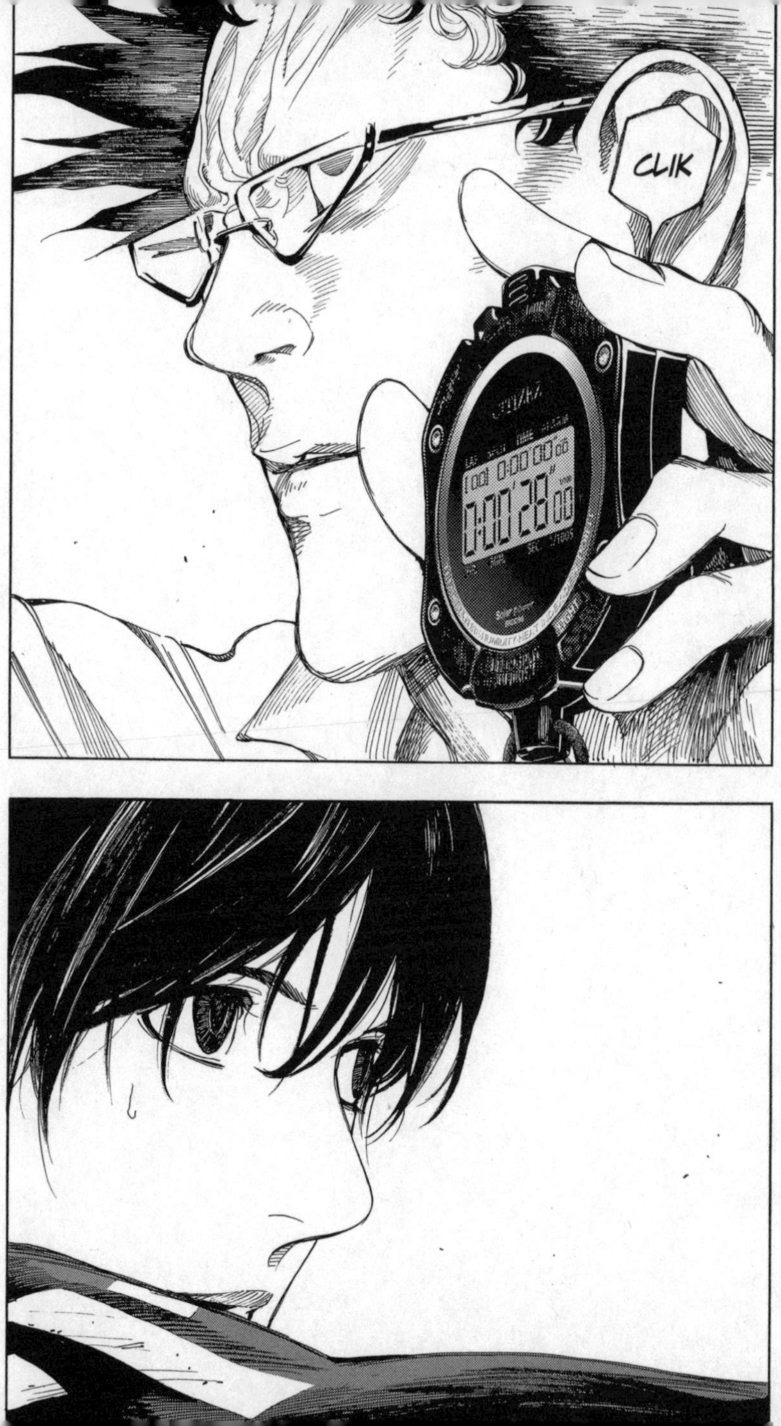
CLIK

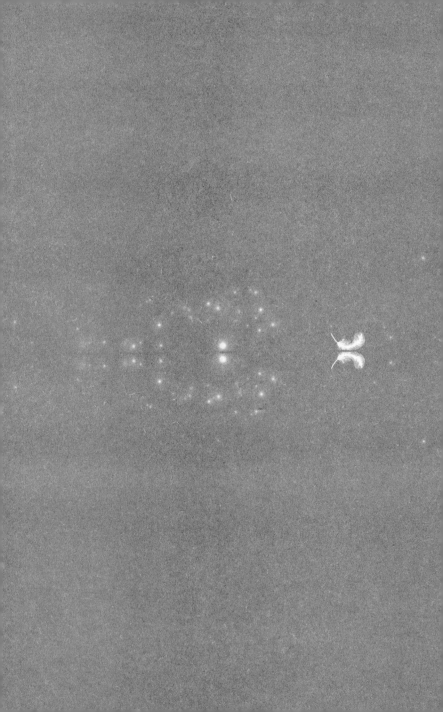

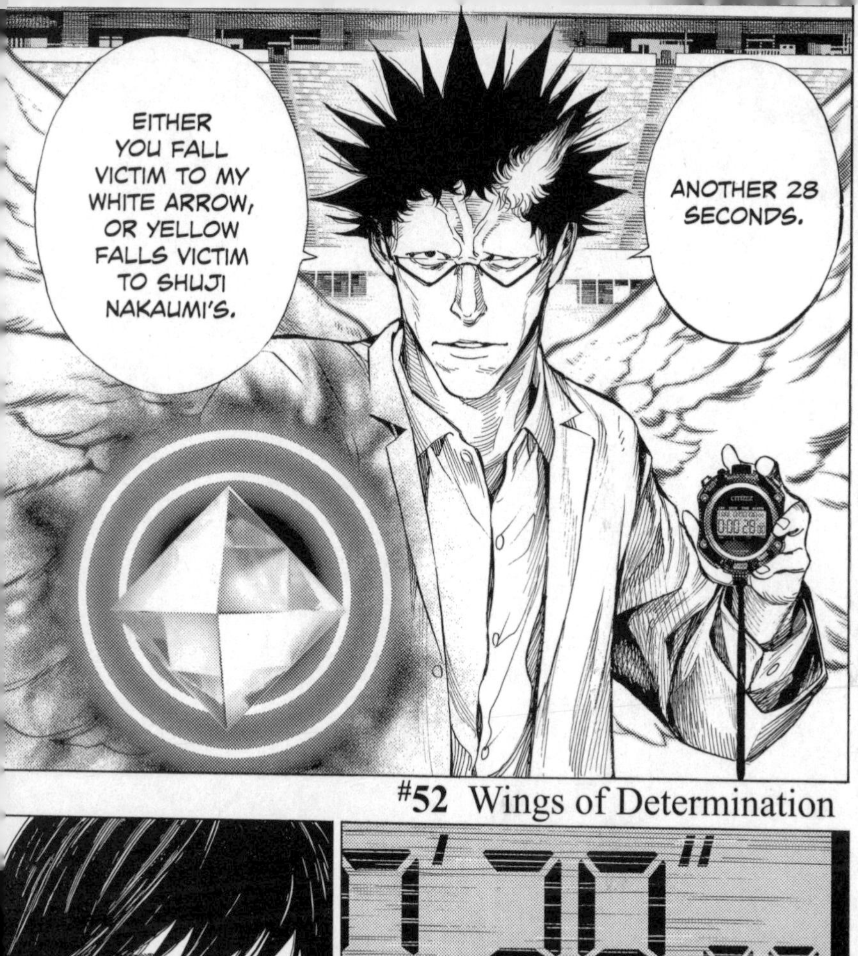
ANOTHER 28 SECONDS.
EITHER YOU FALL VICTIM TO MY WHITE ARROW, OR YELLOW FALLS VICTIM TO SHUJI NAKAUMI'S.

#52 Wings of Determination

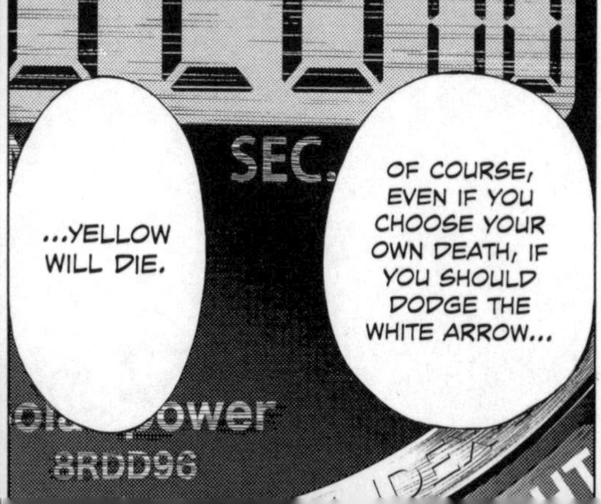
SEC.
OF COURSE, EVEN IF YOU CHOOSE YOUR OWN DEATH, IF YOU SHOULD DODGE THE WHITE ARROW...
...YELLOW WILL DIE.
8RDD96

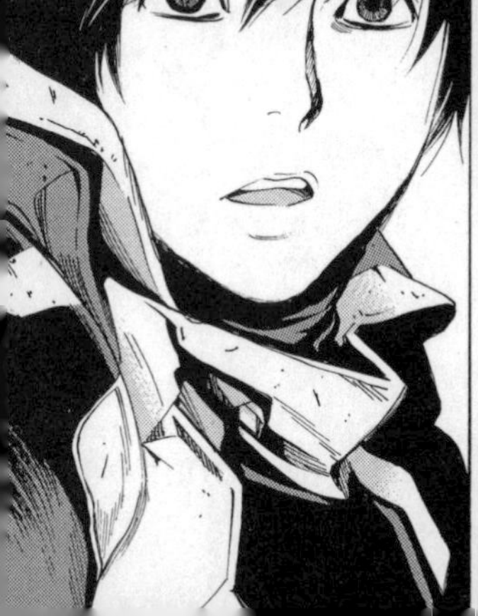

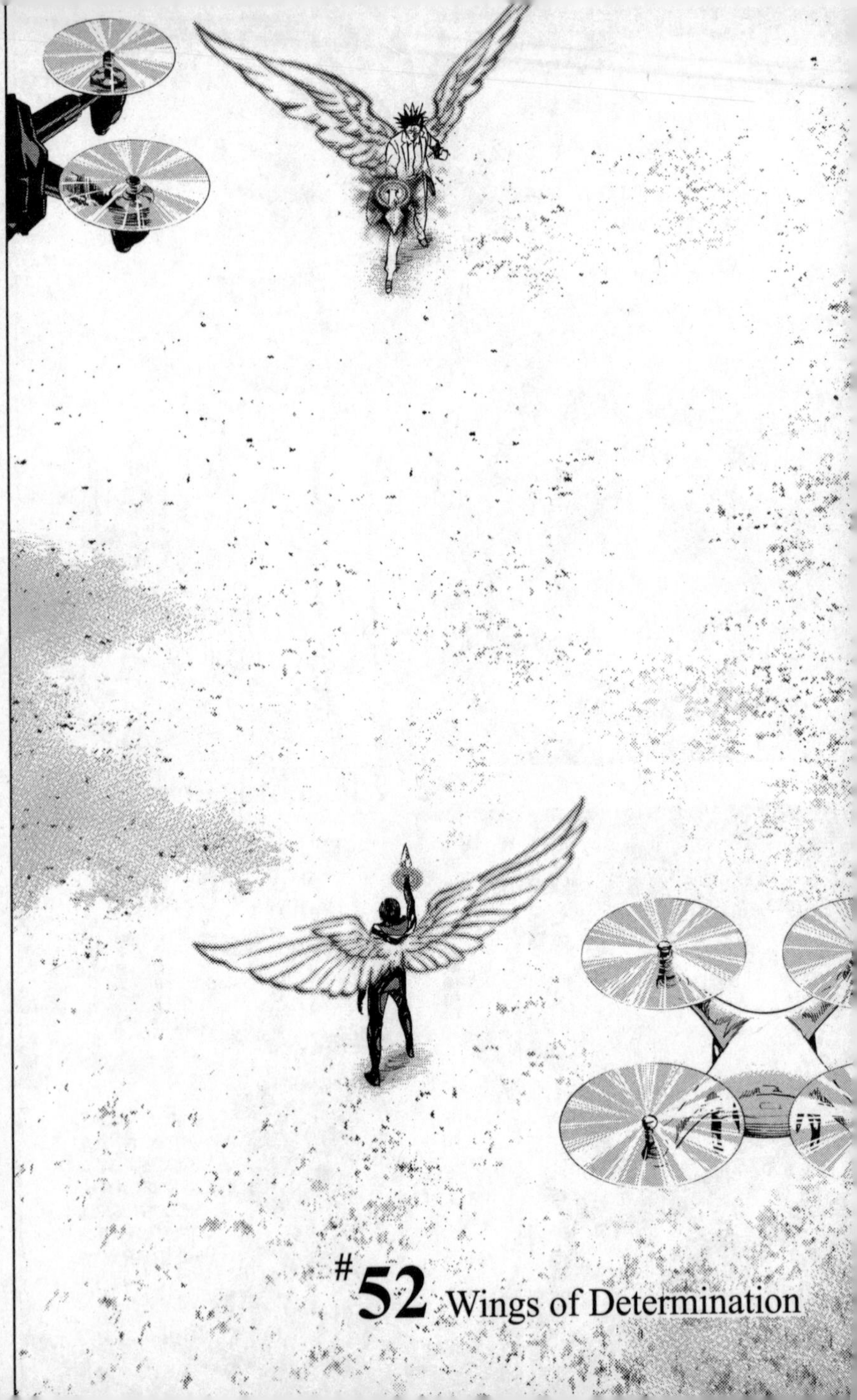

#52 Wings of Determination

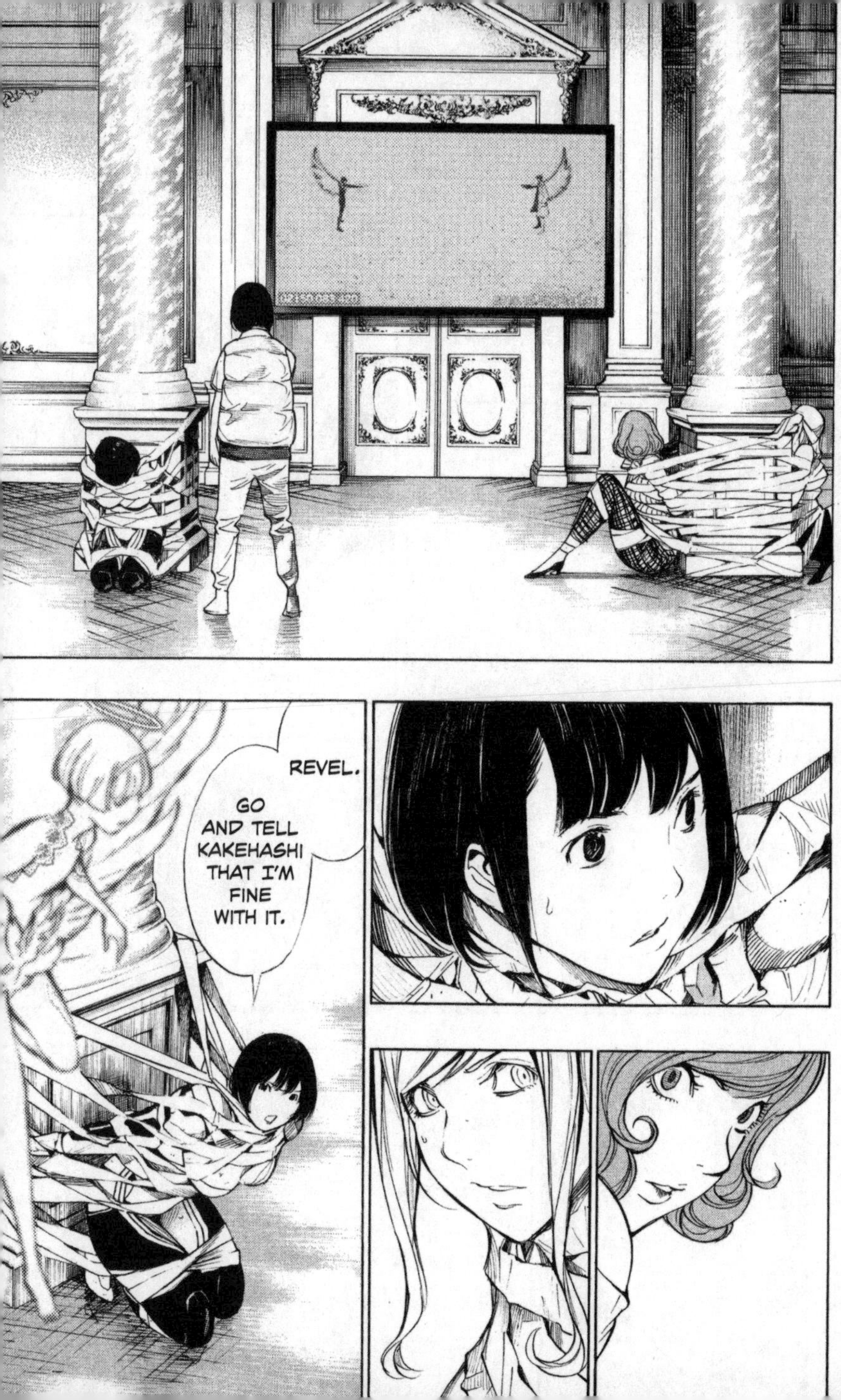
REVEL.
GO AND TELL KAKEHASHI THAT I'M FINE WITH IT.

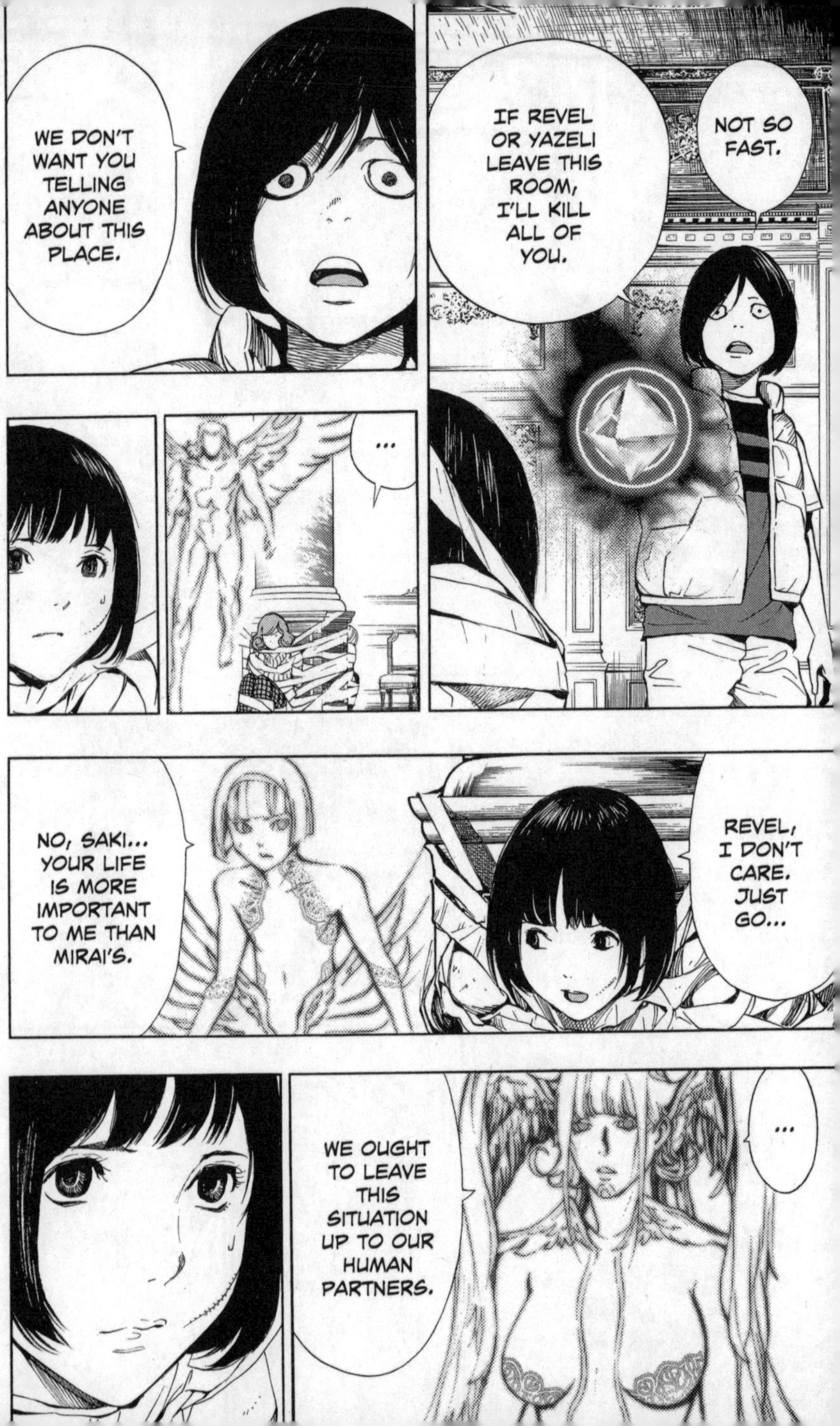
NOT SO FAST.
IF REVEL OR YAZELI LEAVE THIS ROOM, I'LL KILL ALL OF YOU.
WE DON'T WANT YOU TELLING ANYONE ABOUT THIS PLACE.
...
REVEL, I DON'T CARE. JUST GO...
NO, SAKI... YOUR LIFE IS MORE IMPORTANT TO ME THAN MIRAI'S.
...
WE OUGHT TO LEAVE THIS SITUATION UP TO OUR HUMAN PARTNERS.

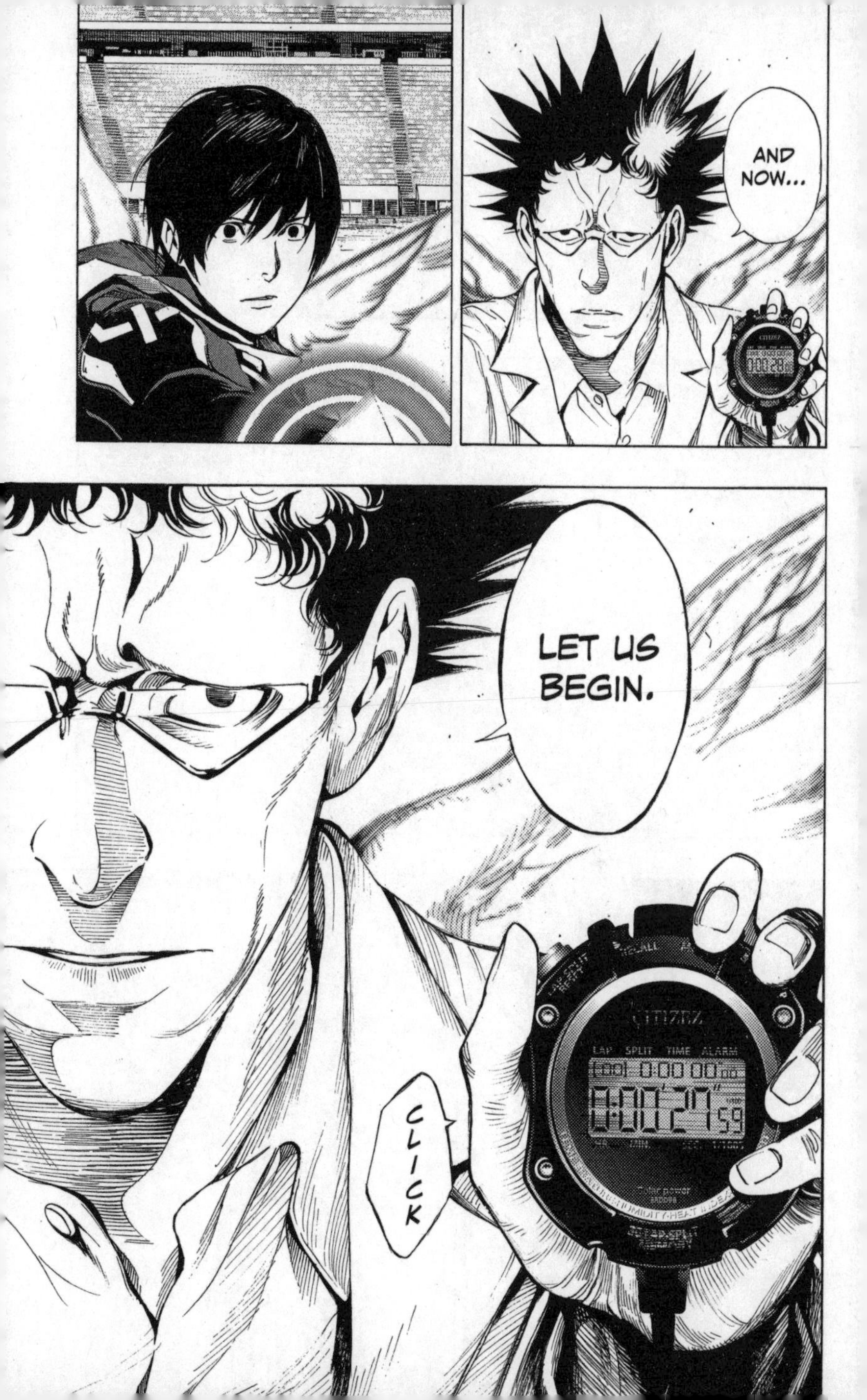
AND NOW...
LET US BEGIN.
CLICK

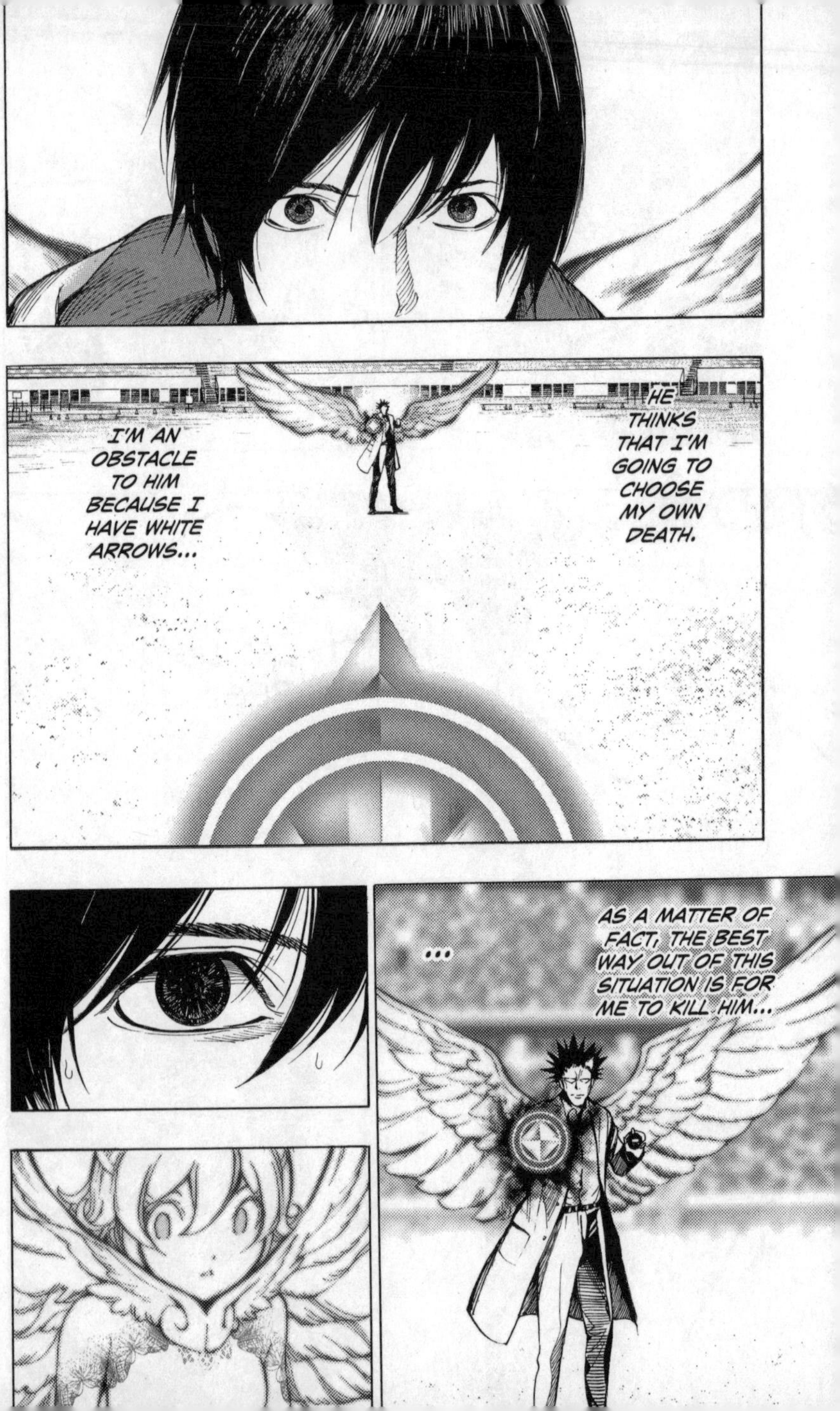
HE THINKS THAT I'M GOING TO CHOOSE MY OWN DEATH.
I'M AN OBSTACLE TO HIM BECAUSE I HAVE WHITE ARROWS...
AS A MATTER OF FACT, THE BEST WAY OUT OF THIS SITUATION IS FOR ME TO KILL HIM...
...

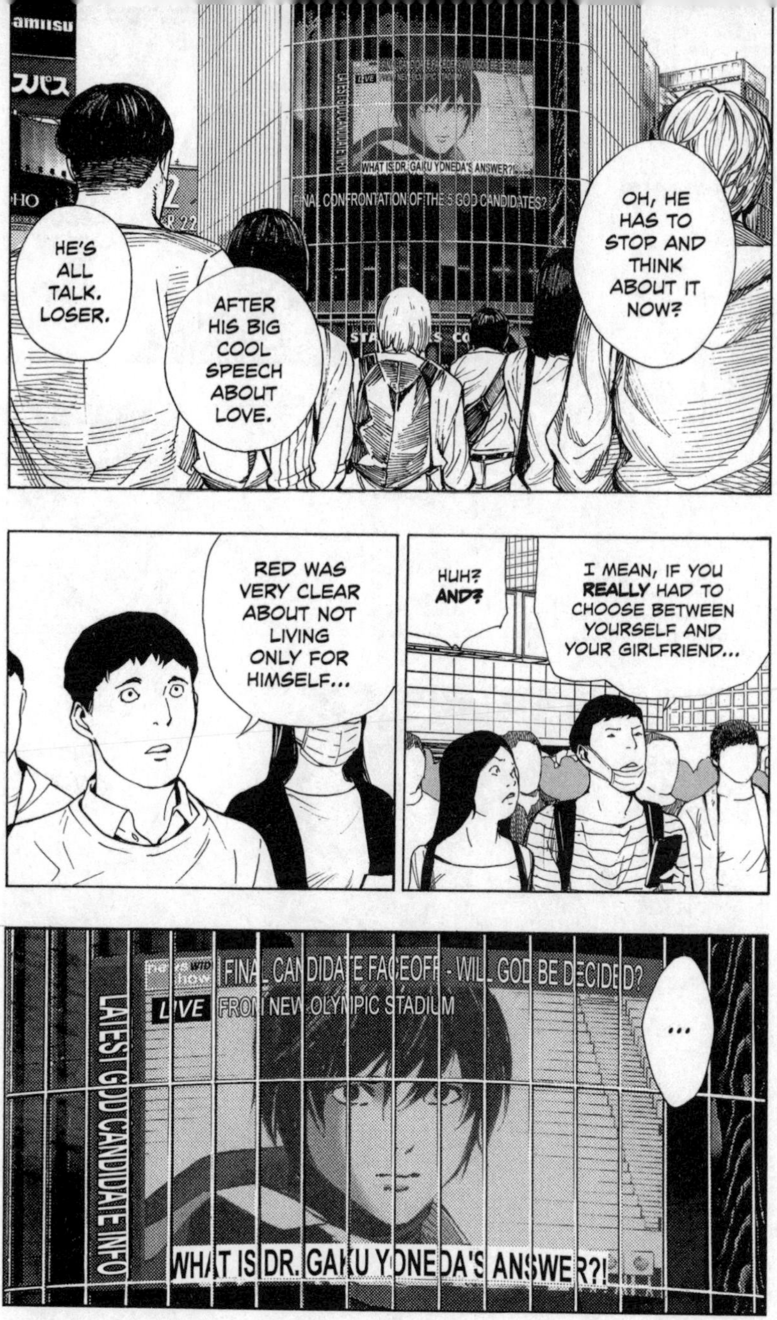
WHAT IS DR. GAKU YONEDA'S ANSWER?!
FINAL CONFRONTATION OF THE 5 GOD CANDIDATES?
OH, HE HAS TO STOP AND THINK ABOUT IT NOW?
AFTER HIS BIG COOL SPEECH ABOUT LOVE.
HE'S ALL TALK. LOSER.
I MEAN, IF YOU REALLY HAD TO CHOOSE BETWEEN YOURSELF AND YOUR GIRLFRIEND...
HUH? AND?
RED WAS VERY CLEAR ABOUT NOT LIVING ONLY FOR HIMSELF...
FINAL CANDIDATE FACEOFF - WILL GOD BE DECIDED?
LIVE FROM NEW OLYMPIC STADIUM
LATEST GOD CANDIDATE INFO
...
WHAT IS DR. GAKU YONEDA'S ANSWER?!

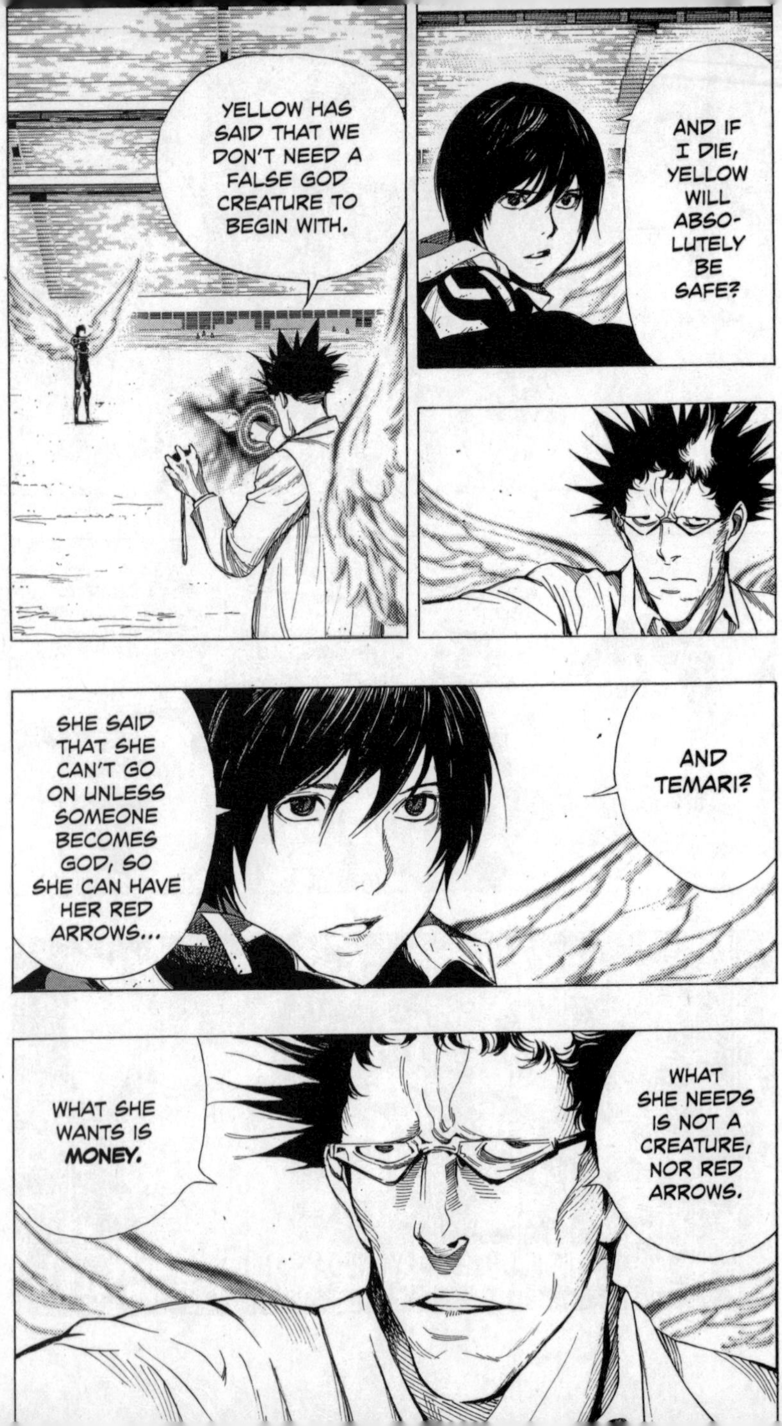
AND IF I DIE, YELLOW WILL ABSO-LUTELY BE SAFE?
YELLOW HAS SAID THAT WE DON'T NEED A FALSE GOD CREATURE TO BEGIN WITH.
AND TEMARI?
SHE SAID THAT SHE CAN'T GO ON UNLESS SOMEONE BECOMES GOD, SO SHE CAN HAVE HER RED ARROWS...
WHAT SHE NEEDS IS NOT A CREATURE, NOR RED ARROWS.
WHAT SHE WANTS IS **MONEY.**

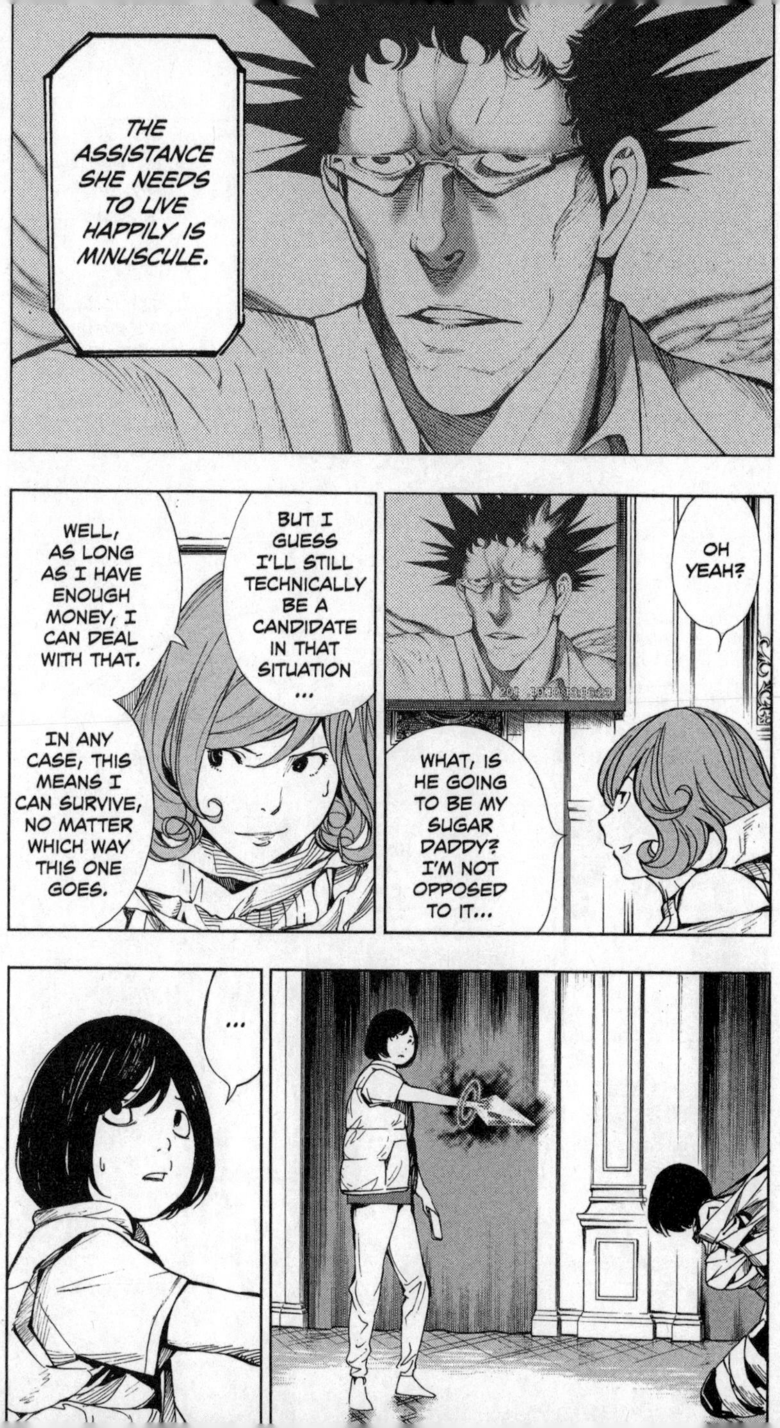
THE ASSISTANCE SHE NEEDS TO LIVE HAPPILY IS MINUSCULE.
OH YEAH?
WHAT, IS HE GOING TO BE MY SUGAR DADDY? I'M NOT OPPOSED TO IT...
BUT I GUESS I'LL STILL TECHNICALLY BE A CANDIDATE IN THAT SITUATION...
WELL, AS LONG AS I HAVE ENOUGH MONEY, I CAN DEAL WITH THAT.
IN ANY CASE, THIS MEANS I CAN SURVIVE, NO MATTER WHICH WAY THIS ONE GOES.
...

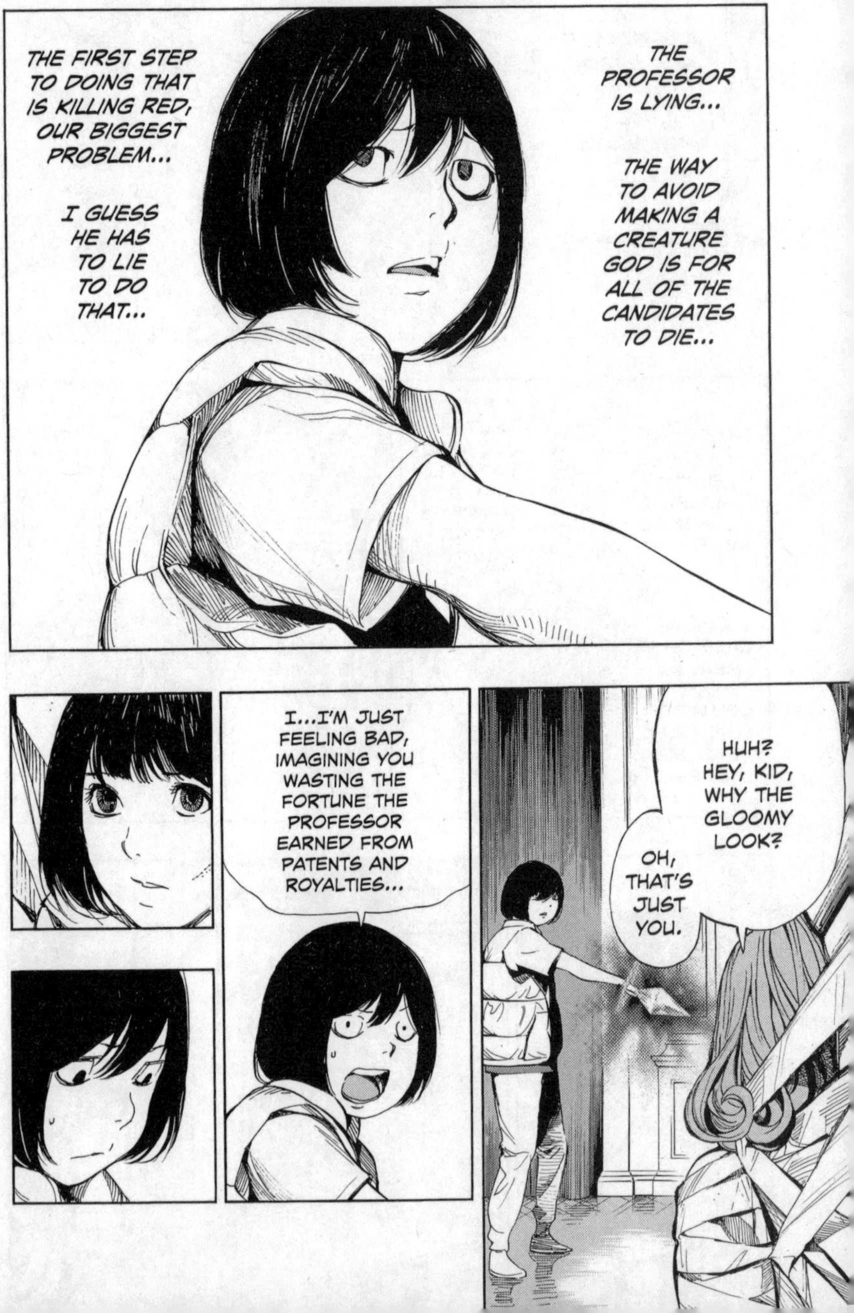
THE PROFESSOR IS LYING...
THE WAY TO AVOID MAKING A CREATURE GOD IS FOR ALL OF THE CANDIDATES TO DIE...
THE FIRST STEP TO DOING THAT IS KILLING RED, OUR BIGGEST PROBLEM...
I GUESS HE HAS TO LIE TO DO THAT...
HUH? HEY, KID, WHY THE GLOOMY LOOK?
OH, THAT'S JUST YOU.
I...I'M JUST FEELING BAD, IMAGINING YOU WASTING THE FORTUNE THE PROFESSOR EARNED FROM PATENTS AND ROYALTIES...

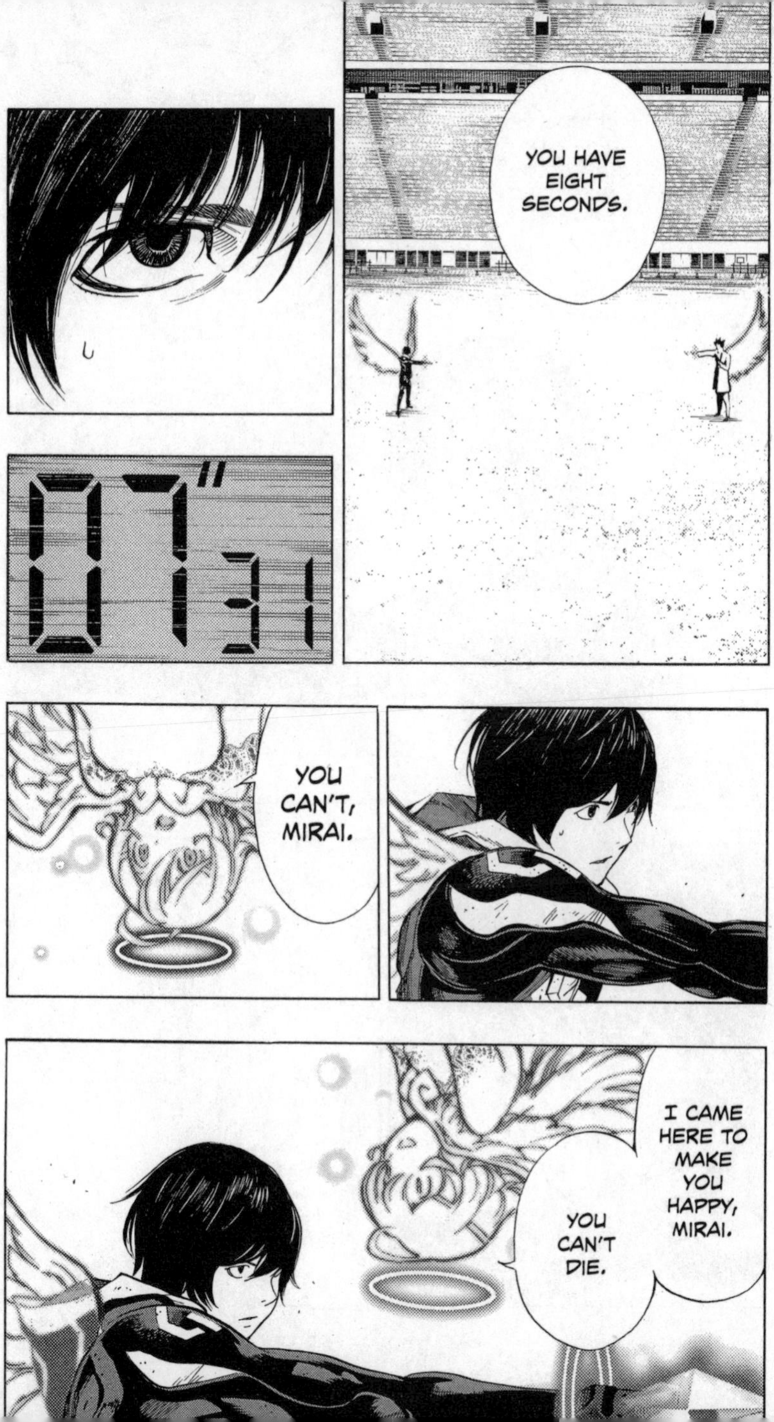
YOU HAVE EIGHT SECONDS.
07"31
YOU CAN'T, MIRAI.
I CAME HERE TO MAKE YOU HAPPY, MIRAI.
YOU CAN'T DIE.

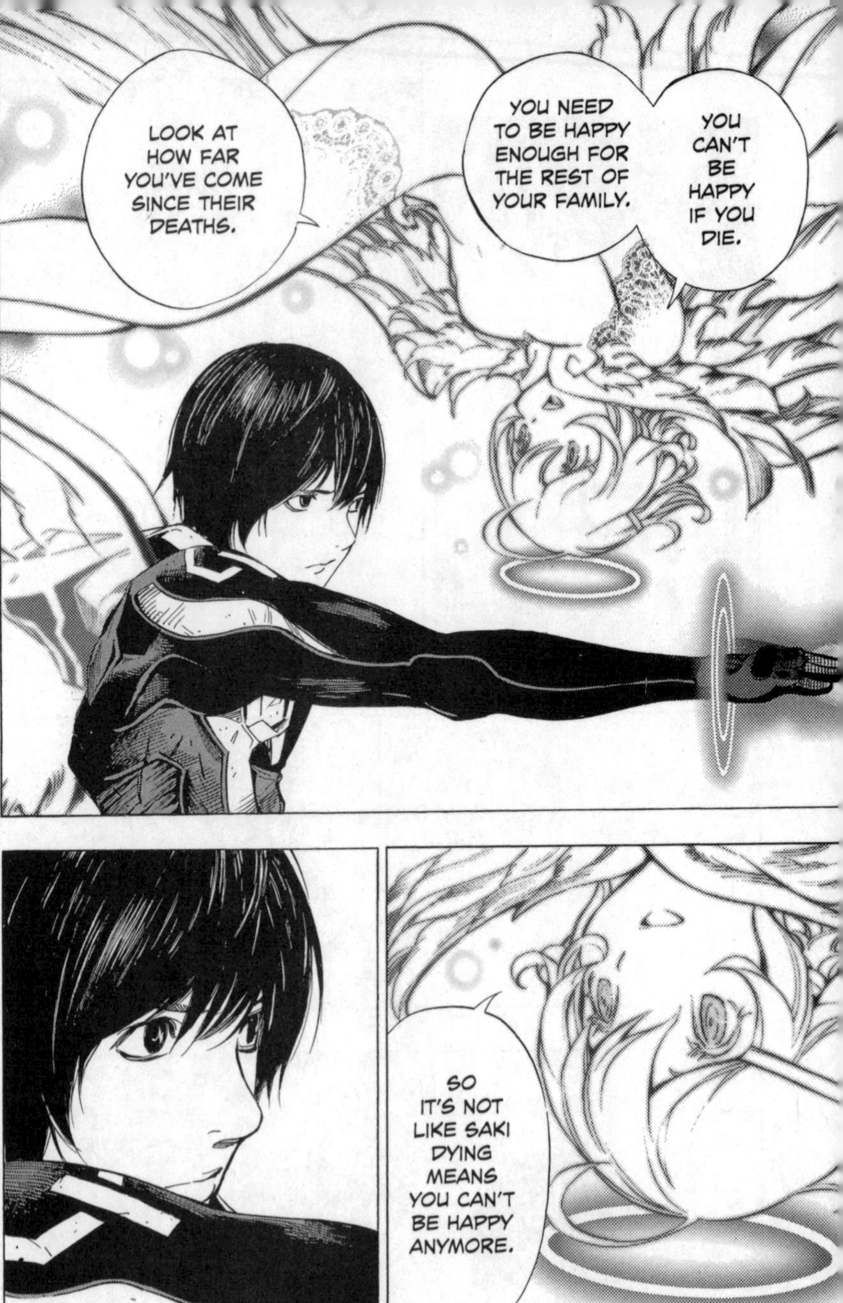
YOU CAN'T BE HAPPY IF YOU DIE.
YOU NEED TO BE HAPPY ENOUGH FOR THE REST OF YOUR FAMILY.
LOOK AT HOW FAR YOU'VE COME SINCE THEIR DEATHS.
SO IT'S NOT LIKE SAKI DYING MEANS YOU CAN'T BE HAPPY ANYMORE.

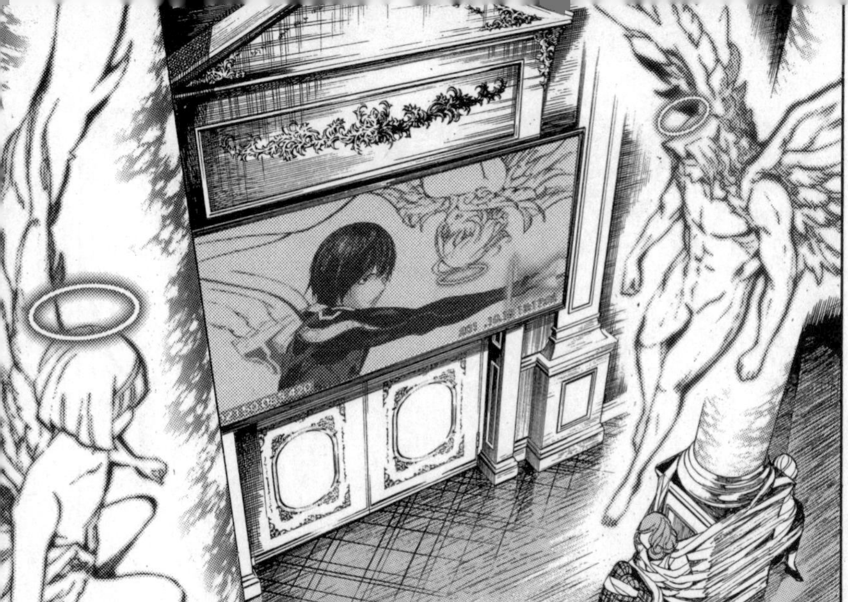

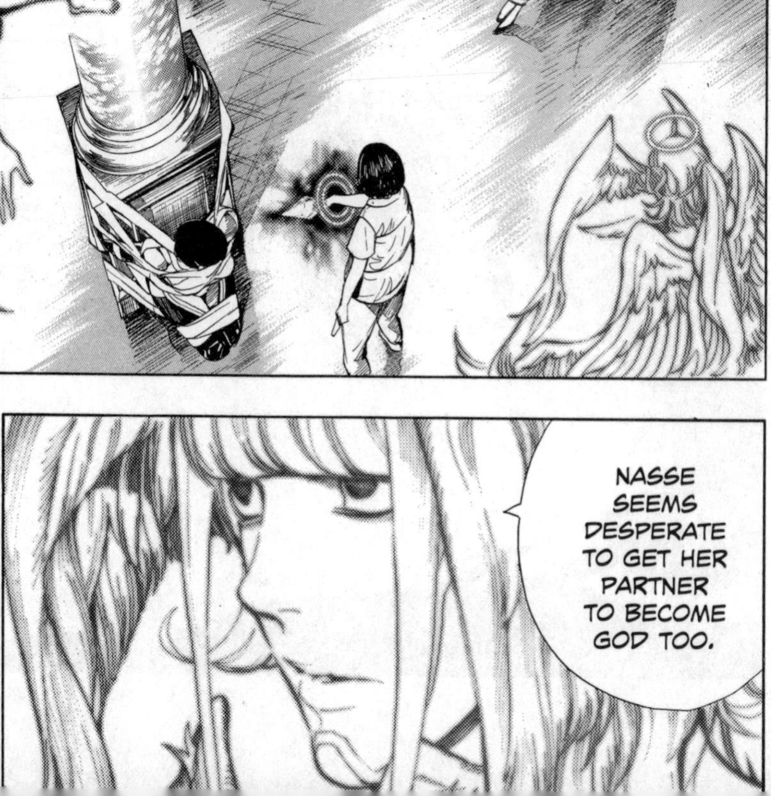
NASSE SEEMS DESPERATE TO GET HER PARTNER TO BECOME GOD TOO.

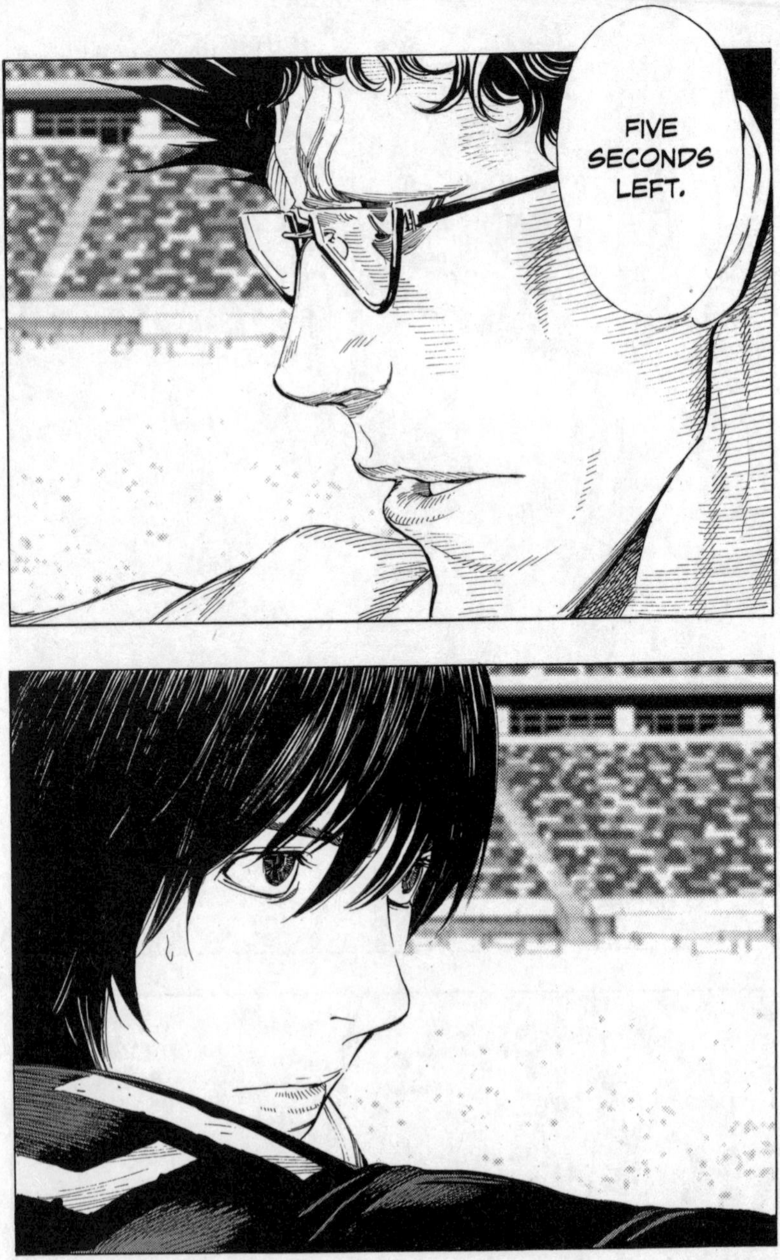
FIVE SECONDS LEFT.

I FOUND A FOUR-LEAF CLOVER.

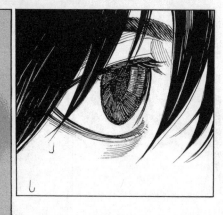

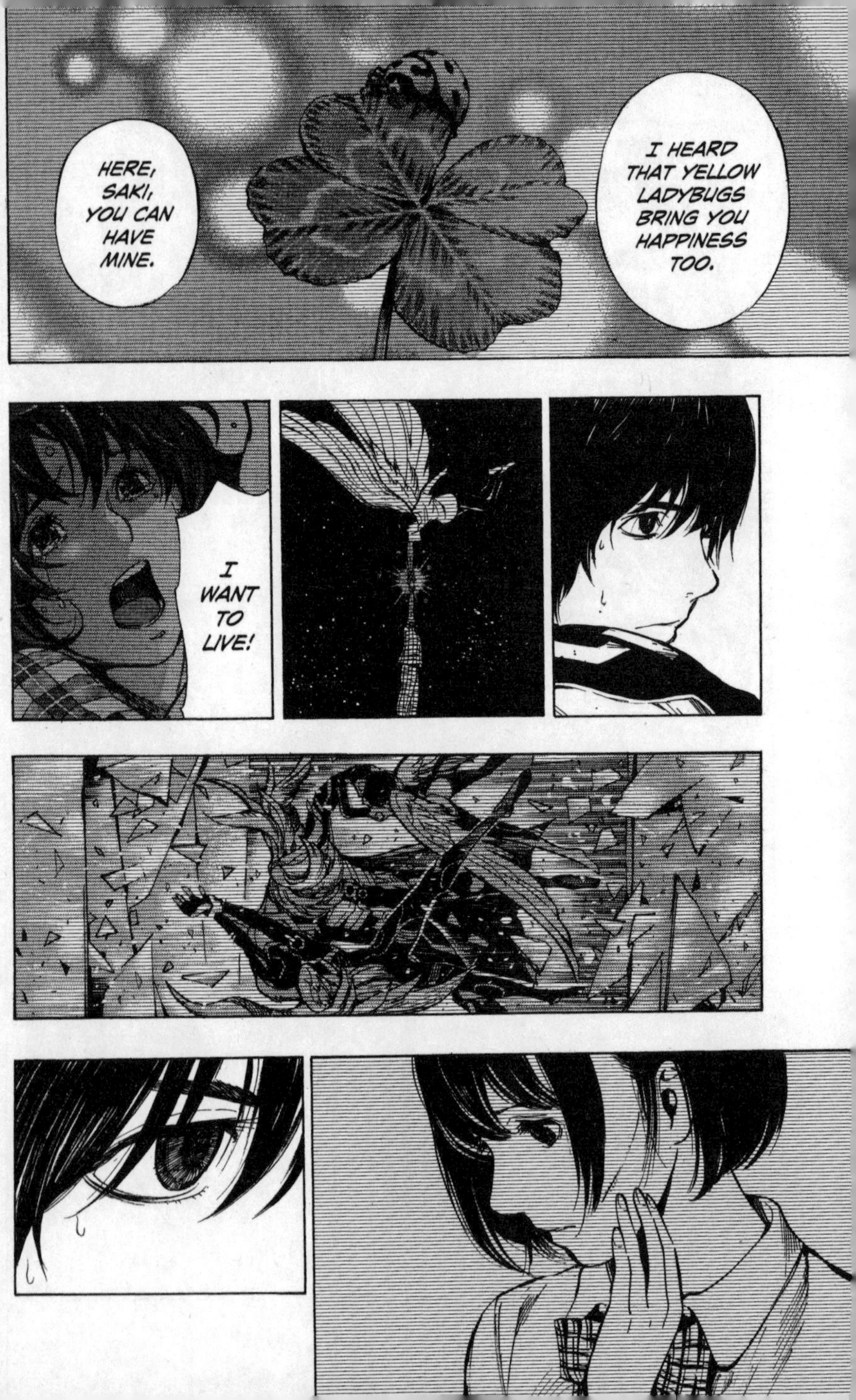
I HEARD THAT YELLOW LADYBUGS BRING YOU HAPPINESS TOO.
HERE, SAKI, YOU CAN HAVE MINE.
I WANT TO LIVE!

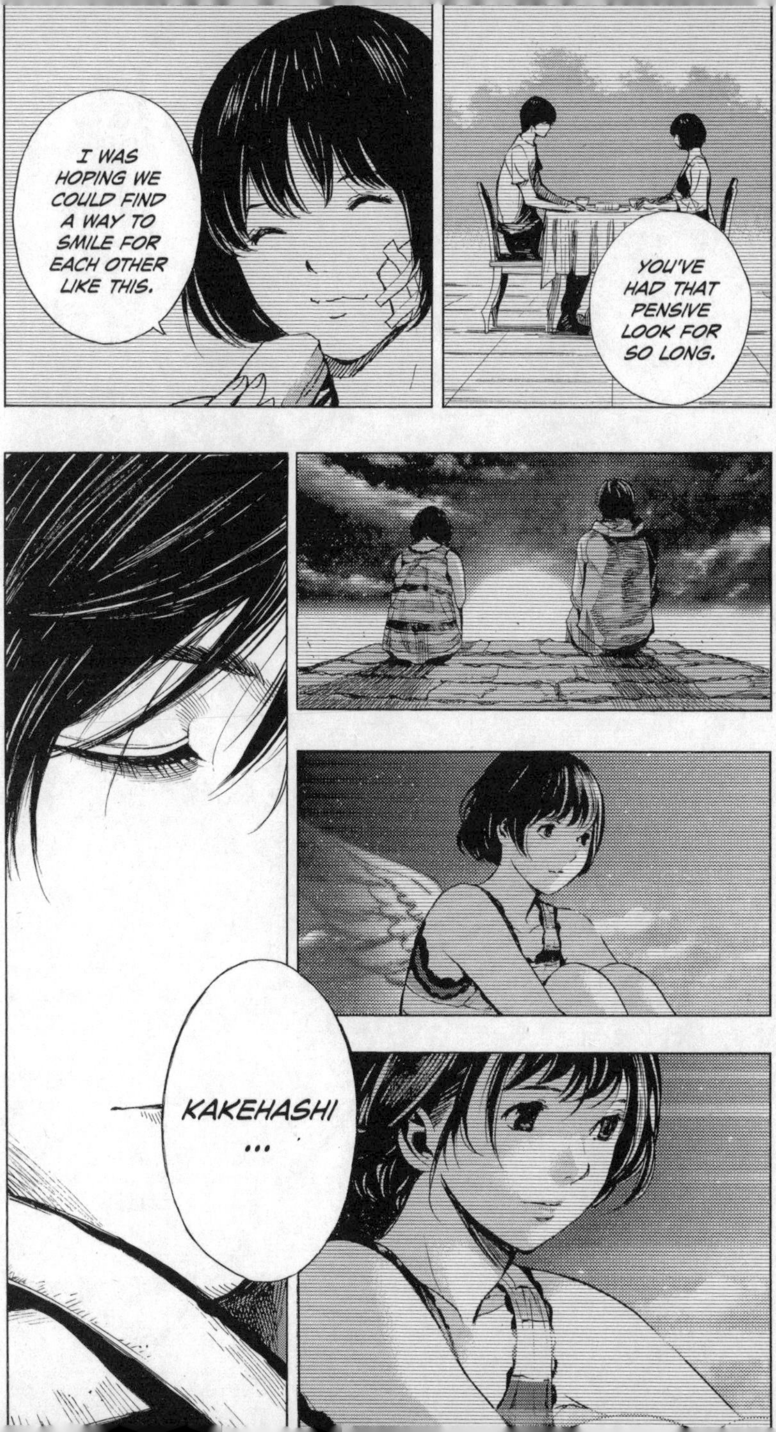
YOU'VE HAD THAT PENSIVE LOOK FOR SO LONG.
I WAS HOPING WE COULD FIND A WAY TO SMILE FOR EACH OTHER LIKE THIS.
KAKEHASHI ...

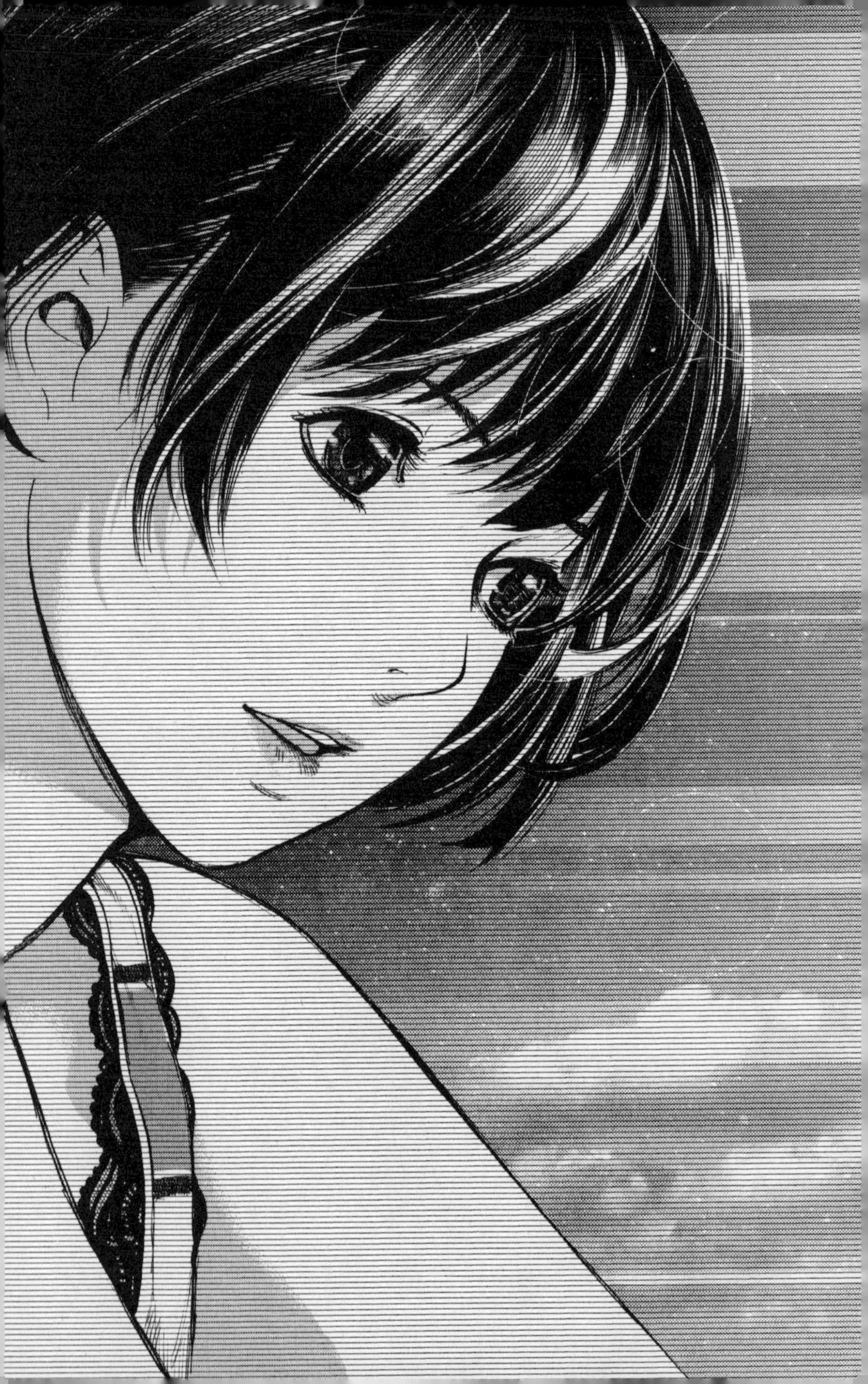

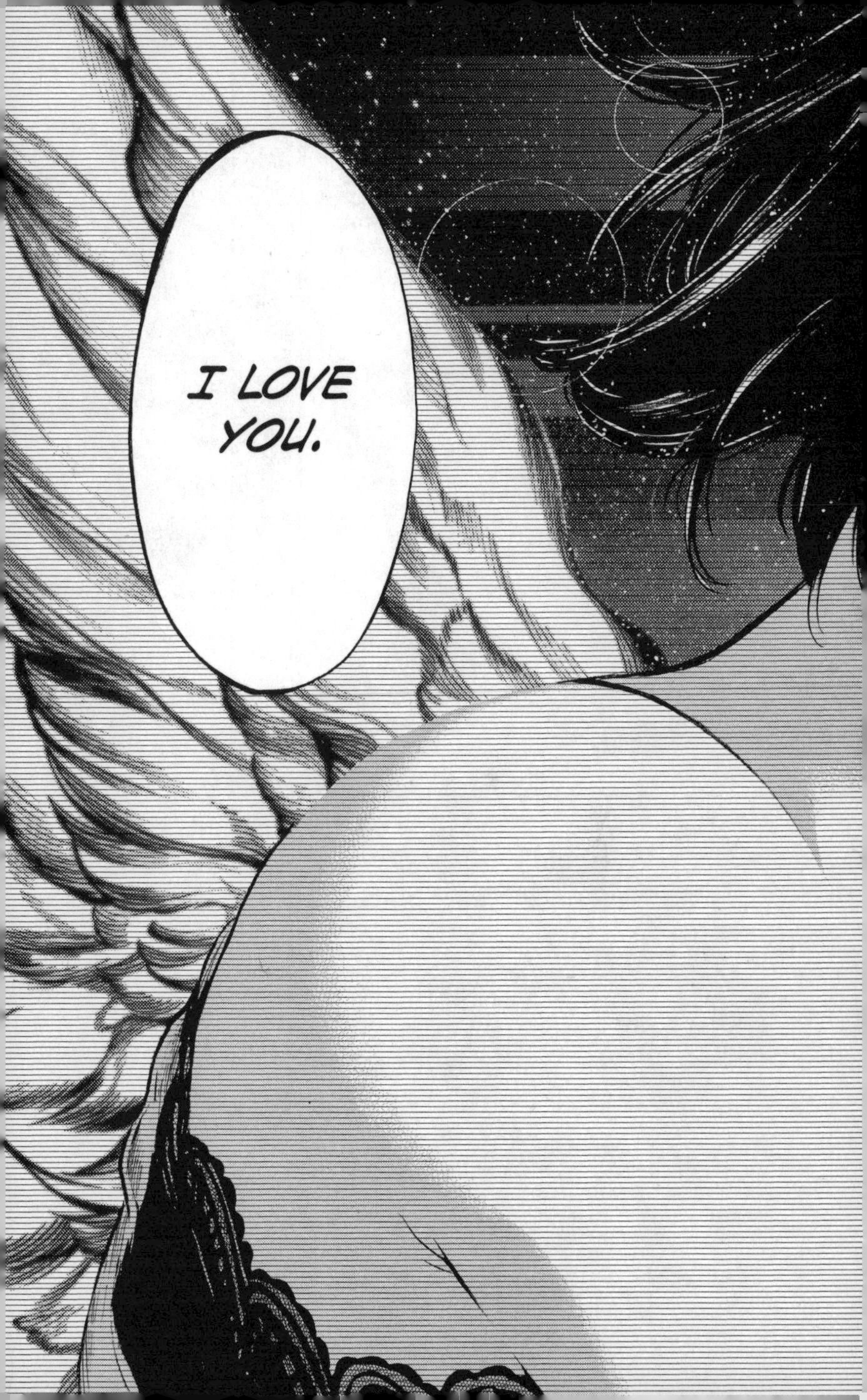
I LOVE YOU.

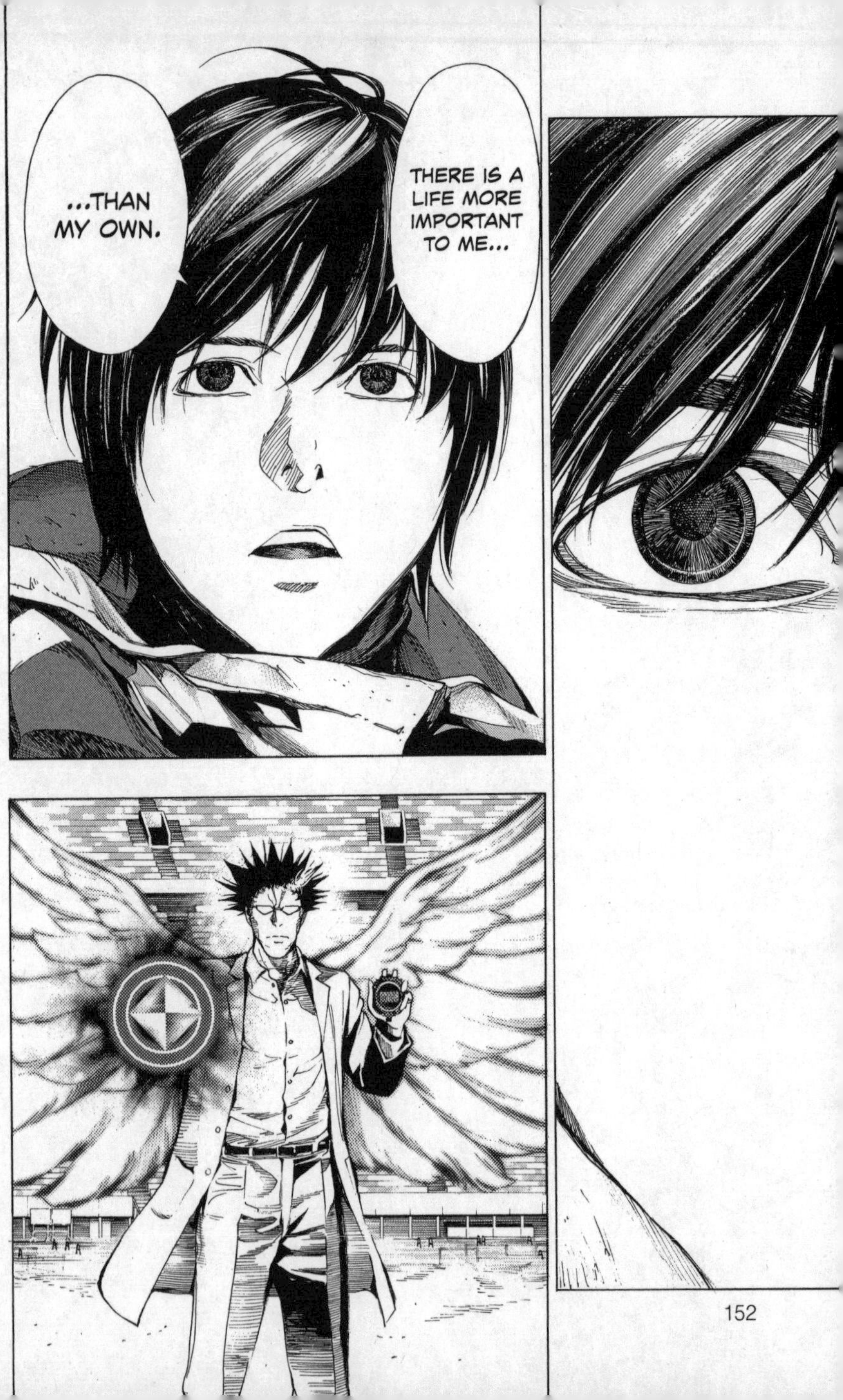
THERE IS A LIFE MORE IMPORTANT TO ME...
...THAN MY OWN.

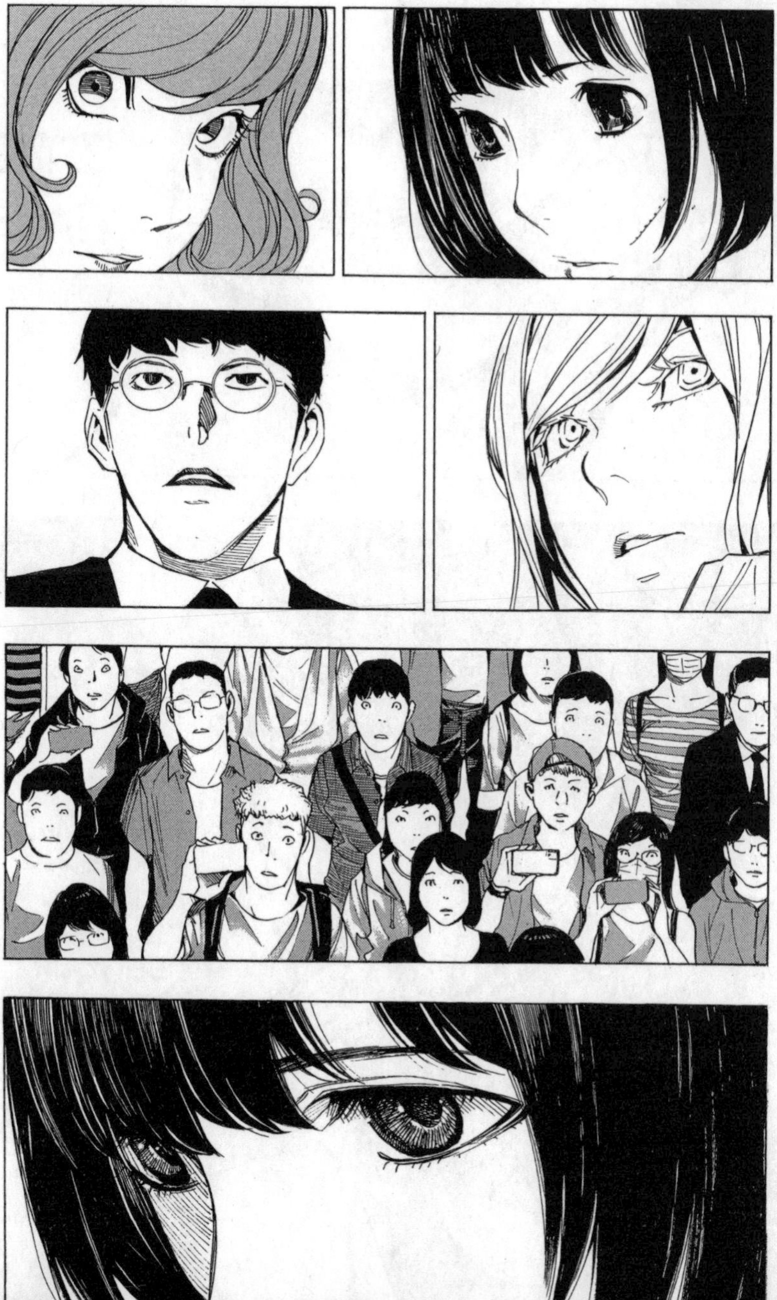

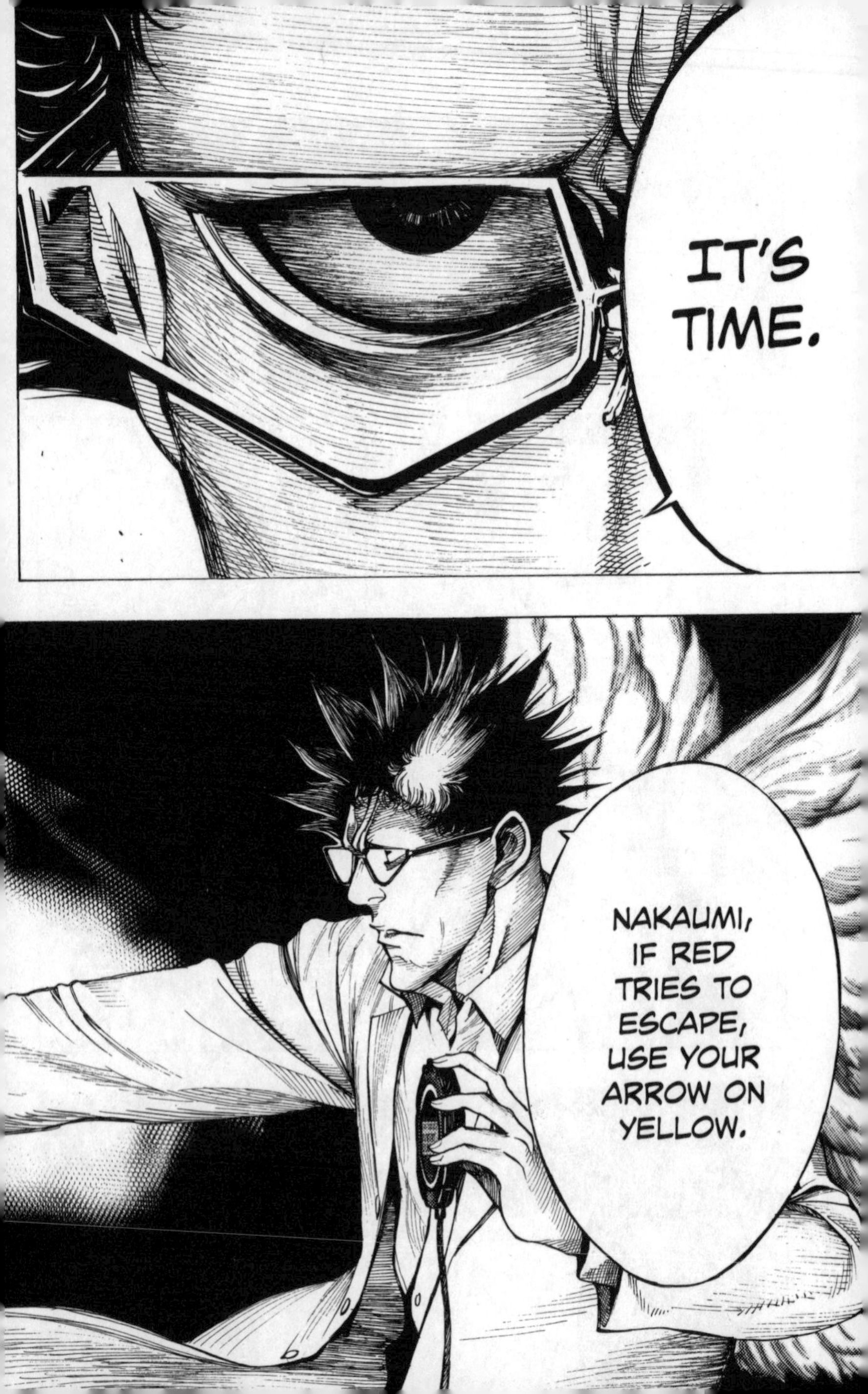
IT'S TIME.
NAKAUMI, IF RED TRIES TO ESCAPE, USE YOUR ARROW ON YELLOW.

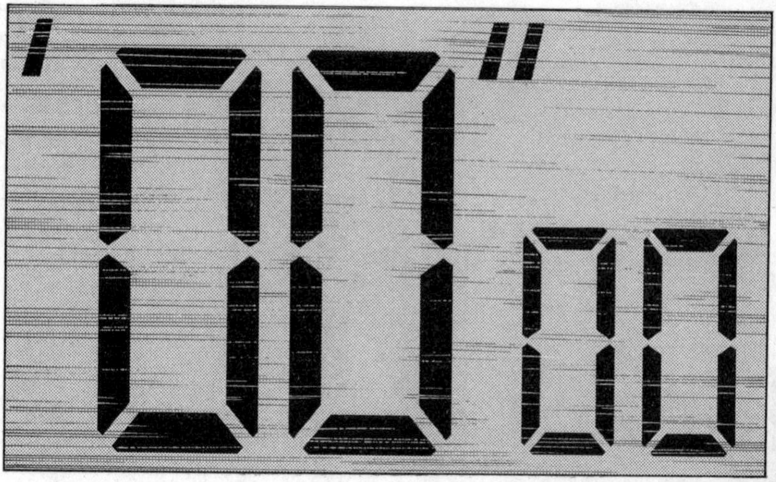
'00"00
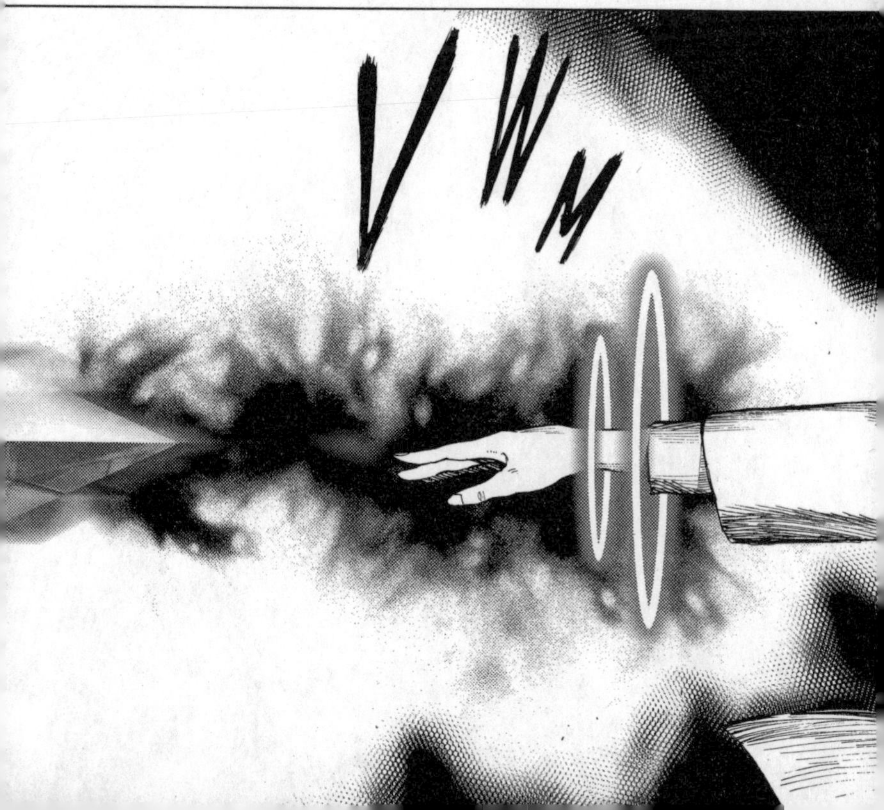
VWM

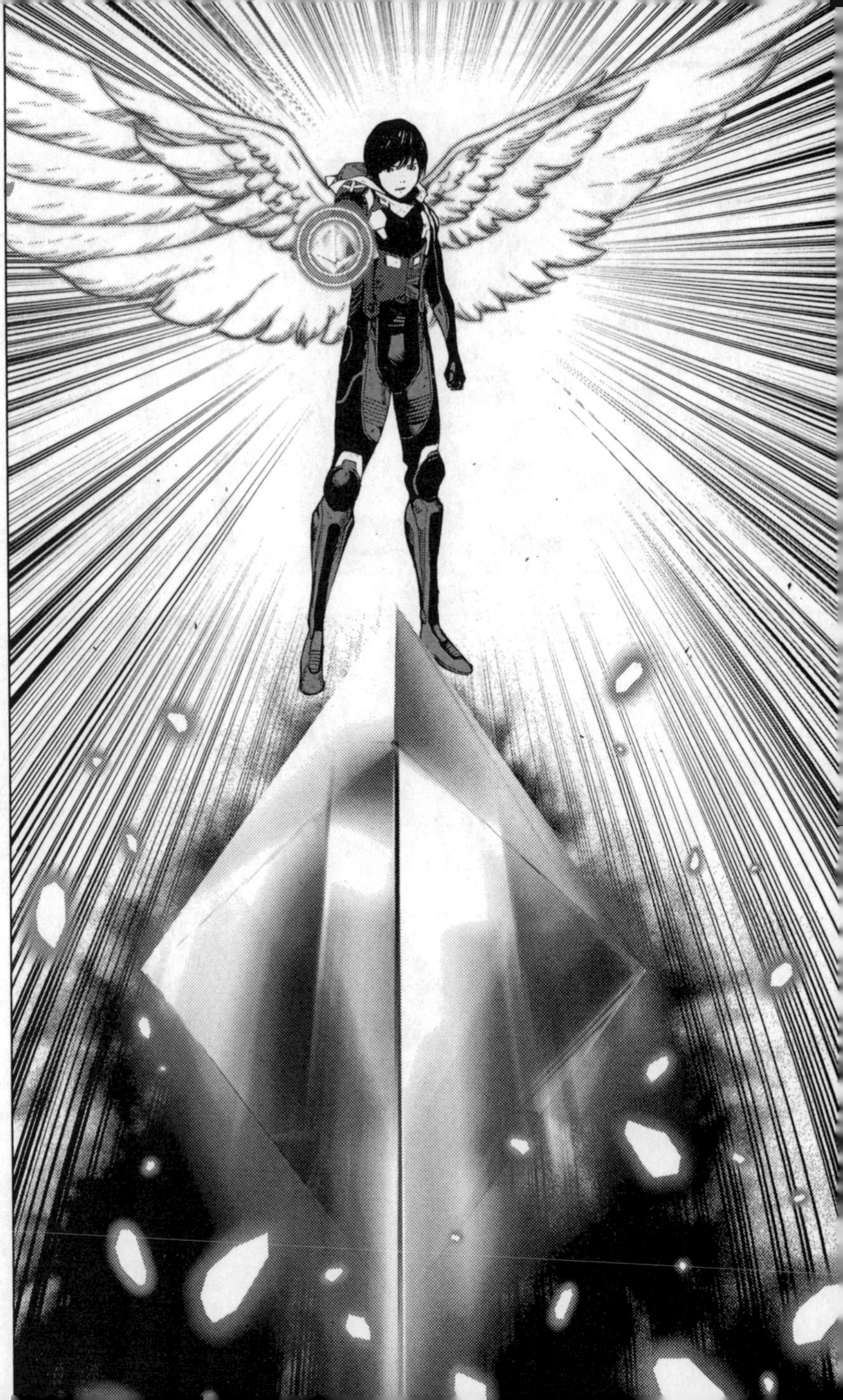

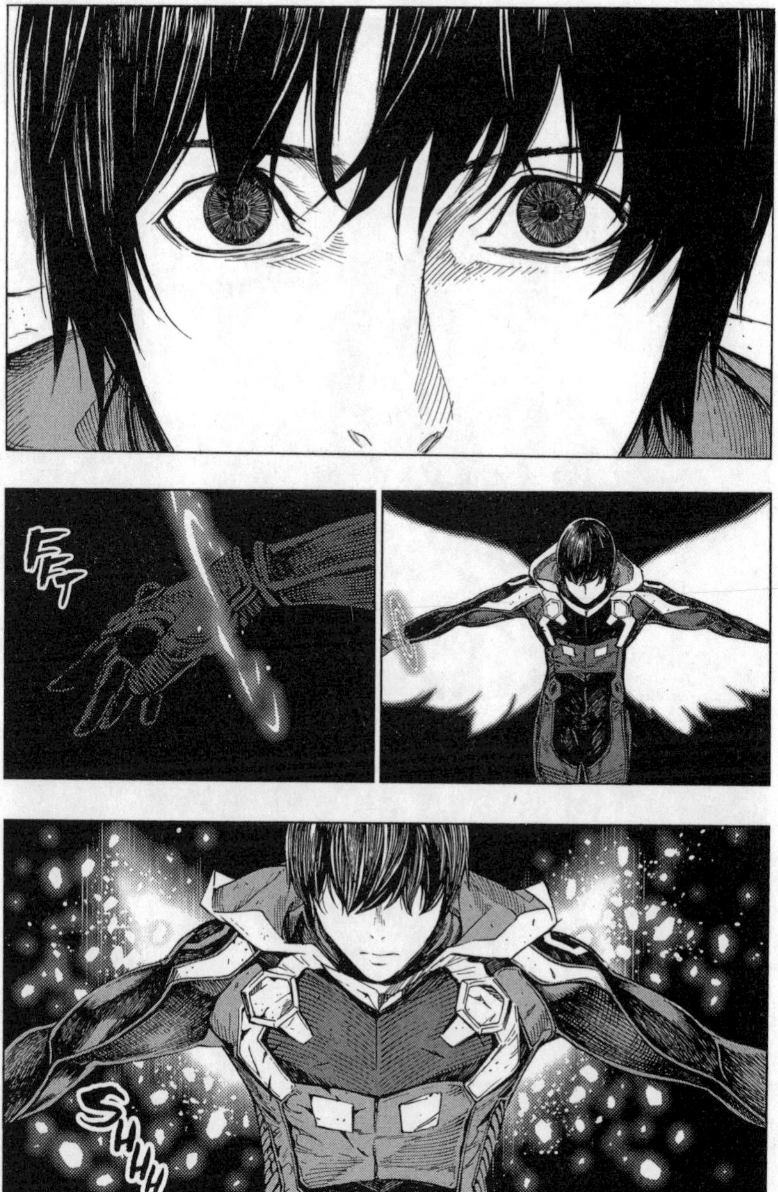
FFT
SHHH

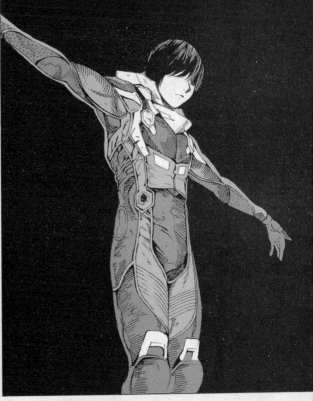

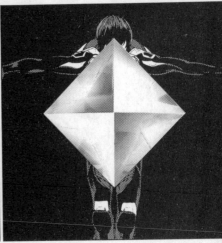

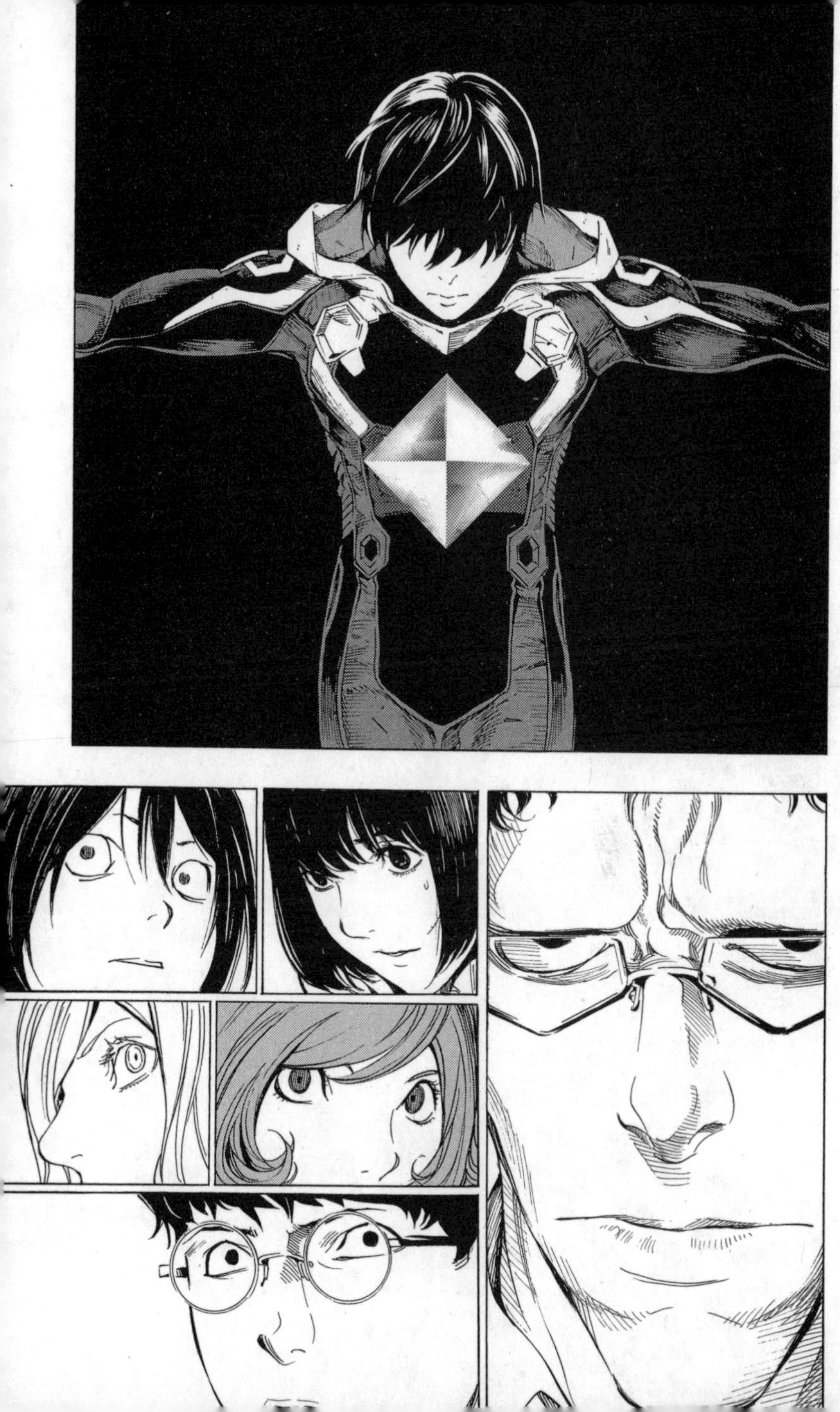

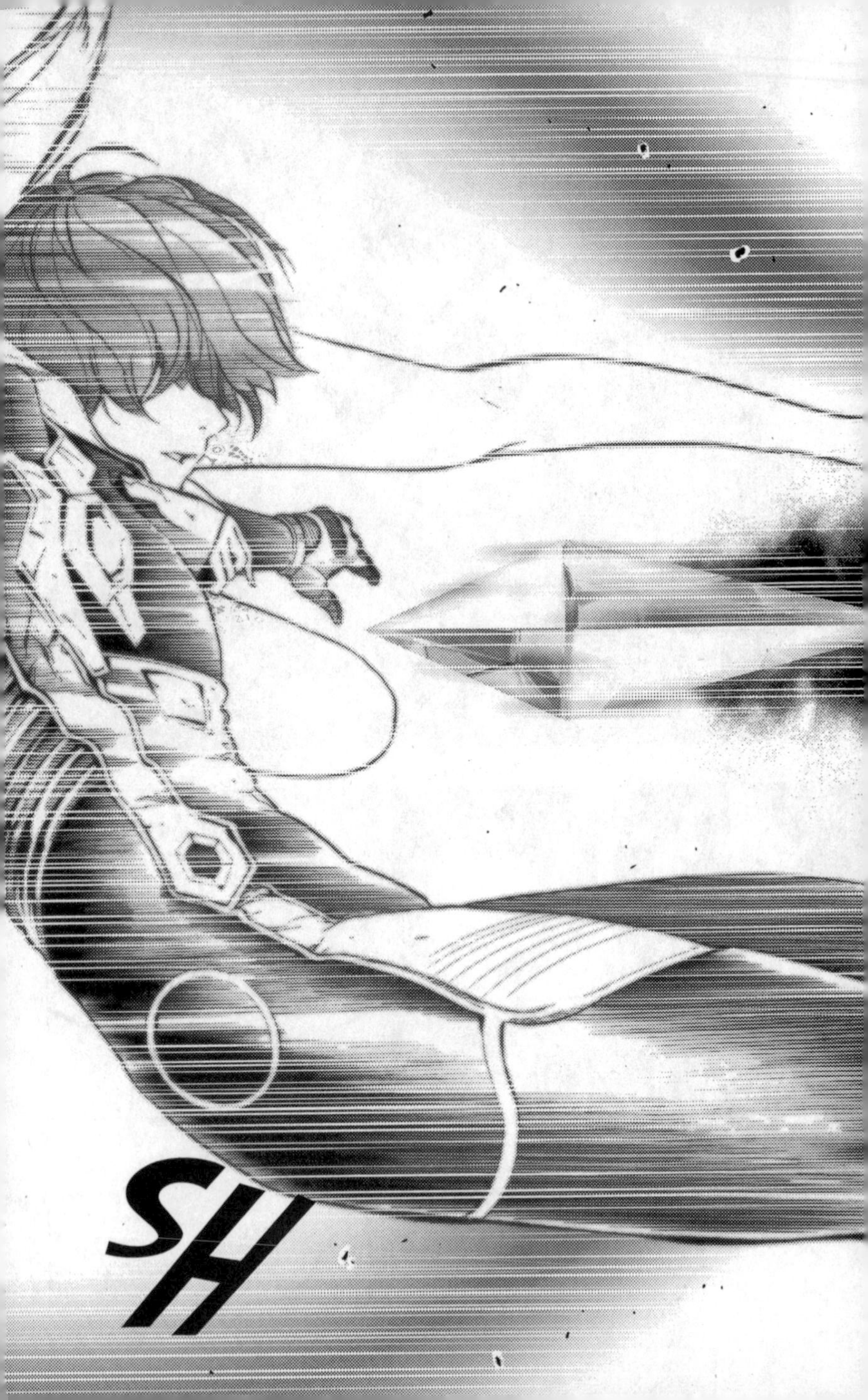
SH

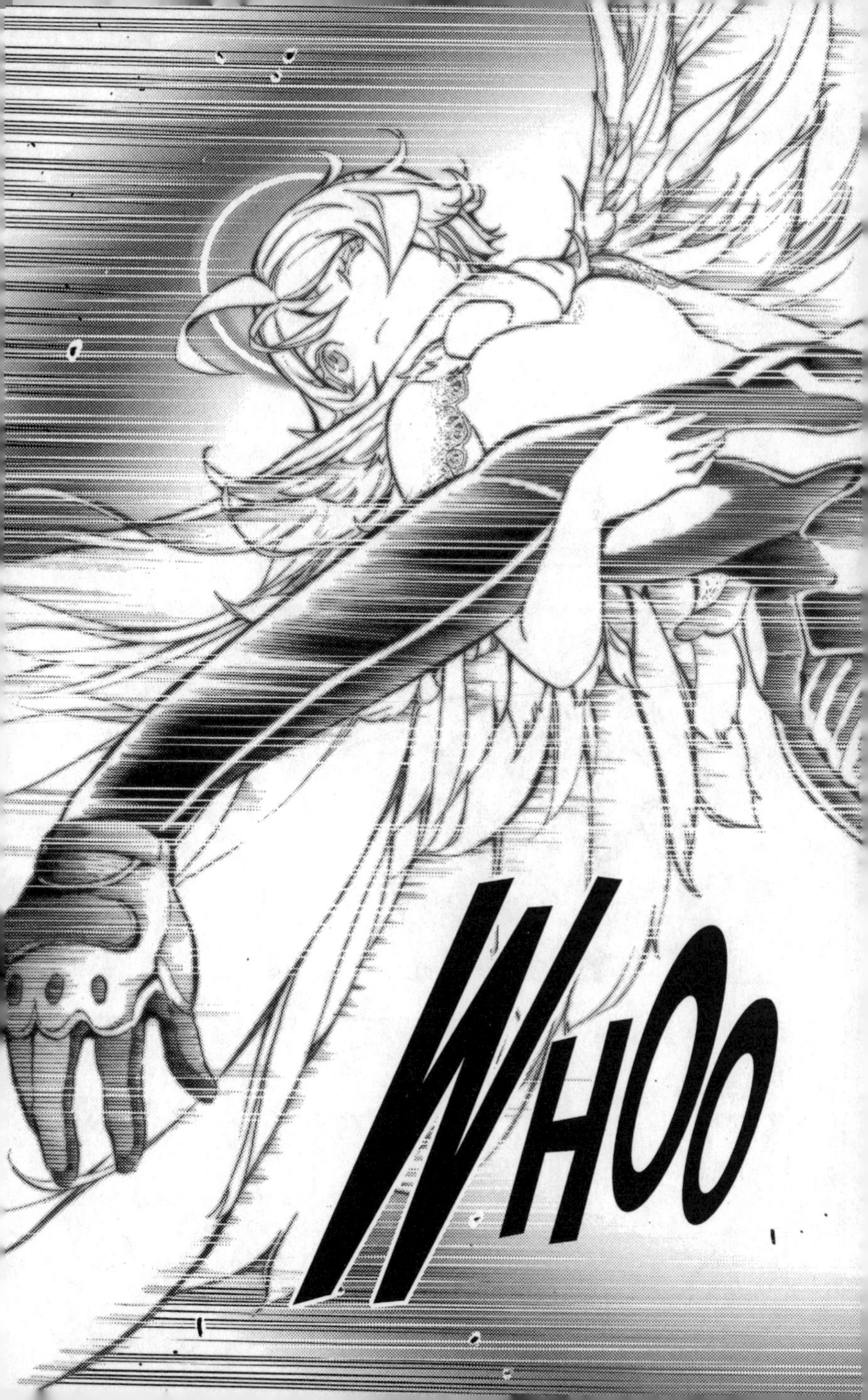
WHOO

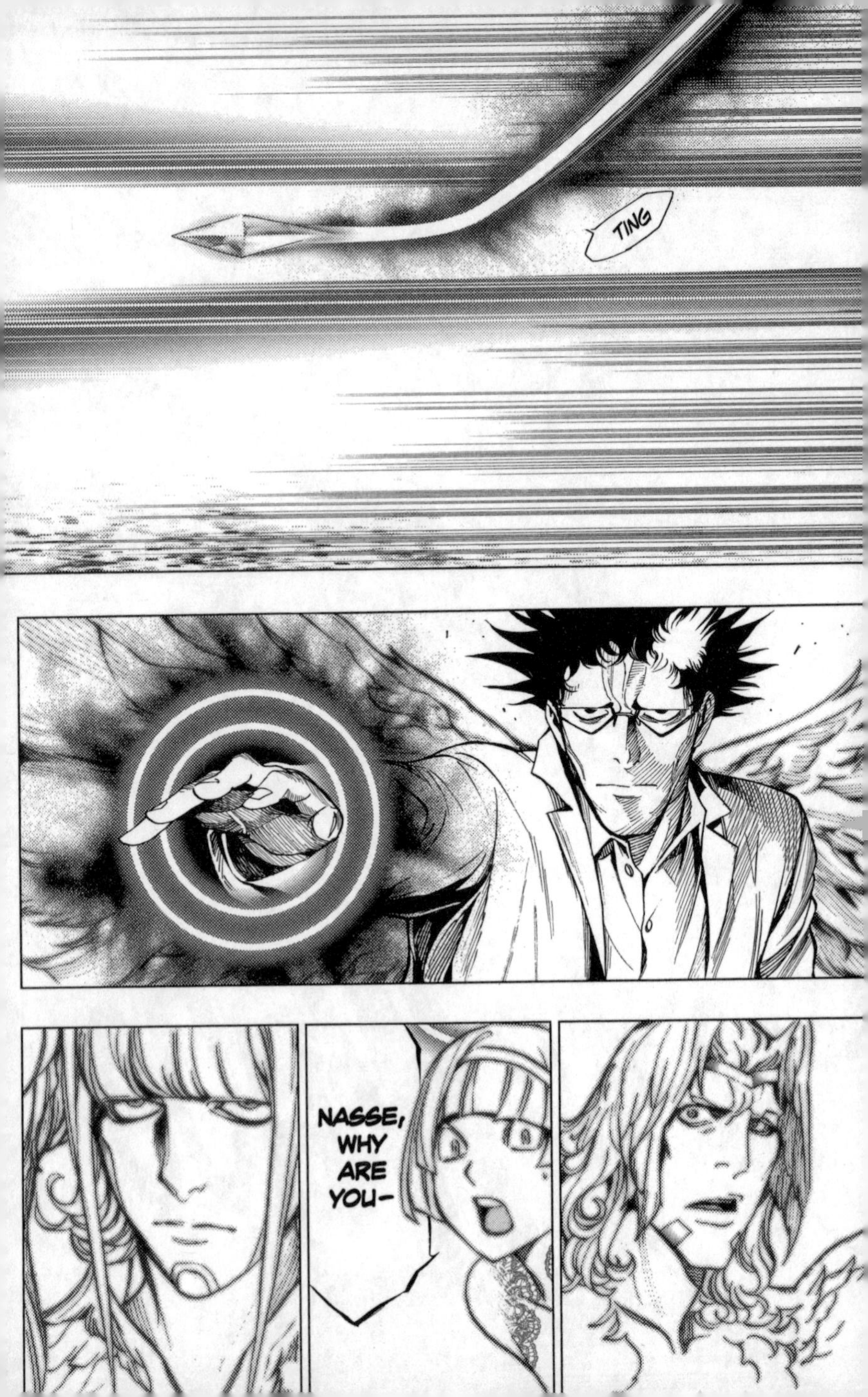
TING
NASSE, WHY ARE YOU-

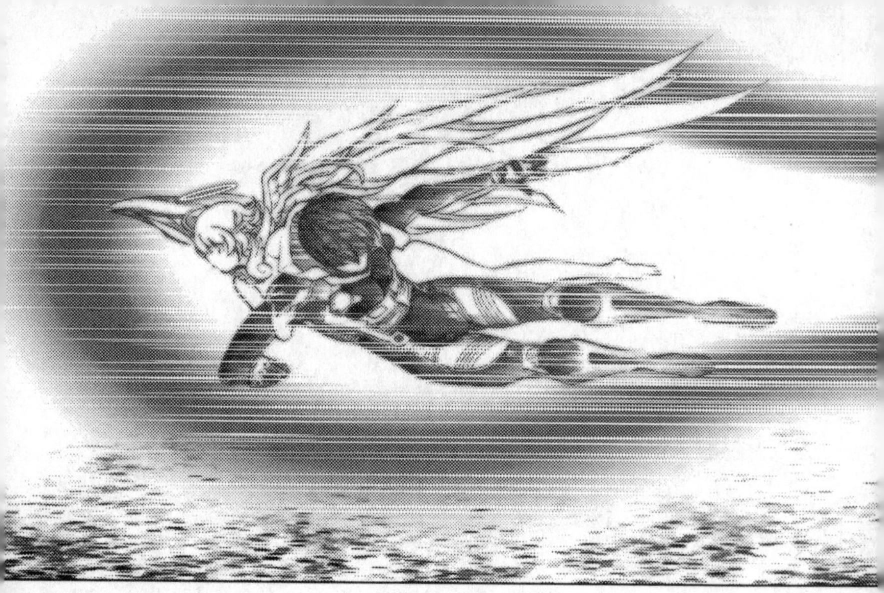

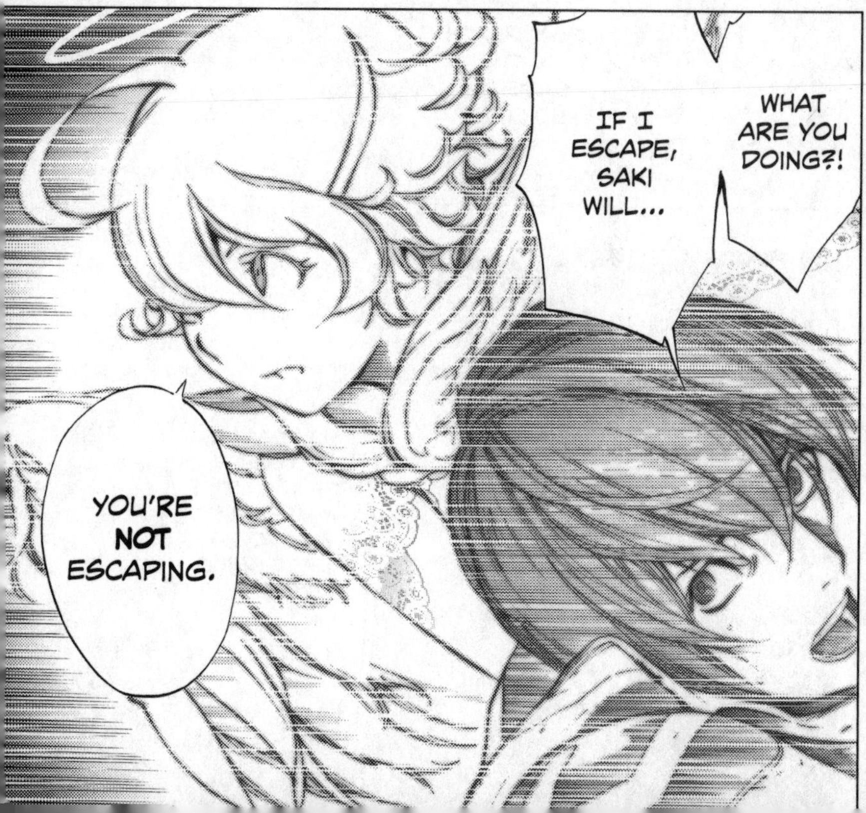
WHAT ARE YOU DOING?!
IF I ESCAPE, SAKI WILL...
YOU'RE **NOT** ESCAPING.

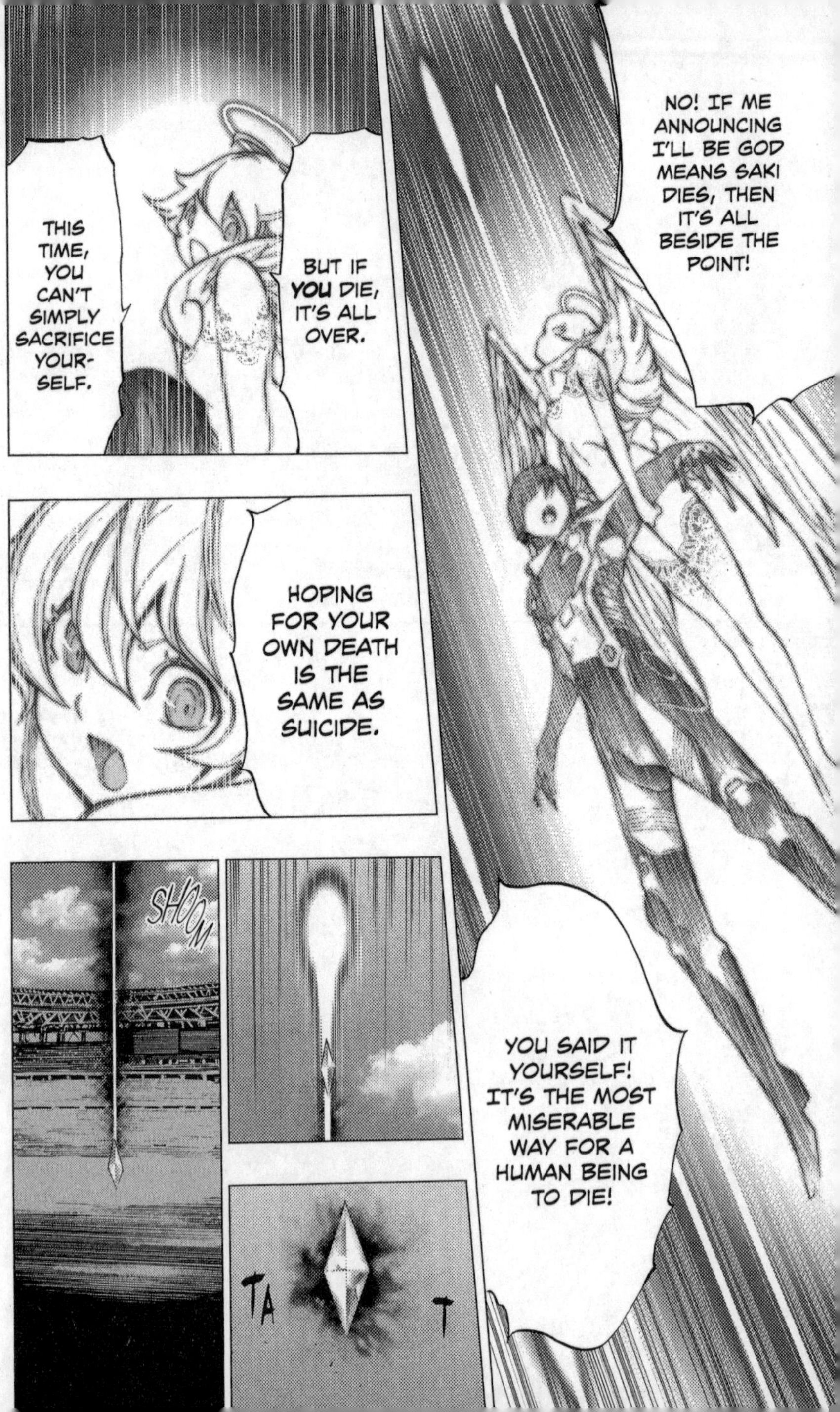

NO! IF ME ANNOUNCING I'LL BE GOD MEANS SAKI DIES, THEN IT'S ALL BESIDE THE POINT!
YOU SAID IT YOURSELF! IT'S THE MOST MISERABLE WAY FOR A HUMAN BEING TO DIE!
BUT IF YOU DIE, IT'S ALL OVER.
THIS TIME, YOU CAN'T SIMPLY SACRIFICE YOUR-SELF.
HOPING FOR YOUR OWN DEATH IS THE SAME AS SUICIDE.
TA T
SHOOM

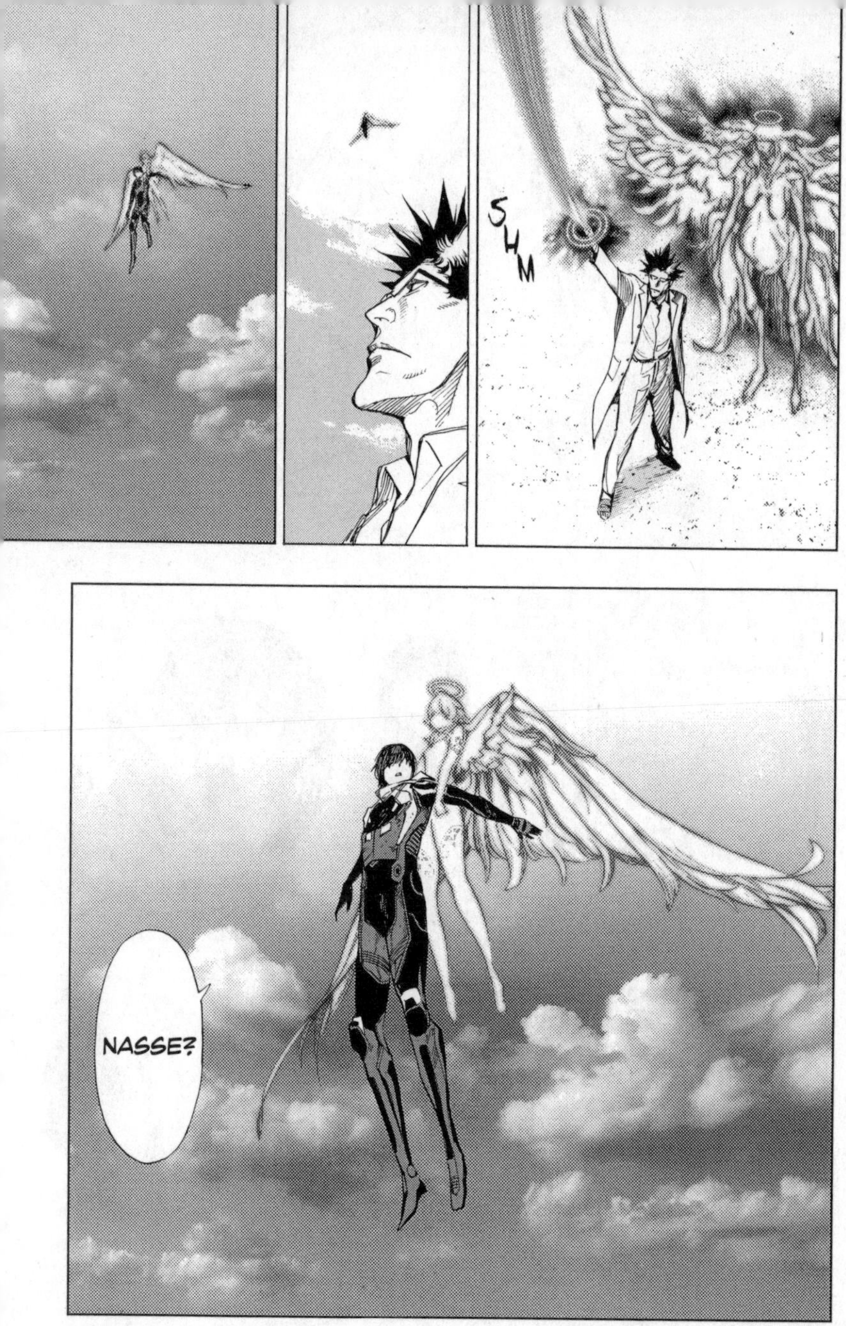
SHM
NASSE?

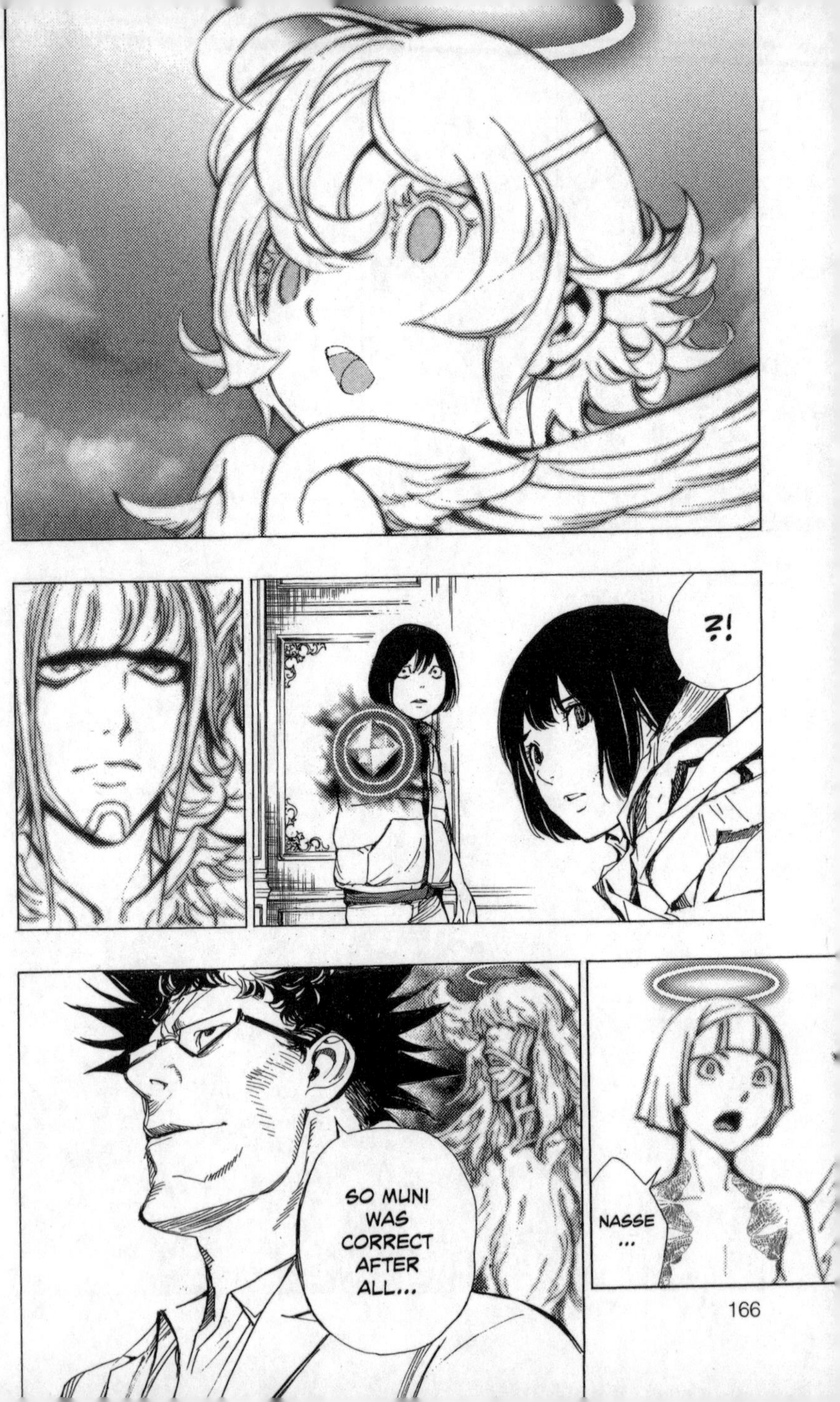
?!
NASSE ...
SO MUNI WAS CORRECT AFTER ALL...

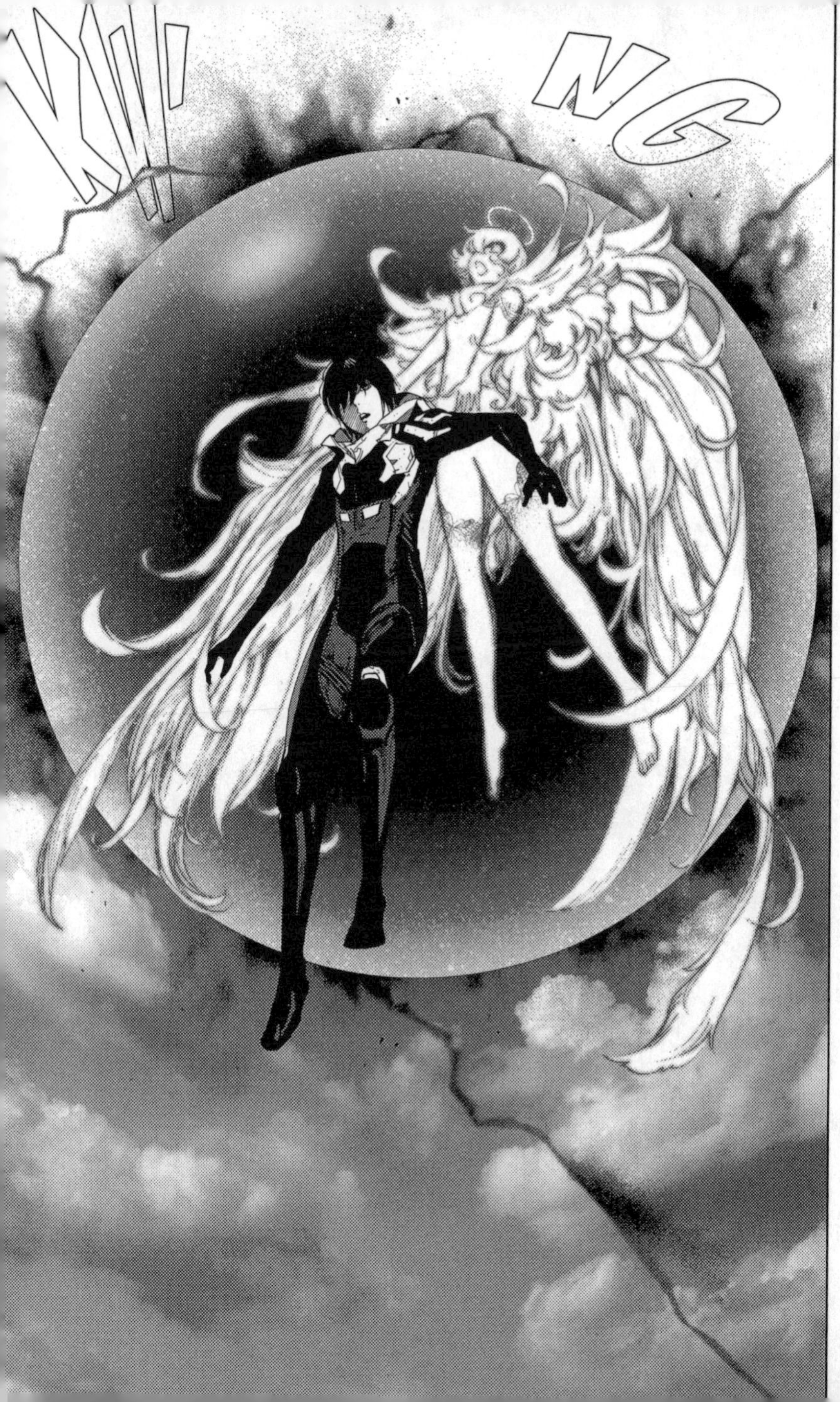
KWII
NG

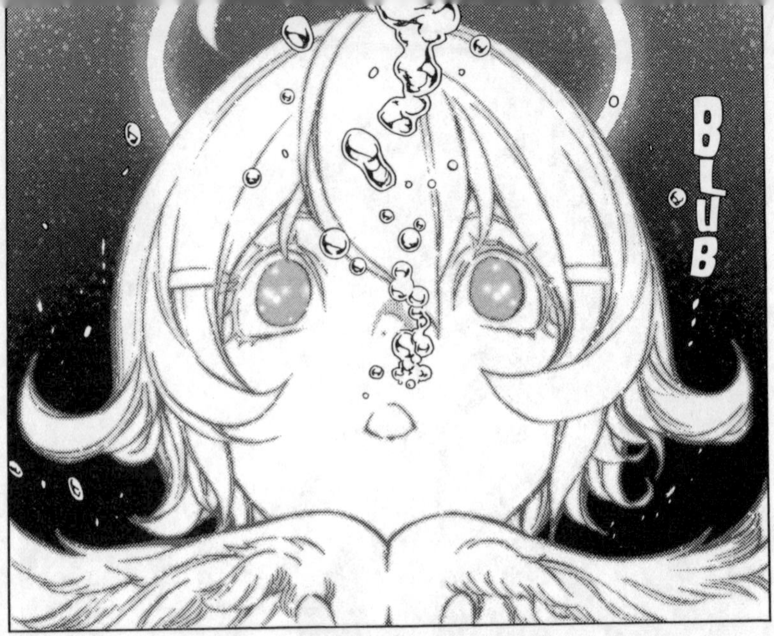
BLUB
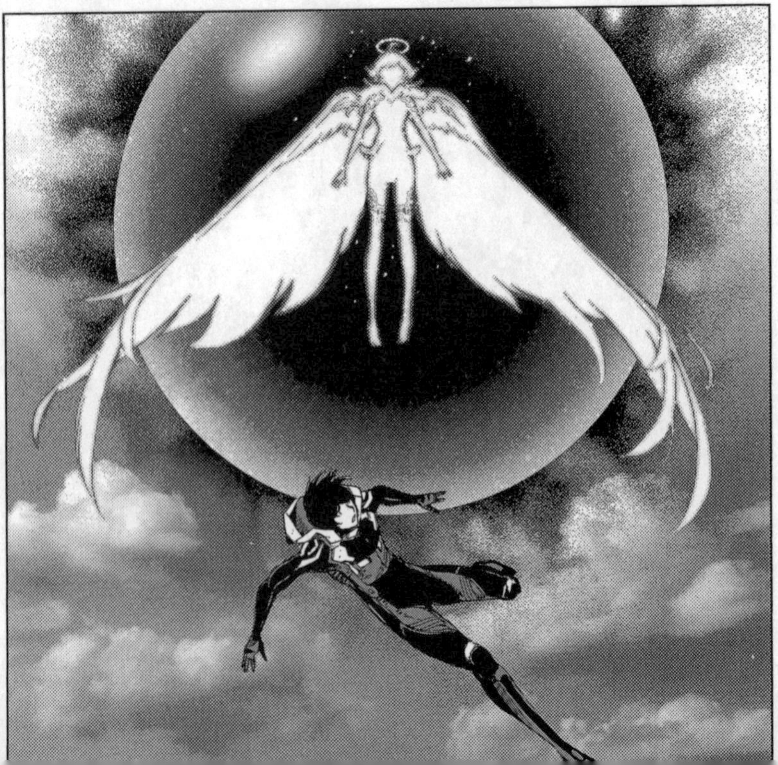

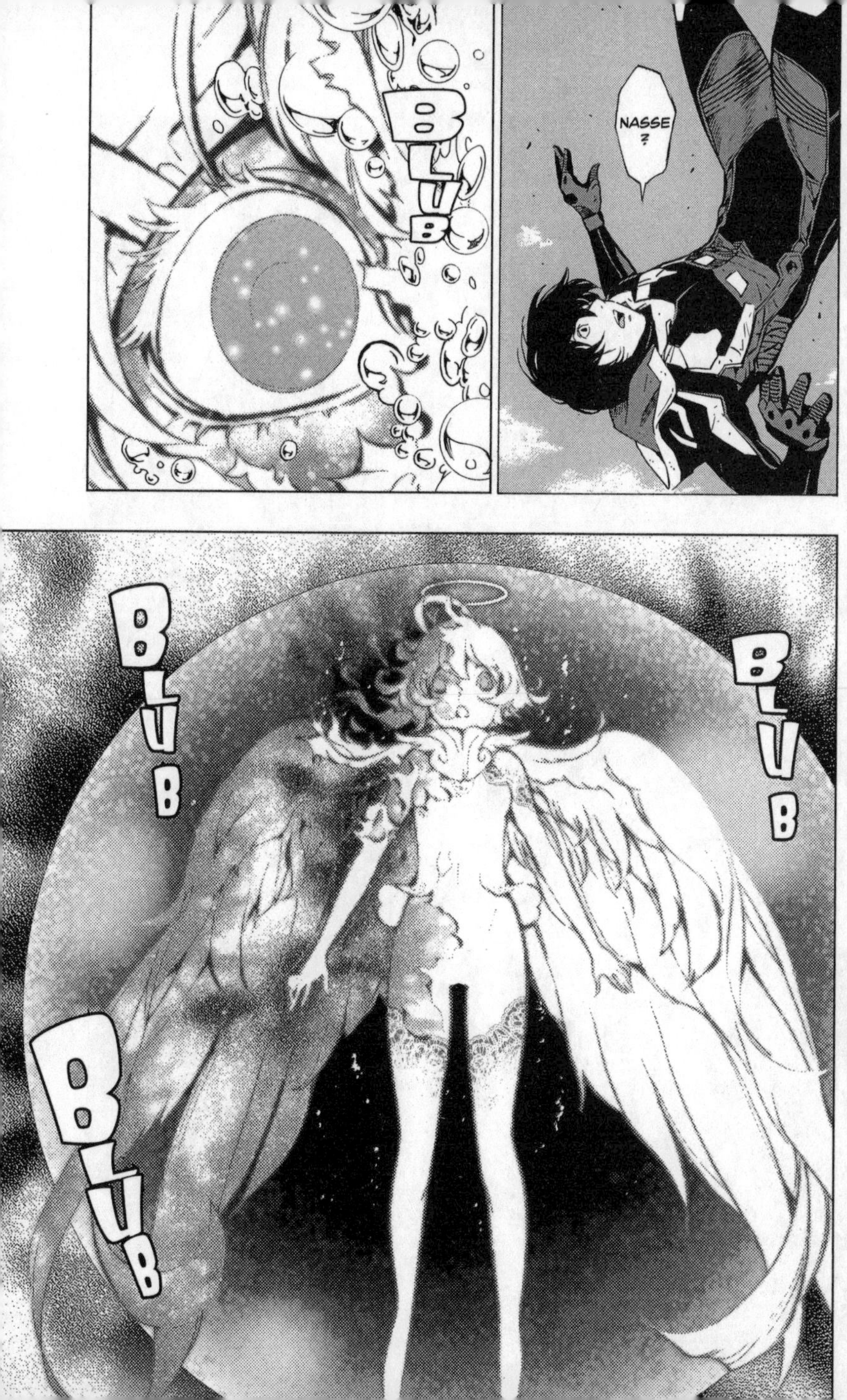
NASSE?
BLUB
BLUB
BLUB
BLUB

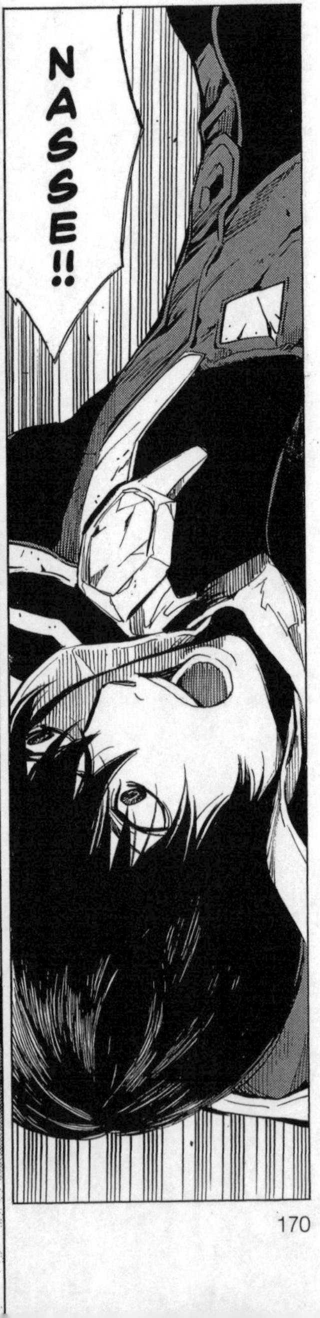
NASSE!!

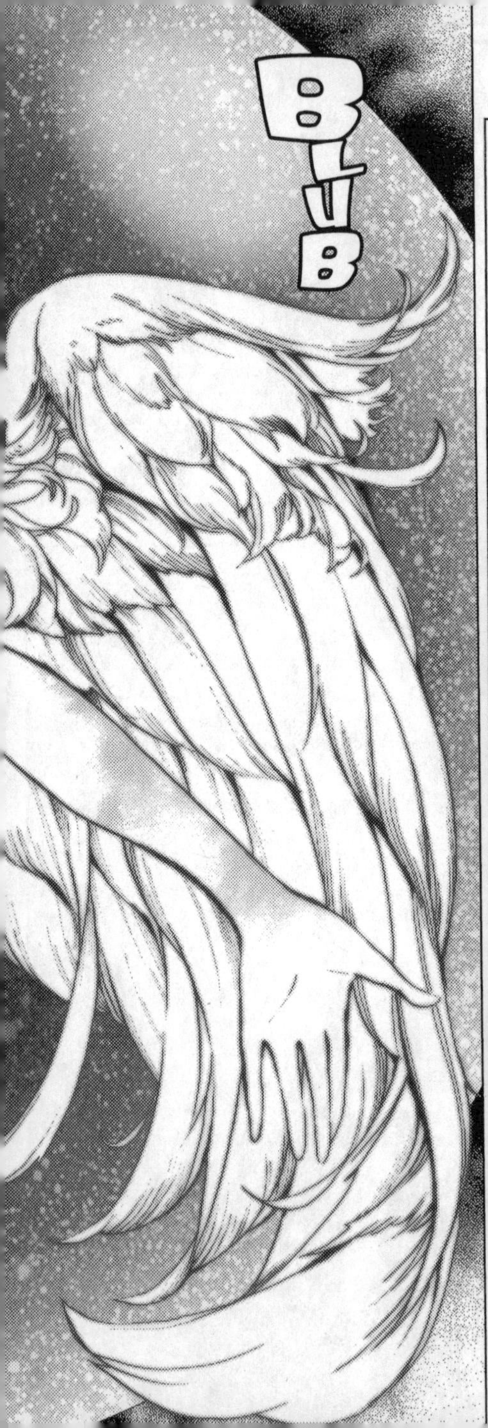
BLUB

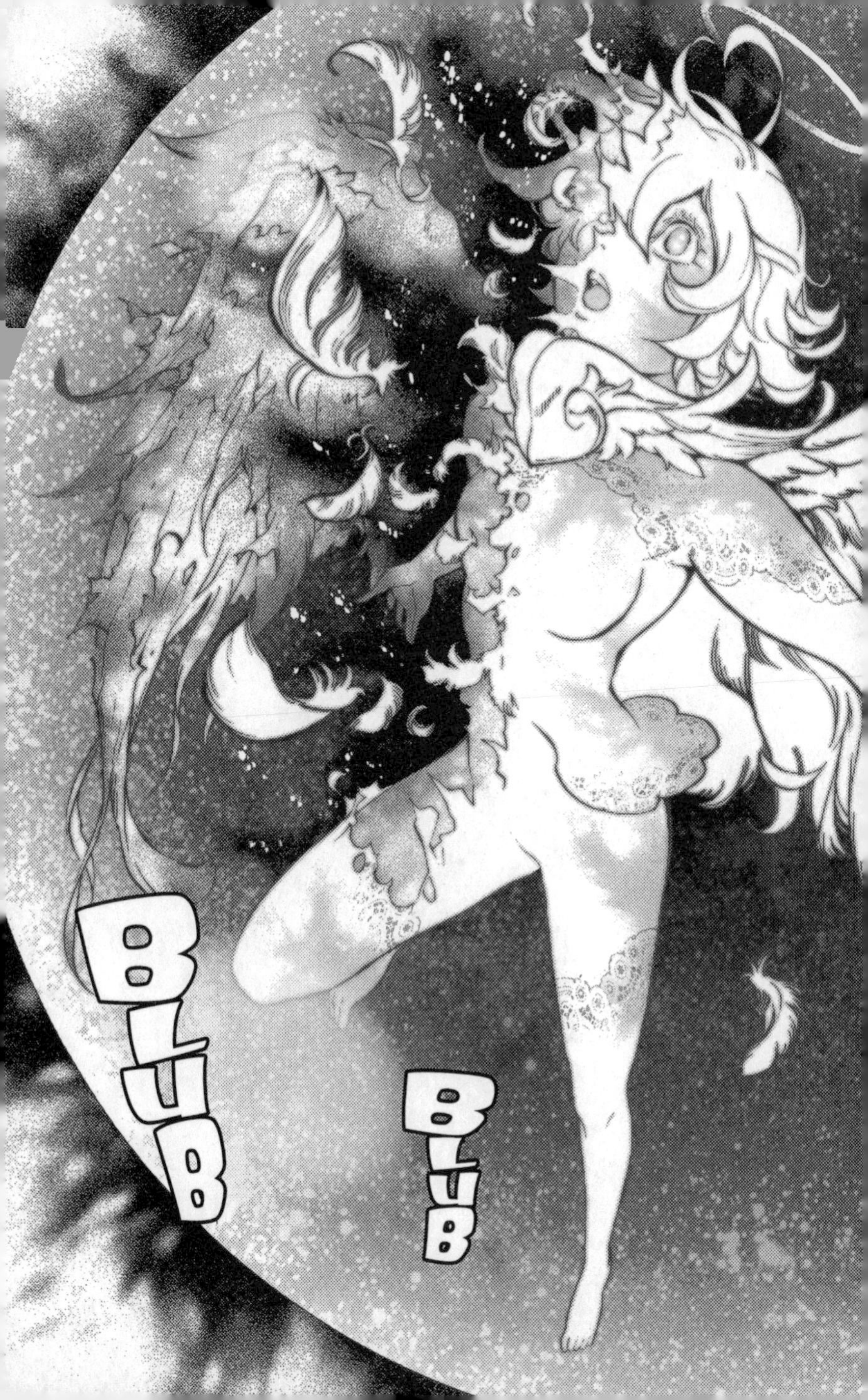
BLUB
BLUB

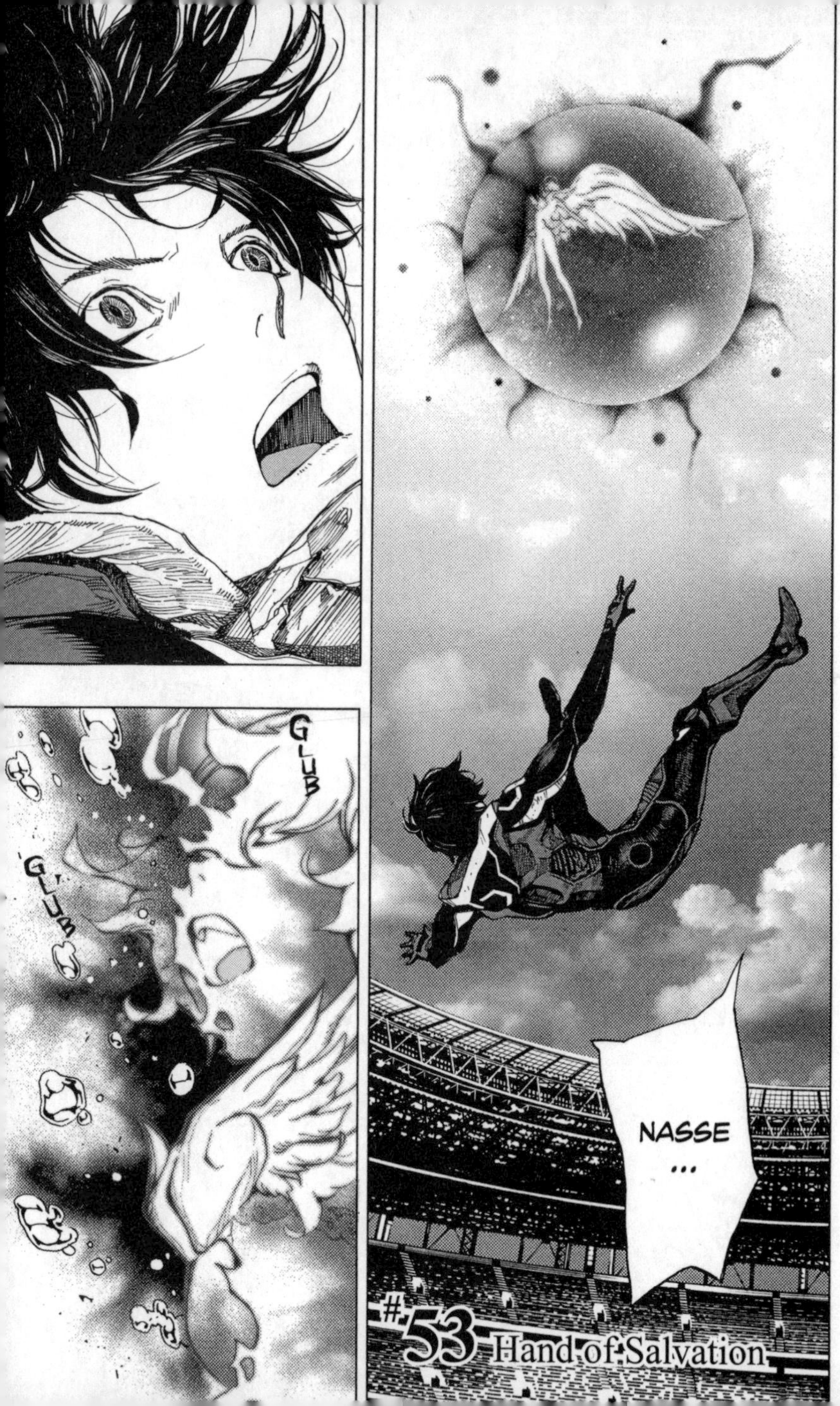
NASSE ...
#53 Hand of Salvation
GLUB
GLUM

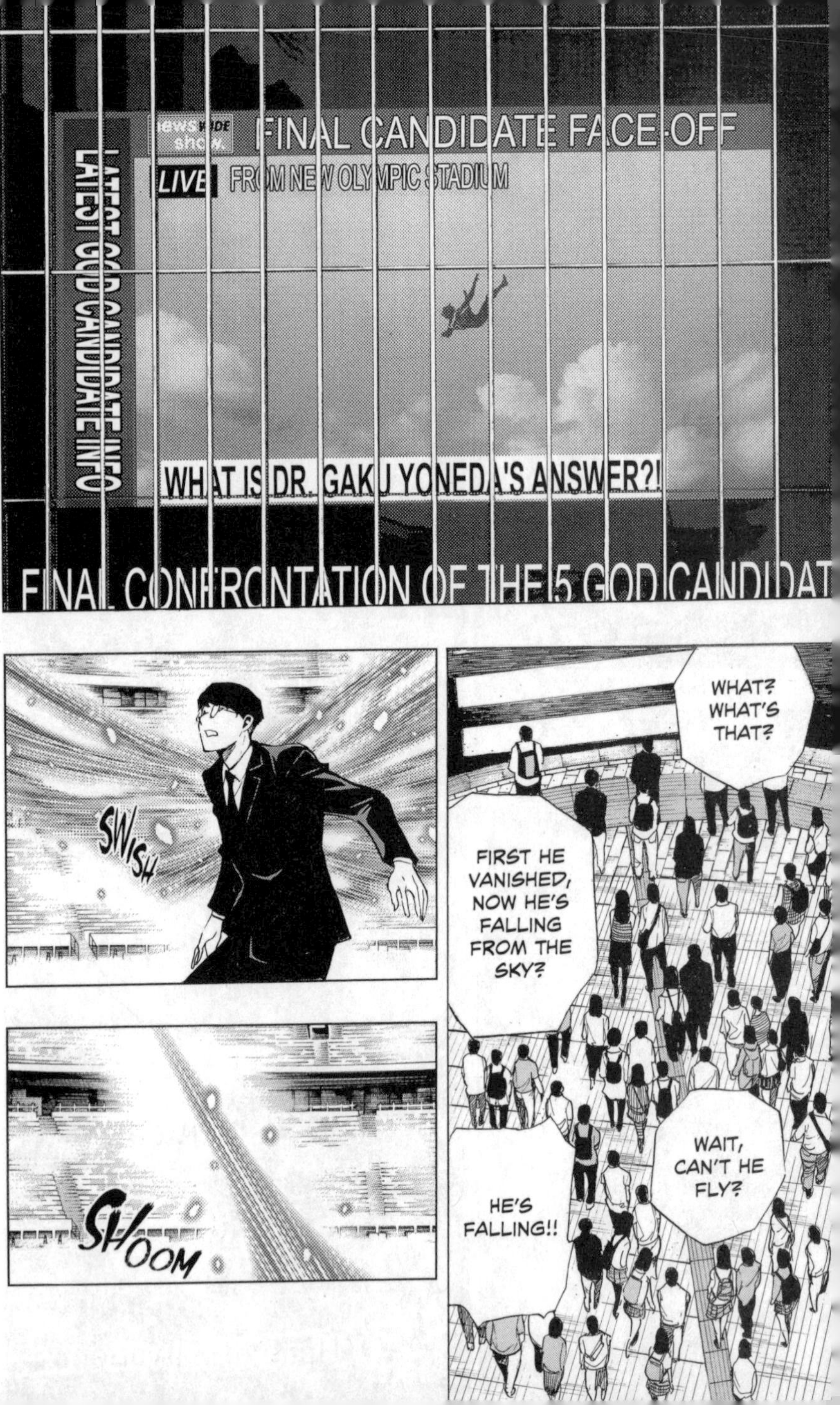
news WIDE show
FINAL CANDIDATE FACE-OFF
LIVE
FROM NEW OLYMPIC STADIUM
LATEST GOD CANDIDATE INFO
WHAT IS DR. GAKU YONEDA'S ANSWER?!
FINAL CONFRONTATION OF THE 5 GOD CANDIDAT
WHAT? WHAT'S THAT?
FIRST HE VANISHED, NOW HE'S FALLING FROM THE SKY?
WAIT, CAN'T HE FLY?
HE'S FALLING!!
SWISH
SHOOM

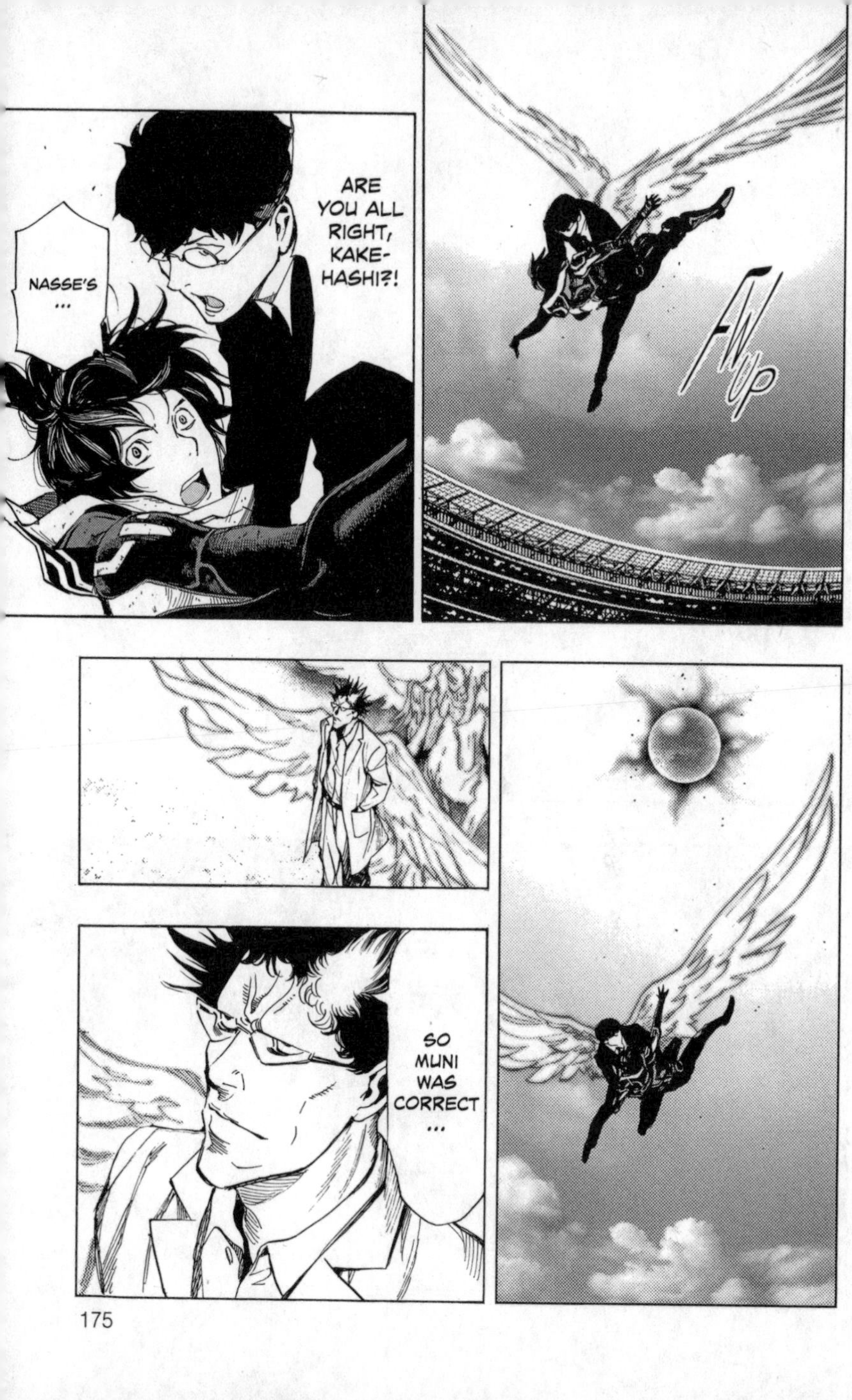
FWUP
ARE YOU ALL RIGHT, KAKE-HASHI?!
NASSE'S ...
SO MUNI WAS CORRECT ...

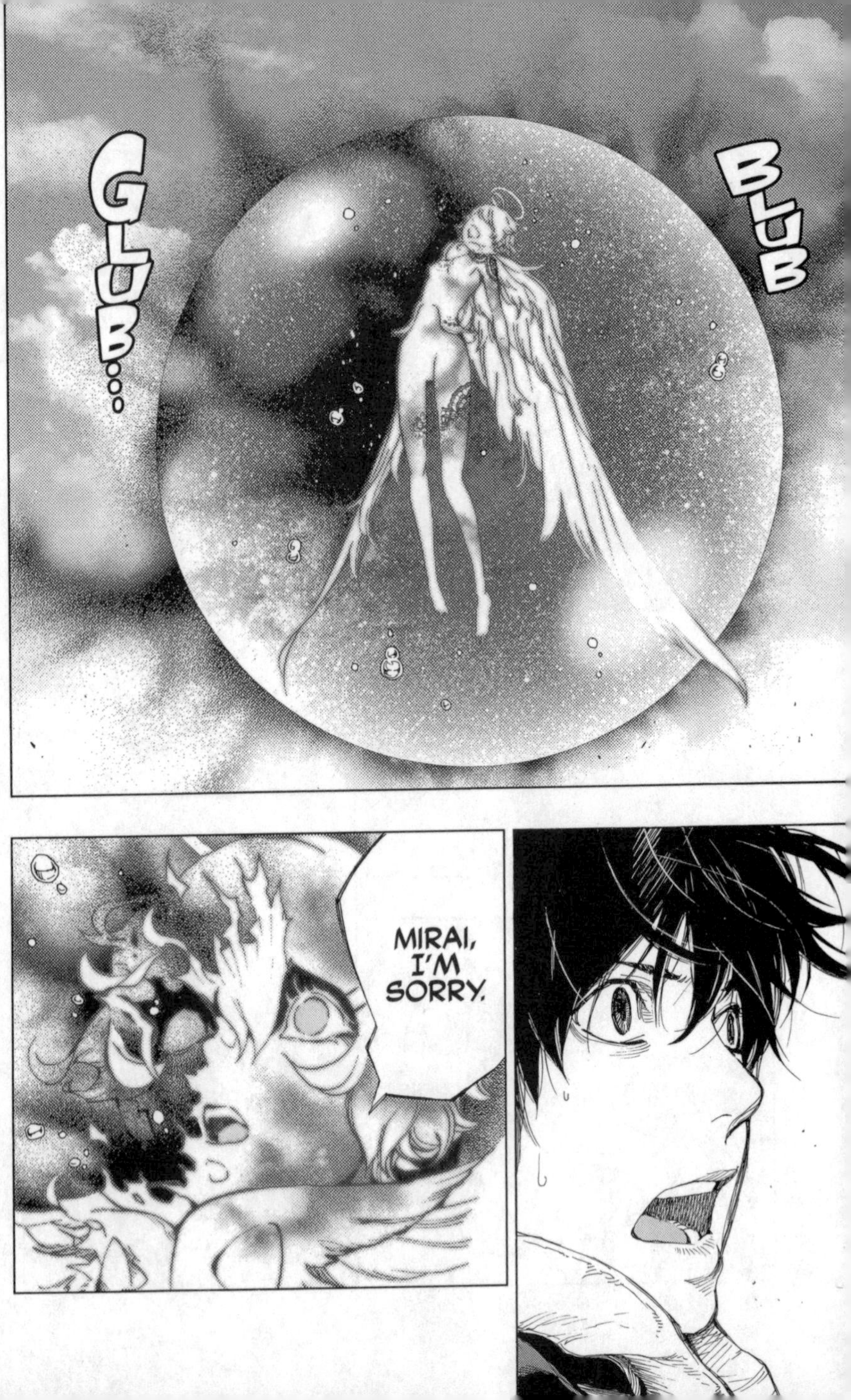
BLUB
GLUB...
MIRAI, I'M SORRY.

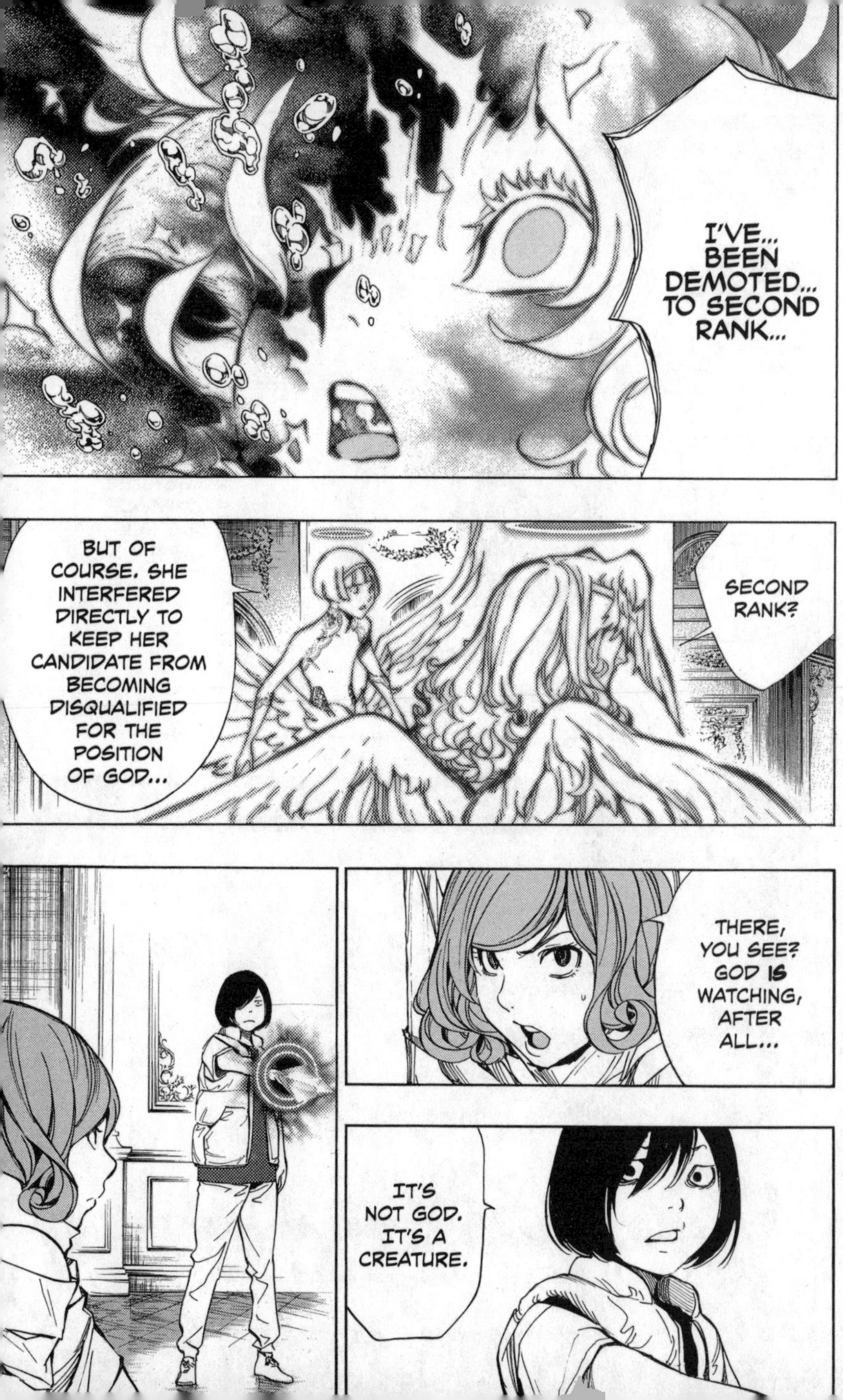
I'VE... BEEN DEMOTED... TO SECOND RANK...
SECOND RANK?
BUT OF COURSE. SHE INTERFERED DIRECTLY TO KEEP HER CANDIDATE FROM BECOMING DISQUALIFIED FOR THE POSITION OF GOD...
THERE, YOU SEE? GOD IS WATCHING, AFTER ALL...
IT'S NOT GOD. IT'S A CREATURE.

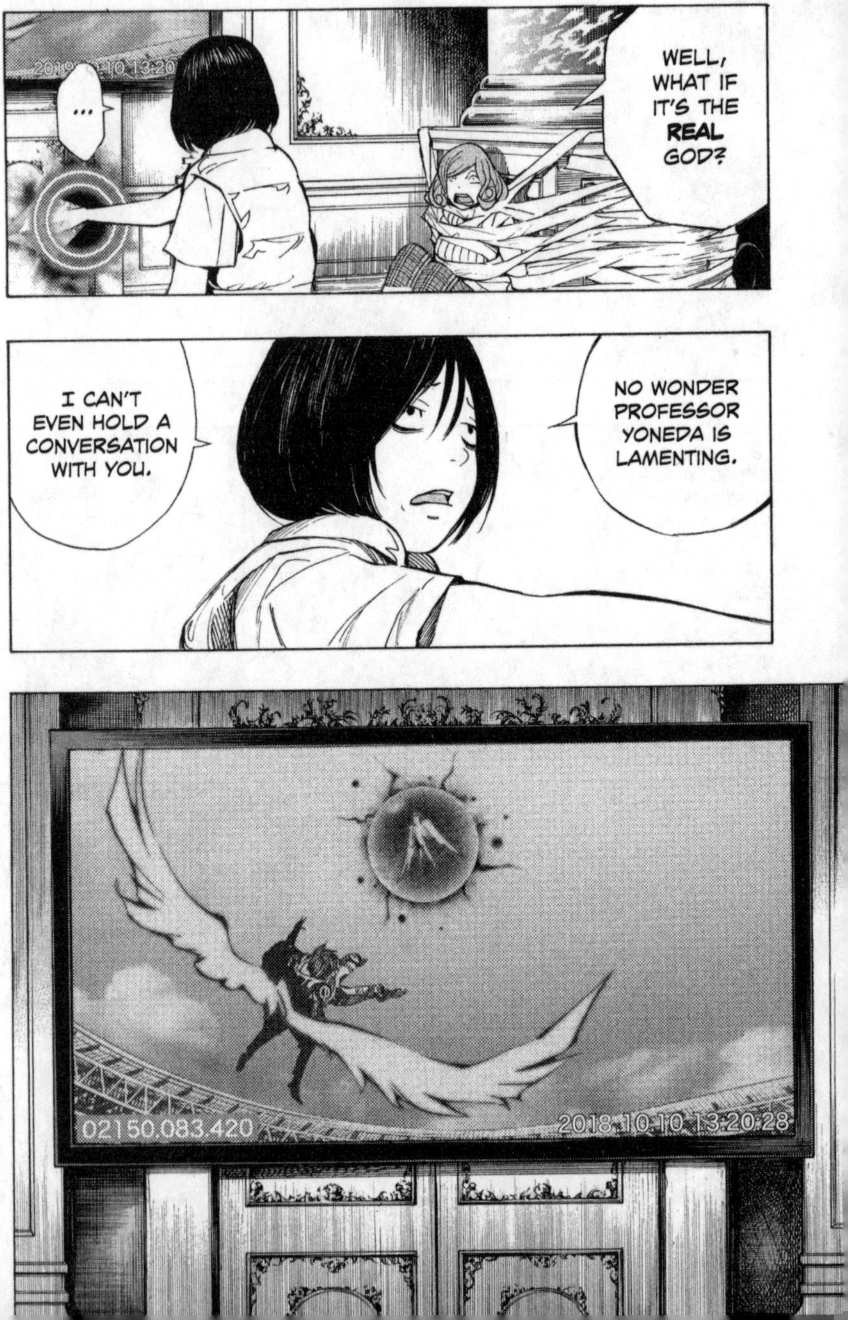
WELL, WHAT IF IT'S THE **REAL** GOD?
...
NO WONDER PROFESSOR YONEDA IS LAMENTING.
I CAN'T EVEN HOLD A CONVERSATION WITH YOU.
2018.10.10.13:20:28
02150.083.420

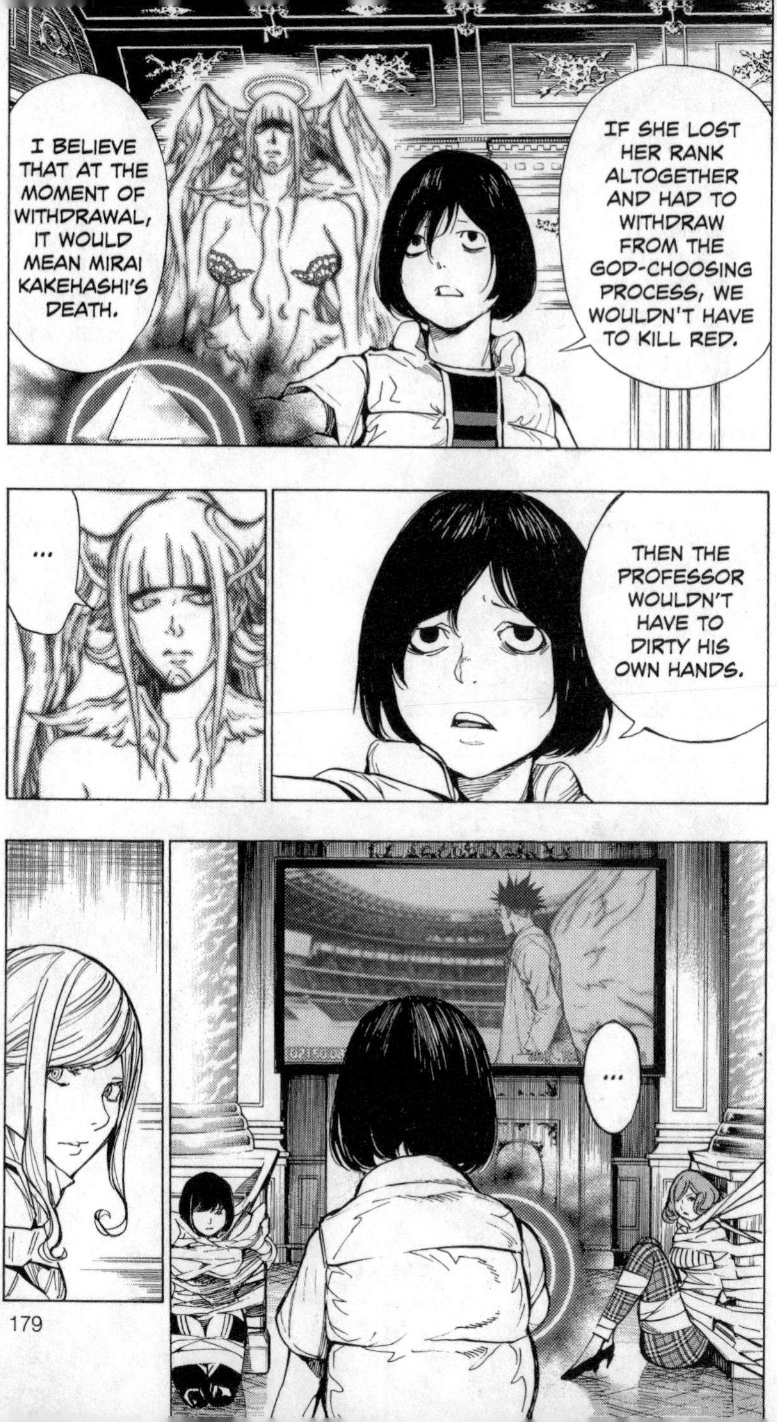
IF SHE LOST HER RANK ALTOGETHER AND HAD TO WITHDRAW FROM THE GOD-CHOOSING PROCESS, WE WOULDN'T HAVE TO KILL RED.
I BELIEVE THAT AT THE MOMENT OF WITHDRAWAL, IT WOULD MEAN MIRAI KAKEHASHI'S DEATH.
THEN THE PROFESSOR WOULDN'T HAVE TO DIRTY HIS OWN HANDS.
...
...

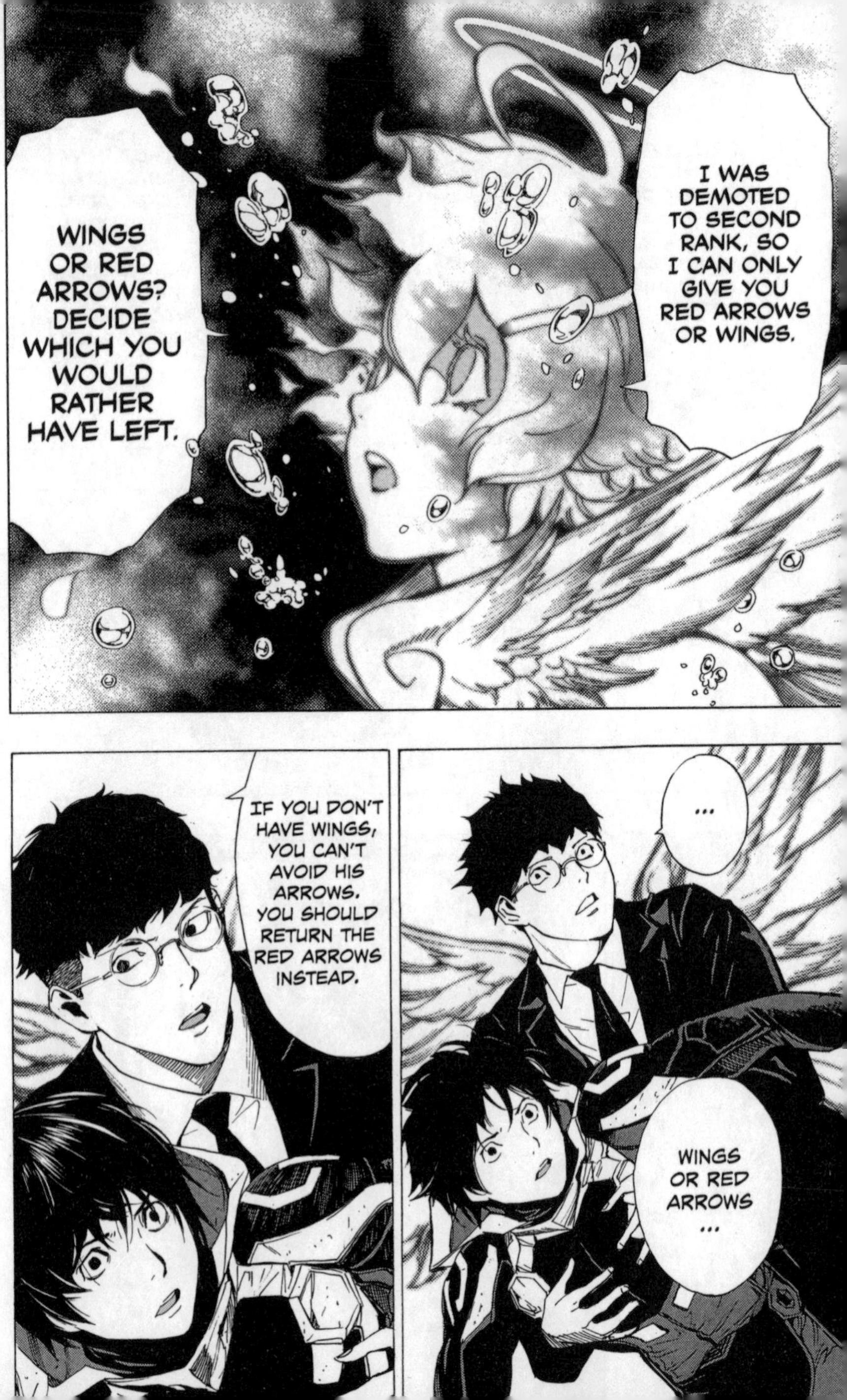
I WAS DEMOTED TO SECOND RANK, SO I CAN ONLY GIVE YOU RED ARROWS OR WINGS.
WINGS OR RED ARROWS? DECIDE WHICH YOU WOULD RATHER HAVE LEFT.
...
WINGS OR RED ARROWS ...
IF YOU DON'T HAVE WINGS, YOU CAN'T AVOID HIS ARROWS. YOU SHOULD RETURN THE RED ARROWS INSTEAD.

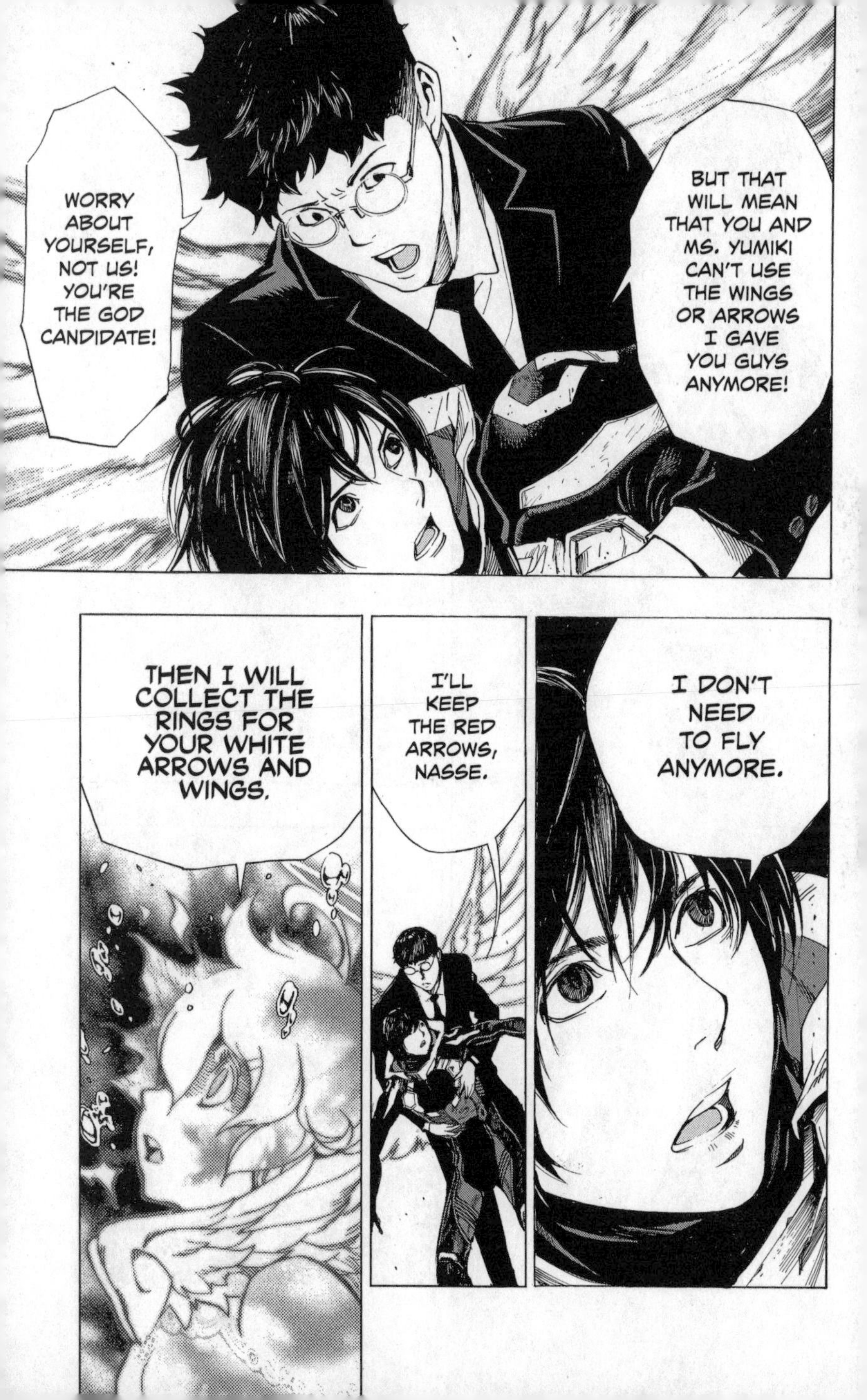
BUT THAT WILL MEAN THAT YOU AND MS. YUMIKI CAN'T USE THE WINGS OR ARROWS I GAVE YOU GUYS ANYMORE!
WORRY ABOUT YOURSELF, NOT US! YOU'RE THE GOD CANDIDATE!
I DON'T NEED TO FLY ANYMORE.
I'LL KEEP THE RED ARROWS, NASSE.
THEN I WILL COLLECT THE RINGS FOR YOUR WHITE ARROWS AND WINGS.

SHING--

SHING

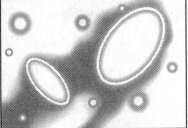

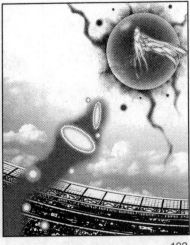

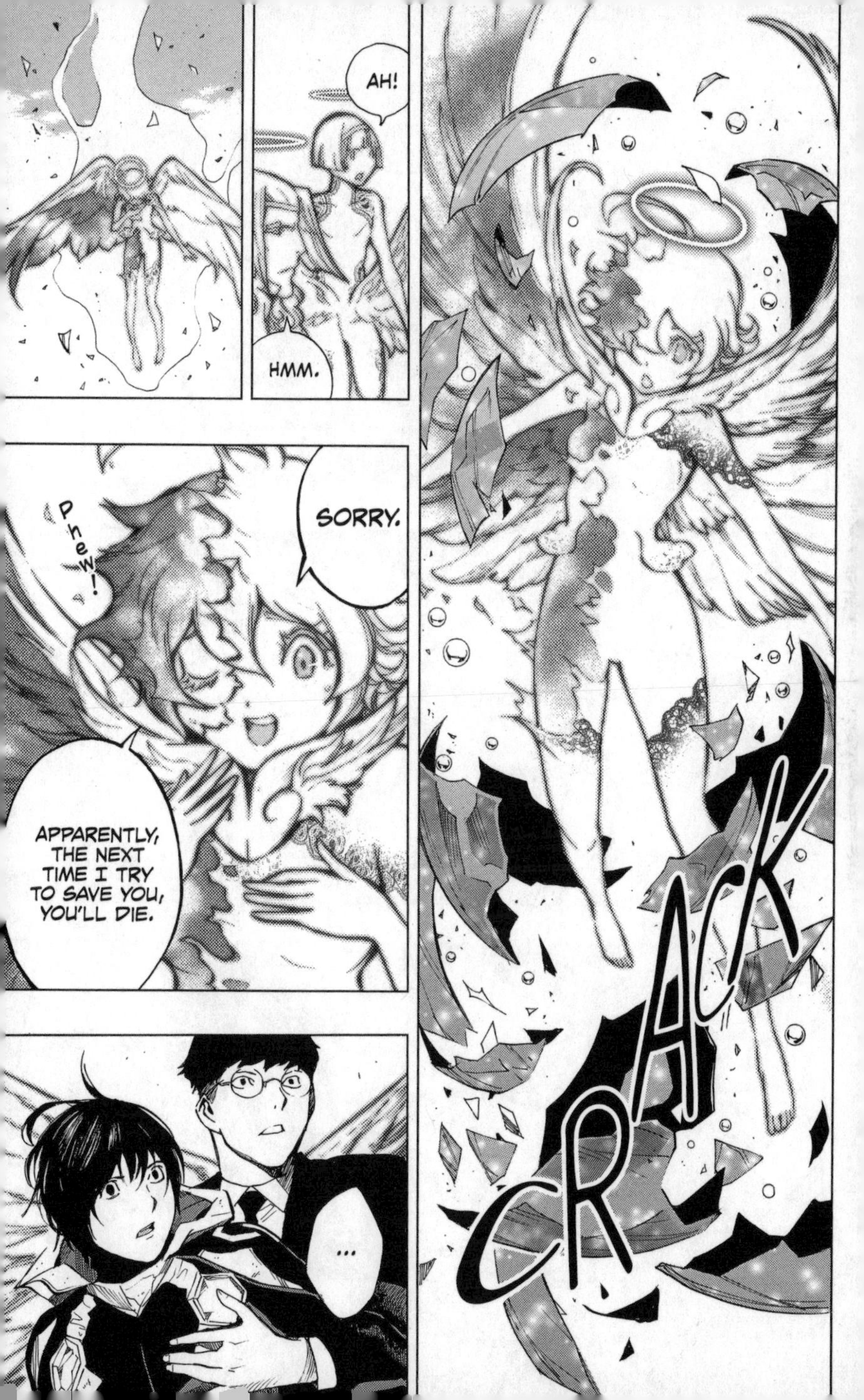
CRACK
AH!
HMM.
SORRY.
Phew!
APPARENTLY, THE NEXT TIME I TRY TO SAVE YOU, YOU'LL DIE.
...

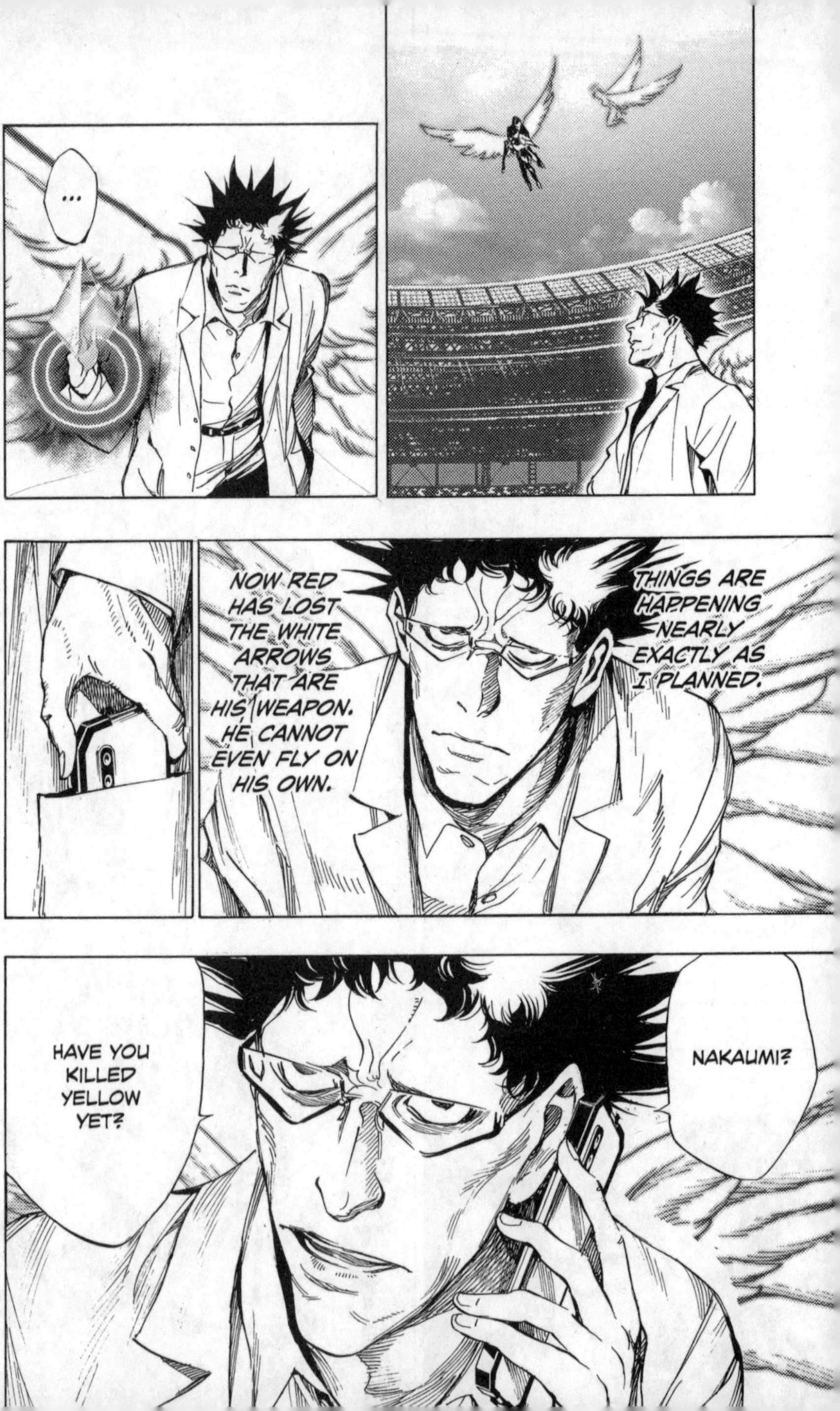
...
THINGS ARE HAPPENING NEARLY EXACTLY AS I PLANNED.
NOW RED HAS LOST THE WHITE ARROWS THAT ARE HIS WEAPON. HE CANNOT EVEN FLY ON HIS OWN.
NAKAUMI?
HAVE YOU KILLED YELLOW YET?

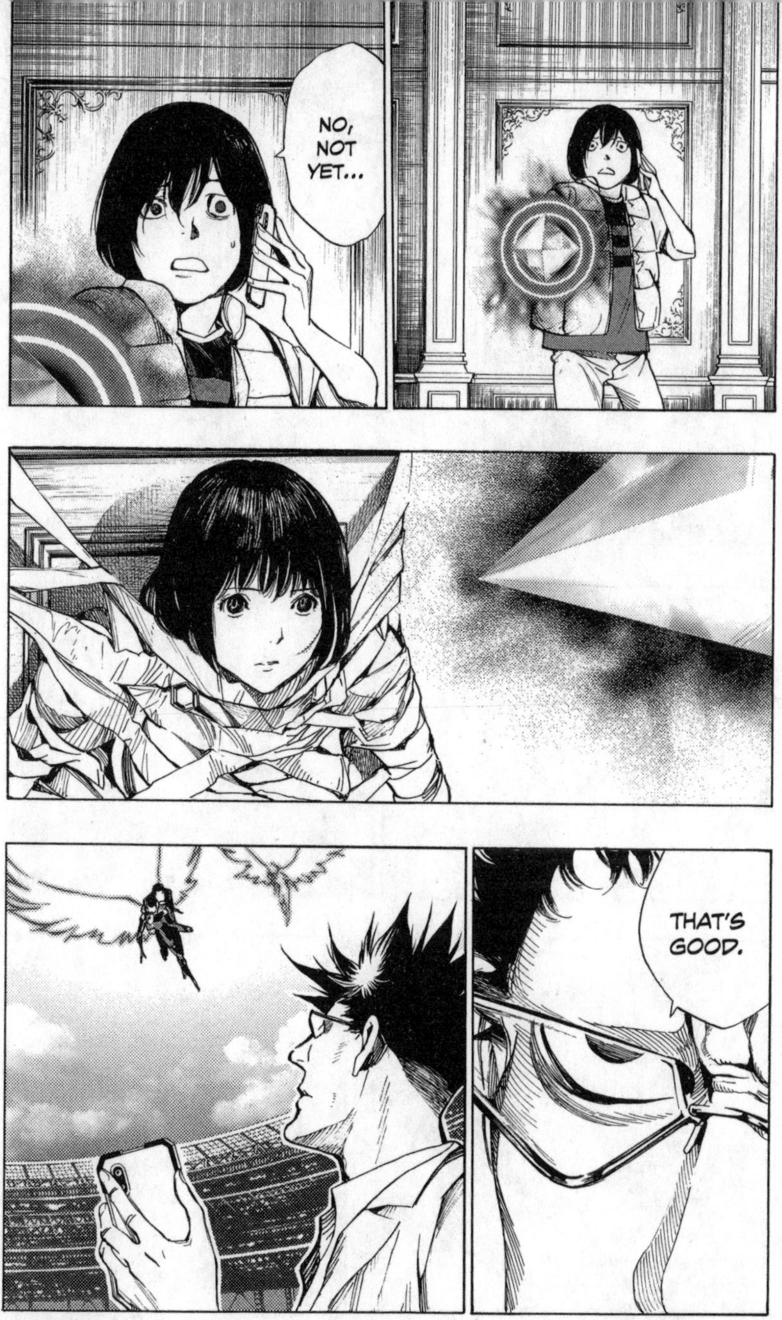
NO, NOT YET...
THAT'S GOOD.

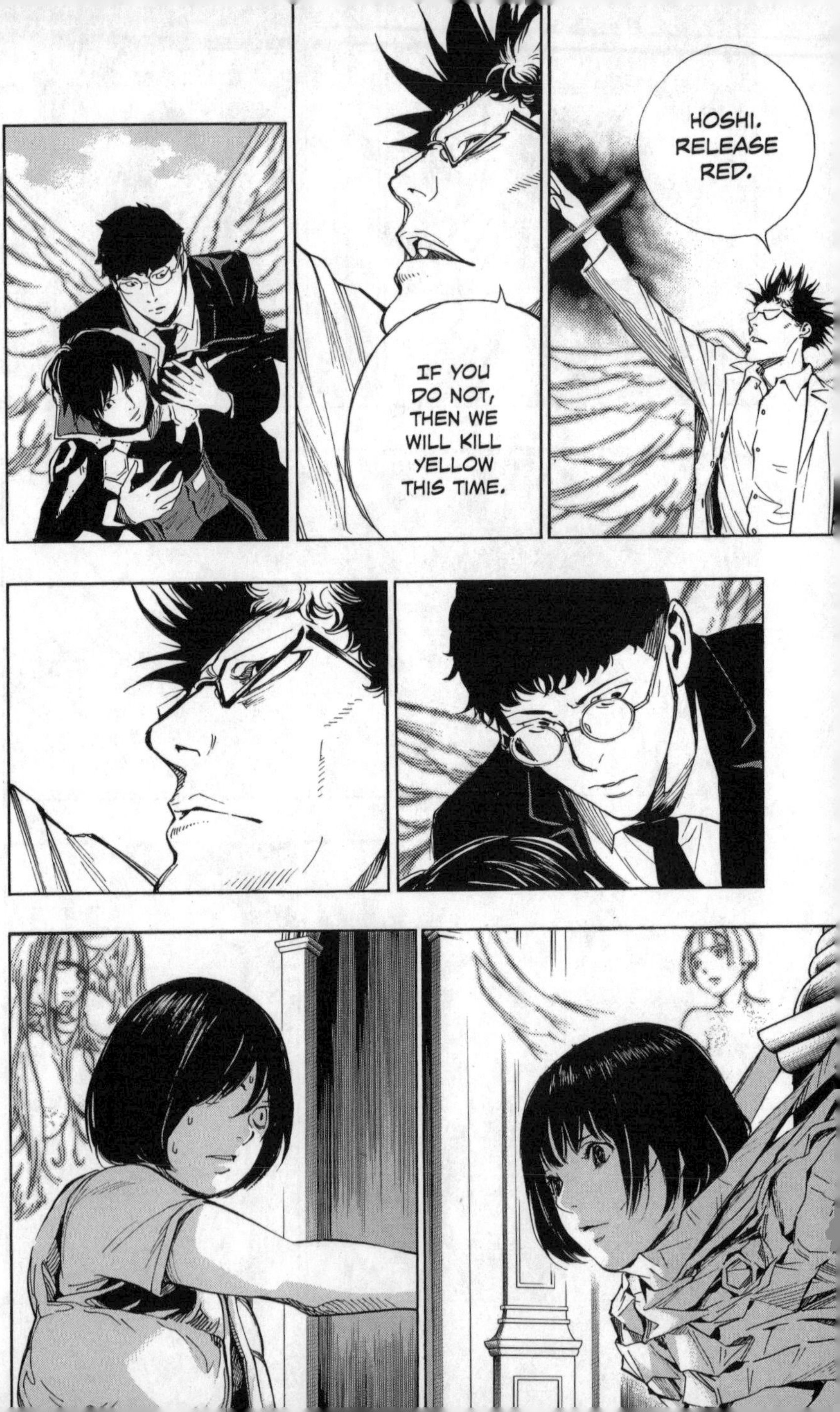
HOSHI. RELEASE RED.
IF YOU DO NOT, THEN WE WILL KILL YELLOW THIS TIME.

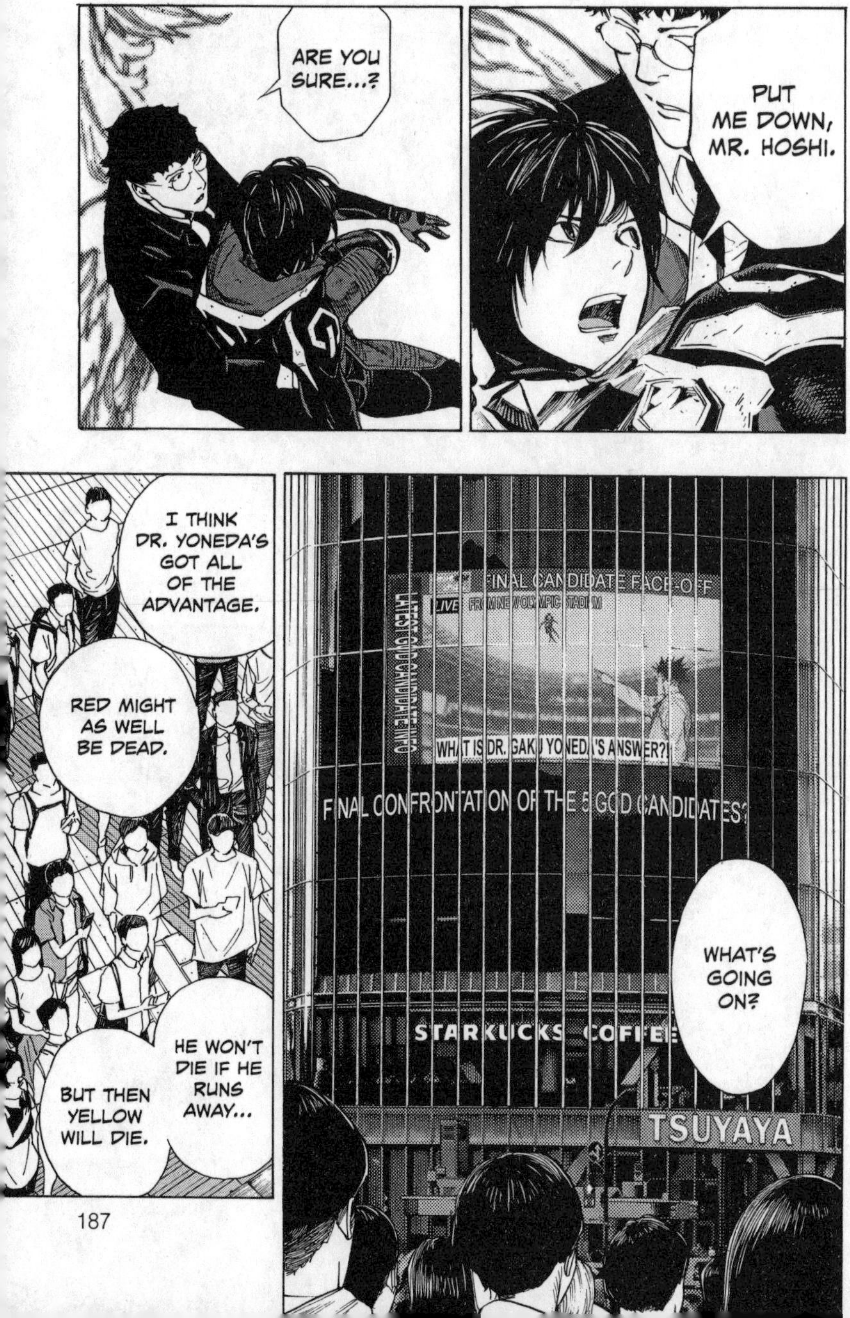
PUT ME DOWN, MR. HOSHI.
ARE YOU SURE...?
FINAL CANDIDATE FACE-OFF
LIVE FROM NEW OLYMPIC STADIUM
WHAT IS DR. GAKU YONEDA'S ANSWER?!
FINAL CONFRONTATION OF THE 5 GOD CANDIDATES?
STARKUCKS COFFEE
TSUYAYA
WHAT'S GOING ON?
I THINK DR. YONEDA'S GOT ALL OF THE ADVANTAGE.
RED MIGHT AS WELL BE DEAD.
HE WON'T DIE IF HE RUNS AWAY...
BUT THEN YELLOW WILL DIE.

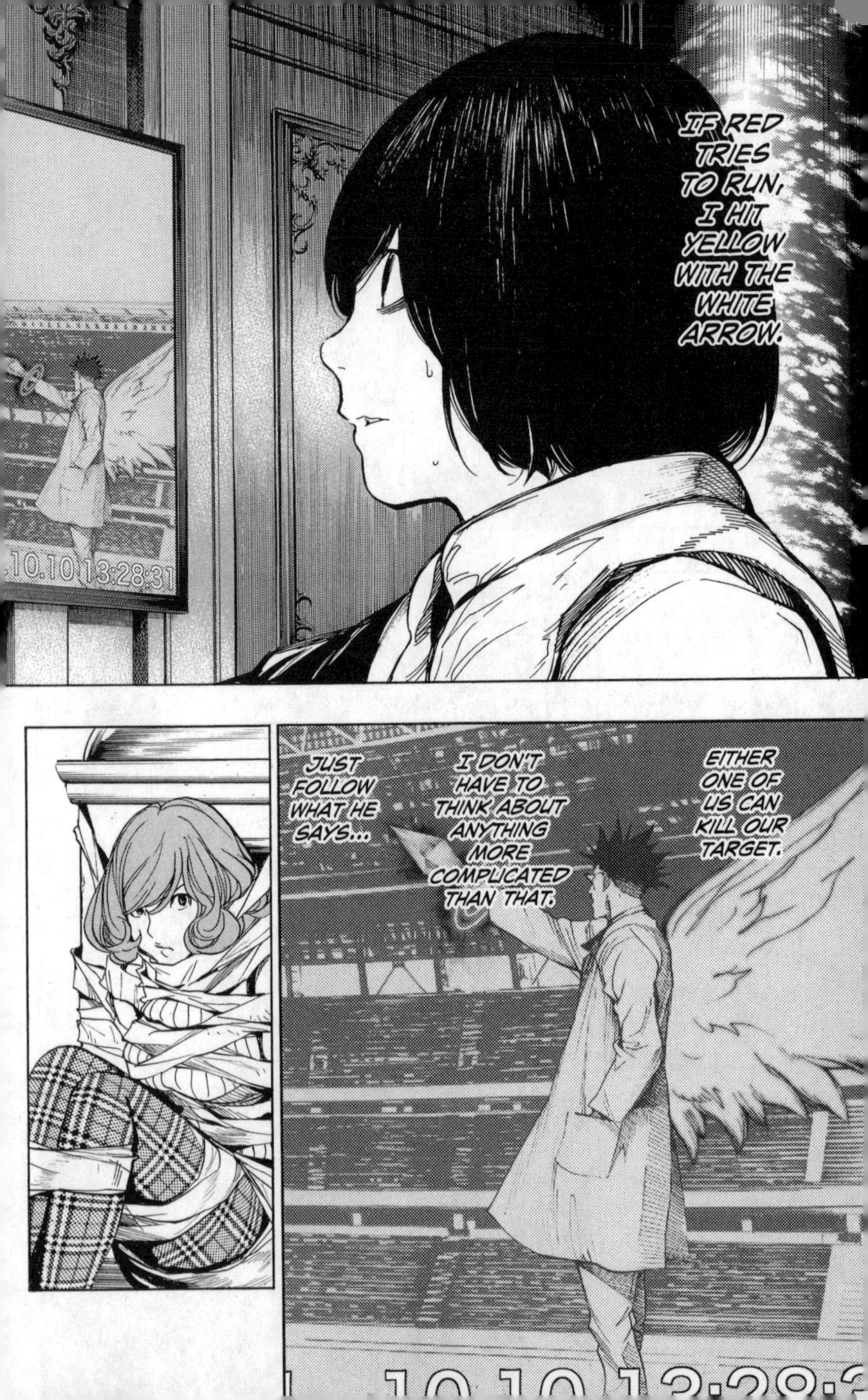
IF RED TRIES TO RUN, I HIT YELLOW WITH THE WHITE ARROW.
.10.10 13:28:31
EITHER ONE OF US CAN KILL OUR TARGET.
I DON'T HAVE TO THINK ABOUT ANYTHING MORE COMPLICATED THAN THAT.
JUST FOLLOW WHAT HE SAYS...

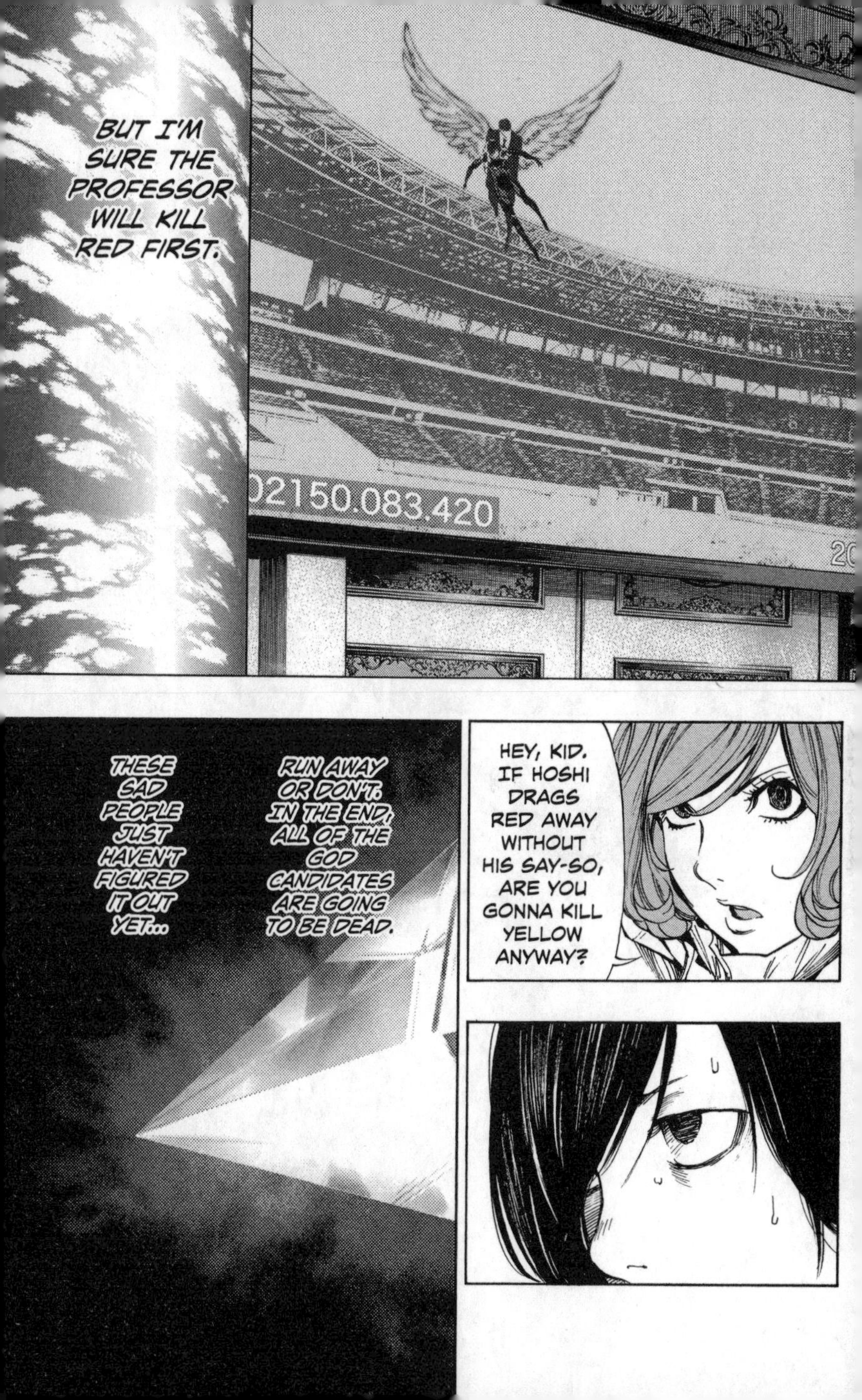
02150.083.420
BUT I'M SURE THE PROFESSOR WILL KILL RED FIRST.
HEY, KID. IF HOSHI DRAGS RED AWAY WITHOUT HIS SAY-SO, ARE YOU GONNA KILL YELLOW ANYWAY?
RUN AWAY OR DON'T. IN THE END, ALL OF THE GOD CANDIDATES ARE GOING TO BE DEAD.
THESE SAD PEOPLE JUST HAVEN'T FIGURED IT OUT YET...

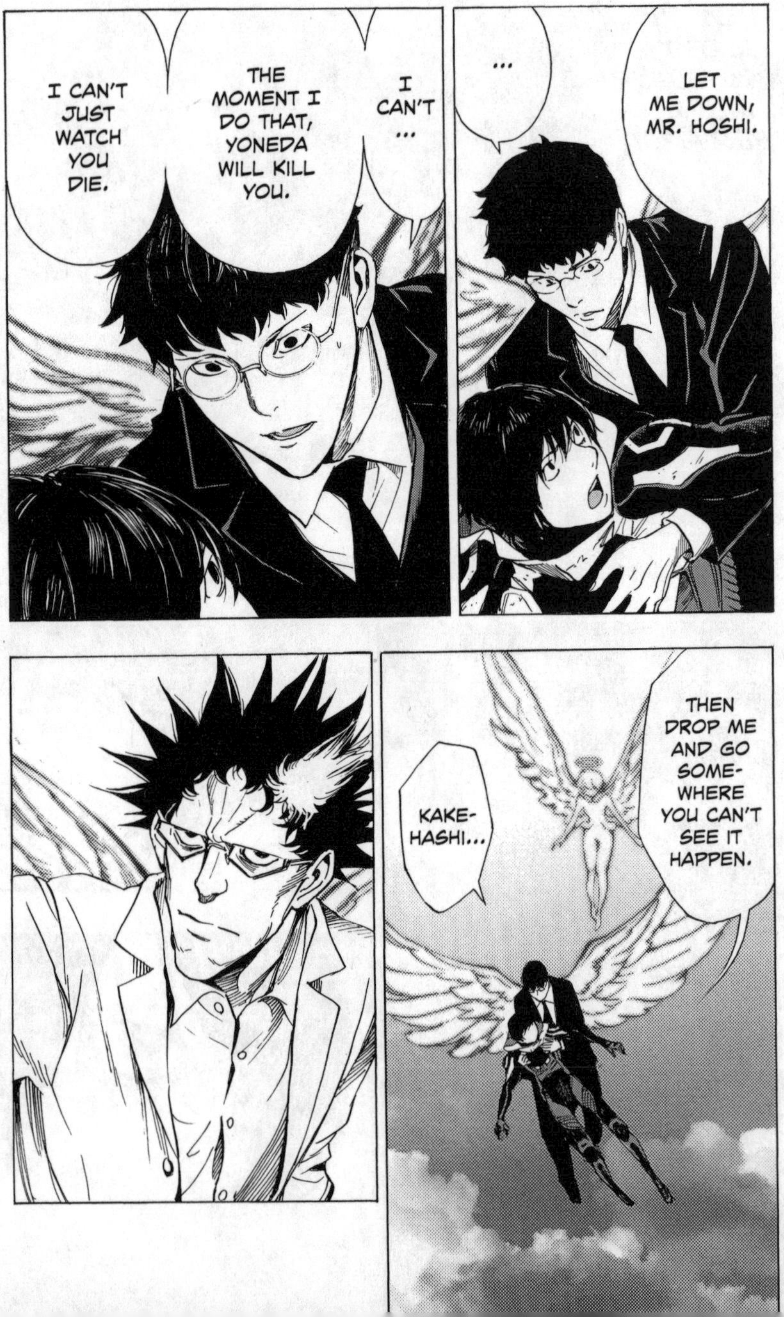
LET ME DOWN, MR. HOSHI.
...
I CAN'T ...
THE MOMENT I DO THAT, YONEDA WILL KILL YOU.
I CAN'T JUST WATCH YOU DIE.
THEN DROP ME AND GO SOME-WHERE YOU CAN'T SEE IT HAPPEN.
KAKE-HASHI...

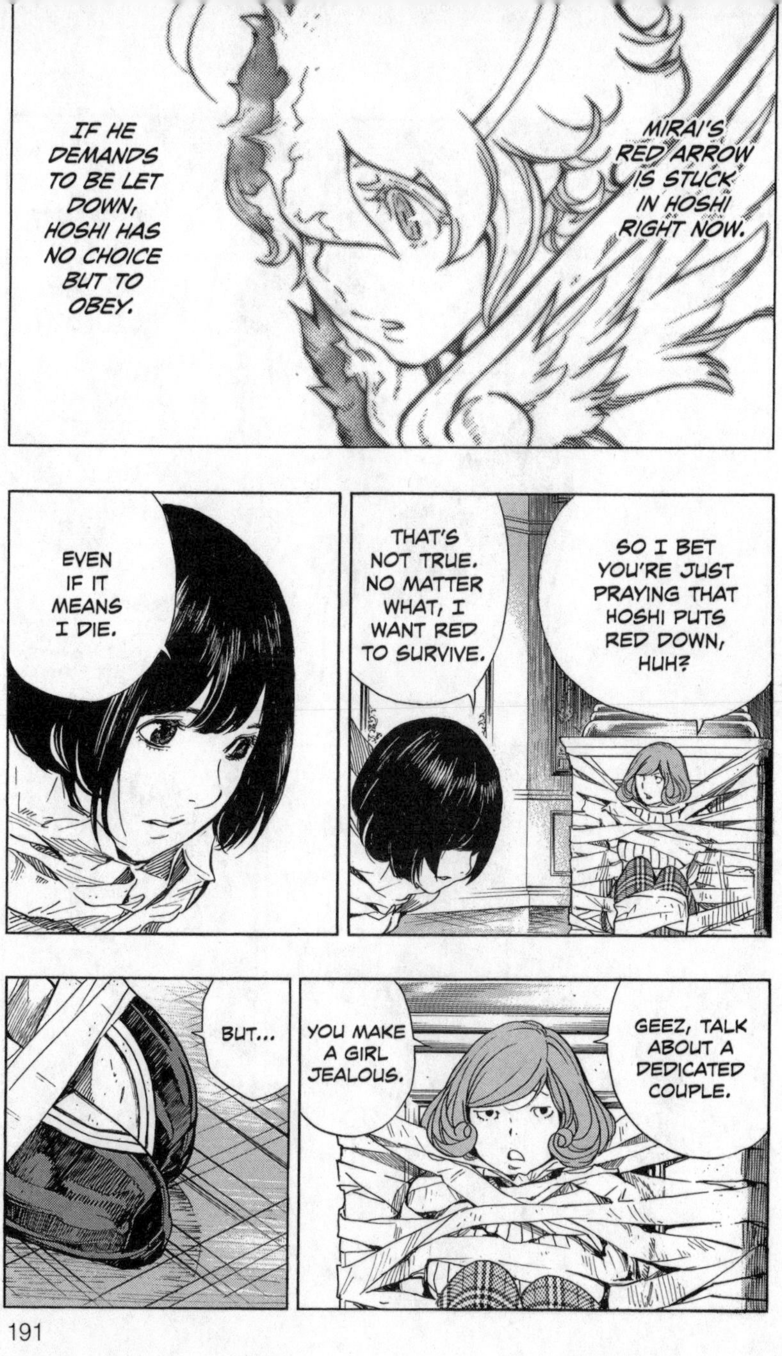
MIRAI'S RED ARROW IS STUCK IN HOSHI RIGHT NOW.
IF HE DEMANDS TO BE LET DOWN, HOSHI HAS NO CHOICE BUT TO OBEY.
SO I BET YOU'RE JUST PRAYING THAT HOSHI PUTS RED DOWN, HUH?
THAT'S NOT TRUE. NO MATTER WHAT, I WANT RED TO SURVIVE.
EVEN IF IT MEANS I DIE.
GEEZ, TALK ABOUT A DEDICATED COUPLE.
YOU MAKE A GIRL JEALOUS.
BUT...

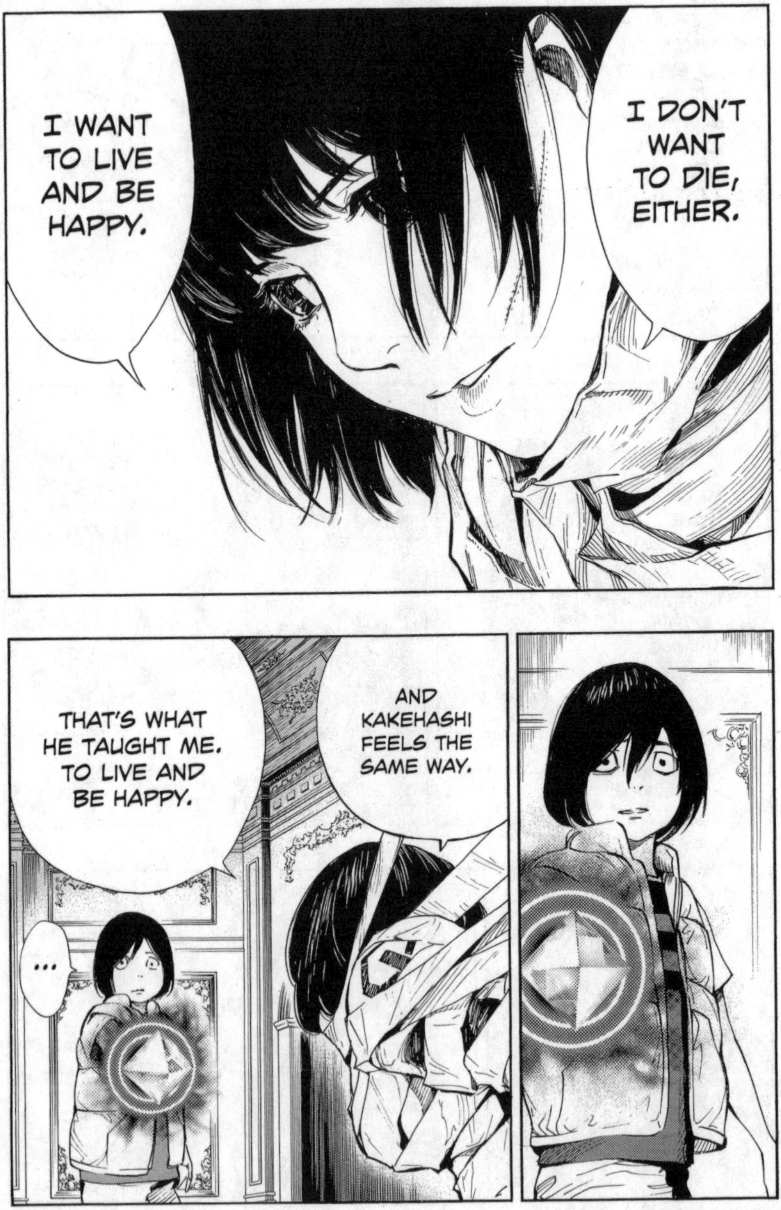
I DON'T WANT TO DIE, EITHER.
I WANT TO LIVE AND BE HAPPY.
AND KAKEHASHI FEELS THE SAME WAY.
THAT'S WHAT HE TAUGHT ME. TO LIVE AND BE HAPPY.
...

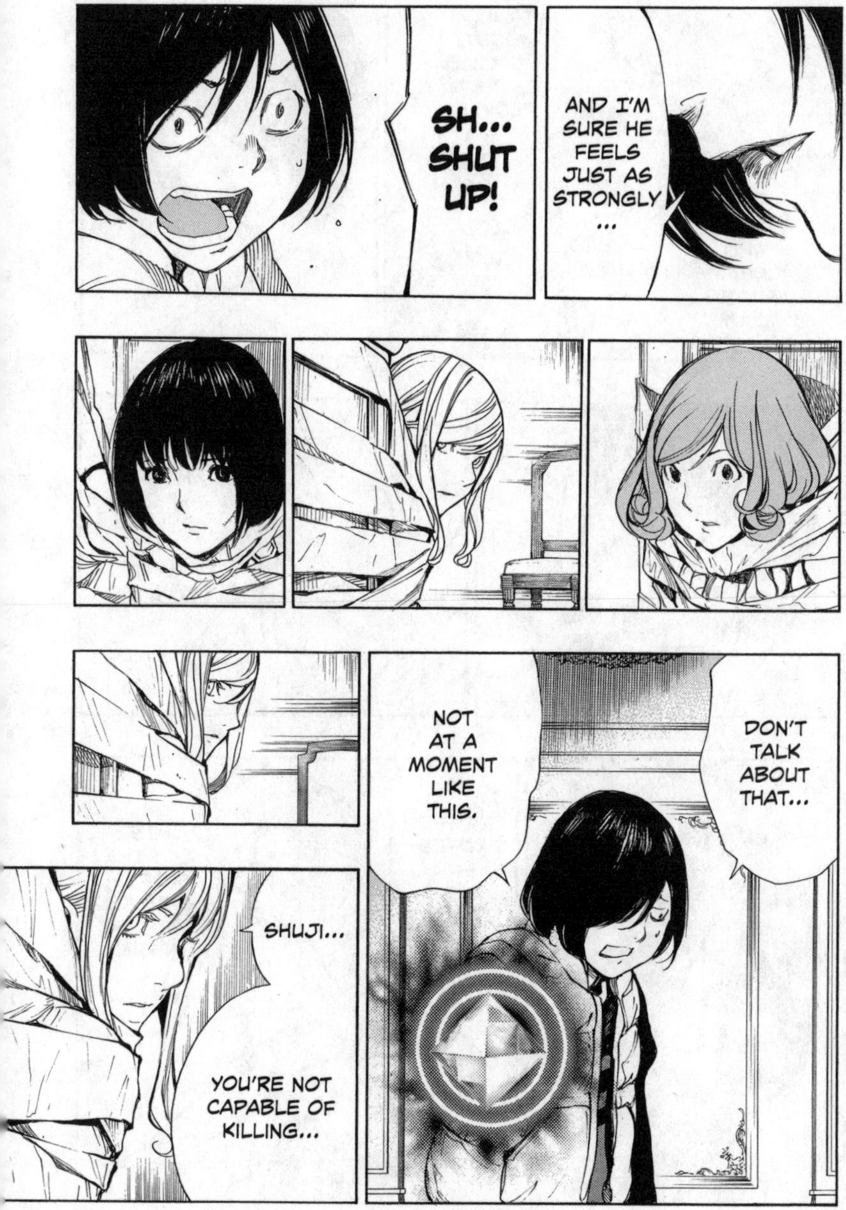
AND I'M SURE HE FEELS JUST AS STRONGLY ...
SH... SHUT UP!
DON'T TALK ABOUT THAT...
NOT AT A MOMENT LIKE THIS.
SHUJI...
YOU'RE NOT CAPABLE OF KILLING...

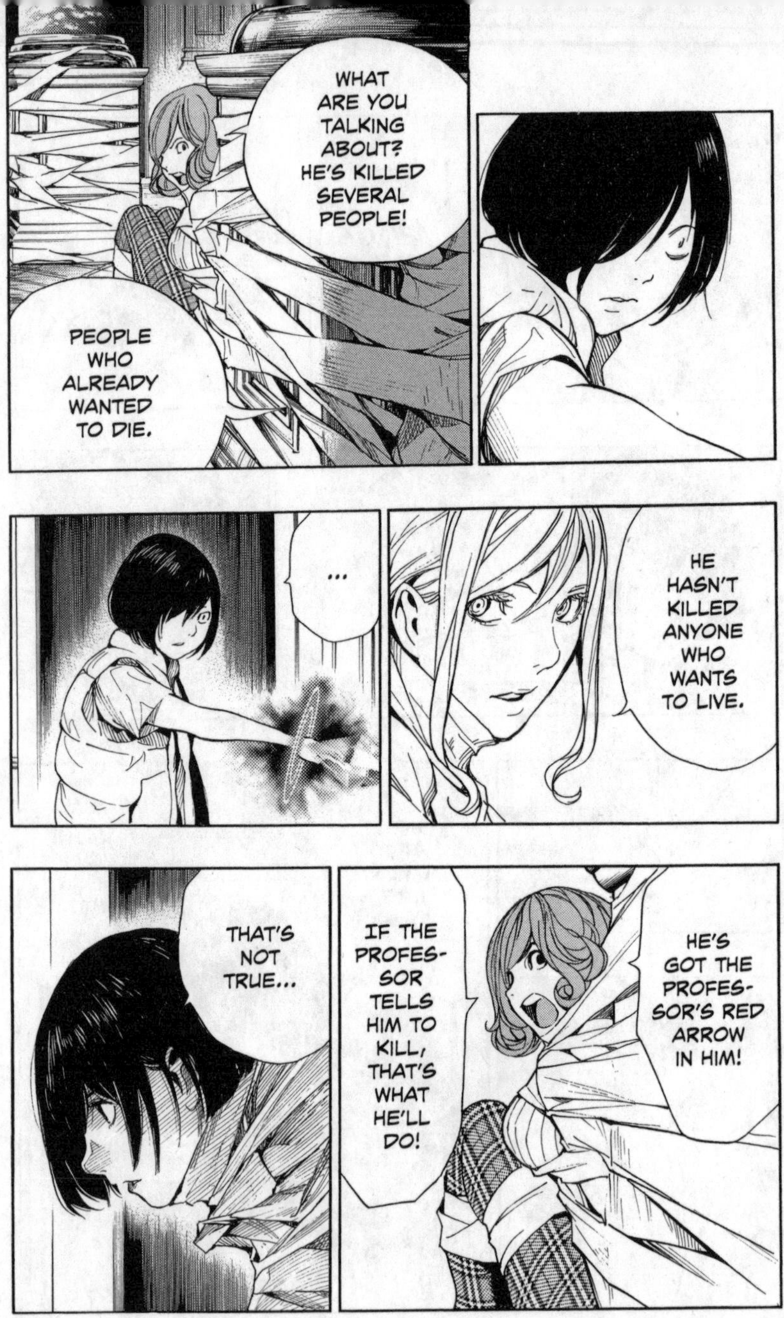
WHAT ARE YOU TALKING ABOUT? HE'S KILLED SEVERAL PEOPLE!
PEOPLE WHO ALREADY WANTED TO DIE.
HE HASN'T KILLED ANYONE WHO WANTS TO LIVE.
...
HE'S GOT THE PROFES-SOR'S RED ARROW IN HIM!
IF THE PROFES-SOR TELLS HIM TO KILL, THAT'S WHAT HE'LL DO!
THAT'S NOT TRUE...

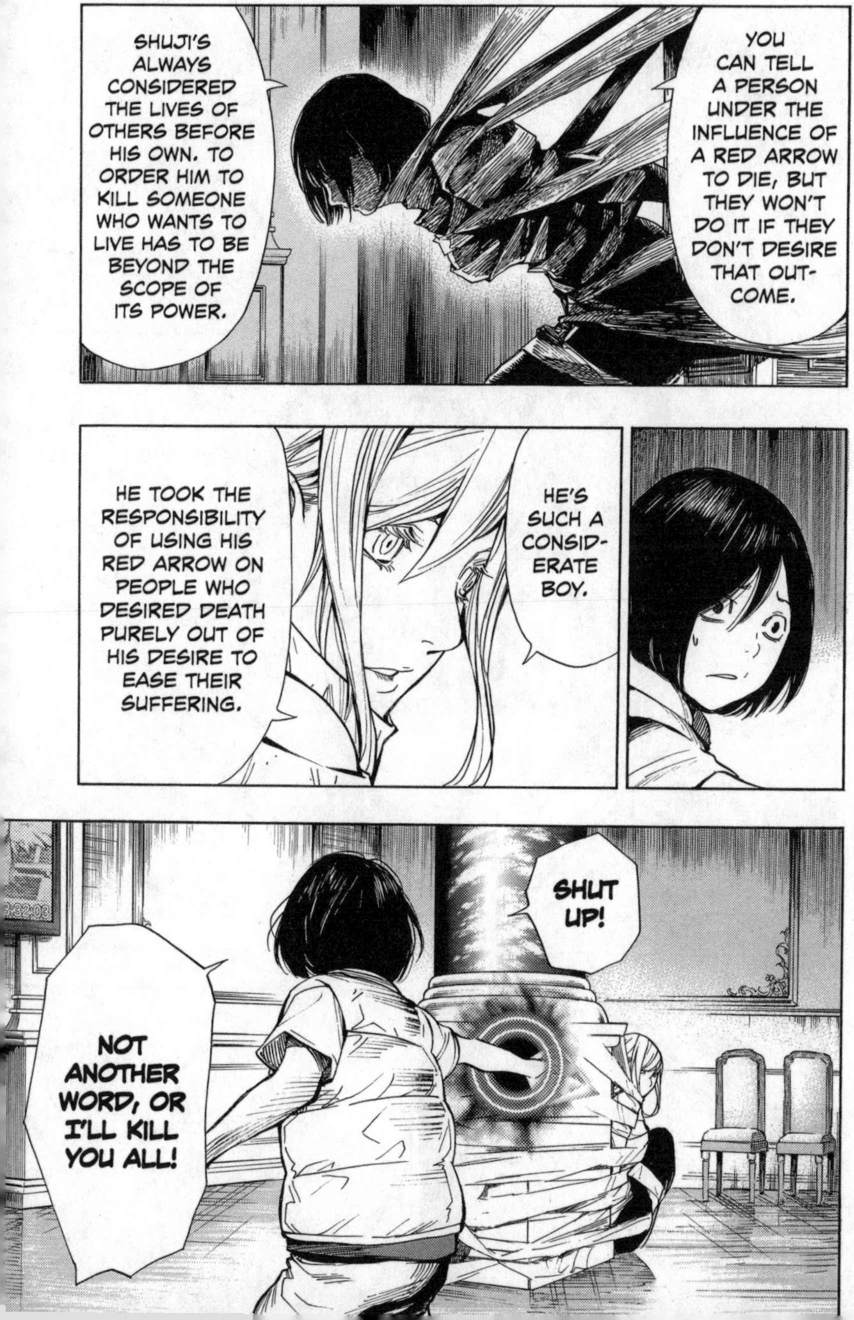
YOU CAN TELL A PERSON UNDER THE INFLUENCE OF A RED ARROW TO DIE, BUT THEY WON'T DO IT IF THEY DON'T DESIRE THAT OUT-COME.
SHUJI'S ALWAYS CONSIDERED THE LIVES OF OTHERS BEFORE HIS OWN. TO ORDER HIM TO KILL SOMEONE WHO WANTS TO LIVE HAS TO BE BEYOND THE SCOPE OF ITS POWER.
HE'S SUCH A CONSID-ERATE BOY.
HE TOOK THE RESPONSIBILITY OF USING HIS RED ARROW ON PEOPLE WHO DESIRED DEATH PURELY OUT OF HIS DESIRE TO EASE THEIR SUFFERING.
SHUT UP!
NOT ANOTHER WORD, OR I'LL KILL YOU ALL!

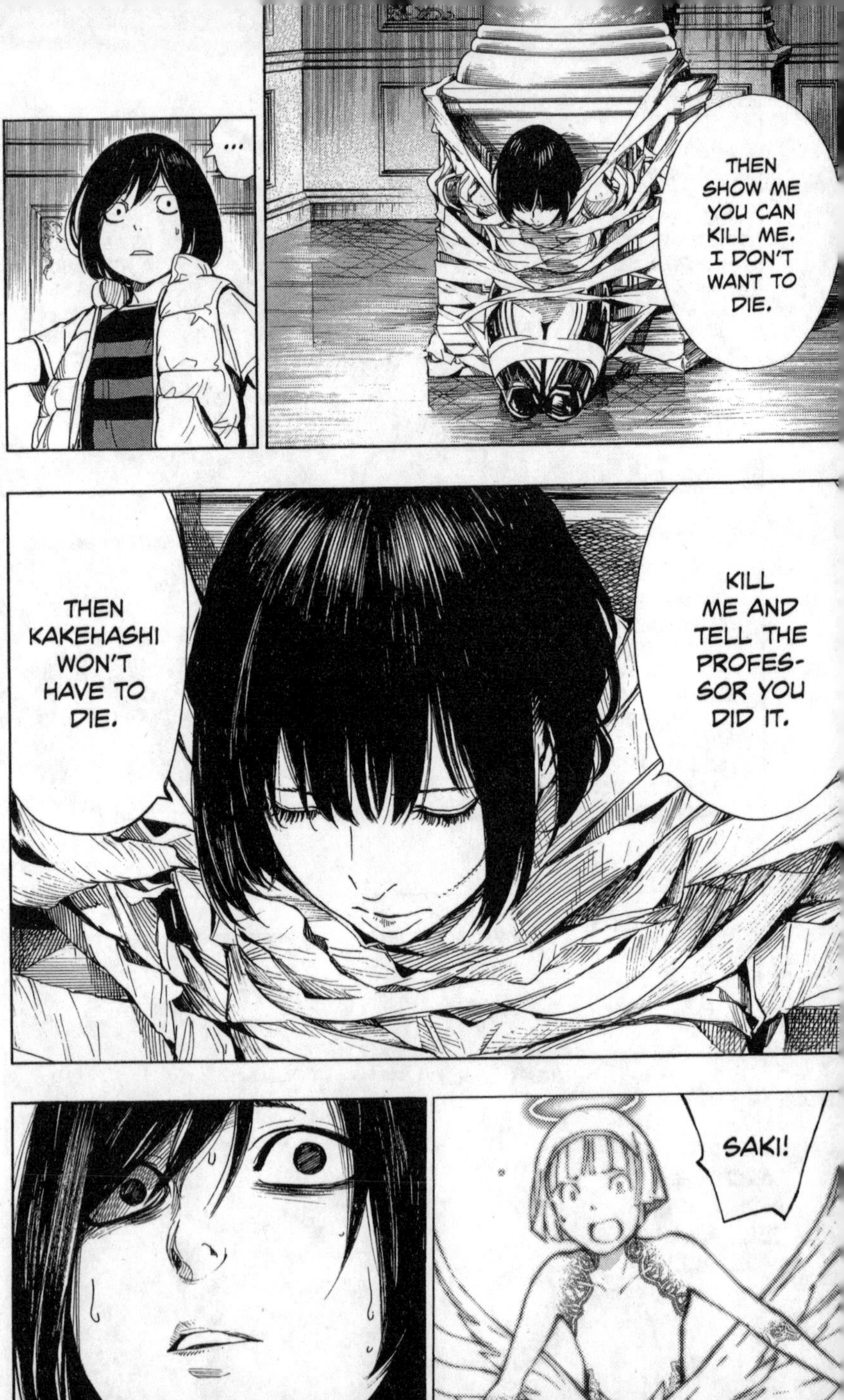
THEN SHOW ME YOU CAN KILL ME. I DON'T WANT TO DIE.
...
KILL ME AND TELL THE PROFES-SOR YOU DID IT.
THEN KAKEHASHI WON'T HAVE TO DIE.
SAKI!

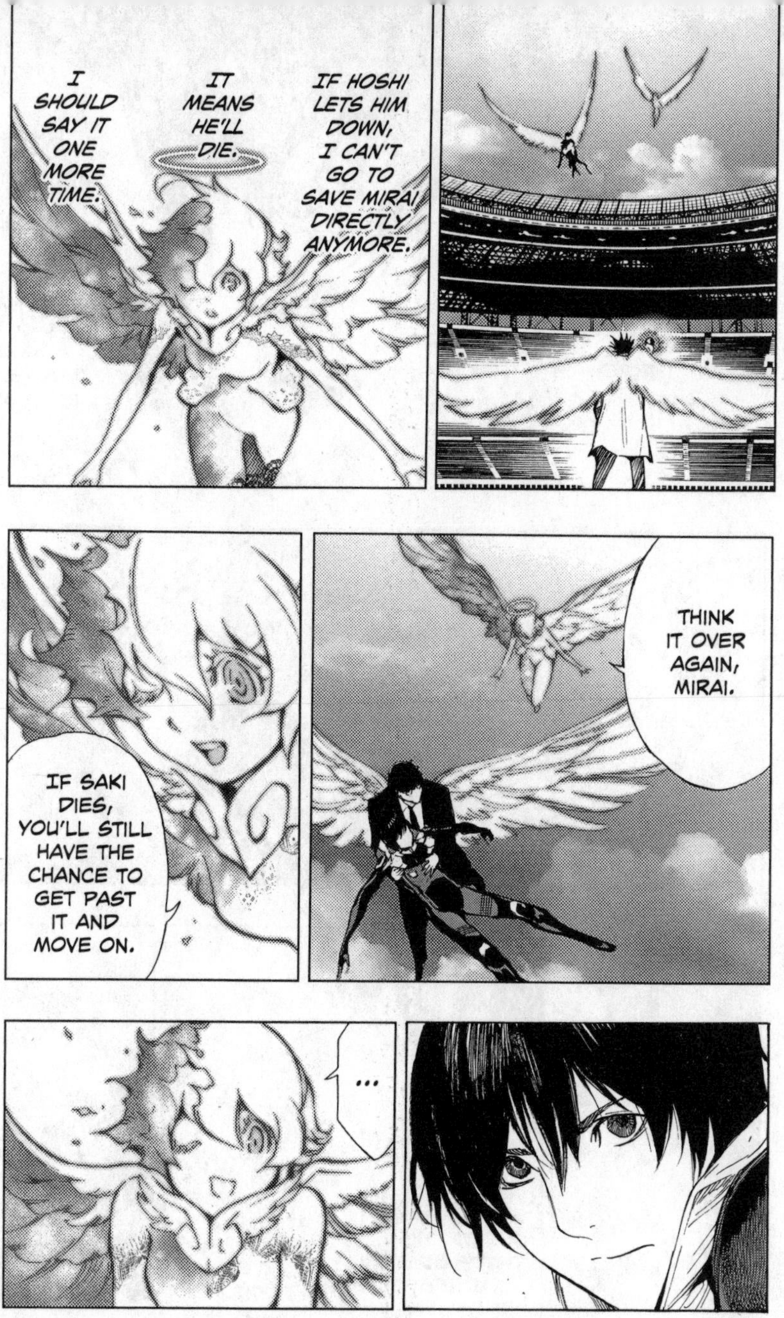
IF HOSHI LETS HIM DOWN, I CAN'T GO TO SAVE MIRAI DIRECTLY ANYMORE.
IT MEANS HE'LL DIE.
I SHOULD SAY IT ONE MORE TIME.
THINK IT OVER AGAIN, MIRAI.
IF SAKI DIES, YOU'LL STILL HAVE THE CHANCE TO GET PAST IT AND MOVE ON.
...

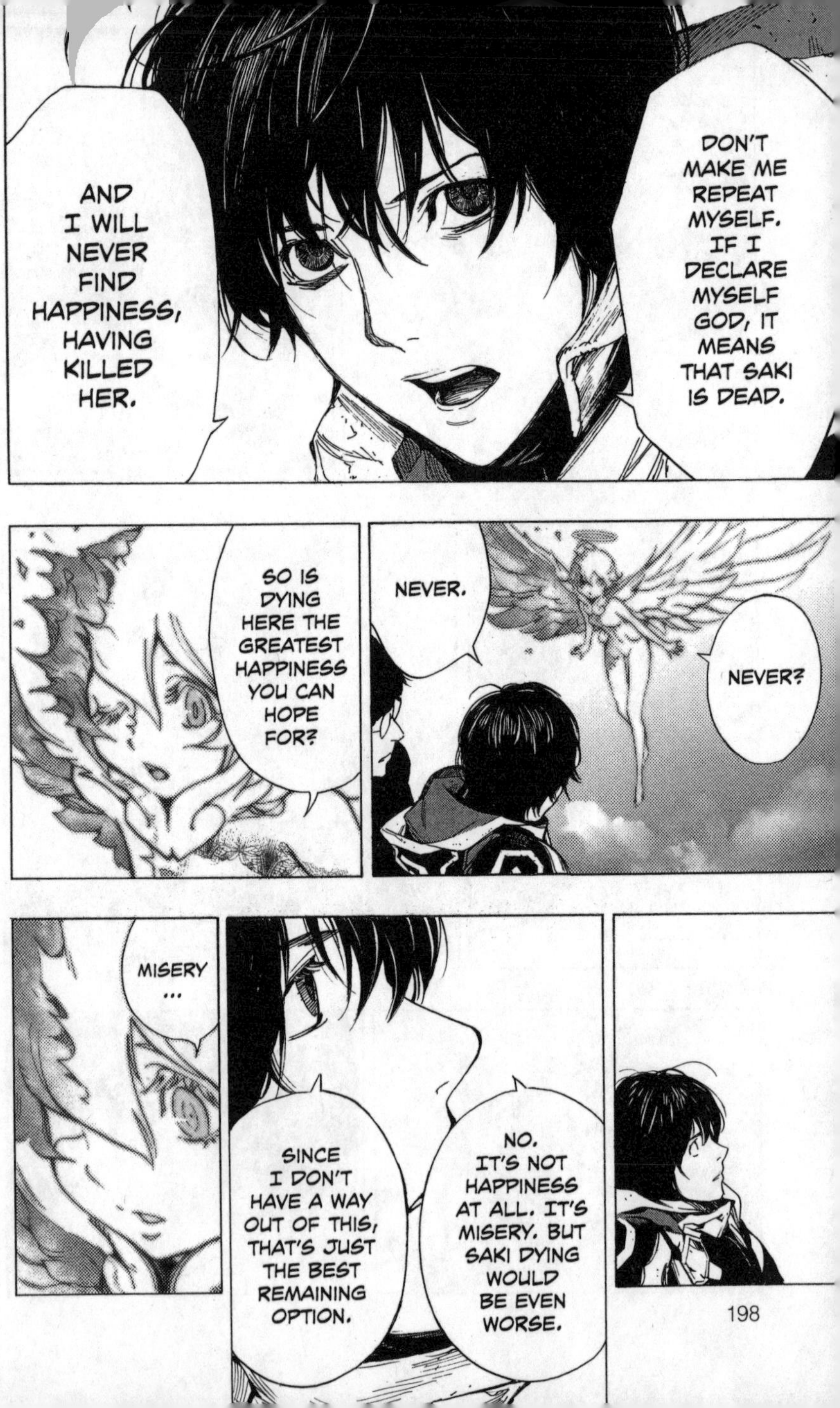

DON'T MAKE ME REPEAT MYSELF. IF I DECLARE MYSELF GOD, IT MEANS THAT SAKI IS DEAD.
AND I WILL NEVER FIND HAPPINESS, HAVING KILLED HER.
NEVER.
NEVER?
SO IS DYING HERE THE GREATEST HAPPINESS YOU CAN HOPE FOR?
NO. IT'S NOT HAPPINESS AT ALL. IT'S MISERY. BUT SAKI DYING WOULD BE EVEN WORSE.
SINCE I DON'T HAVE A WAY OUT OF THIS, THAT'S JUST THE BEST REMAINING OPTION.
MISERY ...

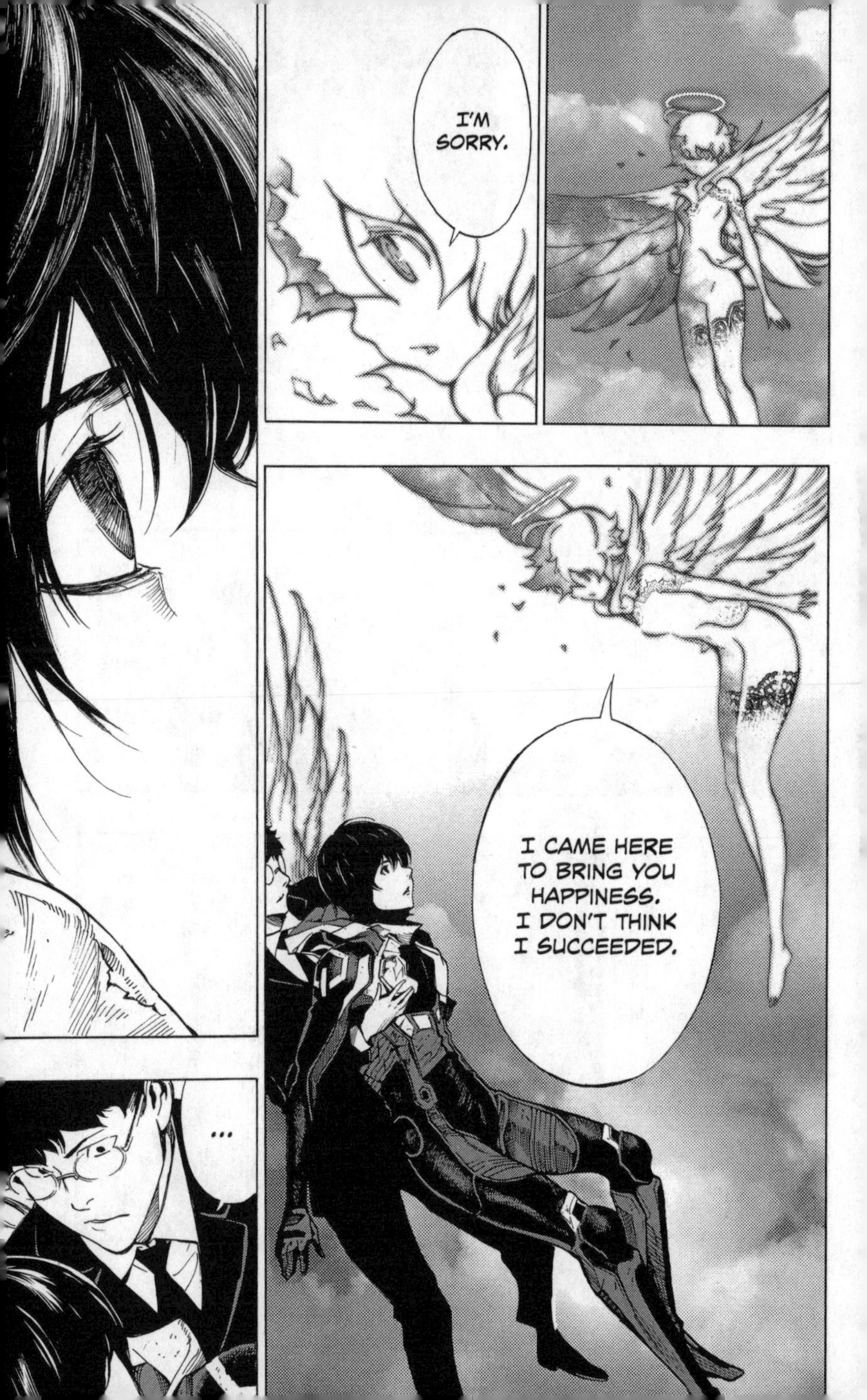
I'M SORRY.
I CAME HERE TO BRING YOU HAPPINESS. I DON'T THINK I SUCCEEDED.
...

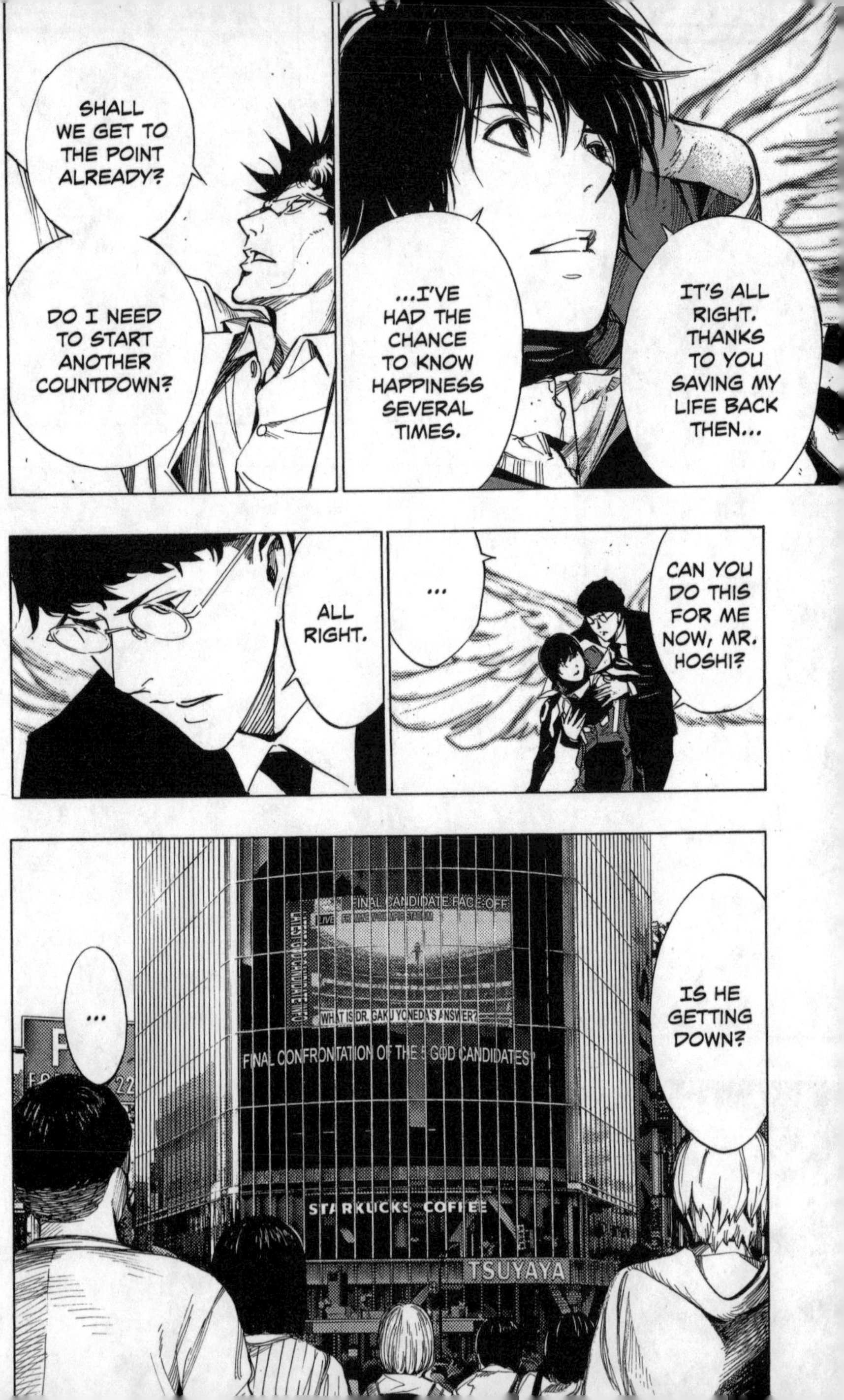
IT'S ALL RIGHT. THANKS TO YOU SAVING MY LIFE BACK THEN...
...I'VE HAD THE CHANCE TO KNOW HAPPINESS SEVERAL TIMES.
SHALL WE GET TO THE POINT ALREADY?
DO I NEED TO START ANOTHER COUNTDOWN?
CAN YOU DO THIS FOR ME NOW, MR. HOSHI?
...
ALL RIGHT.
IS HE GETTING DOWN?
...
FINAL CANDIDATE FACE-OFF
LIVE
WHAT IS DR. GAKU YONEDA'S ANSWER?
FINAL CONFRONTATION OF THE 5 GOD CANDIDATES
STARKUCKS COFFEE
TSUYAYA

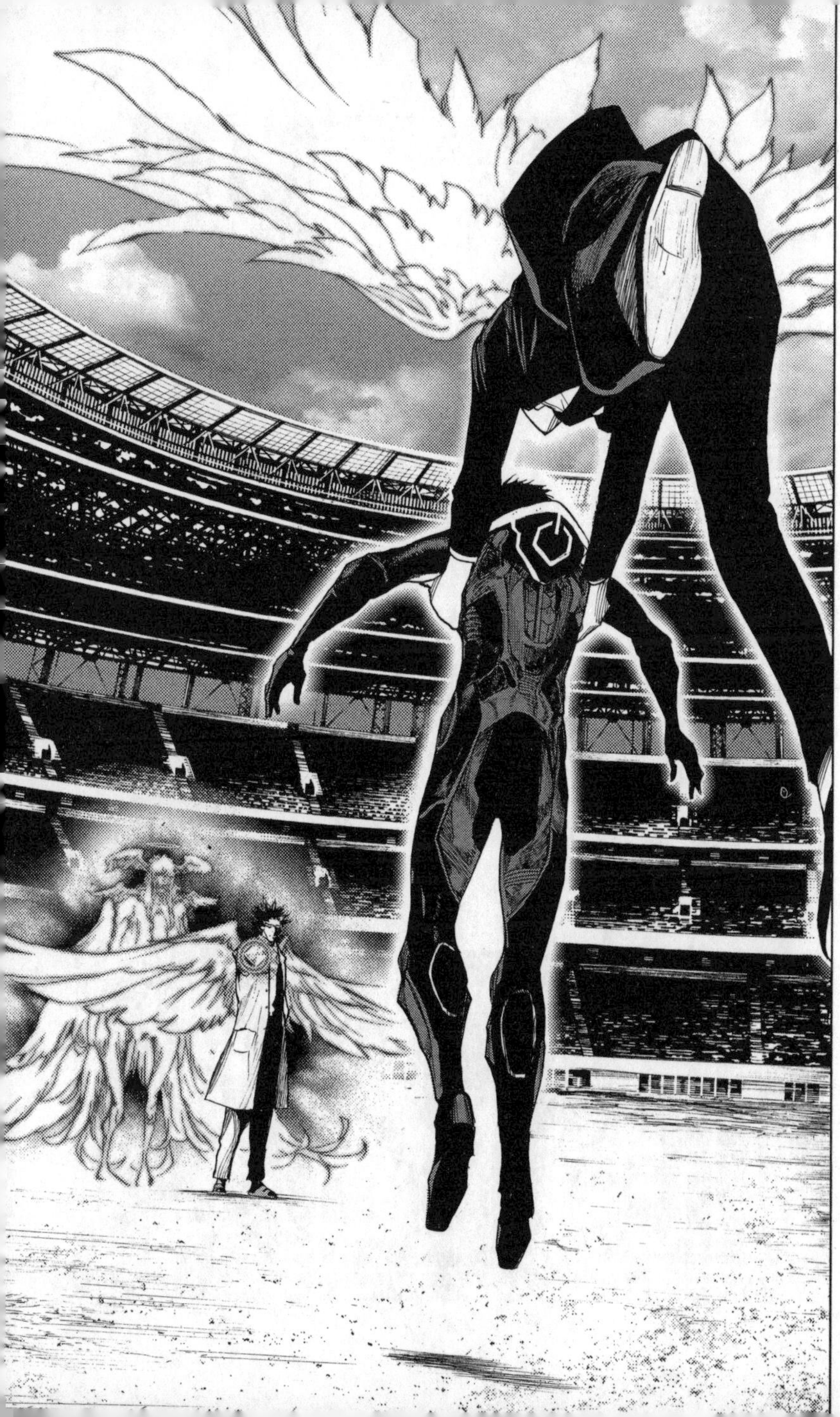

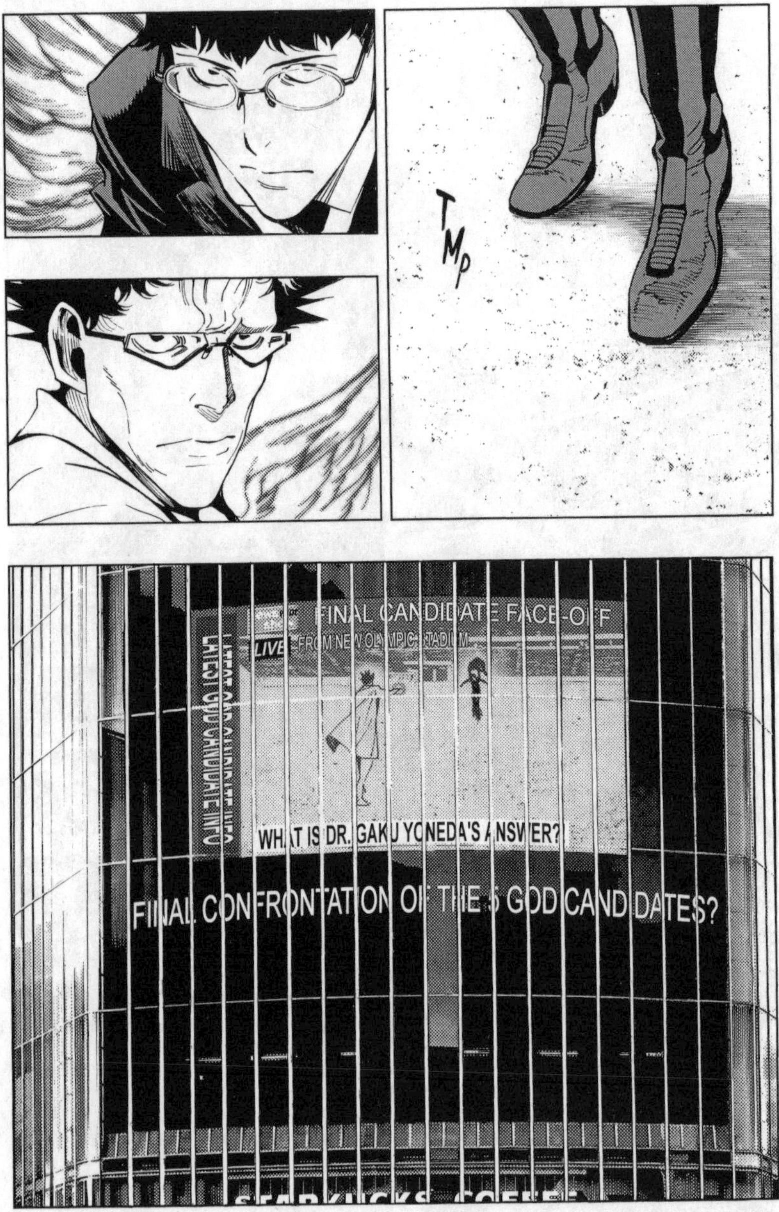
TMP
FINAL CANDIDATE FACE-OFF
LIVE
FROM NEW OLYMPIC STADIUM
LATEST GOD CANDIDATE INFO
WHAT IS DR. GAKU YONEDA'S ANSWER?!
FINAL CONFRONTATION OF THE 5 GOD CANDIDATES?

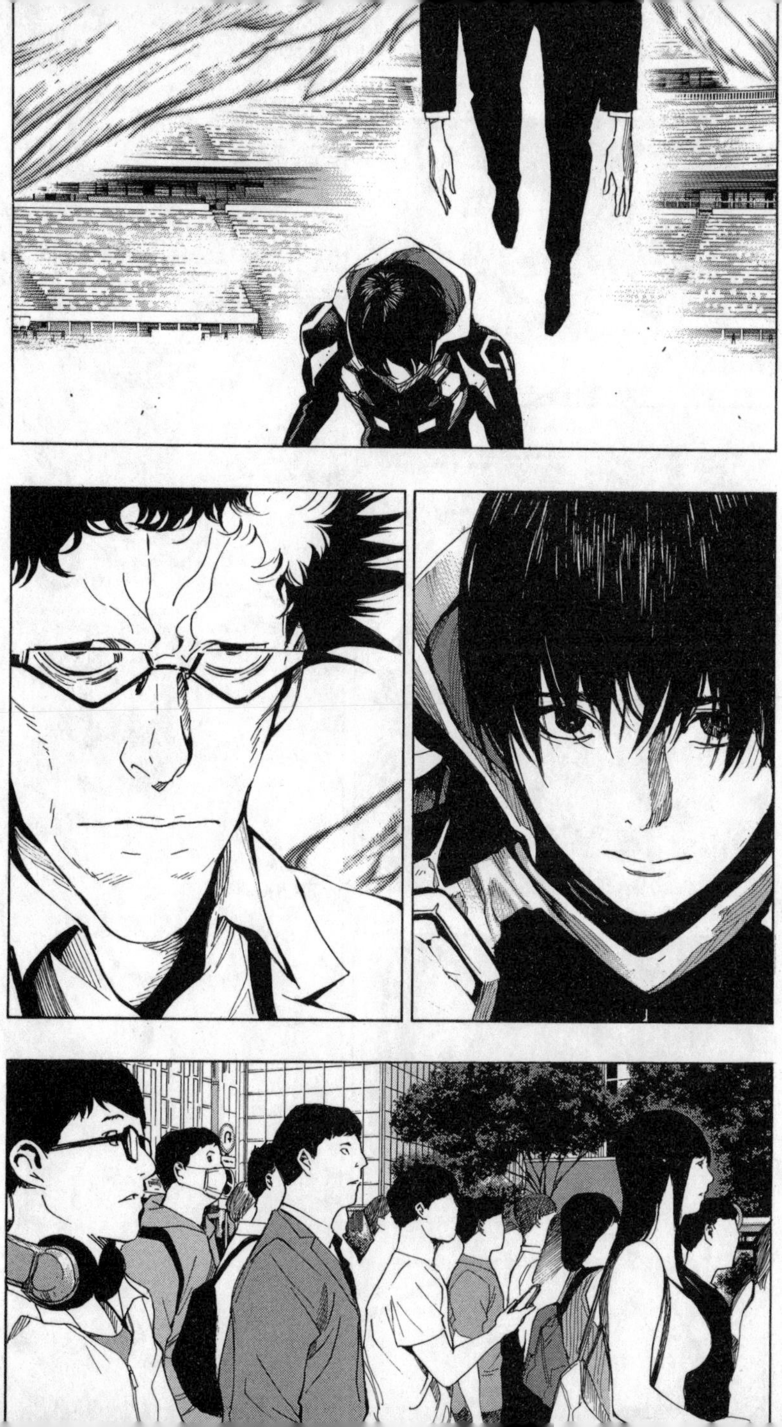

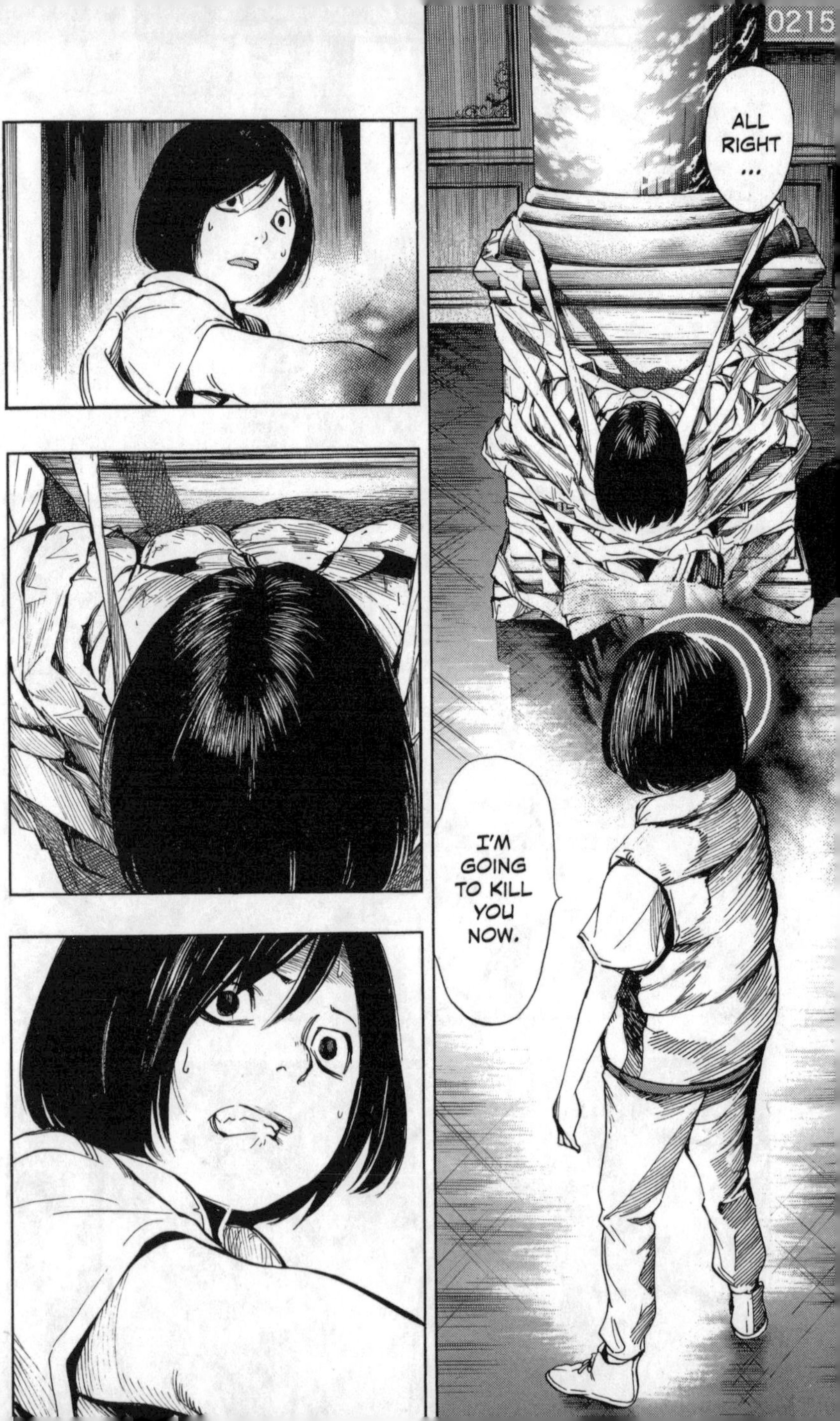
ALL RIGHT ...
I'M GOING TO KILL YOU NOW.

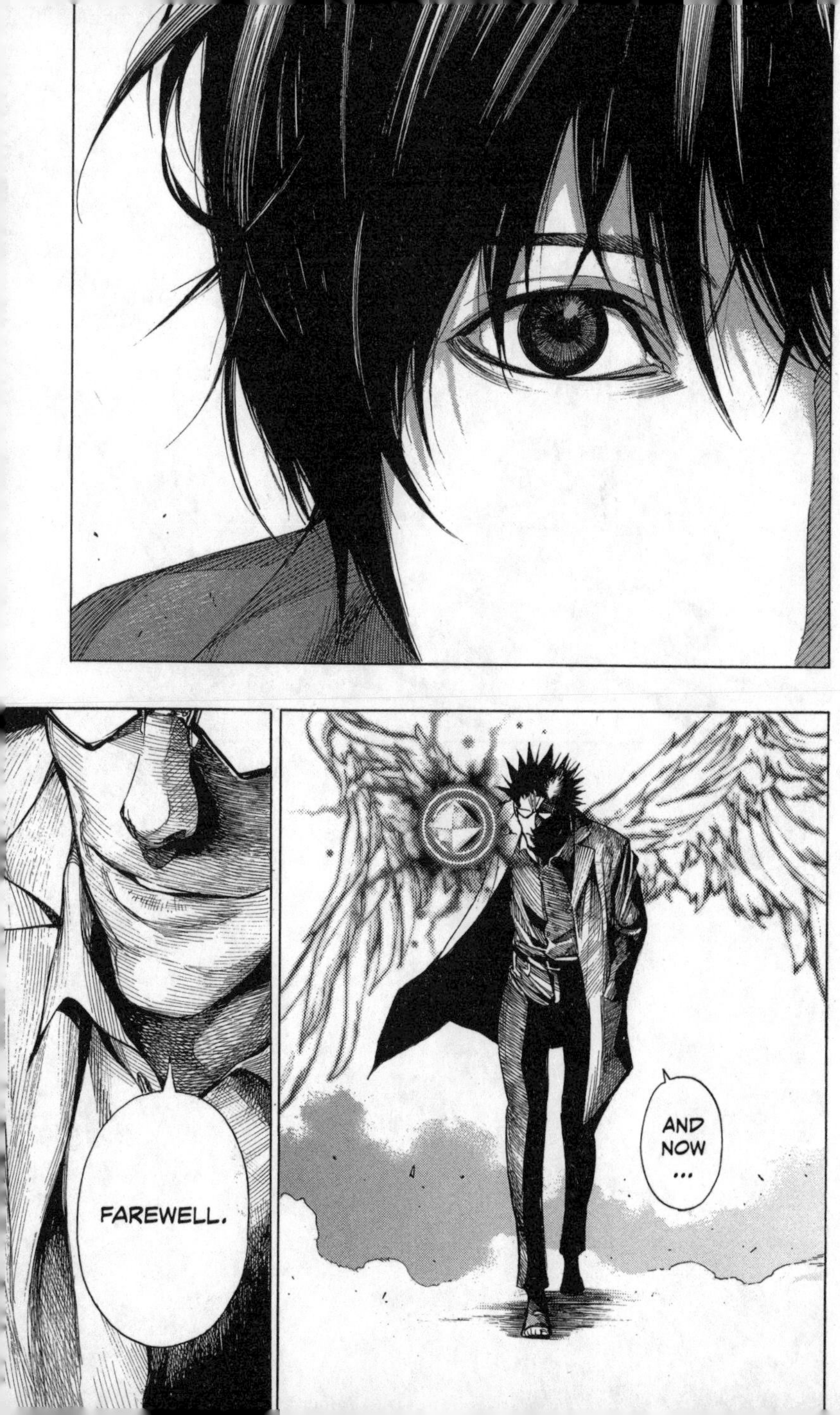
AND NOW ...
FAREWELL.

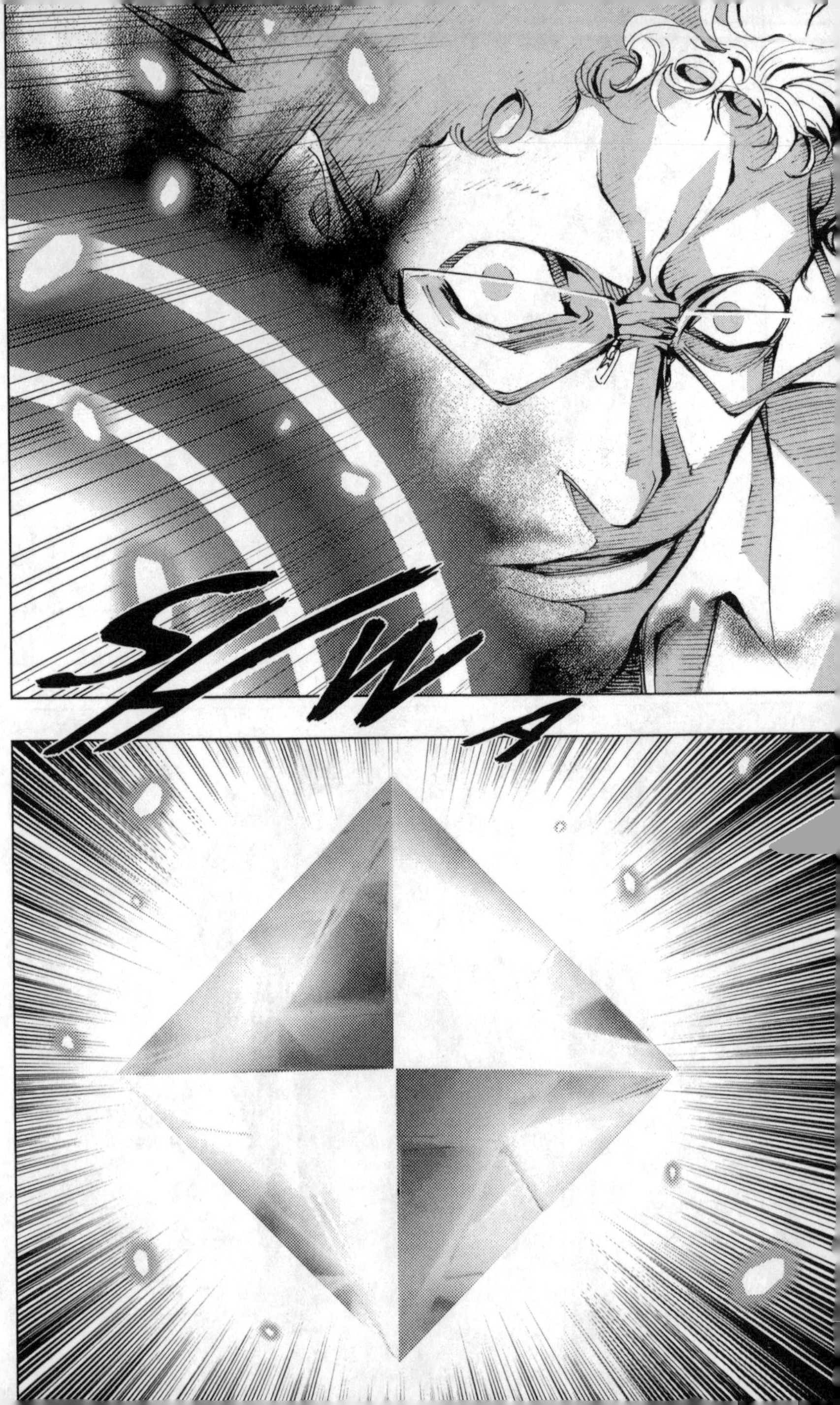
SHWA

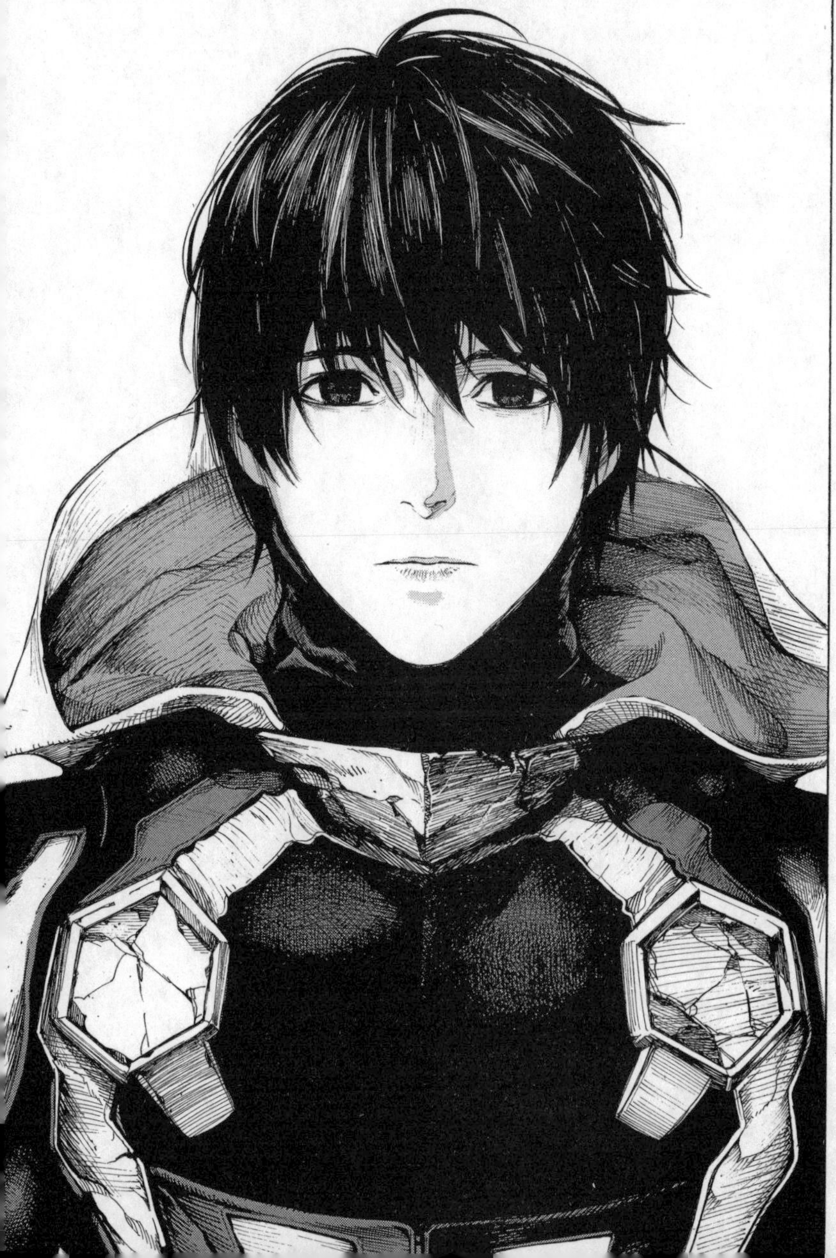

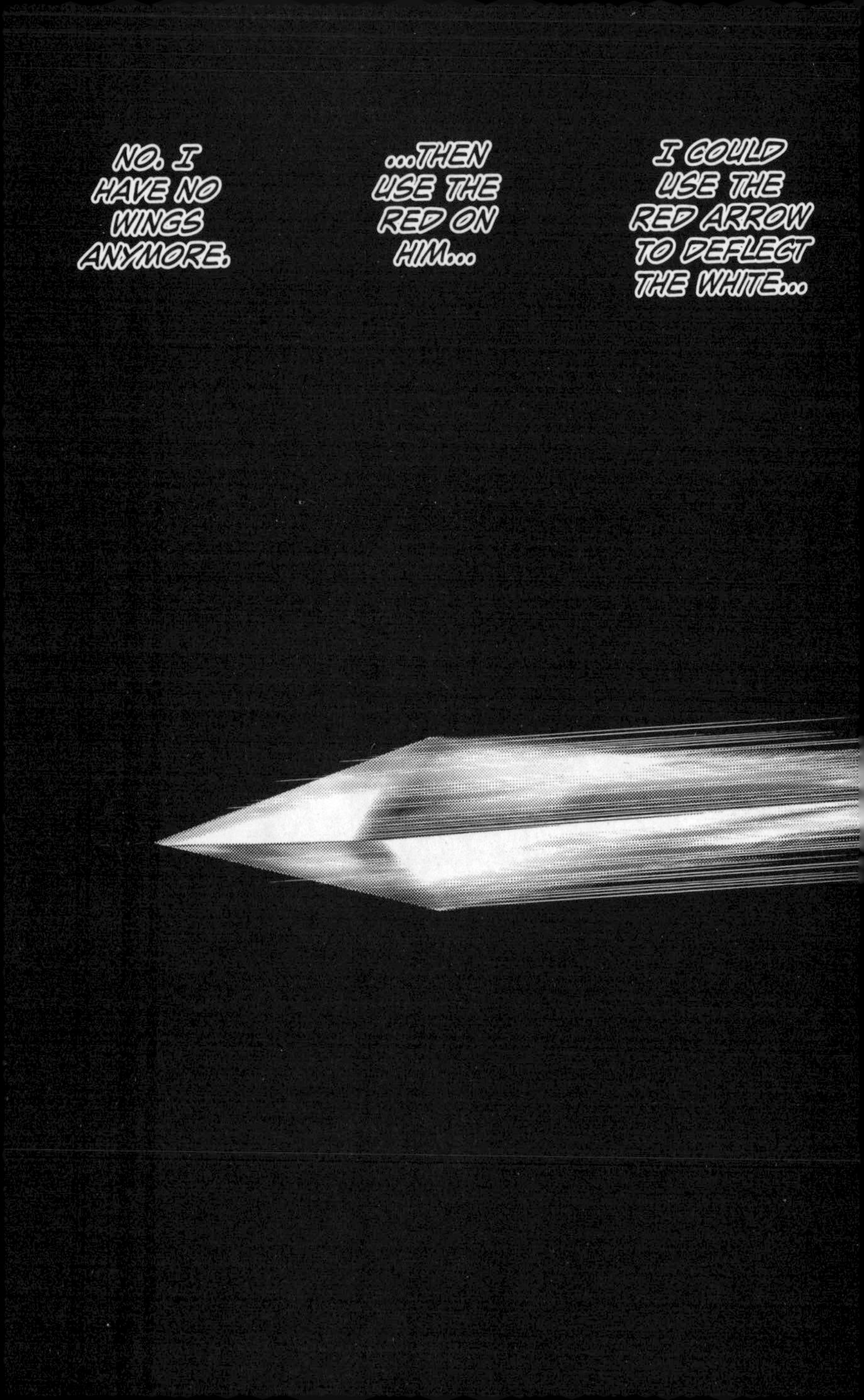
I COULD USE THE RED ARROW TO DEFLECT THE WHITE...
...THEN USE THE RED ON HIM...
NO. I HAVE NO WINGS ANYMORE.

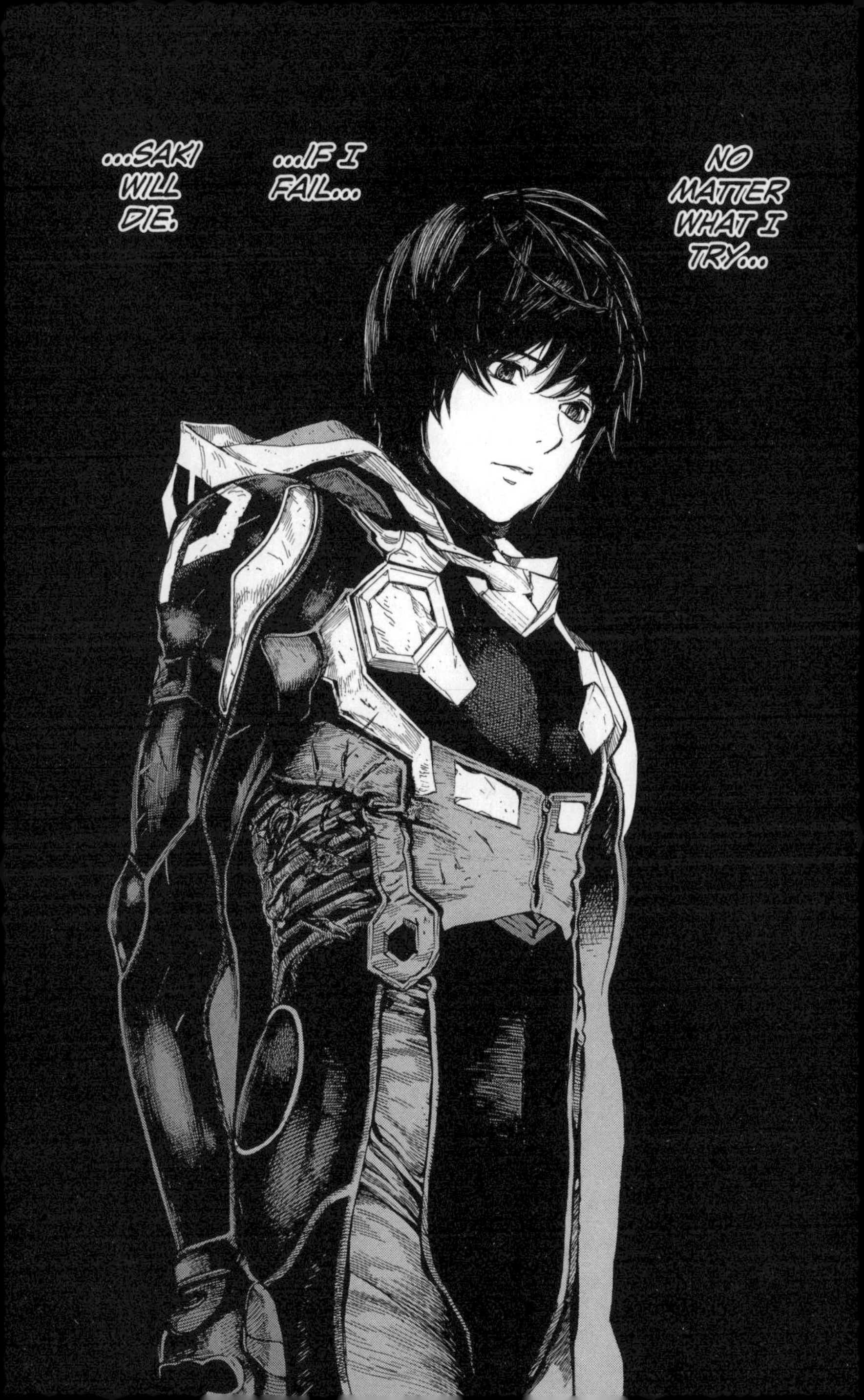
NO MATTER WHAT I TRY...
...IF I FAIL...
...SAKI WILL DIE.

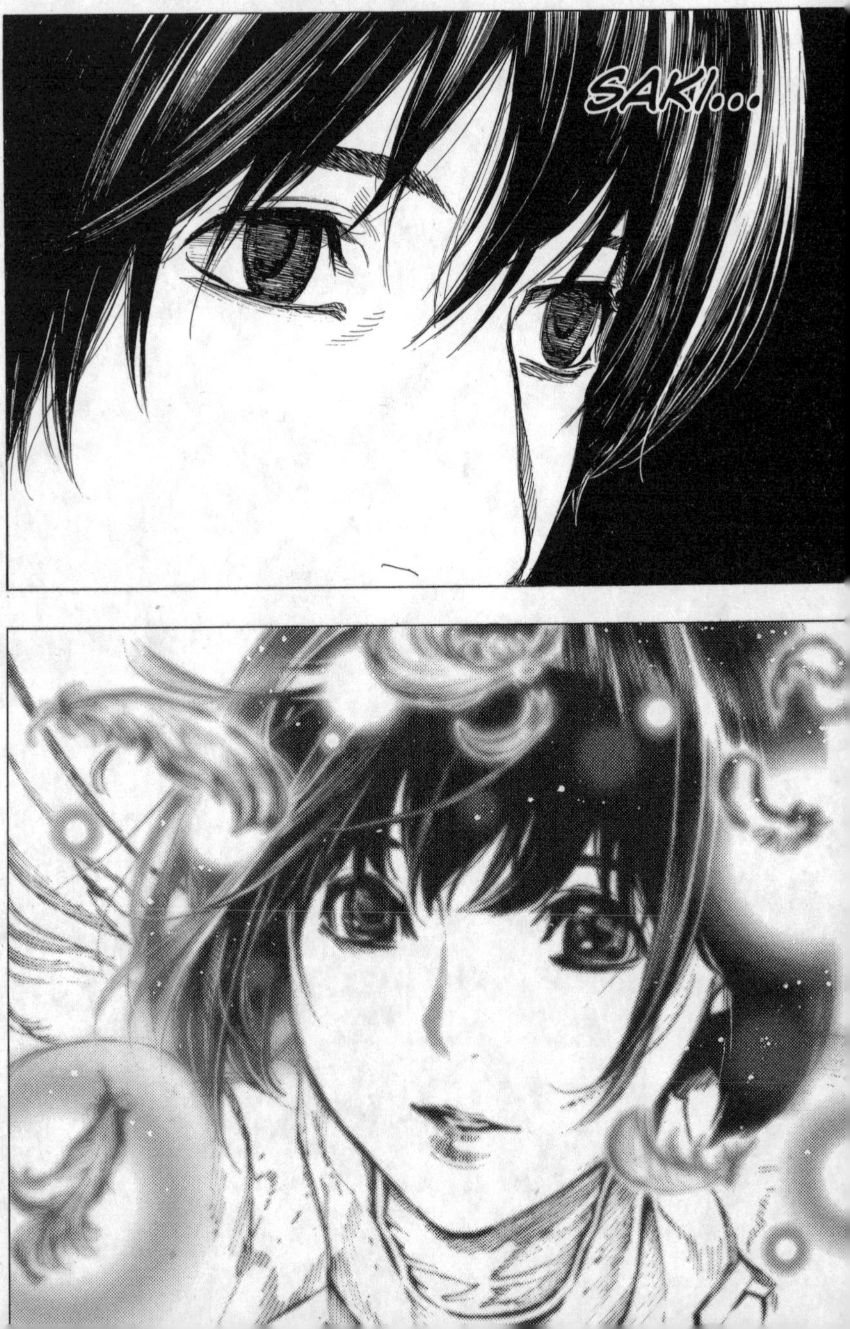
SAKI...

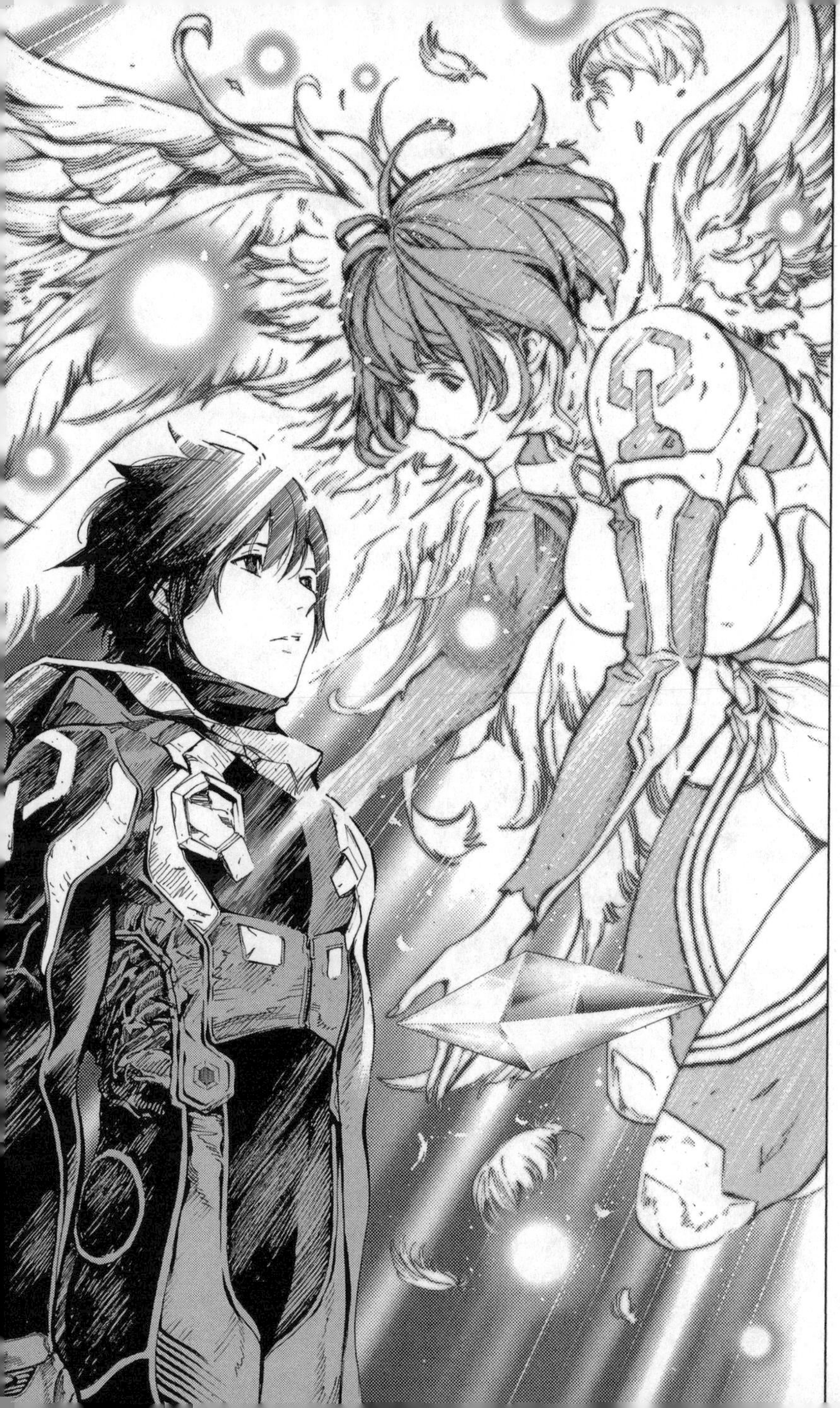

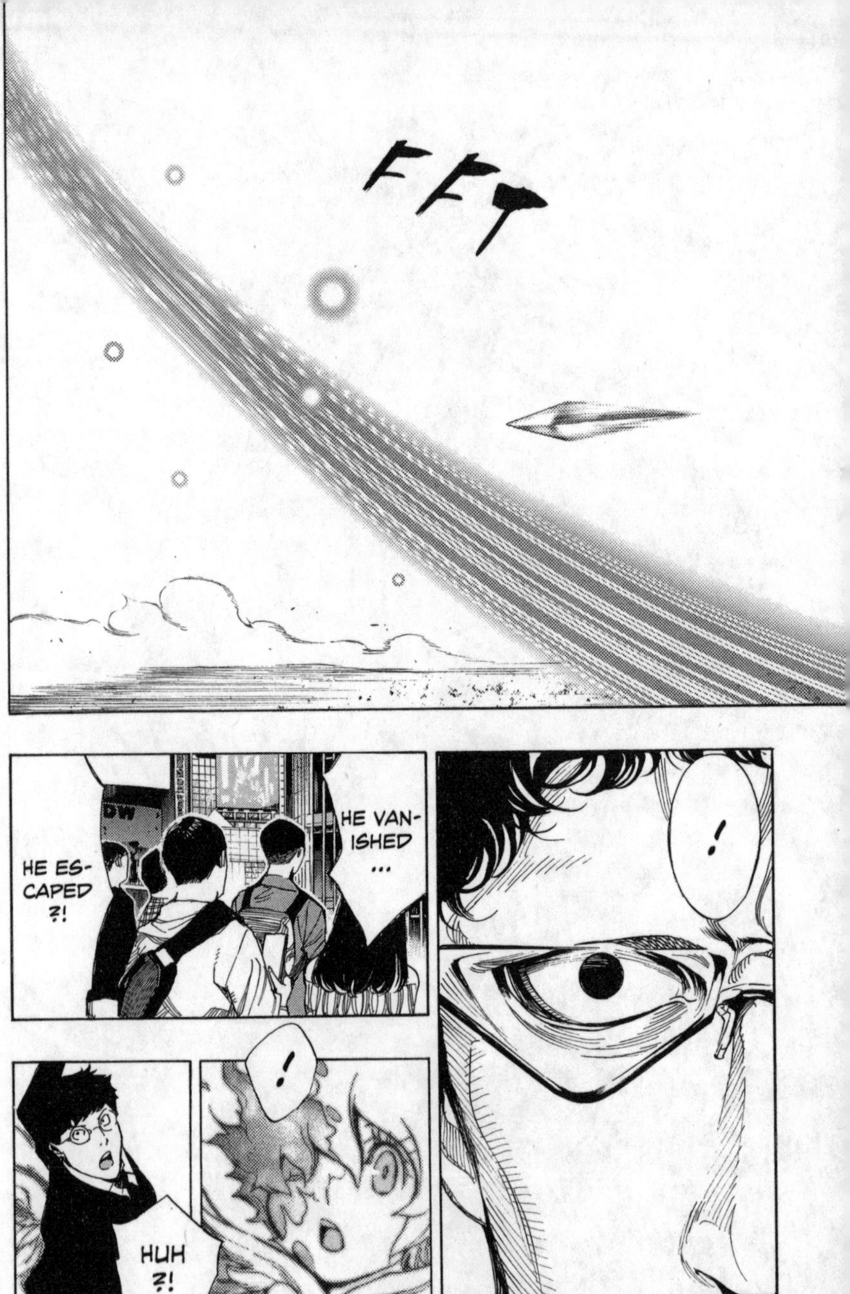
FFT
!
HE VAN-ISHED ...
HE ES-CAPED ?!
!
HUH ?!

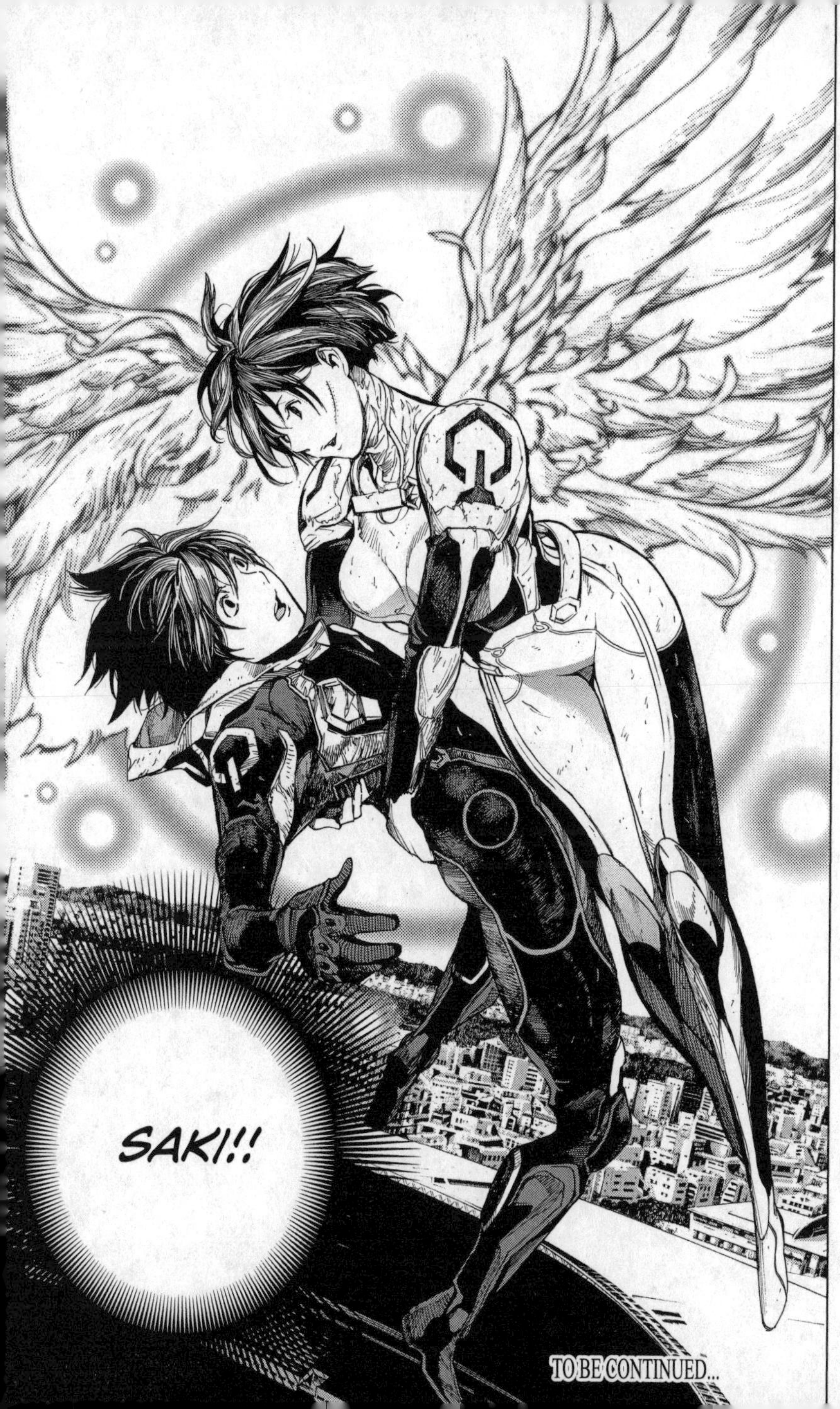
SAKI!!
TO BE CONTINUED...

Tsugumi Ohba

Born in Tokyo, Tsugumi Ohba is the author
of the hit series *Death Note* and *Bakuman。*

Takeshi Obata

Takeshi Obata was born in 1969 in Niigata,
Japan, and first achieved international
recognition as the artist of the wildly popular
Shonen Jump title *Hikaru no Go*, which won the
2003 Tezuka Osamu Cultural Prize: Shinsei
"New Hope" Award and the 2000 Shogakukan
Manga Award. He went on to illustrate the smash
hit *Death Note* as well as the hugely successful
manga *Bakuman。* and *All You Need Is Kill*.

PLATINVM END

VOLUME 13
SHONEN JUMP Manga Edition

○

STORY **T**sugu**mi** O**h** b**a**
ART Ta**ke** s**hi** O**ba**ta

○

TRANSLATION Stephen Paul
TOUCH-UP ART & LETTERING James Gaubatz
DESIGN Shawn Carrico
EDITOR Alexis Kirsch

○

ORIGINAL COVER DESIGN Narumi Noriko

○

PLATINUM END © 2015 by Tsugumi Ohba, Takeshi Obata
All rights reserved.
First published in Japan in 2015 by SHUEISHA Inc., Tokyo.
English translation rights arranged by SHUEISHA Inc.

○

The stories, characters and incidents mentioned in this
publication are entirely fictional.

○

Printed in the U.S.A.

Published by VIZ Media, LLC
P.O. Box 77010
San Francisco, CA 94107

○

10 9 8 7 6 5 4 3 2 1
First printing, July 2021

 MEDIA
viz.com

PARENTAL ADVISORY
PLATINUM END is rated M for Mature
and is recommended for mature readers.
This volume contains suggestive themes.

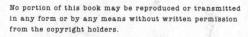

YOU'RE READING THE
WRONG WAY!

PLATINUM END
reads from right to left,
starting in the upper-right
corner. Japanese is read
from right to left, meaning
that action, sound effects
and word-balloon order
are completely reversed
from English order.

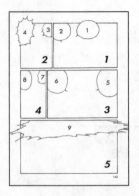

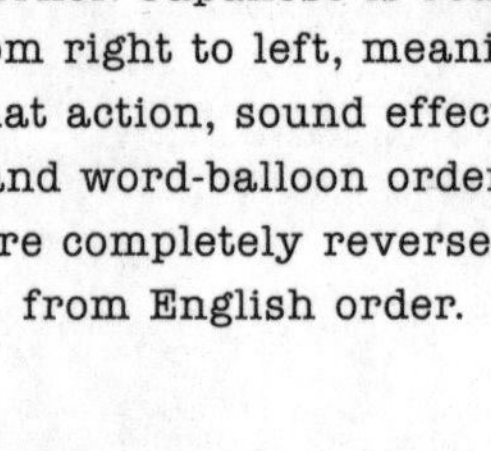